Industrial and Organizational Psychology

IB

Industrial and Organizational Psychology
Linking Theory with Practice

Edited by

Cary L. Cooper
University of Manchester Institute of Science & Technology, UK

Edwin A. Locke
University of Maryland, USA

BLACKWELL
Business

Copyright © Blackwell Publishers Ltd 2000
Editorial matter and organization copyright © Cary L. Cooper and Edwin A. Locke 2000

First published 2000

2 4 6 8 10 9 7 5 3 1

Blackwell Publishers Ltd
108 Cowley Road
Oxford OX4 1JF
UK

Blackwell Publishers Inc.
350 Main Street
Malden, Massachusetts 02148
USA

British Library Cataloguing in Publication Data

A CIP catalogue record for this book is available from the
British Library.

Library of Congress Cataloging-in-Publication Data has been applied for

0-631-20991-3 (hbk)
0-631-20992-1 (pbk)

Typeset in 10 on 12 pt Galliard
by Graphicraft Limited, Hong Kong
Printed in Great Britain by T.J. International Ltd., Padstow, Cornwall

This book is printed on acid-free paper

CONTENTS

ABOUT THE EDITORS

Cary L. Cooper is currently BUPA Professor of Organizational Psychology and Health in the Manchester School of Management, and Pro-Vice-Chancellor (External Activities) of the University of Manchester Institute of Science and Technology (UMIST). He is the author of over 80 books (on occupational stress, women at work and industrial and organizational psychology), has written over 300 scholarly articles for academic journals, and is a frequent contributor to national newspapers, TV and radio. He is currently Founding Editor of the *Journal of Organizational Behavior*, Co-Editor of the medical journal *Stress Medicine*, and Co-Editor of the *International Journal of Management Review*. He is a Fellow of the British Psychological Society, The Royal Society of Arts, The Royal Society of Medicine and the Royal Society of Health. Professor Cooper is the President of the British Academy of Management, is a Companion of the (British) Institute of Management and one of the first UK-based Fellows of the (American) Academy of Management (having also won the 1998 Distinguished Service Award for his contribution to management science from the Academy of Management). Professor Cooper is the Editor (jointly with Professor Chris Argyris of Harvard Business School) of the international scholarly *Blackwell Encyclopedia of Management* (12 volume set). He has been an advisor to the World Health Organisation, ILO, and recently published a major report for the EU's European Foundation for the Improvement of Living and Work Conditions on "Stress Prevention in the Workplace."

Edwin A. Locke is Dean's Professor of Motivation and Leadership at the Robert H. Smith School of Business at the University of Maryland and is also affiliated with the Department of Psychology. He received his undergraduate degree in Psychology from Harvard (1960) and his MA (1962) and Ph.D. (1964) degrees from Cornell. He has published over 200 articles, chapters and books, including (with G. Latham) *A Theory of Goal Setting and Task Performance*, (with others) *The Essence of Leadership, and Prime Movers: The Traits of the Great Wealth Creators* (to appear in spring 2000).

Dr Locke is a Fellow of the American Psychological Association (Division of Industrial and Organizational Psychology), The American Psychological Society and the Academy of Management. He has received the Distinguished Scientific Contribution Award from the Society for Industrial Organizational Psychology and the H. Heneman Career Contribution Award from the Academy of Management (Human Resource Division). He has also received the Outstanding Teacher-Scholar Award from the University of Maryland and numerous teaching awards. He serves on the editorial board of *Organizational Behavioral and Human Performance* and has served on the board of the *Journal of Applied Psychology*.

CONTRIBUTORS

Ram N. Aditya, Louisiana Tech University

Alison E. Barber, Michigan State University

Kathryn M. Bartol, University of Maryland

Christopher J. Collins, University of Maryland

Allan H. Church, W. Warner Burke and Associates

Cathy C. Durham, California State University

Daniel C. Ganster, University of Arkansas

Jane George-Falvy, University of Washington

Marilyn E. Gist, University of Washington

Jerald Greenberg, The Ohio State University

J. Richard Hackman, Harvard University

Robert J. House, University of Pennsylvania

John E. Hunter, Michigan State University

Michele E. A. Jayne, Ford Motor Company

Timothy A. Judge, University of Iowa

Steven Kerr, General Electric Corporation

Gary Latham, University of Toronto

Soosan (Daghighi) Latham, J.P. Morgan, Canada

E. Allan Lind, Duke University

Dana McDonald-Mann, Center for Creative Leadership

Terence R. Mitchell, University of Washington

Larry Murphy, National Institute for Occupational Safety and Health

John M. Rauschenberger, Ford Motor Company

Charles L. Ray, Xerox Corporation

Thomas M. Ruddy, Xerox Corporation

Sara L. Rynes, University of Iowa

Frank L. Schmidt, University of Iowa

M. Susan Taylor, University of Maryland

Kenneth R. Thompson, DePaul University

Gale H. Varma, Prudential Insurance Corporation

Ruth Wageman, Dartmouth College

EDITORIAL FOREWORD

CARY L. COOPER AND EDWIN A. LOCKE

Industrial psychology originated in the first half of the twentieth century, applying basic psychological knowledge and principles to the personnel selection process during World War I. Subsequently, the use of generic psychological theory and research spread into industry, commerce, and the public sector, and extended beyond selection to leadership, motivation, attitudes and job satisfaction, learning and training, and performance behavior. Organizational psychology has a shorter but no less distinguished past and pedigree, stemming primarily from social psychology. The theories and research on inter-personal behavior, group dynamics, inter-group behavior and macro-organizational behavior formed the bedrock for extending the field of industrial and occupational (I/O) psychology into the organizational psychology domain. Increasingly, from about the 1950s onwards (Argyris, 1960), scholars in a variety of disciplines, particularly in social psychology, began to take an interest in developing some scientific understanding of the nature of modern organizations (Cooper, 1991). In 1973 Division 14 of the APA extended its name from Division of the Industrial Psychology to Division of Industrial and Organizational Psychology, while in the UK the Division of Occupational Psychology was formed in 1971 along similar lines. Indeed, if we look at the annual Review of Industrial and Organizational Psychology (Cooper and Robertson, 1986–99), the research topics with broader organizational emphases such as organizational change, job redesign, occupational stress, performance appraisal, corporate culture, and so on, have been increasingly in evidence.

Many textbooks (for example, Dipboye et al., 1994; Arnold et al., 1998) have been written describing and developing the field of I/O psychology, and the subjects now covered are extensive, including job/organizational stress, goal setting, performance appraisal, recruitment, organizational change, and much more. What has been missing in this development is the combining of theory with practice, trying to relate the theory and empiricism of the science of I/O psychology to the practice, how does one inform the other. I/O psychology is in a unique position to integrate theory and practice because the discipline involves large numbers of researchers/ theorists and practitioners, and the two types interact with one another and can establish some common ground, unlike many other areas of psychology.

The purpose of this volume is novel in that it attempts to bring together the leading scientists in various key areas of I/O psychology together with leading practitioners to explore this inter-relationship. For each chapter, one author of the writing team focuses on the theory and research and attempts to answer some of the following questions: What do we know about this topic from basic and applied research? What principles or theories have been established? What degree of confidence can we have in them? The practitioner-based author then explores some of the following issues: What have been the practice benefits of these principles and research in "real" organizations? What difficulties arise when trying to apply these principles or findings? What context factors determine the effectiveness of these principles? What unanswered questions need to be addressed by the I/O scientists?

We have chosen 12 major areas of I/O psychology for collaborative exploration: incentives; leadership; leadership training and development; team effectiveness; job satisfaction; the employment interview; performance appraisal; intelligence/motivation/job performance; organizational recruitment; goal setting; organizational justice; and workplace interventions to prevent stress-related illness. We have also chosen the leading international scholars and scientists in each of these 12 areas to work with the leading practitioners to answer some of the questions above in an effort to integrate theory and practice. We hope that you will find this novel approach helps in exploring what is practically relevant stemming from the science of industrial and organizational psychology, in what context it is or is not appropriate, and what needs to be done in the future.

REFERENCES

Argyris, C. 1960: *Understanding organizational behavior*, Homewood, IL: Dorsey.

Arnold, J., Cooper, C. L., and Robertson, I. 1998: *Work psychology: Understanding human behavior in the workplace*, London: FT/Pitman Publishing.

Cooper, C. L. 1991: *Industrial and organizational psychology*, Vols. 1 and 2, Aldershot, Hampshire: Edward Elgar Publishing; New York: New York University Press.

Cooper, C. L., and Robertson, I. R. 1986–99: *The international review of industrial and organizational psychology*, Chichester and New York: John Wiley & Sons.

Dipboye, R. L., Smith, C. S., and Howell, W. C. 1994: *Understanding industrial and organizational psychology*, Fort Worth, TX: Harcourt Brace.

chapter 1

INCENTIVES: THEORY AND PRACTICE

KATHRYN M. BARTOL AND CATHY C. DURHAM

Compensation is a key aspect of the employer's side of the bargain in the exchange agreement with employees for their efforts. Employers typically design pay systems with several objectives in mind, including legal compliance, labor cost control, perceived fairness toward employees, and the enhancement of employee perform- ance to achieve high levels of productivity and customer satisfaction (Milkovich and Newman, 1999). In this chapter we first discuss theory and research relating to organizations' attempts to achieve their compensation objectives. We next consider compensation practices, assessing the major types of incentive delivery systems currently in use and suggesting conditions under which they are most likely to be effective. Finally, we draw some overall conclusions regarding compensation and note areas in which future research is needed.

■ MOTIVATION THEORIES RELATING TO COMPENSATION

Although striving toward multiple objectives for compensation can be a daunting task, there are several theories that offer guidance for pay system designers, especially with regard to the objectives of promoting fairness perceptions and motivation to perform. In this section we briefly discuss levels of analysis issues. We then consider major theories of motivation and organization that relate to compensation, briefly reviewing each theory, noting its level of analysis, highlighting key research findings, and deriving from the theory principles for compensation practice.

Levels of analysis

As organizations increasingly flatten their structures and redesign work to be per- formed by teams rather than by individuals alone, compensation must be considered not only at the individual level but also at the group and organizational levels. Thus, this chapter will consider compensation theories and organizational practices at all three of these levels – the individual, the group, and the organization. In the terminology of Klein et al. (1994), considering the individual level implies examining how theories apply when individuals are viewed as *independent* (that is, independent of group influence with respect to the attribute of interest). Considering the group and organizational levels means examining how theories apply when individuals are *homogeneous* within a group (that is, sufficiently similar with respect to the attribute in question that they may be characterized as a whole). A third possibility identified by Klein et al. (1994) is that the level of a theory is neither the individual nor the group, but the individual within the group. In this case, group members are viewed as *heterogeneous* and the theoretical focus is on individual attributes as compared to a group average for the attribute. More recently, researchers (for example, Drazin et al., 1999; Kostova, 1999) have considered additional levels of theory beyond the three identified by Klein et al. (1994), and multi-level theory building appears to be on the rise (Klein et al., 1999). Theories relating to compensation, however, have (thus far) generally been articulated at only a single level of analysis. Although the purpose of this chapter is to describe rather than to build theory, we will attempt none the less to follow Klein et al.'s (1994) prescription for researchers to "speculate about alternative conceptualizations [about the level] of their constructs" (p. 208) by suggesting how the theories discussed here may apply at multiple levels.

Although the theories of motivation that we discuss in this chapter intend to explain and predict individual behavior, we propose that they may represent isomorphic models, in that not only individuals, but also groups and organizations, may be influenced by the variables considered in the theories. Rousseau (1985) states that "isomorphism exists when the same functional relationship can be used to represent constructs at more than one level" (p. 8). Klein et al. (1999) note that while isomorphic models are appealing because of their parsimony and their integration of phenomena at diverse levels of analysis, they are difficult to develop because they may appear simplistic, and because of the difficulty of determining the structure and meaning of isomorphic constructs. Morgeson and Hofmann (1999) suggest that a key to isomorphic constructs that span levels of analysis is that, although they may differ in their *structure* (because of the additional aspect of the actions and interactions that are involved at an aggregate level), they have a similar *function* or causal output (that is, the same effect) at all levels. We view the motivation theories discussed below as isomorphic models.

Equity theory

A theory that speaks directly to the issue of individual perceptions of compensation fairness is equity theory (Adams, 1965). Typically, equity theory has been considered at the individual level of analysis, in which individuals are viewed as independent of one another in respect of their fairness evaluations and responses to them. According to the theory, individuals compare their ratios of work outcomes to work inputs to those of referent others, and form judgments about the fairness of their outcomes. If the comparison ratios are equal, the situation is perceived to be equitable and no response occurs. If inequity is perceived, individuals feel a degree of tension which they will be motivated to reduce. Possible reactions to inequity, according to Adams, include: changing one's evaluation of one's own or of the referent other's inputs and/or outcomes; trying to change one's own or the other's actual inputs and/or outcomes; selecting another referent; or reducing one's participation in the employment relationship. Thus, according to the theory, it is not equity but perceived inequity that motivates. And, although the theory suggests that positive outcomes are possible when the perceived inequity favors the individual, most of the predicted consequences of perceived inequity are negative.

Although equity theory has traditionally been studied at the individual level of analysis, one may consider the theory at the group level as well. Recall that, according to Klein et al. (1994), the group level implies homogeneity within a group, so that members are sufficiently similar with respect to the variable of interest to be characterized as a whole. It is possible to imagine work teams comparing their input/outcome ratios with those of other groups, and feeling justly or unjustly rewarded as a team. This group-level view of equity may underlie the prescription that employers should not offer variable pay plans, such as gainsharing, to certain employee groups within a business unit to the exclusion of other groups, because the groups not under the plan may perceive outcome inequity unless equivalent pay arrangements of some type are available. At a higher level of aggregation, the organizational level, labor unions would appear to influence a workforce's equity perceptions when the input/output ratio for one organization's workers is compared to those of other organizations' workers. At the organizational level, inequity perceptions can lead to negative outcomes such as slowdowns or strikes.

Research

Early laboratory studies primarily examined overpayment inequity and generally found support for the theory's predictions that overpaid hourly workers would increase the quality and/or quantity of their output, while overpaid piece-rate workers would decrease quantity and increase quality (Adams and Freedman, 1976). Few people seem to feel overpaid, however (Locke, 1976), and thus equity theory's predictions concerning overpayment seem to be less relevant for organizations than do those concerning underpayment. The few early laboratory studies that examined underpayment found, as the theory predicted, that underpaid hourly workers decreased quantity and/or quality and that underpaid piece-rate workers increased quantity and decreased quality. There has been little research in actual work settings concerning the results of perceived inequity. Bartol and Locke (2000) argue that the most likely effect of perceived inequity is dissatisfaction, and in support of that view Summers and Hendrix (1991) found that perceptions of pay inequity affected not performance, but job and pay satisfaction. Dissatisfaction, in turn, may have many possible consequences besides diminished performance, such as complaining or expressing hostility, being uncooperative, committing sabotage, or, in line with equity theory predictions regarding reducing one's participation in the employment relationship, being absent from work or quitting. Greenberg (1990), for example, found that perceived inequity regarding pay cuts was associated with increased employee theft. Also, Cowherd and Levine (1992) found that large differentials between top managers' pay and the pay of hourly employees was negatively related to organizational citizenship behaviors among lower-level employees, presumably because the employees felt inequitably treated.

Principles

The implication of the theory, therefore, is that organizations should positively influence equity perceptions to the extent possible (both among individuals and groups), in order to avoid the negative results of perceived inequity. One way of accomplishing this is by exercising care in allocating rewards, so that both procedures for determining outcomes and the outcomes themselves will be viewed as fair (Cropanzano and Folger, 1989). This may imply, for example, giving employees voice in the design of their compensation plan (such as through representation on design committees, use of pilot projects, and so on) and/or providing an appeals mechanism through which employees can challenge decisions they see as unjust (Leventhal et al., 1980). At a minimum, it implies showing empathy for employees' concerns and providing the rationale for pay changes. This suggestion is supported by Greenberg's (1990) study, which found the highest level of theft within an organizational unit in which pay was cut without explanation and without expressions of remorse by management, as compared to units that either received no pay cut or received a pay cut with explanation and remorse. A second way to positively influence equity perceptions regarding pay is to help individual workers and teams make realistic assessments of their own inputs (for example, through performance feedback). This implies training supervisors to discriminate among subordinates in performance as well as motivating them and equipping them to provide feedback to employees about performance. A third possibility is to provide outcome information concerning referent others. Bartol and Locke (2000) note, however, that there are pitfalls associated with providing such comparative information (for example, the cost of continually updating the information, or the risk that the data will reveal that the organization's pay scale is below average).

Expectancy (VIE) theory

Expectancy theory (Vroom, 1964) predicts that an individual's motivation to expend a given level of effort is a function of the valence of outcomes to the individual (that is, the desirability of rewards associated with performance at a given level), instrumentality (the individual's belief that performance at the desired level will actually result in the valued rewards), and expectancy (the belief that a specific level of effort will lead to a desired level of performance). Thus, the theory suggests that workers will expend greater effort when they believe they are capable of accomplishing the task at hand and when they are confident that valued rewards will result from performance. The implication for compensation system design, therefore, is that the most motivating incentive plans will be those that make clear linkages between performance and the rewards that workers truly desire. Expectancy theory's emphasis on instrumentality – the perceptual link between performance and rewards – is similar to reinforcement theory's prediction that a response (such as high performance) followed by a reward (such as money) will likely be repeated in the future. Expectancy theory, however, explains as well as predicts behavior by emphasizing that it is the belief by employees that rewards will follow performance that motivates their efforts.

Expectancy theory was originally designed to explain and predict behavior within rather than across individuals. In other words, the theory predicts an individual's choice from among a group of alternative actions – not which individual in a group will exert the greatest overall effort when performing a particular task. Thus, given the same set of behavioral options, individuals will differ in their view of which choice is in their best interest, depending on their values and on their beliefs concerning the efficacy of their efforts, both for task accomplishment and for securing the reward. Campbell and Pritchard (1976) suggest that early studies of expectancy theory, which generally failed to find strong support for its validity, were flawed methodologically in many ways, but particularly for measurement problems associated with testing the theory across rather than within individuals. Later studies provide greater support for the theory as a valid representation of work-related attitudes and behaviors (Pinder, 1984; Van Eerde and Thierry, 1996).

As noted previously, we propose that expectancy theory is an isomorphic model, in that the relationship between an individual's motivation to expend a given level of effort and the three expectancy theory variables (valence, instrumentality, and expectancy) is replicated at group and organizational levels. It should be noted that at the aggregate levels the isomorphic model assumes homogeneity among group or organization members, which is most likely to exist when groups are cohesive and when organizations have a strong organizational culture. Homogeneity cannot always be assumed, however, and herein lies a challenge for incentive system designers. There may be individuals within a group who feel out of syncronization with their perceptions of the group's valence, instrumentality, or expectancy evaluations (for example, "They all think we'll receive the promised bonus if we meet our goals, but I think management will find a way to renege"; or "No one else desires this outcome as much as I do"; or "They all think we can do this, but in my view, there's no way"). Unless consensus is reached, such variance from the group average can dilute group members' motivation to expend effort and thus diminish the group's effectiveness. A management implication would be to address this possibility explicitly and, to the extent possible, to take action that will not only increase the mean level of but also reduce the within-group variance on VIE evaluations.

Principles

Organizations can try to affect the motivation of employees by addressing any or all of the three causal variables: valence; instrumentality; or expectancy. In regard to valence, expectancy theory at the least reminds organizations of the importance of offering rewards (both in type and in amount) that are in fact valued by employees. Fortunately, employees do tend to have some common values, such as an appreciation of money, that organizations can generally count on. Further, expectancy theory stresses the importance of enhancing instrumentality beliefs by demonstrating that high-level performance is consistently rewarded. Finally, the theory reminds organizations to strengthen the expectancy (that is, effort-performance) linkage by equipping (for example, by training) and empowering employees to accomplish their work goals. Expectancy beliefs may be more difficult to achieve at team and organizational levels because of line-of-sight difficulties. Employees may question whether their efforts will in fact lead to the desired level of group or organizational performance because there are likely to be many factors other than their own efforts that are influencing performance as well. Thus, it is important to make clear how group efforts will in fact lead to the desired level of performance.

Goal-setting theory

A key component of many pay plans is the setting of performance goals. Goal-setting theory (Locke and Latham, 1990) suggests that specific, difficult goals, accompanied by feedback on performance, lead to higher performance by focusing individuals' attention, increasing effort, and strengthening persistence toward task accomplishment. For more complex tasks, goals lead individuals to engage in more planning and enhance strategy development. Critical factors in the success of goal setting are individuals' commitment to the goal and their self-efficacy (that is, task-specific self-confidence). A related and complementary theory, social cognitive theory (Bandura, 1986; 1997), suggests that self-efficacy influences both personal (that is, self-set, as compared to assigned) goals and goal commitment. Research has shown that goal setting and incentives are related, in that making pay contingent on goal attainment can increase commitment to goals (Locke and Latham, 1990; Riedel et al., 1988; Wright, 1992). However, there are complex interactions between goal difficulty and type of incentive as they combine to influence performance, so that the expected positive effect of hard goals on performance occurs under piece-rate and hourly pay systems, but not under all-or-nothing bonus pay systems. When a bonus is at stake, a hard goal (as compared to a goal of moderate difficulty) can lead to poor performance, presumably because individuals may doubt their capability to attain the goal and thus earn the bonus (Lee et al., 1997; Mowen et al., 1981).

A difficult issue in the design of performance-contingent pay is determining what the assigned goals will be. Research generally shows that self-efficacy is influenced by assigned goals (presumably because assigned goals provide information about what is considered possible) and that personal goals are influenced by both assigned goals and self-efficacy. Because performance is usually affected either directly or indirectly by all three factors, setting the assigned goal properly is critical. If goals are too easy, self-efficacy may be high but personal goals and thus performance will be lower than if goals are difficult. However, if assigned goals are viewed not only as hard but as unattainable, self-efficacy and personal goals (and thus performance) will likely be considerably lowered because effort seems futile (Lee et al., 1997). Performance-contingent rewards can best have their desired performance effects when what constitutes a difficult-but-attainable goal is identifiable.

Increasingly, goal setting is being studied at the group level, under the implicit assumption that the theory is isomorphic, that is, that goals have the same function or outcomes at the group level as at the individual level. Also, management by objectives (MBO) suggests the relevance of goal setting at a higher level of aggregation – that of the business unit. Thus, the expectation is that incentives that are contingent upon the attainment of assigned group goals will lead to higher group efficacy, to higher personal (group-set) goals, to greater goal commitment, and to higher group performance. When members of groups or organizations are juggling multiple goals at multiple levels (individual, group, and/or organizational), an additional function of group rewards may be to increase group homogeneity by aligning the interests of members toward the achievement of a common goal. As evidence of the positive effects of goal alignment, Crown and Rosse (1995) found that when individual and group goals were congruent, group members were more committed to maximizing group performance and developed more cooperative strategies than when group and individual goals were incongruent. Shalley and Johnson (1996) found that when individual and group goals were incongruent, individuals gave priority to a specific goal over a more ambiguous or overarching goal. They propose that if incentives are based on goal attainment (whether group or individual), group members will likely give priority to the goal that offers the greatest potential for reward. Similarly, Gomez-Mejia and Balkin (1992) suggest that team-based pay is used to align the interests of multiple individuals into a common goal, and Mitchell et al. (1990) report that one reason that gainsharing is thought to be effective is because it creates organizational goals that lead to teamwork and cooperation.

Principles

Concerning the use of incentives to foster high goal setting among employees, Bartol and Locke (2000) present three possibilities. The first alternative is to use all-or-nothing bonuses with difficult assigned goals. As suggested above, a danger associated with such an approach is that, if the goal is considered too difficult, an all-or-nothing system may discourage employees and cause them to greatly reduce their efforts because the bonus is seen as unattainable. The authors thus note that it is important when using this alternative to provide an organizational environment that facilitates success, especially by hiring only highly capable people, all the while discouraging inordinate risk taking or dishonest practices. Bartol and Locke's second recommendation is to assign a difficult goal but to reward for degrees of success in relation to the goal rather than on an all-or-nothing basis, so that there is a proportionate pay increment for every performance increment above a certain minimally acceptable goal level. Their third alternative, which they acknowledge is contrary to expectancy theory, is appropriate when management is uncertain about how to specify what should be accomplished or how to reward performance in advance. In such a case, employees set their own goals and management determines rewards after the fact, based on the value employees have created for the company. At the group level, goal-setting theory suggests that offering rewards that are contingent upon given levels of team or organizational performance will strengthen members' commitment to team or organizational goals, increase the likelihood that members are all working toward the same ends, and encourage members to set high personal goals for team or organizational performance.

ORGANIZATIONAL THEORIES RELATING TO COMPENSATION

Agency theory

Agency theory (Eisenhardt, 1989; Jensen and Meckling, 1976) is concerned with determining the most efficient contract between a principal (one who delegates work) and an agent (one who performs the work). The theory addresses two problems associated with agency relationships. First is the agency problem, which occurs when the principal and agent have conflicting desires or goals and it is difficult or expensive for the principal to monitor the behavior of the agent. Second is the problem of risk sharing, which occurs when the principal and agent have different risk preferences. Agents, because they cannot diversify their employment, are generally considered to be more risk averse than are principals, who can diversify their investments.

The unit of analysis for agency theory is the contract that governs the principal–agent relationship, and the theory predicts the relative efficiency of a behavior-oriented contract as compared to an outcome-oriented contract. Behavior-oriented contracts imply that the principal will monitor the agent's behavior to be sure that the agent acts in the principal's interest, and that the principal will incur the costs associated with such monitoring (for example, the cost of development of information systems). Outcome-oriented contracts seek to ensure the agent's acting in the interest of the principal by aligning the two parties' interests and goals by basing the agent's pay on performance outcomes. This makes the rewards for both parties dependent on appropriate actions by the agent. Because performance outcomes can be affected by factors other than the agent's actions, outcome-based contracts mean greater risk for agents, who therefore demand the opportunity to earn higher pay (for example, through bonuses, commissions, or stock options) in exchange for bearing greater risk.

Research

In regard to agency theory's predictions regarding compensation, research has generally been supportive. Eisenhardt (1985, 1988) found in support of the theory that job programmability, the presence of information systems, the cost of outcome measurement, and outcome uncertainty predicted incentive system (salary versus commission) in retail stores. In a laboratory study, Conlon and Parks (1990) found that the ability to monitor was negatively related to performance-contingent (that is, outcome-based) compensation. Concerning effectiveness, Tosi et al. (1997) found in a laboratory study that incentives effectively aligned agents' decisions with the interests of the principal, while monitoring did not (and also, the combination of incentives and monitoring did not, except for agents with long tenure).

Principles

Agency theory is often seen as more descriptive than normative. We believe, how-ever, that because it specifies which type of contract is more efficient for given situations, the theory has implications for compensation practice. Eisenhardt (1989) suggests that the most efficient contracts will be behavior-based more than outcome-based under the following conditions: when information systems are in place (because the agent's behavior can be easily monitored by the principal); when outcome uncertainty is high (because of the expense of shifting the risk to the agent in an outcome-based contract); when the agent is highly risk averse (also because of the expense of risk shifting); when the principal is not risk averse (because he or she is more willing to bear the risk than the cost of shifting the risk); when the goal conflict between principal and agent is low (because the agent is more likely to behave as the principal desires); when the task is programmable (that is, appropriate agent behaviors are specifiable in advance and are easily observed and evaluated); when outcomes are difficult to measure or require a long time to measure (which makes outcome-based contracts less attractive); and when the principal and agent have been in an agency relationship for a long period of time, so that the principal knows the agent well and can readily assess his or her behavior. In terms of com-pensation, therefore, salary (a behavior-based contract) is more suitable under the conditions noted above. When the opposite conditions exist, performance-based incentives, such as bonuses, commissions, and stock options, will be preferable. Bartol and Locke (2000) note, for example, that because high-level executive posi-tions are likely to be characterized by low task programmability, agency theory would recommend outcome-based contracts for executives.

Prospect theory

Prospect theory (Kahneman and Tversky, 1979) is a theory of individual judgment and decision making under conditions of risk, when it is difficult to predict exactly what the outcomes or consequences of events will be. The theory directly addresses how alternatives are framed and evaluated in the decision-making process. Kahneman and Tversky argue that although expected utility theory – a rational choice model of decision making – has been generally accepted as normative and widely applied as descriptive, it in fact fails to provide an adequate understanding of individuals' *actual* decision choices. They therefore offer prospect theory as an alternative model that makes no claims about how individuals should make decisions but more accur-ately describes what they actually do.

Because few employees determine their own compensation plans, prospect theory does not address choices about which plan among a set of alternatives will be implemented. Rather, it addresses employees' judgments about plans that are in place or that are being modified. In regard to compensation, prospect theory has mainly been applied to how employees evaluate at-risk pay plans (Bartol and Locke, 2000; Wiseman and Gomez-Mejia, 1998), which explicitly discount (place at risk) employees' base pay by a certain percentage and then offer performance-based incentives that give employees the opportunity to earn back and then exceed their base-pay earnings.

Fundamentally, prospect theory suggests that an individual's risk propensity varies depending on whether an alternative is defined as a gain or as a loss. The theory states that individuals tend to be risk averse in the domain of gains, and risk seeking in the domain of losses. Support for these notions has been found in numerous experiments dealing with framing effects in decisions about money, usually in the form of payoffs, bets, and gambles (for example, Kahneman and Tversky, 1979; Levin et al., 1987; Neale et al., 1987).

Kahneman and Tversky (1979) suggest several tendencies in regard to framing. Particularly relevant to compensation is the tendency of decision makers to categorize outcomes in terms of gains and losses rather than in terms of final absolute states of wealth or welfare. Gains and losses are defined relative to some neutral reference point, which usually corresponds to one's "current asset position" (p. 274), such as one's current pay. Thus, when facing a pay system change, employees will not consider, "What will my financial condition be under this new system?" but rather, "How much more or less will I make than I do now?" McDermott (1998) notes how strikingly different this is than expected utility theory, which assumes that the final asset position is critical in predicting choice. Prospect theory's emphasis on change from the reference point, she also notes, is in keeping with basic human perceptual processes, which tend to notice shifts more than resting states.

We noted above that individuals are risk averse in situations involving the possibility of gain and risk seeking in situations involving the threat of loss. Prospect theory further suggests that loss aversion is greater than gain attraction, or, as McDermott (1998) suggests, that "losing hurts more than a possible gain pleases" (p. 29). Thus, to avoid a loss, individuals may choose a higher-risk alternative than they would in the pursuit of a gain. Also, McDermott notes that individuals tend to adjust to and become satisfied with the status quo, and thus become averse to losing any component part of their present situation. They value what they possess to a greater degree than they value an equally attractive alternative, so that equal trade is seen as unattractive. Thus, for an alternative to be acceptable, it must be perceived as clearly superior to the status quo.

Research

Although prospect theory is to a large extent based on experimental studies of individuals' choices regarding hypothetical monetary payoffs under conditions of risk, no research studies to date have explicitly tested the theory as it relates to pay systems in actual organizations. Bartol and Locke (2000), however, use the theory to explain two failed pay-at-risk plans. In the first (Koenig, 1990; McNutt, 1990), DuPont Corporation's Fibers Division instituted a plan that put a portion of employees' base pay at risk if minimal divisional performance goals were not met, but that also offered employees the opportunity to earn a bonus above the base rate of pay for high levels of divisional performance. Although successful in the first year when goals were achieved and bonuses paid, the plan was discontinued in the second year due to employee discontent when the division lost money and employees faced the prospect of certain losses. In the second pay-at-risk plan (Brown and Huber, 1992), a similar system was installed and then terminated at a large US bank, also due to employee discontent (even among employees who had earned equal or greater pay under the new plan). Bartol and Locke (2000) explain that, in accordance with prospect theory's predictions, employees in both cases were likely to devalue the loss of their expected pay more strongly than they valued the possible gain of bonus pay, especially when a loss was imminent.

Principles

The key principle suggested by prospect theory is that organizations should consider framing issues when making changes to pay systems. It is important to consider what the employee's likely reference point is, because this point determines whether changes are framed as gains or losses. Prospect theory suggests that if the reference point is one's current salary and a portion of it is suddenly placed at risk, the employee will be averse to the potential loss more than seeking of the potential gain and will likely reject the plan, even if his or her expected utility is greater under the new system. It is not enough for the change to be framed as a non-loss or as an alternative that is equally attractive to the status quo; it must clearly be viewed as a probable gain for there to be acceptance. Thus, replacing a no-pay-at-risk system with an at-risk system may be doomed to failure. Pay-at-risk systems may be better-suited to start-ups where no reference point has yet been established.

Institutional theory

Institutional theory seeks to explain why organizations take the forms that they do. According to Hall (1991), the institutional perspective views organizational design not as a rational process but rather as one by which organizations in a field respond to both external and internal pressures in such a way that the organizations resemble each other over time. DiMaggio and Powell (1983) give three reasons why organizations in a given field develop similar practices and procedures. First, environmental forces such as government regulations and cultural expectations define what constitutes responsible management and thus require a degree of standardization of practices (either by law or by pressure to conform to accepted ways of doing business). Second, sameness develops due to mimicry among organizations as they seek the best way to handle (and receive similar advice from consultants and other experts about how to handle) challenges that they all face. Third, there is increased homogeneity among members of the workforce – particularly managers – due to their receiving similar professional training, their participating together in trade and professional organizations, and their movement from job to job among organizations within the field. A fourth reason is offered by Meyer and Rowan (1977), who suggest that once a policy or procedure is established within an individual organization, it may be perpetuated not necessarily for rational or instrumental reasons (that is, it leads to positive outcomes) but simply because it comes to be unquestioningly viewed by organizational members as the only acceptable way of getting things done. Institutional theory would predict, therefore, that organizations within a given field would tend to employ similar pay practices in order to appear legitimate from both without and within.

Although the theory focuses on irrational elements influencing compensation and other business practices, we argue that all the factors noted above are not of necessity irrational. Responding to environmental (such as legal) requirements is reasonable, as is mimicry, when it is a choice based on an analysis of the situation rather than mindless copying. Gerhart et al. (1996) suggest that by imitating or benchmarking with other organizations they see as more legitimate or successful (for example, by determining pay levels based on market surveys or implementing a pay plan that has been endorsed in the business community as a "best practice"), organizations can save valuable resources (for example, for focusing on new or more pressing problems). Further, Gerhart et al. indicate that firms sometimes tailor the imitated pay practices to their own situations, so that they gain additional benefits from them. Imitation of this sort cannot be considered an irrational exercise. Unquestioningly adopting the most recent compensation fad is irrational, however, and may preclude the adoption of a more efficient and value-creating alternative. The theory's assertion about the dominance of emotion over rationality in the perpetuation of a practice, once it has been institutionalized, suggests that compensation system designers may face considerable resistance from organizational members when attempting to change established pay practices within a particular organization.

Research

Institutional theory has been applied to a wide variety of situations (for example, civil service reform, Tolbert and Zucker, 1983; accounting practices, Kaplan, 1984; the development of organizational roles, Zucker, 1977; the use of cesarean surgeries, Goodrick and Salancik, 1996), and some researchers have used the perspective of institutional theory to study compensation practices. Based on a case-survey analysis of the introduction of a formal job evaluation plan to a Canadian provincial government, Quaid (1993) applied the theory to conclude that the true function of job evaluation is not to achieve the rational goal of determining an internally equitable and externally competitive pay structure but rather to "manage meaning" about the comparative value of jobs within the organization. In her field study of compensation contracts governing retail salespeople, Eisenhardt (1988) found that an institutional variable – an industry's or a firm's pay traditions – predicted the form of compensation (salary versus commission) used to control salespeople. In a laboratory study, Conlon and Parks (1990) found, in support of agency theory, that the ability to monitor was negatively related to performance-contingent compensation and, in support of institutional theory, that there was an interaction between tradition and monitoring, so that the effect of monitoring was obtained only when no pay tradition was present. They also found that the effect of tradition increased over time. Conlon and Parks concluded that institutional factors, such as pay traditions, are powerful forces that can inhibit economically rational thinking about what practices will lead to optimal outcomes.

Principles

Institutional theory points to the importance of recognizing two sets of factors that affect pay systems, the environmental factors exerting pressure toward standardization within fields and the organizational factors causing resistance to change within organizations, both of which may have rational and non-rational components. The key principle that we draw from this theory is that to the extent possible, organizations should avoid the trap of institutionalization, which is designing and maintaining compensation systems based not on rational or instrumental reasons (such as they lead to better performance) but on non-rational or emotional ones (for example, tradition, other companies use the system, organizational members resist change). This is not to suggest that organizations cannot learn from others' experiences and practices or that they should ignore employees' legitimate concerns, but rather that they should make well-considered choices that fit their individual strategies and cultures.

■ INCENTIVE DELIVERY SYSTEMS

The theoretical perspective just discussed outlines some basic parameters for effective compensation delivery systems and yet leaves considerable latitude in the way in which systems can be designed. In this section we use the theoretical perspective and other relevant research to assess what is known about the strengths and shortcomings of major compensation delivery systems in terms of fostering increased performance and productivity. We also briefly consider other factors, such as satisfaction, organizational justice, and retention issues when they are particularly germane to the delivery system under discussion. As a basis for future research, we draw conclusions regarding the circumstances under which each delivery system is likely to be effective in facilitating higher levels of performance.

To facilitate our analysis, we divide compensation delivery systems into four categories. First, we consider systems that focus on rewarding individual performance. Second, we examine systems that reward individual development. Third, we investigate systems that base rewards on the performance of small groups. Finally, we discuss systems in which rewards are based on division or organizational performance. Of course, we recognize that it is often possible to use more than one type of system simultaneously, an issue that we will point out is in need of further research.

Pay for individual performance

A variety of compensation systems have been designed to deliver pay to reward individual outcomes. Among the most prominent are merit pay, traditional incentives, and the emerging use of variable pay, including "at risk" approaches.

Merit pay

Merit pay rewards individuals for past work behaviors and outcomes by adding dollar amounts to their base pay (Milkovich and Newman, 1999). Surveys indicate that merit pay is the most widely used pay system in US organizations (Bretz et al., 1992; O'Dell, 1987).

Heneman (1992) reviewed 25 studies that have assessed the impact of merit pay plans on satisfaction, motivation, and/or performance. He concluded that, overall, merit pay plans are only "moderately effective" because they have been consistently related to positive attitudes, but they have not been consistently related to performance. Institutional theory suggests that merit pay may continue to be used by organizations because it is "legitimated" or accepted practice, rather than because it is effective in motivating performance.

In practice, a number of factors tend to weaken the connection between performance and pay under merit pay plans (Heneman, 1990). For example, contrary to prescriptions from expectancy theory regarding instrumentality, some merit pay systems consider non-performance factors, such as longevity and cost of living, although the use of cost of living increases is declining. The linkage between pay and performance is often further diluted when adjustments for market comparability are folded into merit pay systems without being identified as such. Research by Harris et al. (1998) suggests that cross-sectional studies focusing on merit pay increases may understate pay and performance linkages because such studies do not adequately capture the cumulative impact of pay adjustments, including the effects of promotions and market adjustments.

Adding to the difficulties in establishing pay-for-performance instrumentalities with merit pay is the fact that managers are frequently reluctant to differentiate among workers in assigning performance ratings (Murphy, 1992). Part of the reason is that they are concerned about disrupting the working relationships in the work group. As a result, managers tend to avoid awarding widely different percentage increases even when performance differences warrant it (Kopelman et al., 1991), raising the specter of unfairness perceptions addressed by equity theory.

Even when performance factors are given heavy weight, they are frequently addressed only retrospectively. That is, contrary to goal-setting theory, performance goals and standards for evaluation often are not adequately specified at the beginning of the merit pay cycle. This means that employees may not have a solid understanding of what performance is expected or what will be rewarded. The lack of up-front standards may render performance judgments all the more difficult to make and defend, leading to perceptions of both procedural and distributive injustice.

With merit pay, there is also a continuing issue regarding the potential valence of the merit pay raises available. Various attempts have been made to assess the size of a meaningful pay raise (Mitra et al., 1997; Worley et al., 1992; Zedeck and Smith, 1968). Despite the fact that the studies were conducted at different points in time, they are somewhat consistent in concluding that the amount necessary to elicit positive perceptual and attitudinal responses is somewhere in the 5–7 percent range. This issue needs to be researched further in terms of the adjustments (or lack thereof) that individuals make for inflation in evaluating the amounts of merit pay received. For example, while recent pay raises have averaged somewhat below 5 percent (Healey, 1997), inflation has been relatively low.

In considering *conditions for effectiveness* regarding merit pay, agency theory provides some perspective. As merit pay plans are practiced in many organizations, there is actually relatively little differentiation based on performance outcomes, with most of the raise amounts actually constituting market adjustments. Such plans – that is, salary and "merit" (mostly market adjustment) – may be appropriate when it is possible to monitor behaviors. In such situations, it may not be necessary or desirable to pay a monetary performance premium to obtain specific outcomes. Rather, a salary and some "merit" for market adjustments and as a reward for consistency of appropriate behaviors may be warranted. Agency theory suggests other circumstances under which a salary and market adjustment "merit" approach may be appropriate, such as a highly risk-averse agent or low conflict between principal and agent.

As also suggested by agency theory, merit pay may also be appropriate in situations of high outcome uncertainty. In such cases, retrospective judgments regarding performance, coupled with merit raises, may be appropriate because the extremely high uncertainty regarding outcomes makes pre-specified outcome-based pay impractical. In such situations, it would still be useful to set somewhat verifiable goals. Of course, the use of merit pay to cover up for the lack of planning (that is, failure to set outcome goals in advance when outcome-based pay is appropriate) is likely to lead to low instrumentality and subsequent poor performance (Cameron and Pierce, 1997; Eisenberger and Cameron, 1996).

Traditional incentive plans

Incentive plans offer pay as a prior inducement, with actual payout contingent on achieving very specific pre-specified performance outcomes. Incentive plans can be short term or long term and can be used to reward performance at the individual, group, or business unit level. We address group and business unit incentives in later sections of this paper. Two major types of relatively short-term incentive plans are piece-rate plans and commissions. Here we discuss piece-rate plans. For an analysis of commission pay systems, see Bartol (1999).

Piece-rate plans

With piece-rate incentive plans, an employee is paid a specified rate for each unit produced or each service provided. There are a number of variations, such as paying at a higher or lower rate once a standard has been achieved. Much of the evidence regarding the effectiveness of piece-rate systems is based on case studies. Mitchell et al. (1990) estimate that performance gains associated with the proper use of piece-rate plans fall in the 10–25 percent range. A study by Locke et al. (1980) found that the median productivity improvement from piece-rate plans is 30 percent. There is some anecdotal evidence from high-profile companies such as Lincoln Electric and Nucor, as well as theoretical evidence that offering incentives encourages more productive workers to join an organization and encourages others to leave (Lazear,

1998). Thus, some of the impact of incentive plans in organizations may be due to a self-selection process in which only employees who perceive a high likelihood of exceeding the going market rate for pay remain.

While piece-rate incentives appear to be associated with higher performance, evidence also points to counterproductive behaviors as apparent byproducts of incentive systems. Such behaviors include establishing production norms that limit productivity, hiding work method innovations to avoid increases in standards, working slowly to protest standards that are perceived as too high, and focusing only on job facets that are directly rewarded (Mitchell et al., 1990; Wilson, 1992). However, data are unclear regarding causal directions. It is possible that such behaviors are the result of the way in which incentive programs are designed, implemented, and managed rather than necessary outcomes of piece-rate systems themselves. Expectancy theory, goal-setting theory and equity theory all appear to support the potential effectiveness of piece-rate systems. Yet, with inputs and outcomes so closely aligned, perceptions regarding procedural justice may be particularly important. Many of the difficulties, particularly setting and changing the outcome standards that form the basis for pay under piece-rate systems, are related to procedural issues. Thus, procedural justice may be particularly important with piece-rate plans.

As implied above, individuals tend to make higher wages under incentive systems than under time-based pay systems (Mitchell et al., 1990). Yet such differentials may be less when there are multiple pay plans in effect in the organization (Pencavel, 1977). Therefore, there is the possibility that equity considerations across worker groups may lead to tempering the magnitude of the incentives offered, thus perhaps blunting their effectiveness. Moreover, Lawler (1987) has noted the tendency for organizations with part of the work force on incentives and part on straight pay to experience conflict between the two worker segments. Thus, there may be group-level phenomena associated with equity theory that actually lessen the effectiveness of piece-rate systems and that are worthy of future research.

From the point of view of *conditions for effectiveness*, piece-rate systems are likely to be most useful when the work requires significant skill, can be done independently, is repetitive, does not change rapidly, requires a short time period to complete, and has output that can be easily measured in a way that captures all of the essential functions of the job (Henderson, 1997; Mitchell et al., 1990). Piece-rate systems should also be confined to situations in which increased effort clearly makes an important difference in outcomes. Due to group level equity issues, they may be most compatible in organizations in which employees in many types of jobs have the potential to earn extra pay based on performance. Agency theory suggests that when the work is simple, monitoring may be effective and it may not be necessary to pay the wage premium inherent in piece-rate systems to obtain acceptable performance.

Variable and "at-risk" pay plans

The concept of variable pay has been gaining in popularity in recent years. Variable pay is performance-related compensation that does not permanently increase base pay, and that must be re-earned to be received again. For example, a form of variable pay might be a lump-sum bonus for achieving particular goals; but unlike a merit pay raise, the variable pay bonus does not represent an increase in base salary. Although we are discussing variable pay in this section mainly as an individual level phenomenon, it can apply to individuals, teams, business units, and entire organizations. Actually, traditional types of incentive pay systems, such as piece-rate and commissions, fit into the definition of variable pay because the pay must be continually re-earned with new performance.

Part of the recent attraction to the notion of variable pay is that it allows organizations greater flexibility and control over labor costs. For example, if pay is tied to important organizational goals and the goals are not reached, then, with variable pay, the organization will pay employees less, thereby incurring lower costs. Variable pay, in essence, shifts part of an organization's payroll costs from fixed to variable. By having more money allocated to bonuses or other forms of variable pay, an organization can shrink its payroll costs during downturns. In fact, there is evidence that variable pay programs are associated with less organizational employment variability, such as downsizing, allowing employment levels to be more stable over time (Gerhart and Trevor, 1996). Firms requiring high financial flexibility are more likely to make greater use of variable pay (Balkin and Gomez-Mejia, 1987).

Variable pay is typically instituted in one of two major ways (Schuster and Zingheim, 1992). One approach is to discount present base pay by some amount (for example, 5 percent) and then offer variable pay that provides employees with the potential to not only meet, but also exceed their base pay earnings. A second approach is to discount potential base pay by adding only part of the normal merit increase amount to base pay (for example, 2 percent) and reserving the rest (for example, 3 percent) to be given as variable pay. If this is done over several years, the portion of variable pay can grow substantially, allowing the offering of sizable variable pay bonuses for performance.

With base pay moving up more slowly in a variable pay plan, a greater portion of the money formerly used for merit pay can be allocated to variable forms of performance pay. Keeping base salaries lower also can save on those benefits that are often tied to base salary levels, such as pension plans. Another argument in favor of variable pay is that, by requiring continued high performance to receive the extra pay, it reduces the entitlement mentality that sometimes becomes associated with merit pay. In that sense, variable pay fits more closely the prescriptions inherent in expectancy theory. Of necessity, variable pay plans must clarify instrumentality – that is, what performance is required for specified rewards.

On the other hand, as suggested by equity theory and institutional theory, employees may consider the pay plan to be unfair compared to traditional merit pay plans that provide greater base salary growth. Not surprisingly in view of prospect theory, Brown and Huber (1992) found that employees in a bank reacted quite negatively to an at-risk pay plan that reduced their base pay even though they had the potential to earn more under the at-risk system. This was true even among individuals who earned at least as much or more under the new system. As agency theory indicates, keeping base pay at relatively low levels and incorporating risk is likely to be unattractive to employees and potential employees unless there is a fairly attractive "upside" potential to the variable pay portion.

Schuster and Zingheim (1992) argue that several circumstances govern whether new variable pay should be current base pay at risk or potential base pay at risk. They also point out that an add-on is a third option. With the add-on approach, variable pay is extra compensation that can be earned over what is available through a typical merit pay plan. The circumstances regarding which approach to use include the organization's ability to pay, the readiness of employees for variable pay, and the competitiveness of the organization's total compensation. They argue that the higher the performance standards before the variable pay plan begins to pay out, the more feasible it is to offer variable pay as an add-on because the higher productivity justifies the higher pay. Caution is needed to avoid inflating payroll costs to high levels without registering corresponding productivity gains. Otherwise, variable pay plans will lead to less, rather than more flexibility for organizations and their members. Agency theory suggests that offering variable pay may be unnecessary when behavioral monitoring is possible.

In considering *conditions for effectiveness*, individual variable pay is likely to work best when performance outcomes that are ultimately important to the bottom line can be reliably measured at the individual level. Caution is needed to ensure that the measurement includes all of the important aspects of the job, so that the pay system does not neglect important job functions. Unless further research demonstrates that discounting current base pay leads to better performance without causing serious negative affective reactions, prospect theory suggests it should be avoided.

It may be more reasonable for an organization that generally sets base pay in the upper quartiles of the market to gradually move to the average or median of the market and channel the money saved to variable pay. It may also be possible to allow salaries to lag behind the market somewhat as long as the upside potential of the variable pay is sufficiently high to offset the added risk. As indicated by goal-setting theory, under variable pay arrangements, it is important that employees have some reasonable hope of attaining total compensation that exceeds market pay if they expend extra effort.

Skill- and competency-based pay

In most compensation schemes, job evaluation is used to determine the worth of the job and individuals are paid within the job's pay range based on how well they perform the job's duties. One relatively new compensation orientation is to base pay on the characteristics of the person rather than the job. Part of the underlying logic is that organizations need to be flexible in order to compete and, therefore, it makes sense to establish pay systems that encourage individual development of the knowledge, skills, and abilities that are strategically important to the organization (Barney, 1991; von Krogh, 1998). Two emerging methods for basing pay on the person are skill-based pay and competency-based pay.

Skill-based pay

Skill-based pay compensates employees for the breadth and depth of relevant skills they can use in the organization rather than for the particular job that they may be doing at a given point in time (Gupta et al., 1992). Skill-based pay is used mainly with operators, technicians, and office workers, in situations in which the work can be fairly well specified and defined (Milkovich and Newman, 1999). With skill-based pay, employees can learn various skill units, which are collections of tasks, duties, and responsibilities. Once they are certified as having mastered a particular skill unit, they receive an increment in pay associated with that unit. One study of 97 skill-based plans showed that certification of mastery of skills units is done by the immediate supervisor (84 percent), co-workers (52 percent) and/or the employee (40 percent) (Gupta et al., 1992). The same study indicated that, on average, employees can master the maximum number of allowed skill units within three years.

In addition to the desire to have flexible employees from a strategic point of view, there are several other major reasons cited by companies for adopting skill-based pay plans (O'Neill and Lander, 1993/94). One is the requirement to improve and maintain production efficiencies while also implementing leaner and flatter organization structures. Another is the need to more effectively maintain productive capability in the face of absenteeism, turnover, or production bottlenecks. Still another is the desire to foster involvement, commitment, increased teamwork, and the development of enriched jobs that will be more rewarding to employees. In the Gupta et al. (1992) survey mentioned previously, about 41 percent of respondents reported that their skill-based pay plans were highly successful and only 6 percent characterized their plans as unsuccessful. Respondents gave their skill-based pay plans high marks for increasing employee flexibility, satisfaction, and commitment. Almost 50 percent credited skill-based pay as having achieved "a lot" of success in increasing output per hour worked. Some of the apparent increase in productivity is likely to be due to greater flexibility in handling work. Using time series data, Murray and Gerhart (1998) found that a plant with a skilled-based pay program outperformed a comparison plant without skill-based pay on several dimensions – productivity, labor costs per part, and quality (scrap reduction).

Although the available data suggest that skill-based pay has a positive effect on productivity and worker satisfaction, most of these data are based on the perceptions of individuals responsible for these compensation programs (the study by Murray and Gerhart, 1998, is an exception). Because surveys assessing skill-based pay plans have tended to focus on plans that are still in operation, they may understate the difficulties and failure rates. Some organizations, such as Motorola, have abandoned skill-based pay, largely because they found they were paying for skills that they were not utilizing sufficiently to justify the higher wages being paid (Davidson, 1993). Moreover, skill-based pay plans have added costs, such as training and higher levels of pay, that must be considered in assessing their true effectiveness. In the plant they studied, however, Murray and Gerhart (1998) found that the higher costs were offset by higher productivity.

From an expectancy theory perspective, skill-based pay plans appear to be particularly useful in addressing the expectancy element because the skills training is likely to enhance the belief that one's efforts will lead to the desired level of performance. Skill-based pay also typically creates a situation in which the employees under skill-based plans make higher wages than other employees do in similar types of jobs in the local labor market or industry (Gupta et al., 1992). Thus, in the short run, the system also provides a strong focus on the instrumentality and valence elements in spelling out the link between learning new skills and achieving higher pay. Once the new skills are learned, however, it is not clear how skill-based pay systems will continue to motivate performance.

In assessing *conditions for effectiveness*, skill-based pay is likely to be most useful in situations in which there is a major productivity benefit to be derived from having a staff with interchangeable skills. Nevertheless, the focus of skill-based pay is mainly on inputs to the system – that is, employee development. Unless the system is also combined with some means of measuring and rewarding outcomes, the long-term link to performance is likely to be tenuous other than possibly encouraging retention of the skilled workers because of the higher wages.

Competency-based pay

In addition to the proliferation of skill-based pay plans, the concept of paying for the capabilities of the person rather than the job is currently being explored for work that is more difficult to define. Pay systems of this type are called competency-based pay. Competency-based pay compensates knowledge workers for the breadth and depth of relevant knowledge, skills, and competencies they possess, rather than the particular job they hold at a particular point in time. Although the approach has roots in skill-based pay, the term competency is used to denote the broader and more non-programmed nature of managerial and professional work. Ledford (1995) defines competencies as "demonstrable characteristics of the person, including knowledge, skills, and behaviors, that enable performance" (p. 56).

Interest in competency-based pay is rising in part because organizations are becoming more concerned with developing core competencies from a strategic point of view. Hence pay systems that might encourage employees to develop their competencies in areas of strategic importance to the organization might have long-term benefits. This type of an approach fits particularly well with the resource-based strategic model of the firm (Barney, 1991). The perceived success of skill-based plans has also encouraged some companies to look for ways to extend the concept of paying for the person to professional and managerial employees. The growing importance of knowledge workers is another catalyst for exploring means of pay based more heavily on the person rather than the specific duties of the job.

Efforts to create competency-based organizations are in their embryonic stages. One of the questions that will need to be answered is: what competencies are strategically important to the organization? It will then be necessary to develop or at least facilitate training so individuals can acquire the desired skills. A competency certification process will need to be developed, so that organizations can be sure that the necessary competencies are acquired and maintained, particularly if pay will be used to reward their acquisition.

Because of the extra costs both in development and pay, it is important that the competencies add sufficient value to the organization to justify the additional costs both in development and pay. Otherwise the organization will find itself at a disadvantage because of higher labor costs than its competitors and possibly also wasted efforts aimed at acquiring non-pivotal skills (Lawler, 1994). Moreover, human capital theory

(Becker, 1975) suggests that organizations should allocate resources to training that is specific to the needs of the organization and that is not readily transferable to other organizations. An example might be to acquire in-depth knowledge about and the ability to design applications using an organization's proprietary software. Otherwise, individuals may use the training they have obtained to negotiate better paying positions in competing organizations that then reap the training benefits without the costs.

At the present time, many organizations are experimenting with the competency approach, but there is little concrete data available with which to evaluate its effectiveness. Clearly more research is needed to appraise both the design and implementation of competency-based assessment and training systems, as well as the advisability of linking pay to competencies development.

In considering *conditions for effectiveness*, competency-based pay is likely to be most beneficial in situations in which it is possible to identify competencies of strategic importance. Ideally the competencies would be organizationally specific and difficult for others to imitate, making it particularly worthwhile for the organization to provide resources, including pay, for their development. Still, as noted earlier, competencies are characteristics of a person that "enable performance" (Ledford, 1995). There is a difference between being able to perform and doing so. Therefore, as suggested by goal-setting theory and expectancy theory, it will be important for such systems also to be tied to specific goals, outcomes, and related rewards. Otherwise the potential benefits of the acquired competencies may not be realized.

Pay for small group effectiveness

For competitive reasons, many organizations are seeking ways to encourage greater cooperation within and across work units by altering compensation systems to emphasize group outcomes. Much of this focus has centered on seeking better ways to link compensation with the growing emphasis on teamwork (Bartol and Hagmann, 1992).

Limited data exist on the use of small group incentives in organizations. One Conference Board study (Peck, 1990) indicates that 12 percent of the 435 responding companies use small group incentives. Another study indicates that 70 percent of the Fortune 1000 are using some type of work group/team incentives (Lawler et al., 1995). For the purposes of this paper, teams or work groups are multi-person work units that are designated or recognized by management and others in the organization, that are composed of individuals who operate interdependently as group members, and that perform tasks that affect others associated with the organization (Guzzo and Dickson, 1996; Hackman, 1987). As Guzzo and Dickson do, we use the terms "teams" and "work groups" interchangeably.

As has been pointed out by a number of authors, small groups or teams can differ greatly from one another. For example, work groups include autonomous work groups, cross-functional teams, project teams, and task forces (Guzzo and Dickson, 1996). Moreover, a number of different views have been advanced regarding how team pay should be configured (for example, Lawler, 1996; Zingheim and Schuster, 1997).

For example, Montemayor (1994) argues that one of the most important factors to consider in designing pay systems for teams and work groups is the degree of task interdependence: pooled (members work generally independently but combine their output); sequential (members perform tasks in a predetermined serial order); or reciprocal (doing the task requires a high level of interaction). He maintains that pooled interdependence calls for pay based on individual productivity, whereas sequential interdependence lends itself to team bonuses as a percentage of base pay (because base pay can reflect the differences in skill levels involved in the process). Montemayor argues that reciprocal interdependence warrants team bonuses based on dollars per capita or dollars per hour because significant differences in pay can highlight status differences and hinder collaboration.

Lawler (1996) notes that a key decision in adopting teams is the extent of reward for individual performance versus team performance. He suggests using skill-based pay and competency-based pay to encourage individual development, while using pay based on team performance to reinforce the need for teamwork. He notes that gainsharing or profit sharing (discussed further below) may be appropriate for rewarding group achievement in all but project teams. For project teams, he argues that team-based pay tied to project performance is critical; otherwise team members will concentrate on their functional areas. For the coordinating/overlay teams, he recommends possibly adding stock ownership opportunities for team performance and also rewarding individual achievements because these teams typically do not produce specific products. None of these prescriptions has been tested empirically.

Wageman (1995) investigated interdependence issues among service groups or teams at Xerox by selecting existing groups that had individual, group, or hybrid tasks (a mix of individual and group tasks). She found that groups performed best when their tasks and outcomes were either purely group oriented or purely individual oriented. Hybrid groups actually performed poorly, experienced low-quality interaction processes, and experienced low group member satisfaction. One possibility is that the hybrid task design was not as compatible with the type of work involved. The study results illustrate the challenges associated with mixing levels of analysis when designing pay systems.

Research related to goal-setting theory suggests that congruence between individual and group goals can enhance goal commitment (Crown and Rosse, 1995). On the other hand, when individual and group goals are in conflict, it appears likely that individuals will give priority to the type of goal that is seen as offering the most reward potential (Shalley and Johnson, 1996). There is a critical need for further research on group incentives and particularly the viability of mixing individual and group pay schemes.

From the viewpoint of *conditions for effectiveness*, group incentives are likely to be most useful in situations in which the nature of the task requires a significant amount of sequential or task interdependence. Multiple-level plans involving individual and team pay combinations would seem to be warranted when reaching group goals depends on both cooperative behavior in the group and identifiable individual behaviors/outcomes. Care should be taken to ensure that individual and group goals are congruent; otherwise the performance effect is likely to be different from that which is intended.

Pay for plant, division, or organizational effectiveness

Gainsharing

Gainsharing is a compensation plan in which an organization shares with employees a portion of the added earnings obtained through their collective increases in productivity (Henderson, 1997). Typically gainsharing involves all or a significant number of an organization's employees. Gainsharing plans have been in existence for more than 60 years and their numbers seem to be growing. According to one estimate, there are more than 1,000 gainsharing plans in existence (Lawler and Jenkins, 1992). One survey indicates that 42 percent of the Fortune 1000 had some type of gainsharing in operation in 1993, up from 26 percent in 1987 (Lawler et al., 1995).

The available research on gainsharing indicates that the approach has been fairly successful in raising productivity in organizations (US General Accounting Office, 1981; Graham-Moore and Ross, 1990; Kaufman, 1992; Welbourne and Gomez-Mejia, 1988). Bullock and Lawler (1984) estimate that the success rate for gainsharing programs is about 70 percent. These conclusions must be tempered by the fact that most of the available studies tend to be case studies and/or are based on data collected after the programs had already been implemented (Welborne and Gomez-Mejia, 1988). The growth of gainsharing plans should open up opportunities for more rigorous studies of their effectiveness.

Most gainsharing plans are adaptations of one of three major approaches, each using a different type of formula to determine bonuses (Milkovich and Newman, 1999). Scanlon plans, the oldest approach, focus on labor costs, while Rucker plans emphasize value added per dollar of total wage. Both Scanlon and Rucker plans place heavy emphasis on employee participation through worker committees that play a major role in evaluating suggestions for cost savings and productivity improvements. They consider participation to be a critical ingredient in their success. Improshare, a newer approach, establishes production standards and ties bonuses to improvements. Interestingly, the Improshare approach places less explicit emphasis on participation, considering it to be an outcome of efforts to achieve bonus-earning results rather than a necessary input.

Although the available evidence suggests that gainsharing is successful in raising productivity, the mechanisms through which it does so are unclear. For example, Lawler and Jenkins (1992) note that some of the improvement may be due to the motivational impact of tying pay more clearly to performance. They note, however, that the motivational impact may be limited because gainsharing is tied to the aggregate performance of a number of people. Gainsharing encompasses the elements of expectancy theory to some degree. Yet the expectancy element may be somewhat problematic in the context of gainsharing because the line of sight between organization members' efforts and productivity impact (and thus on the bonus amount) may be blunted in a gainsharing environment.

Locke et al. (1997) suggested that much of the positive impact of participation on performance may actually be due to the enhanced information available through participation. The success of both the highly participatory Scanlon and Rucker plans, and even the Improshare plans that place less overt emphasis on participation, provide some support for the idea that something besides simply the motivational impact of participation is at work here. Part of the apparent success of such plans is probably attributable to goal setting, because gainsharing involves setting targets for improvement.

Gainsharing also tends to alter the structure of decision making and control, in the sense of frequently allowing decisions to be made and actions taken at lower levels in the organization than before. There can also be greater feedback, both because of the suggestion committees that are part of many gainsharing plans and because heads of units or facilities with gainsharing plans often hold monthly plant-wide meetings to discuss progress, operational issues, and bonus results (Collins et al., 1993).

Gainsharing focuses on relatively short-term specific productivity gains that must be generated before payout. Some companies, such as Corning, Inc., have been experimenting with "goalsharing" plans that allow goals which may have more long-term benefits – such as improvements in customer service (Altmansberger and Wallace, 1995). Under the plan, business units are encouraged to set no more than five goals that will have long-term impact. Achievement of the goals accounts for 75 percent of the payout. The other 25 percent is based on the corporate return on equity (ROE), with the maximum profit-sharing bonus being distributed only if Corning's ROE is in the top quartile of its peer companies.

Congruent with agency theory, Welbourne et al. (1995) found that gainsharing leads to mutual monitoring among peers who have greater surveillance capabilities at relatively low monitoring costs because they, too, are engaged in the activity. Their findings also indicated that individuals were more likely to engage in mutual monitoring when they perceived both procedural and distributive justice – that is, they could count on the system to be fair in the manner in which rewards were determined and in the level of rewards awarded. Thus, part of the benefit of gainsharing may derive from encouraging mutual monitoring. The sharing of the benefits of productivity gains also likely has benefits in terms of positive justice perceptions regarding the organization.

In considering *conditions for effectiveness*, gainsharing will be most effective when there is a clear line of sight regarding what individuals and/or groups can do to influence productivity improvement goals. It will likely work best when information sharing is encouraged among employees and in situations of sequential or reciprocal interdependence that offer good prospects for productivity improvements through collaborative efforts. Such plans may require extra communication regarding procedural and distributive justice issues because of the number of individuals involved.

Profit sharing

Profit-sharing plans provide payments to employees based on the profitability of the business. Payments can be made through current distribution plans, deferred plans, or a combination of both. For tax reasons, the majority of companies with profit-sharing plans use the deferred option and it is the fastest growing type of profit-sharing plan (Milkovich and Newman, 1999). According to Lawler et al. (1995), approximately 66 percent of the Fortune 1000 have some type of profit-sharing plan.

The existing research on the effectiveness of profit sharing suffers from a number of limitations largely related to almost exclusive reliance on case studies. Moreover, these generally lack appropriate pre- and post-plan measures (Florkowski, 1987). A meta-analysis of existing profit-sharing studies by Weitzman and Kruse (1990) suggests that profit sharing has a positive impact on productivity. They estimated a mean average effect on productivity of 7.4 percent. Given the nature of the underlying research, these results must be viewed as tentative. Moreover, the Weitzman and Kruse study included gainsharing, which we would argue potentially provides a much greater line of sight than that offered by profit sharing. Even while arguing that profit sharing has positive effects on performance, Weitzman and Kruse acknowledge that the mechanisms through which profit sharing may affect productivity are poorly understood. Indeed, more rigorous studies of profit sharing are sorely needed. Florkowski (1987) offers a framework that includes a number of variables which may be of interest.

A weakness of profit sharing is that it may be difficult to establish a clear line of sight so that individuals and work groups know what they can do to affect profits. In this sense, both the expectancy and instrumentality elements of expectancy theory may be somewhat weak in a profit-sharing context. Indeed, profit levels can be affected by a variety of variables, such as accounting procedures and economic conditions, over which operating employees may have little control. To the extent that profit-sharing plans incorporate targets, it may be possible to harness some of the benefits of goal setting. However, the line-of-sight issue remains a potential deficiency.

From the point of view of *conditions for effectiveness*, it is possible that profit sharing may be most useful from an equity theory point of view because it provides some linkages to rewards based on the profit levels of the organization. This may be particularly important for publicly traded companies, for which the salaries of top-level executives are more readily available. It may be best to frame profit sharing in a positive light as sharing the wealth during good times. Thus profit sharing may be useful in helping to convey efforts toward procedural and distributive justice. It is also possible that equity issues relate to productivity somewhat indirectly through procedural and distributive justice mechanisms (Greenberg, 1990), thus raising the possibility of productivity gains via enhanced justice perceptions. Research, however, is needed to verify this possibility.

Employee stock ownership

A growing number of companies are providing ownership opportunities for employees through stock ownership programs. A study of Fortune 1000 companies indicated that 71 percent had stock ownership programs of some type, up from 61 percent in 1987 (Lawler et al., 1995). The three main vehicles are Employee Stock Ownership Plans (ESOPs), stock purchase plans, and stock options. Each is subject to a variety of complex securities and tax provisions (see, for example, Henderson, 1997). We focus our attention on stock options because they are increasingly the vehicle of choice for providing rewards through stock ownership.

Stock options give employees the right to purchase a specific amount of stock at a specific price, but over a longer period of time than is typically the case with stock purchase plans. Organizations use stock options as compensation when the opportunity exists for future stock appreciation and the organization wants the recipients of the stock options to participate in that appreciation. Although stock options have been used widely as a vehicle for rewarding corporate executives, recently an increasing number of companies are awarding options to employees at middle and lower levels in the organization (Chingos and Engel, 1998). Options are sometimes issued with vesting periods, which specify a time period that must elapse before the options can be exercised. When an organization's stock price is appreciating, the impact of vesting periods is to discourage individuals from leaving the organization (Ellig, 1998).

Under most circumstances, an individual will exercise option rights only if the stock price has increased. When the market stock price is higher than the option price, the stock is said to be "in the money;" when the market stock price is below the option price, the stock is said to be "underwater" (Ellig, 1998). Under many plans, the option recipient must produce the cash to purchase the stock at the option. Some plans allow cashless exercise through such mechanisms as allowing the option receiver to simultaneously buy the stock under the option and sell it at the market price (Ellig, 1998). The individual then receives cash or stock for the difference.

The growing trend toward expanding both the magnitude of awards and the levels of the organization to which stock options are offered is causing some concerns (Morgenson, 1998). One is the resulting stock dilution, whereby the additional shares outstanding cause a reduction in earnings per share. To counter the dilution effects and boost earning per share, some companies have been buying back stock at high market prices. For example, Microsoft recently repurchased 37 million shares for $3.1 billion. The average repurchase price was $84, while the average exercise price for all outstanding options was $31. These trends are alarming stockholders and causing increasing shareholder votes against stock-option plans (Bryant, 1998). At the same time, one study by accounting professors Steven Huddart and Mark Lang showed that two-thirds of lower level employees exercised their options within six months of vesting when the stocks were "in the money," while senior managers exercised their options at about half that rate (cited in Gill, 1998). Such scenarios cast doubt on the long-term ownership impact of stock options for employees, particularly those at lower levels.

In terms of *conditions for effectiveness*, at this point there is little evidence regarding the degree to which employee stock options below top management lead to improved organizational or individual performance. Therefore, future studies are sorely needed. Generally, the same line of sight, equity, and justice issues cited for profit sharing apply to stock options. Because actual stock prices influence the value of stock options, one advantage of stock options may be that they likely focus employee attention on the organization's daily stock price (Gill, 1998). Whether this leads to better organizational performance and productivity remains an empirical question in need of investigation.

Special case: top management (CEO) compensation

One of the most controversial aspects of employee compensation in recent years centers on the sizable amounts of pay afforded to CEOs and other members of top management. The controversy has two major aspects (Crystal and Cook, 1996). One is the seeming lack of sufficient linkage between top management compensation and organizational performance. The second is the growing pay gap between CEOs and other employees in the organization.

Numerous studies have examined the connection between CEO pay and performance. Tosi and Gomez-Mejia (1989) assess that the total explained variance in performance accounted for by compensation in these studies has rarely exceeded 15 percent and is frequently well below 10 percent. For the most part, these studies have involved the use of publicly available archival data. Gomez-Mejia (1994) points out that there are many methodological limitations associated with these studies, including problems of comparability among the data reported by firms, lack of systematic qualitative data about CEO performance, and shortcomings in operationalizing theoretical constructs because of reliance on existing databases. He speculates that underlying theory may be inadequate, noting that agency theory is less concerned about pay level than about how the risk features and criteria associated with compensation packages influence management decisions. To overcome the limitations associated with archival data, there is a need to explore alternative methodologies, in particular to help hone theory development. For example, Tosi et al. (1997) recently used a laboratory study to test the degree to which incentive alignments recommended by agency theory influence managerial (agent) decision making. In congruence with agency theory, the study results indicated that when a compensation arrangement offered to agents aligns the interests of both agents and owners, managers make profit-maximizing decisions. On the other hand, when the compensation arrangement is linked to decisions that produce low returns to the owners, agents will nevertheless make those decisions because they are in their own best interest.

In terms of *conditions for effectiveness*, one outgrowth of the debate over the apparent weak linkages between CEO pay and performance has been pressure for compensation packages that more heavily link CEO pay with both short- and long-term company performance. A study by KPMG Peat Marwick of 133 public and privately owned companies found that long-term incentives, most of which are stock-based, constituted the largest single component in the compensation packages of senior management. In public companies, the present value of the long-term incentives exceeded base salary and was two to four times larger than annual incentives, such as bonuses. In private companies, the trend was similar, but to a lesser degree. Chingos and Engel (1998) report that these long-term incentives represent "a dramatic increase over the typical compensation mix five years ago, when long-term incentives were much less prominent in the total compensation picture" (p. 15). Further research will now be critical to assess the effectiveness of this shift.

CONCLUSIONS

We have reviewed the various major theories that are relevant to the design of pay and incentive systems and identified the principles that can be induced from such theories. We have also assessed the major types of incentive delivery systems, pointing to circumstances under which they are likely to be effective as a basis for future research. In the process we have pointed to a number of areas in which further research is needed.

There are, however, several major issues that cross the boundaries of the various pay systems which also are in need of investigation. For example, although we have alluded to level of analysis issues throughout the paper, it is useful to reiterate here the need for further research that attempts to assess the impact of simultaneous pay plans at multiple levels (for example, merit pay, team pay, and profit sharing or other combinations). We also need to better understand how pay difference and issues of pay dispersion affect perceptions of justice within and across levels (Bloom, 1999).

Another important related area is the influence of homogeneity versus heterogeneity among group members with respect to various expectancy theory elements and the impact on pay plan success. Along these lines, we know very little about how employees within large group pay plans, such as gainsharing and profit sharing, think about expectancy, instrumentality, and valence issues related to such plans. Nor do we fully understand the potential benefits in terms of justice perceptions.

The issue of risk as it relates to pay plans also needs further investigation. Although agency theory and prospect theory provide frameworks for thinking about risk issues, we actually know very little about the degree to which pay plans encourage useful versus inordinate risk taking. This is particularly true with respect to high level managers in organizations, who increasingly have higher amounts of variable pay at stake. Moreover, evidence suggests that individuals differ in their risk-taking propensity (Bromiley and Curley, 1992), but have little understanding of how this might affect individual decision making or approaches in group contexts.

As institutional theory suggests, there often are major difficulties associated with changing pay plans. We need to know more about how to change pay plans in a way that will overcome the inherent inertia and yet provide positive justice perceptions.

Finally, as we have outlined, theory and research offer suggestions regarding the characteristics of effective pay systems and the circumstances under which the various pay systems are likely to be effective. Future research needs to evaluate and further refine these prescriptions. More carefully contrived pay systems and better matching with the appropriate context constitute steps that are likely to greatly increase both the motivational impact of and satisfaction with pay systems. Given the massive amounts of pay distributed by organizations each year, a stepped-up pace of research on the issues addressed in this chapter would seem to be well warranted.

REFERENCES

Adams, J. S. 1965: Inequity in social exchange. In L. Berkowitz (ed.), *Advances in experimental social psychology*, New York: Academic Press, Vol. 2.

Adams, J. S., and Freedman, S. 1976: Equity theory revisited: Comments and annotated bibliography. In L. Berkowitz and E. Walster (eds.), *Advances in experimental social psychology*, New York: Academic Press, Vol. 9, 43–90.

Altmansberger, H. N., and Wallace, M. J. 1995: Strategic use of goalsharing at Corning. *American Compensation Association Journal*, 4, Winter, 64–73.

Balkin, D. B., and Gomez-Mejia, L. R. 1987: Toward a contingency theory of compensation strategy. *Strategic Management Journal*, 8, 169–82.

Bandura, A. 1986: *Social foundations of thought and action: A social-cognitive view*, Englewood Cliffs, NJ: Prentice Hall.

Bandura, A. 1997: *Self-efficacy: The exercise of control*. New York: W.H. Freeman.

Barney, J. 1991: Firm resources and sustained competitive advantage. *Journal of Management*, 17, 99–120.

Bartol, K. M. 1999: Reframing salesforce compensation systems: An agency theory-based performance management perspective. *Journal of Personal Selling and Sales Management*, 19, issue 3, 1–16.

Bartol, K. M., and Hagmann, L. L. 1992: Team-based pay plans: A key to effective teamwork. *Compensation and Benefits Review*, November–December, 24–9.

Bartol, K. M., and Locke, E. A. 2000: Incentives and motivation. In S. Rynes and B. Gerhart (eds.), *Compensation in organizations: Progress and prospects*, San Francisco: New Lexington Press, 104–147.

Becker, G. S. 1975: *Human capital*, Chicago: University of Chicago Press.

Bloom, M. 1999: The performance effects of pay dispersion on individuals and organizations. *Academy of Management Journal*, 42, 25–40.

Bretz, R. D., Milkovich, G. T., and Read, W. 1992: The current state of performance appraisal research and practice: Concerns, directions, and implications. *Journal of Management*, 18, 321–52.

Bromiley, P., and Curley, S. P. 1992: In J. F. Yates (ed.), *Risk-taking behavior*, New York: Wiley & Sons, 87–132.

Brown, K. A., and Huber, V. L. 1992: Lowering floors and raising ceilings: A longitudinal assessment of the effects of an earnings-at-risk plan on pay satisfaction. *Personnel Psychology*, 45, 279–311.

Bryant, A. 1998: Some second thoughts on options. *American Compensation Association Journal*, 7, Spring, 96–100.

Bullock, R. J., and Lawler, E. E., III 1984: Gainsharing: A few questions and fewer answers. *Human Resource Management*, 23, 23–40.

Cameron, J., and Pierce, W. D. 1997: Rewards, interest and performance: An evaluation of experimental findings. *American Compensation Association Journal*, 6, Winter, 6–15.

Campbell, J. P., and Pritchard, R. D. 1976: Motivation theory in industrial and organizational psychology. In M. D. Dunnette (ed.), *Handbook for industrial and organizational psychology*, Chicago: Rand McNally, 63–130.

Chingos, P. T., and Engel, M. M. 1998: Trends in stock option plans and long-term incentives. *American Compensation Association Journal*, 7, Spring, 13–18.

Collins, D., Hatcher, L., and Ross, T. L. 1993: The decision to implement gainsharing: The role of work climate, expected outcomes, and union status. *Personnel Psychology*, 46, 77–101.

Conlon, E., and Parks, J. 1990: Effects of monitoring and tradition on compensation arrangements: An experiment with principal-agent dyads. *Academy of Management Journal*, 33, 603–22.

Cowherd, D. M., and Levine, D. I. 1992: Product quality and pay equity between lower-level employees and top management: An investigation of distributive justice theory. *Administrative Science Quarterly*, 37, 302–20.

Cropanzano, R., and Folger, R. 1989: Referent cognitions and task decision autonomy: Beyond equity theory. *Journal of Applied Psychology*, 74, 293–9.

Crown, D. F., and Rosse, J. G. 1995: Yours, mine, and ours: Facilitating group productivity through the integration of individual and group goals. *Organizational Behavior and Human Decision Processes*, 64, 138–50.

Crystal, G. S., and Cook, F. W. 1996: The growing pay gap: Are CEOs paid too much relative to other employees? *American Compensation Association Journal*, 5, Summer, 22–9.

Davidson, K. M. 1993: Motorola transitions from skill-based pay. *American Compensation News*, 3, July.

DiMaggio, P. J., and Powell, W. W. 1983: The iron cage revisited: Institutional isomorphism and collective rationality in organizational fields. *American Sociological Review*, 48, 147–60.

Drazin, R., Glynn, M. A., and Kazanjian, R. K. 1999: Multilevel theorizing about creativity in organizations: A sensemaking perspective. *Academy of Management Review*, 24, 286–307.

Eisenberger, R., and Cameron, J. 1996: Detrimental effects of reward: Reality or myth? *American Psychologist*, 51, 1153–66.

Eisenhardt, K. M. 1985: Control: Organizational and economic approaches. *Management Science*, 31, 134–49.

Eisenhardt, K. M. 1988: Agency- and institutional-theory explanations: The case of retail sales compensation. *Academy of Management Journal*, 31, 488–511.

Eisenhardt, K. M. 1989: Agency theory: An assessment and review. *Academy of Management Review*, 14, 57–74.

Ellig, B. R. 1998: Employee stock options: An overview. *American Compensation Association Journal*, 7, 8–12.

Florkowski, G. W. 1987: The organizational impact of profit sharing. *Academy of Management Review*, 12, 622–36.

Gerhart, B., and Trevor, C. O. 1996: Employment variability under different compensation systems. *Academy of Management Journal*, 39, 1692–1712.

Gerhart, G., Trevor, C. O., and Graham, M. E. 1996: New directions in compensation research: Synergies, risk, and survival. *Research in Personnel and Human Resources Management*, 14, 143–203.

Gill, E. S. 1998: Cashless exercise: Why so few people keep shares. *American Compensation Association Journal*, 7, Spring, 31–3.

Gomez-Mejia, L. R. 1994: Executive compensation: A reassessment and a future research agenda. *Research in Personnel and Human Resources Management*, 12, 161–222.

Gomez-Mejia, L. R., and Balkin, D. B. 1992: *Compensation, organizational strategy, and firm performance*. Cincinnati, OH: South-Western.

Goodrick, E., and Salancik, G. R. 1996: Organizational discretion in responding to institutional practices: hospitals and cesarean births. *Administrative Science Quarterly*, 41, 1–28.

Graham-Moore, B. E., and Ross, T. L. 1990: *Gainsharing*. Washington, DC: The Bureau of National Affairs.

Greenberg, J. 1990: Employee theft as a reaction to underpayment inequity: The hidden cost of pay cuts. *Journal of Applied Psychology*, 75, 561–8.

Gupta, N., Ledford, G. E., Jenkins, G. D., and Doty, D. H. 1992: Survey-based prescriptions for skill-based pay. *American Compensation Association Journal*, 1, 48–59.

Guzzo, R. A., and Dickson, M. W. 1996: Teams in organizations: Recent research on performance and effectiveness. *Annual Review of Psychology*, 47, 307–38.

Hackman, J. R. 1987: The design of work teams. In J. W. Lorsch (ed.), *Handbook of Organizational Behavior*, Englewood Cliffs, NJ: Prentice Hall, 315–42.

Hall, R. H. 1991: *Organizations: Structures, processes, and outcomes*. Englewood Cliffs, NJ: Prentice Hall.

Harris, M. M., Gilbreath, B., and Sunday, J. A. 1998: A longitudinal examination of a merit pay system: Relationships among performance ratings, merit increases, and total pay increases. *Journal of Applied Psychology*, 83, 825–31.

Healey, A. 1997: U.S. salary increases continue slow climb. *American Compensation Association News*, September, 14–17.

Henderson, R. I. 1997: *Compensation management in a knowledge-based world*, 7th edn., Upper Saddle River, NJ: Prentice Hall.

Heneman, R. L. 1990: Merit pay research. *Research in Personnel and Human Resources Management*, 8, 203–63.

Heneman, R. L. 1992: *Merit pay: Linking pay increases to performance ratings*. Reading, MA: Addison-Wesley.

Jensen, M., and Meckling, M. 1976: Theory of the firm: Managerial behavior, agency costs and ownership structure, *Journal of Financial Economics*, 3, 305–60.

Kahneman, D., and Tversky, A. 1979: Prospect theory: An analysis of decisions under risk. *Econometrica*, 47, 262–91.

Kaplan, R. S. 1984: The evolution of management accounting. *Accounting Review*, 59, 390–480.

Kaufman, R. 1992: The effects of Improshare on productivity. *Industrial and Labor Relations Review*, 45, 311–22.

Klein, K. J., Dansereau, F., and Hall, R. J. 1994: Levels issues in theory development, data collection, and analysis. *Academy of Management Review*, 19, 195–229.

Klein, K. J., Tosi, H., and Cannella, A. A., Jr. 1999: Multilevel theory building: Benefits, barriers, and new developments. *Academy of Management Review*, 24, 243–8.

Koenig, R. 1990: Du Pont plan linking pay to fibers profit unravels. *The Wall Street Journal*, October 25, B1, B4.

Kopelman, R. E., Rovenpor, J., and Cayer, M. 1991: Merit pay and organizational performance: Is there an effect on the bottom line? *National Productivity Review*, 10, 299–307.

Kostova, T. 1999: Transnational transfer of strategic organizational practices: A contextual perspective. *Academy of Management Review*, 24, 308–24.

Lawler, E. E., III. 1987: Pay for performance: A motivational analysis. In H. R. Nalbantian (ed.), *Incentives, cooperation, and risk sharing*, Totowa, NJ: Rowman and Littlefield, 69–86.

Lawler, E. E., III. 1994: From job-based to competency-based organizations. *Journal of Organizational Behavior*, 15, 3–15.

Lawler, E. E., III. 1996: Teams, pay and business strategy: Finding the best mix to achieve competitive advantage. *American Compensation Association Journal*, 5, Spring, 12–25.

Lawler, E. E., III, and Jenkins, G. D., Jr. 1992: In M. D. Dunnette and L. Hough (eds.), *Handbook of industrial and organizational psychology*, 2nd edn., Palo Alto, CA: Consulting Psychologists Press, Vol. 3, 1009–55.

Lawler, E. E., III, Mohrman, S., and Ledford, G. E., Jr. 1995: *Creating high performance organizations*. San Francisco: Jossey-Bass.

Lazear, E. P. 1998: *Personnel economics for managers*. New York: John Wiley & Sons.

Ledford, G. E., Jr. 1995: Paying for the skills, knowledge, and competencies of knowledge workers. *Compensation and Benefits Review*, July–August, 55–62.

Lee, T. W., Locke, E. A., and Phan, S. H. 1997: Explaining the assigned goal-incentive interaction: The role of self-efficacy and personal goals. *Journal of Management*, 23, 541–59.

Leventhal, G. S., Karuza, J., and Fry, W. R. 1980: Beyond fairness: A theory of allocation preferences. In G. Mikula (ed.), *Justice and social interaction*, New York: Springer Verlag, 167–218.

Levin, I. P., Johnson, R. D., and Davis, M. L. 1987: How information frame influences risky decisions: Between-subjects and within-subjects comparisons. *Journal of Economic Psychology*, 8, 43–54.

Locke, E. A. 1976: The nature and causes of job satisfaction. In M. Dunnette (ed.), *Handbook of industrial and organizational psychology*, Chicago: Rand McNally, 1297–1349.

Locke, E. A., Alavi, M., and Wagner, J. A., III. 1997: Participation in decision making: An information exchange perspective. In G. R. Ferris (ed.), *Research in Personnel and Human Resources Management* (JAI Press), 15, 293–331.

Locke, E. A., Feren, D. B., McCaleb, V. M., Shaw, K. N., and Denny, A. T. 1980: The relative effectiveness of four methods of motivating employee performance. In K. D. Duncan, M. M. Gruneberg, and D. Wallis (eds.), *Changes in working life*. London: Wiley.

Locke, E. A., and Latham, G. P. 1990: *A theory of goal setting and task performance*. Englewood Cliffs, NJ: Prentice Hall.

McDermott, R. 1998: *Risk-taking in international politics: Prospect theory in American foreign policy*. Ann Arbor, MI: University of Michigan Press.

McNutt, R. P. 1990: Sharing across the board: Du Pont's Achievement Sharing Program. *Compensation and Benefits Review*, 22(4), 17–24.

Meyer, J. W., and Rowan, B. 1977: Institutionalized organizations: Formal structure as myth and ceremony. *American Journal of Sociology*, 83, 340–63.

Milkovich, G. T., and Newman, J. M. 1999: *Compensation*, 6th edn., Chicago: Irwin.

Mitchell, D. J. B., Lewin, D., and Lawler, E. E., III. 1990: Alternative pay systems, firm performance, and productivity. In A. S. Blinder (ed.), *Paying for productivity: A look at the evidence*, Washington, DC: The Brookings Institution, 15–94.

Mitra, A., Gupta, N., and Jenkins, G. D., Jr. 1997: A drop in the bucket: When is a pay raise a pay raise? *Journal of Organizational Behavior*, 18, 117–37.

Montemayor, E. F. 1994: A model for aligning teamwork and pay. *American Compensation Association Journal*, 3(2), 18–25.

Morgenson, G. 1998: Stock options are not a free lunch. *Forbes*, May 18, 212–17.

Morgeson, F. P., and Hofmann, D. A. 1999: The structure and function of collective constructs: Implications for multilevel research and theory development. *Academy of Management Review*, 24, 249–65.

Mowen, J. C., Middlemist, R. D., and Luther, D. 1981: Joint effects of assigned goal level and incentive structure on task performance: A laboratory study. *Journal of Applied Psychology*, 66, 598–603.

Murray, B., and Gerhart, B. 1998: An empirical analysis of a skill-based pay program and plant performance outcomes. *Academy of Management Journal*, 41, 68–78.

Murphy, K. J. 1992: Performance measurement and appraisal: Motivating managers to identify and reward performance. In W. J. Bruns, Jr. (ed.), *Performance measurement, evaluation, and incentives*, Boston: Harvard Business School Press, 37–62.

Neale, M. A., Huber, V. L., and Northcraft, G. B. 1987: The framing of negotiations: Contextual vs. task frames. *Organizational Behavior and Human Decision Processes*, 39, 228–41.

O'Dell, C. 1987: *People, performance and pay*. Houston, TX: American Productivity Center.

O'Neill, G. L., and Lander, D. 1993/94: Linking employee skills to pay: A framework for skill-based pay plans. *American Compensation Association Journal*, 2, Winter, 14–26.

Peck, C. 1990: *Variable pay: New performance rewards*. The Conference Board, Research Bulletin No. 246.

Pencavel, J. H. 1977: Work effort, on-the-job screening and alternative methods of remuneration. *Research in Labor Economics*, 225–58.

Pinder, C. C. 1984: *Work motivation*. Glenview, IL: Scott, Foresman.

Quaid, M. 1993: Job evaluation as institutional myth. *Journal of Management Studies*, 30, 239–60.

Riedel, J. A., Nebeker, D. M., and Cooper, B. L. 1988: The influence of monetary incentives on goal choice, goal commitment, and task performance. *Organizational Behavior and Human Decision Processes*, 42, 155–80.

Rousseau, D. M. 1985: Issues of level in organizational research: Multi-level and cross-level perspectives. *Research in Organizational Behavior*, 7, 1–37.

Schuster, J. R., and Zingheim, P. K. 1992: *The new pay: Linking employee and organizational performance.* New York: Lexington Books.

Shalley, C. E., and Johnson, P. R. 1996: *The dilemma of dual goals: An investigation of resource allocation between competing goals.* Paper presented at the meeting of the Eleventh Annual Conference of the Society for Industrial and Organizational Psychology, San Diego, CA, April.

Summers, T. P., and Hendrix, W. H. 1991: Modelling the role of pay equity perceptions: A field study. *Journal of Occupational Psychology*, 64, 145–57.

Tolbert, P. S., and Zucker, L. G. 1983: Institutional sources of change in the formal structure of organizations: The diffusion of civil service reform, 1880–1935. *Administrative Science Quarterly*, 28, 22–39.

Tosi, H. L., and Gomez-Mejia, L. R. 1989: The decoupling of CEO pay and performance: An agency theory prespective. *Administrative Science Quarterly*, 34, 169–89.

Tosi, H. L., Katz, J. P., and Gomez-Mejia, L. R. 1997: Disaggregating the agency contract: The effects of monitoring, incentive alignment, and term in office on agent decision making. *Academy of Management Journal*, 40, 584–602.

US General Accounting Office 1981: *Productivity sharing programs: Can they contribute to productivity improvement?* (AFMD-81-22), Washington, DC: US General Accounting Office.

Van Eerde, W., and Thierry, H. 1996: Vroom's expectancy models and work-related criteria: A meta-analysis. *Journal of Applied Psychology*, 81, 575–86.

Von Krogh, G. 1998: Care in knowledge creation. *California Management Review*, 40, 133–53.

Vroom, V. 1964: *Work and motivation.* New York: Wiley.

Wageman, R. 1995: Interdependence and group effectiveness. *Administrative Science Quarterly*, 40, 145–80.

Weitzman, M. L., and Kruse, D. L. 1990: Profit sharing and productivity. In A. S. Blinder (ed.), *Paying for productivity: A look at the evidence*, Washington, DC: The Brookings Institution, 95–141.

Welbourne, T. M., Balkin, D. B., and Gomez-Mejia, L. R. 1995: Gainsharing and mutual monitoring: A combined agency-organizational justice interpretation. *Academy of Management Journal*, 38, 881–99.

Welbourne, T. M., and Gomez-Mejia, L. R. 1988: Gainsharing revisited. *Compensation and Benefits Review*, 20, July–August, 19–28.

Wilson, T. 1992: Is it time to eliminate the piece rate incentive system? *Compensation and Benefits Review*, 24, March–April, 43–9.

Wiseman, R. M., and Gomez-Mejia, L. R. 1998: A behavioral agency model of managerial risk taking. *Academy of Management Review*, 23, 133–53.

Worley, C. G., Bowen, D. E., and Lawler, E. E., III. 1992: On the relationship between objective increases in pay and employees' subjective reactions. *Journal of Organizational Behavior*, 13, 559–71.

Wright, P. M. 1992: An examination of the relationships among monetary incentives, goal level, goal commitment and performance. *Journal of Management*, 18, 677–93.

Zedeck, S., and Smith, P. C. 1968: The psychophysical determination of equitable payment: A methodological study. *Journal of Applied Psychology*, 52, 343–7.

Zingheim, P. K., and Schuster, J. R., Jr. 1997: Best practices for small-team pay. *American Compensation Association Journal*, 6, Spring, 40–9.

Zucker, L. G. 1977: The role of institutionalization in cultural persistence. *American Sociological Review*, 42, 726–43.

chapter 2

WORKPLACE INTERVENTIONS TO PREVENT STRESS-RELATED ILLNESS: LESSONS FROM RESEARCH AND PRACTICE

DANIEL C. GANSTER AND LARRY MURPHY

We have good news and bad news about going to work. First, the good news. After controlling for socioeconomic status and health, people who have paid employment (that is, jobs) report having a significantly higher quality of life (Ruchlin and Morris, 1991). Having a full-time job also is associated with slower declines in perceived health and physical functioning as one approaches old age (Ross and Mirowsky, 1995). These patterns prevail for both men and women. The healthful effects of work are perhaps even more compelling for women, however, who suffer significantly lower rates of preterm delivery when they have full time jobs (Marbury et al., 1984; Saurel-Cubizolles and Kaminski, 1986). In short, work is good for you. If you have a job you are likely to live longer and healthier, be happier, and even have healthier babies. Of course, work usually brings income and that brings better health care and generally a better social environment. But the beneficial effects of paid work hold even after controlling for income. In fact, work provides opportunities for self-fulfillment, meaningful social ties, and independence.

Now the bad news. Your job might be killing you if you picked the wrong occupation. For example, in England the Whitehall studies of thousands of civil servants (for example, Bosma et al., 1998; Marmot et al., 1997) have demonstrated an inverse social gradient in mortality from coronary heart disease (CHD). Those employees in the highest grade (administrators) had age-adjusted CHD rates that were significantly lower than those in the lowest grades (clerical and office support staff). Of all the factors examined, the largest contributors to this social gradient were work characteristics, especially personal control in the workplace. This factor had a larger impact than the standard CHD risk factors.

The evidence from the Whitehall studies is provocative, but there could be factors unrelated to the demands of the occupations but linked to the difference in social status that might explain these occupational differences. Kasl (1984), however, has noted that occupations roughly equivalent in terms of physical environment and social status often have widely divergent morbidity and mortality rates. For example, professors and others in the teaching fields have mortality rates for arteriosclerotic heart disease that are about one-half the rates of physicians, lawyers, pharmacists, and insurance agents. General practitioners also have much higher disease-related mortality than specialty fields within the medical profession. Kasl (1978) noted that suicide rates for refracting opthamologists are roughly *ten times* the rates found among optometrists. The work in these two professions is very similar; the only obvious difference is the higher level of education among the opthamologists. These striking differences in occupational mortality and morbidity are not easily explained by differences in income, education, or social class.

Thus, data from large-scale epidemiological research make a good case for the general proposition that something about the demands and conditions of work might cause serious health problems for individual employees. Health risks caused by psychosocial work conditions can harm the corporate bottom-line as well as the employees themselves. Manning et al. (1996) found that work stress and strain and lack of social support at work were predictive of various categories of employee health care costs over a two-year period. In a more recent and larger study, Goetzel and his colleagues (reported in Winslow, 1998) surveyed more than 46,000 workers in large US companies. All respondents had completed questionnaires about their work stress, health habits, and depression, and were assessed for traditional risk factors such as cholesterol, blood pressure, blood glucose, smoking, and body fat. They found that those reporting high job stress and depression had health costs that were 2.5 times higher than those who did not.

With such evidence mounting it is not surprising that employees are filing civil tort suits as well as workers' compensation claims for work stress-related disabilities. In fact, workers' compensation costs are growing faster than regular health care costs. In 1982 workers' compensation costs were $20 billion, increasing to $60 billion by 1990 (Bordwin, 1996). One of the reasons for this increase is the growth of claims for so-called "cumulative trauma injuries." These are injuries involving both mental and physical symptoms (such as anxiety, depression, gastrointestinal disorders) that are attributed to the effects of chronic exposures to psychosocial demands in the workplace. These demands can range from requirements to work long hours to mental abuse by co-workers and supervisors.

In short, there are compelling reasons for both researchers and practitioners to understand how work demands might exert such a negative toll and to devise effective prevention and intervention strategies for reducing these potentially costly problems. In this chapter we will briefly review what we know about how a constellation of work and occupational characteristics, generally grouped under the rubric of work stress, might cause mental and physical health problems. We will also review the relatively few empirical studies that have tested ways of reducing stressful demands, or their impact, in the workplace. And although work stress might be suspected of causing job performance deficits and even such problems as workplace violence, the evidence is so scant in these areas as to convince us to focus our attention on the health outcomes as our primary dependent variables of interest. It is for these outcomes that the most convincing theoretical and empirical basis for a stress effect exists. The far-reaching impacts of mental and physical health problems on quality of life and organizational costs, moreover, make them worthy targets for intervention and prevention even if no other indicators of organizational effectiveness were affected. In keeping with the theme of this book, we will then review the actions that practitioners are taking to reduce the harmful effects of work stress and how these are informed by and might possibly inform the research literature.

■ DEFINITIONS AND THEORIES OF JOB STRESS

Stress is a difficult concept to define for it often refers to physiological and psychological reactions of individuals as well as to the environmental conditions that elicit them. Typically, investigators have referred to the situational demands that provoke these responses as "stressors" and the responses themselves as "strains" (Ganster and Schaubroeck, 1991). Stressors generally mean environmental factors that cause the individual to muster a coping response because they pose threat or harm. In the work domain examples of such stressors are high workloads, requirements for working fast and meeting strict deadlines, conflicting demands, and interruptions. Many theorists believe that such stressors are especially harmful when they are uncontrollable, but we will speak more of this later. Other common demands arise from interpersonal interactions with supervisors, co-workers, and customers. Throughout all of these environmental demands runs the idea that the individual interprets them as posing some level of threat or challenge. In the most common paradigm (Lazarus, 1991), this cognitive appraisal of threat or challenge triggers a set of coping responses. Stress might then be described as the process whereby individuals respond to demands from their environment. In many respects this response process is a normal and benign part of life, and in fact some stressors, such as physical exercise, are regarded as promoting health and well being. Problems are seen to arise, though, when exposure to such demands is chronic and elicits a strong enough pattern of responses to strain the individual's physical and mental resources.

Hans Selye (1976) was among the first to posit that chronic exposures to environmental demands could have a cumulative negative impact on health through a process he described as the General Adaptation Syndrome (GAS). The three-part response of alarm, resistance, and exhaustion, if chronically elicited, could produce wear and tear that eventually leads to illness. This model, which involves the fluctuation of physiological systems in the body to meet demands, can be described as an allostatic load model. In recent years researchers have directed much of their attention to the effects that chronic exposures have on fluctuations in neuroendocrine arousal, as these, and their sequelae, are believed to produce a host of pathological conditions ranging from CHD to cancer. The immune system is also thought to respond to psychosocial stressors (Cohen and Herbert, 1996), suggesting an even more pervasive role for chronic stress in health.

Another route from chronic stress to disease is through the direct impact of stressful exposures on mental distress. Negative emotional states in themselves can be debilitating, with depression thought to be affecting about one-quarter of the population. As noted earlier, depression is also linked to higher employee health care costs (Winslow, 1998). In addition, negative emotions such as depression, hostility, and anxiety are implicated in the etiology of a variety of physical disorders including CHD and mortality from all causes (Martin et al., 1995). In this perspective chronic stressors elicit negative emotions which in turn trigger allostatic processes, mostly in the neuroendocrine system. Thus, chronic exposures to work demands can generate both mental and physical illness, and both arenas are likely mediated by allostatic responses of the neuroendocrine system, especially in the adrenomedullary and adrenocortical axes (Cohen and Herbert, 1996).

There is theoretical and empirical support for the proposition that chronic exposures to psychosocial stressors can create significant health problems. This support provides a backdrop for investigating stressors in the workplace and determining whether specific demands in that environment can be identified that produce these problems. This goal – identifying specific workplace demands and linking them to ill-health – has guided what is arguably the most multi-disciplinary effort relevant to the organizational sciences. We briefly review this immense body of research with the particular aims of: (1) assessing whether work demands in general play a causal role in the development of mental and physical illness; (2) identifying what specific workplace characteristics might be most important in this regard; and (3) whether interventions in the workplace are effective in reducing these negative effects. Our review is selective, focusing on the most recent studies conducted after the publication of more extensive reviews (Cooper and Marshall, 1976; Ganster and Schaubroeck, 1991).

■ DO WORK DEMANDS CAUSE ILLNESS?

Studies linking various work demands to health outcomes roughly comprise two broad categories. Most commonly conducted studies by organizational behavior researchers are field surveys of employees in which characteristics of work and occupations are linked at the individual level of analysis to various measures of psychological and physical well being, as well as job attitudes. Most of these studies rely on the self-reports of the respondents for measures of both work stressors and their putative outcomes (see the review by Ganster and Schaubroeck, 1991), although exceptions to this method are appearing more frequently (Fox et al., 1993; Manning et al., 1996; Schaubroeck et al., 1994; Schaubroeck and Ganster, 1993).

The other broad category of work stress research arises from occupational comparisons of health and mortality by epidemiologists having an interest in identifying population risk factors or populations that are most at risk. The tradition here is to compare occupational groups on various measures of health, including mortality. Occupational variation tends to be measured in either of two ways. One approach utilizes fairly objective occupational classifications (for example, retail salesperson) and relates these to aggregate health data. Normally these data have been compiled by responsible government agencies into registries. Variations in this approach include the imputation of finer-grained job classifications to job titles within occupational categories and the use of occupational coding schemes (for example, the stress temperament code from the *Dictionary of Occupational Titles*, US Department of

Labor, 1977; Adelman, 1987). These various codes or classifications may be related to health outcomes as independent variables. Analyses at this occupational level are somewhat crude because they assign the same job characteristics to all incumbents of an occupation, thus ignoring within-occupation variation among employees. Such occupational-level analyses cannot identify the effects of meaningful variation in job demands across different work settings and different supervisors, and thus they can provide little insight into how jobs can be changed to make them less stressful, short of changing an entire occupation. More recent work by epidemiologists, however, has attempted to measure job demands at the individual level of analysis (Marmot et al., 1997).

Both research traditions have come to be guided by a particularly influential theory of job stress known as the demands-control, or job decision latitude model (Karasek, 1979). In its basic form the model specifies two broad constructs that can vary independently in the work environment. Job *demands* are defined as psychological stressors, such as requirements for working fast and hard, having a great deal to do, not having enough time, and having conflicting demands. It must be stressed that these are psychological demands and not physical ones. Thus a fast and hectic workplace may impose physical requirements that lead to fatigue, but the stress-related outcomes predicted by the model are related to the psychological effects of this workload (for example, the anxiety associated with the need to maintain the workpace and the associated consequences of failing to complete the work). Job *decision latitude* comprises two components: the worker's authority to make decisions on the job (decision authority); and the variety of skills used by the worker on the job (skill discretion). In the epidemiological literature these two components are combined into one measure of decision latitude, whereas the organizational researchers generally discriminate between the two components and focus on the decision authority dimension (control).

The central hypothesis of the model is that "strain," which is a stressful condition that leads to mental and physical health problems, occurs when jobs are simultaneously high in demands and low in control. This hypothesis rests on the reasoning that high demands produce an allostatic response. When there is a constraint on the responses of the worker, as would occur under conditions of low control, the arousal cannot be appropriately channelled into a coping response and thus produces an even larger physiological reaction that persists for a longer time.

The demands-control theory has been subjected to several critical reviews (Fox et al., 1993; Schnall et al., 1994), and the validity of its central hypothesis is still not consistently supported. Whether their effects are additive or interactive is still controversial, but recent evidence in both the organizational and epidemiological research streams make a rather compelling case that job demands and control are causally implicated in the development of mental and physical ill-health. We will examine a few of the recent studies from each of these areas to illustrate this conclusion.

Marmot et al. (1997) used occupational and social class data from a sample of over 7,000 civil servants in the UK and related them to three self-reported indicators of coronary heart disease (angina, chest pain, and doctor-diagnosed ischemia) in a 5.3-year follow-up survey. As with the earlier Whitehall studies (for example,

Marmot et al., 1991), they found that those civil servants working in jobs classified in the lowest of three grade levels (clerical and office support staff) had significantly higher incidence rates than those in the higher grades. They examined this "inverse social gradient" by testing how entering variables such as traditional coronary risk factors and social support affected the occupational differences. A self-report control scale that combined decision authority and skill discretion showed the greatest effect on this gradient, larger than those for height and standard coronary risk factors. They concluded that the psychosocial work environment could explain much of the inverse social gradient in coronary heart disease.

Theorell et al. (1998) examined job demands and control in a case-control study of first myocardial infarction in Stockholm, Sweden. They compared the work histories of 1,047 males aged 45–64, who had been working full time for the last five years and experienced their first myocardial infarction during the study period, with an equal number of referent cases chosen randomly from the study base. Decreases in control (decision latitude inferred from occupational histories) during the preceding ten years significantly increased risk of myocardial infarction after controlling for all standard risk factors, including chest pain and social class. Moreover, self-reported job demands and control similarly predicted myocardial infarction. As with other epidemiological studies, however, Theorell et al. (1998) did not test the interaction between demands and control, but rather formed groups based on combinations of demands and control.

These two recent studies from the epidemiological literature are significant because they probe deeper into occupational differences in disease by testing whether the self-reports of workers regarding job demands and control mediate them. They also attempt to control for other risk factors that might be confounded with the occupational differences. Despite such statistical controls, however, one cannot safely rule out the possibility that other personal characteristics might confound these results. Occupations differ in their typical levels of certain demands and control, but their incumbents are also embedded in a broader social context that could affect health status (Taylor et al., 1997). In non-experimental research involving multiple occupations, eliminating all confounding influences is virtually impossible.

Another inferential challenge for job stress researchers is disentangling the effects of work characteristics, *per se*, and the individual characteristics that individuals bring to the workplace and that might be the primary causes of their health status. People's health is at least partly predictable from stable personality traits (Contrada et al., 1990; Friedman and Booth-Kewley, 1987). Recent data also confirm that there are different distributions of personality traits across occupations and organizations, probably arising from differential attraction, selection, and attrition processes (Schaubroeck et al., 1998). Thus, disentangling the effects of work and personality is difficult to accomplish in occupational comparison studies.

Organizational researchers, however, have worried about the possible confounding effects of personality and have taken steps to control them (Brief et al., 1988; Schaubroeck et al., 1992). Usually this control is statistical with the investigators partialling traits while testing the relationships between job demands and health outcomes. Organizational studies, although they tend to be more modest in scope than the epidemiological studies, sometimes have the advantage of eliminating social class and personality confounds when studying samples from a single organization. The study by Fox et al. (1993) is a good example.

Fox et al. (1993) wanted to test the job demands-control model by employing objective as well as subjective assessments of job demands and control and relating them to a set of outcomes that included mental and physical symptoms as well as physiological measures. Their sample was of 136 nurses who all worked in the same institutional setting but were distributed across 15 departments. They found that, as predicted by the theory, neuroendocrine arousal (salivary cortisol) and other outcomes were explained by the interaction of workload demands (both objective and subjective) with perceived control. In fact, they discovered that the interaction of these variables predicted carry-over effects after work. Multiple-day measures of systolic and diastolic blood pressure and salivary cortisol taken several hours after work were predicted by the demands-control interactions. These findings are especially significant in that they demonstrate that heightened physiological arousal elicited by work demands can persist after leaving the work environment. It is just such chronically elevated allostatic responses that are believed to be implicated in the onset of health problems. In fact, in a longitudinal follow-up of this sample, Ganster et al. (1999) found that it was this elevated after-work physiological response that predicted the cumulative health care costs of the nurses for the next five years. These analyses controlled for standard risk factors such as age, relative weight, and smoking. One advantage that this study had was that they could confidently rule out social class effects associated with different occupations because all respondents were in the same occupation and socioeconomic status did not vary across the nursing specialties. Any occupational and organizational differences in personality traits were eliminated as well. Despite all respondents being sampled from the same occupation, different nursing specialties impose significantly different levels of workload demands and control, thus providing plenty of variance on the factors of interest.

Taken together, the large-scale multi-occupation studies reported in the epidemiological literature and the smaller-scale but finer-grained research emerging in the organizational literature convince us that characteristics of jobs and the workplace social environment are implicated in the onset and progression of mental and physical health problems. Specific work characteristics, such as workload demands and personal control, are associated with CHD and depression, as well as the more proximal physiological mediators, such as elevated blood pressure and salivary cortisol. Moreover, such findings replicate across very different methodological strategies and across nationalities, and they are not readily explained by confounding factors such as socioeconomic status and personality traits.

■ WHAT SPECIFIC WORKPLACE CHARACTERISTICS HAVE THE LARGEST IMPACT ON HEALTH?

Having made a case for an etiologic role of work stress on health, our next question is whether we can identify job characteristics that appear to be important contributors to health problems and are common across a wide range of occupations. From a practical standpoint, we gain little by targeting work life as a threat to health without being able to pinpoint things that we might change in order to make work healthier.

In some ways generating a list of very specific stressors is futile because occupations, and different work settings within the same occupation, differ widely in the kinds of demands that they impose. In any practical application individuals desiring to intervene would need to conduct a diagnosis that includes some open-ended, or inductive component. We will speak more of this later. There is a large literature in which investigators search for stressors within specific occupations. For example, studies have reported such descriptions for nurses (for example, McGrath et al., 1989), teachers (Blase, 1986; Brenner and Bartell, 1984; Friesen and Sarros, 1989; Mykletun, 1984), caregivers (Chiriboga et al., 1989), occupational therapists (Rogers and Dodson, 1988), paramedics (Grigsby and McKnew, 1988), firemen (Lim et al., 1987), hospice staff (Yancik, 1984), correctional workers (Brodsky, 1982), and South African educational psychologists (Basson, 1988). These represent a small fraction of such studies. Despite the wide diversity of occupations examined and the inductive approach researchers often take, there is a surprising degree of overlap in the stressors that emerge from such studies. In part, this convergence might arise from the fact that many investigators start from similar conceptual perspectives and use similar measures. But much of the emergence of a common core of stressors probably reflects some basic underlying property of demands that make them stressful. In their broad review of "unhealthy environments," Taylor et al. (1997) make a sweeping statement about what features are common across harmful environments. After reviewing the literature about social class, community, family, peer environment, adult social environment, and work, they conclude that unhealthy environments are "those that threaten safety, that undermine the creation of social ties, and that are conflictual, abusive, or violent. A healthy environment, in contrast, provides safety, opportunities for social integration, and the ability to predict and/or control aspects of that environment" (p. 411). That list does quite a good job of describing the underlying properties of most stressors that appear in the work literature.

The most commonly studied stressors in the work stress field include: (1) role stressors, such as role conflict and ambiguity; (2) workload stressors, such as work overload, tight deadlines, too many hours, and a fast and hectic pace; (3) job insecurity; (4) stressful interpersonal interactions and lack of social support; and (5) lack of control. As one can see, these stressors fit under the Taylor et al. (1997) formulation pretty well. In terms of being linked to mental and physical health outcomes, the workload stressors, lack of social support, and lack of control enjoy the broadest empirical support, from both the work and the non-work literature. How these general characteristics are manifested in a particular work situation can vary greatly, however.

Control is a particularly important characteristic because evidence regarding its impact on health and well being pervades both the epidemiological and the psychological literatures. Moreover, it is a complex construct whose meaning is often unclear and which seems to vary from setting to setting. For example, lack of control might be a serious issue for many employees of the US postal service and primarily be a function of a machine-paced technology (Hurrell, 1985). In a nursing environment, low control might arise mostly from the way that the organization delineates the roles and discretion of nurses in dealing with their patients and with doctors (Fox et al., 1993; Molleman and Van Kippenberg, 1995). These two examples arise from the machine pacing and work design literatures, respectively, but they represent the same underlying basis of stress. The epidemiologists (for example, Theorell et al., 1998) interpret control to mean "job decision latitude," a construct that subsumes both personal discretion and job skill level. To an organizational psychologist this construct resembles job complexity, which combines autonomy as well as skill variety and task identity. Researchers in the organizational behavior tradition, in contrast, have tended toward a narrower conception of control in which it means having the ability to influence one's job environment in significant ways so as to affect the outcomes one experiences (Ganster and Fusilier, 1989).

Although "control over outcomes" might be the critical element, it cannot be assumed that the behavioral control measures that organizational researchers have used have always captured this dimension. A closely related construct, but one that has seldom appeared in the work stress literature, is Bandura's (1997) concept of self-efficacy. Wood and Bandura (1989) defined self-efficacy as "beliefs in one's capabilities to mobilize the motivation, cognitive resources, and courses of action needed to meet given situational demands" (p. 408). Self-efficacy thus can be classified as a belief in one's ability to cope, and that means being able to achieve desired outcomes. The fact that behavioral control measures might not always capture this outcome control could explain the frequent failure of researchers to find a significant interaction between control and demand as predicted by the demands-control model (Karasek, 1979). Schaubroeck and Merritt (1997) recently posed this very hypothesis. Specifically, they hypothesized that job control would buffer the negative health effects of high job demands only for those employees who had high job self-efficacy, and might even exacerbate the effects of demands for those who did not. In two different samples they found this to be the case, with diastolic blood pressure as the outcome. Schaubroeck and Merritt's (1996) conclusions stressed the importance of providing both job control and self-efficacy when designing interventions to reduce the negative health effects of stress. We believe that this is good advice and underscores the importance of designing job stress interventions from a comprehensive perspective that considers how employees will deploy augmented control to achieve outcomes desirable for both themselves and the organization. Often this will mean combining a job redesign intervention with training targeted at increasing job self-efficacy (Gist and Mitchell, 1992, discuss ways to accomplish this).

Similarly, role conflict might arise from incompatible demands from different role senders within the organization (such as, supervisors and co-workers), from outside the organization (for example, citizens and courts for police officers, or conflicting work–family demands), or from a poorly engineered job. Thus, while the work stress literature provides some guidance about the general factors that are important for stress and health, every job environment needs its own careful diagnosis. This diagnosis needs to identify the most salient aspects of the work setting and feasible ways that they can be changed. Any change efforts also need to consider what training is necessary for preparing employees to profit from changes in the work. In the next section we reinforce this theme by illustrating the ways that researchers have attempted to change the work setting.

WHAT DO WE KNOW ABOUT INTERVENING IN STRESSFUL WORK ENVIRONMENTS?

Interventions aimed at changing organizational structures, job design, leadership practices, and many other aspects of work settings occur every day. Some of these are reported in the research literature, but rarely do they examine stress-related outcomes or mental and physical health. There are only a handful of studies that we know of that actually tested an intervention designed to reduce the negative effects of work stress by changing some aspect of the work situation. We will discuss these as a way of illustrating approaches that can be taken and also to gauge how effective such interventions might be.

One of the early field experiments in work stress was not really an intervention designed to make a work setting less stressful, but it is worth noting because it provides one of the rare examples of experimentally testing the impact of a specific work stressor. Timio and Gentili (1976) manipulated the payment methods for 16 confectioners in a repeated measures design. Half the workers started on a piece-rate payment schedule then cycled to a daily pay schedule and then cycled back to a piece-rate schedule, each cycle lasting for four days. The other half of the sample performed under a daily pay/piece-rate/daily pay sequence. Cumulative daily measures of adrenaline, noradrenaline, and 11-hydroxycorticosteroids showed a very large effect for the piece-rate payment method, with levels of adrenaline, for example, being two to three times higher when working on piece-rate. Timio and Gentili (1976) noted that the exertion levels of the workers were identical during each phase of the study, leading them to conclude that the effects reflected a "corresponding augmentation in stress and distress" (p. 264). An experiment by Timio et al., (1979) also showed that neuroendocrine responses are affected by working on an assembly line. But assembly line work entails a number of characteristics (such as forced pacing, repetitiveness, monotony, lack of social interaction), making it harder to pinpoint the exact nature of the stressor than in the Timio and Gentili (1976) experiment. The Timio and Gentili (1976) study raises several interesting questions. For example, how did the workers cognitively appraise the different payment schemes? Did the piece-rate payment system lower their sense of personal control? Did they perceive the piece-rate system as a threat to their pay or job security? We don't know the answers to these questions, but the results do illustrate how changing just one aspect of the work setting (albeit an important one) can trigger a large stress response. Of course, we also do not know how persistent the allostatic reactions to the payment plan would have been over time. On the one hand, they might have exacted a cumulative toll on health over an extended exposure. On the other hand, the workers might have eventually adapted to their changed pay system with a concomitant reduction in their physiological reactivity.

Jackson (1983) was one of the first to report a stress reduction intervention in the organizational literature. She assigned employees of a hospital outpatient facility either to a participation or no-intervention control group. Self-report measures confirmed that employees in the participation condition experienced a greater amount of control over work-related matters. The intervention produced lower levels of self-reported emotional strain at a six-month post-test and a nine-month follow-up. What is enlightening about this study is how significant the effect was of such a seemingly low-key intervention. The participation program consisted of training in the nominal group technique and weekly staff meetings to discuss departmental activities. In this case, there is evidence that the intervention augmented the respondents' sense of control in the workplace, which might very well be the key mediator for its effects on their emotional strain. The broader participation in decision-making literature certainly does not make a strong case for the efficacy of participative interventions in general (Ganster and Fusilier, 1989). Thus, we are reluctant to generalize Jackson's findings to the extent of recommending participation programs as a general strategy for alleviating stress in the workplace. But such interventions might indeed have a significant impact if they truly change the control perceptions of employees in areas that affect their work lives. Once again, a careful diagnosis of the target setting must guide the choice of such an intervention.

Schaubroeck et al. (1993) evaluated a two-stage intervention program that attempted to reduce high levels of role ambiguity. The target population was a group of middle managers and their subordinates in the business services division of a large university. The responsibilities of this division consisted of all purchasing and inventory management for the university, including food services. A new director had recently been appointed and the division was undergoing what turned out to be the penultimate reorganization in a series that started several years earlier. Their last reorganization occurred soon after the study was completed. The reorganizations had created considerable turbulence regarding individual roles and relationships among the various departments within the division. Reported stress levels were very high and many employees reported psychosomatic disorders and frequent sick days, with most being attributed to conditions at work. In a two-and-a-half-year study we conducted two surveys, had countless meetings with staff and managers, and finally implemented a role clarification intervention that began with charting the responsibilities of the managers and their departments and ended with individual role negotiation sessions between each manager and his or her subordinates. We randomly assigned groups of subordinates to treatment and wait-control conditions and evaluated employee stress symptoms several months after implementation. Although the intervention significantly reduced employee perceptions of role ambiguity, it seemed to have little impact on employee health symptoms or sick days.

■ HOW HAS RESEARCH INFORMED STRESS INTERVENTION PRACTICE?

In light of the vast amount of research on job stress, one might expect significant parallels with respect to the nature and scope of stress interventions. However, a review of the stress intervention literature reveals some surprising results (see Murphy, 1996 for details). First, most interventions focus on changing the worker, not the work environment. Usually called "stress management training," these interventions are prescriptive, individual-oriented, relaxation-based techniques, such as progressive muscle relaxation and cognitive-behavioral skills training. Most of these intervention techniques were derived from clinical and counseling psychology, where they are routinely used in the treatment of anxiety and psychosomatic disorders. Training sessions usually last an hour or more and are offered on a weekly basis. They ranged from a few days of training to many weeks, and small group formats were most common.

Second, the design of stress interventions has been guided less by *job* stress theory than stress theory in general. Thus, interventions typically deal with stress from a generic perspective (for example, nature and sources of stress, effects of stress on health, the benefits of relaxation, and so on) and could just as easily have been designed without any reference to the workplace. Indeed, the workplace seems incidental to the content of the intervention; it simply provides a convenient vehicle for administering the intervention.

Nearly 90 percent of the studies used reliable and valid outcome measures, in the form of a physiological/biochemical measure or a validated self-report measure. Over half (60 percent) of the studies included some type of post-training follow-up assessment, but very few extended the follow-up to a full year post-training. Of the studies that used control/comparison groups, over half reported significant effects on outcome measures for the control groups as well as the trained groups, and in many studies, the authors noted that *non-specific factors* clearly contributed to the obtained results. The issue here is whether the outcomes are due to specific elements of the training or to factors such as sitting in a comfortable chair and receiving time off from work to participate in training.

■ WHAT IS THE IMPACT OF STRESS MANAGEMENT TRAINING?

Stress management is often associated with positive and consistent improvements on measures of psychological function like anxiety. Workers report fewer symptoms after stress management training than control/comparison groups, and often report fewer somatic complaints. Stress management does not produce improvements in job/organization-relevant outcomes, such as absenteeism or job satisfaction. This is not surprising since the interventions did not focus on changing job-related sources of stress. The effects of stress management on physiological outcomes like blood pressure are equivocal; some studies report positive effects but others find no effects.

Although only three studies assessed biochemical changes after training (such as catecholamines), all three reported rather impressive results. Similarly, all three studies which measured health-care costs reported significant post-training results. In light of the equivocal effects of stress management interventions on blood pressure and the lack of effects on job/organizational measures, these findings take on added significance and warrant special attention in future studies.

■ WHY IS STRESS MANAGEMENT MORE COMMON THAN JOB/ORGANIZATIONAL CHANGE APPROACHES?

A number of reasons can be offered to explain why practitioners prefer stress management interventions to job redesign/organizational change. First, the prevailing attitude about job stress within a company has a strong influence on whether any such activities will exist, and on what type of activities are offered. For example, the prevalent belief that stress is not a work-related problem but a personal one leads many companies to focus on helping workers cope with stress instead of efforts to reduce job stressors.

Second, the health promotion movement in the early 1980s strongly influenced the type and prevalence of stress intervention activities. Stress management is one of the most often requested health promotion programs by workers (McGuinnis, 1993). These programs are prescriptive, involve little disruption of organization structure and function, can be tailored to the needs of individual workers, and are easy to evaluate. Job/organizational change interventions, on the other hand, require a careful assessment of the sources of stress before an intervention can be designed, and require greater commitment to change on the part of management.

Third, stress management interventions directly address the idiosyncratic nature of stress more so than job redesign/organizational change interventions. One of the major themes emerging from stress research has been the important role of individual perceptions or appraisals of situations or events. The maxim "one person's meat is another person's poison" aptly captures this concept. From a practitioner point of view, this concept is difficult to integrate into many job/organizational change interventions. How does one design an organizational intervention when stress is largely a matter of individual perceptions? How can one insure that stress will be reduced for all workers under study? To what extent could the intervention reduce stress for some workers but increase stress for others? How will this all play out when one performs a bottom-line, cost/benefit analysis? Of course, this is not a dilemma for individual-based interventions because the focus is on the individual, not the job or the organization. So, stress management represents a less risky and less costly choice for practitioners.

Fourth, there are more nationally representative data about the prevalence of stress symptoms (such as depression and anxiety) than stressful job characteristics, and so it is easier to justify stress management than organizational change strategies. The last nationwide study of the quality of work life was conducted in 1977 (Quinn and Staines, 1979), so there is little in the way of current surveillance data on stressful characteristics of work. In the same way, although many companies routinely conduct employee surveys as part of their Human Resource (HR) function, and provide feedback to managers and employees on the results, such surveys rarely contain questions on job stressors. This occurs in part because of the lack of knowledge of job stress among human resource personnel, and in part because job stress is not viewed as an appropriate HR issue. Stress is more often handled by medical staff. Ideas for addressing job stress through collaboration between medical and HR departments can be found in Murphy (1995).

Finally, the research literature offers few demonstrations of effective organizational change interventions. Unlike stress management, one cannot "prescribe" an organizational intervention without first conducting an assessment to determine the main sources of stress in the organization. Although many authors routinely advocate job and organizational change interventions to reduce stressors at work, there is little scientific evidence that such interventions will produce sizable reductions in stress symptoms. Indeed, a careful, honest review of this literature leads to the conclusion that organizational interventions produce small or insignificant effects on symptoms like distress or anxiety (Briner and Reynolds, 1999).

It doesn't make sense for practitioners to exert the substantial time, effort, and resources required to design, implement, and evaluate job/organizational change strategies when the odds of achieving significant reductions in stress symptoms are low or non-existent. It is far easier simply to install a stress management program and demonstrate small but significant reductions in stress symptoms. Moreover, workers usually respond to stress management training in a very positive way: they appreciate the attention, and find the training useful in understanding stress and developing stress coping strategies.

◼ WHAT WOULD CONSTITUTE AN IDEAL STRESS INTERVENTION?

Based on the available evidence, an ideal intervention would have the following characteristics:

1. Be comprehensive and attend to individual and organizational factors. Teaching workers stress-management skills is necessary and serves a useful purpose, but it deals with only part of the problem. The workplace can be a source of important stressors that can be identified and targeted for change.
2. Include an assessment of stressors in the work environment in order to understand the stress–health dynamics. A job stress assessment need not be a major undertaking; an initial assessment could take the form of informal discussions with workers. Opening a channel of communication with employees serves to legitimize stress as a topic for discussion and is a good way to obtain valuable information about job stressors and employee reactions. Group discussions and questionnaire surveys can be used later to pinpoint common areas of stress and to measure the prevalence of the problem.
3. Include workers in the design and evaluation of the intervention. There is sufficient research attesting to the importance of worker involvement in organizational change efforts, and to the importance of the process (that is, *how* the intervention is done) as well as the content of such interventions. In most stress intervention studies, consultants make all the decisions regarding program design, assessment tools, interventions, and evaluation protocols. It is recommended that worker groups (for example, joint labor–management committees) be positioned at the center of the decision-making process, and stress intervention experts relocated to the periphery. Increasing worker participation and involvement in stress interventions will shift some of the emphasis to the process, without ignoring either the content or outcomes of training. Reynolds and Shapiro (1991) have made a convincing case for examining process variables as well as outcome variables in stress intervention research.
4. Be designed and evaluated within the context of a well-defined conceptual model. A conceptual model is useful for defining the stressors, the short- and

long-term consequences of stress, key intervening variables, and the nature of relationships among stressors, outcomes, and intervening variables. Once a model is specified, it guides the choice of which stressors to measure, the targeting of intervention strategies, and decisions on how to implement the intervention and evaluate its effectiveness. A number of authors have proposed conceptual models for stress intervention, but these models remain underutilized by practitioners (Ivancevich et al., 1990; Newman and Beehr, 1979; Stoner and Fry, 1983).

▪ WHAT TYPES OF INFORMATION DO PRACTITIONERS NEED FROM RESEARCHERS?

Practitioners need a good deal more information from the research community to support the design of stress interventions. As noted earlier, there is a need for nationally representative data on job risk factors for worker ill-health. Today's workplace is being shaped by a global economy and heightened competition, resulting in substantial changes in the nature of work, employment practices and the composition of the workforce. New forms of work organization such as lean production and contingent work are becoming commonplace, but their health and safety effects have not been examined. Presently, there exists no national effort to monitor changes in work organization and resultant health and safety consequences. Data collected in national surveys of job stress could be used to identify high risk work practices and suggest interventions to protect and improve worker health and safety. This type of information would provide practitioners with a solid foundation for pursuing the design of job and organizational change programs. In its absence, practitioners will continue to design interventions which address the symptoms, but not the causes of job stress.

Another critical need is for authoritative guidelines on job and organization design to guide the development of stress interventions. These guidelines should be based on a composite of research evidence, not one or two studies, and be applicable to most if not all work organizations. Guidelines developed for the ergonomic interventions provide an example of what is needed (Cohen et al., 1997). The National Institute for Occupational Safety and Health (NIOSH) has offered some general guidelines for reducing work stress (see, for example, Sauter et al., 1990) but more specifics are needed to be more useful to practitioners.

Finally, demonstrations of the efficacy of specific job and organizational change strategies plus cost-benefit calculations are sorely needed. Without better evidence that such interventions will produce notable changes, there is little inducement for practitioners to shift their focus from managing stress to job stressor reduction.

REFERENCES

Adelman, P. K. 1987: Occupational complexity, control, and personal income: Their relation to psychological well being in men and women. *Journal of Applied Psychology*, 72, 529–37.
Bandura, A. 1997: *Self-efficacy: The exercise of control*, New York: W.H. Freeman.

Basson, C. 1988: Potential sources of work-related stress for the educational psychologist in the Republic of South Africa, *School Psychology International*, 9, 203–11.

Blase, J. 1986: A qualitative analysis of sources of teacher stress: Consequences for performance. *American Educational Research Journal*, 23, 13–40.

Bordwin, M. 1996: Overwork: The cause of your next workers' comp claim? *Management Review*, 85, 3–50.

Bosma, H., Peter, R., Siegrist, J., and Marmot, M. 1998: Two alternative job stress models and the risk of coronary heart disease. *American Journal of Public Health*, 88, 68–74.

Brenner, S., and Bartell, R. 1984: The teacher stress process: A cross-cultural analysis. *Journal of Occupational Behaviour*, 5, 183–95.

Brief, A. P., Burke, M. J., George, J. M., Robinson, B. S., and Webster, J. 1988: Should negative affectivity remain an unmeasured variable in the study of job stress? *Journal of Applied Psychology*, 73, 193–8.

Briner, R. B., and Reynolds, S. 1999: The costs, benefits, and limitations of organizational level stress interventions. *Journal of Organizational Behavior*, 20, 647–64.

Brodsky, C. 1982: Work stress in correctional institutions. *Journal of Prison and Jail Health*, 2, 74–102.

Chiriboga, D., Weiler, P., and Nielsen, K. 1989: The stress of caregivers. Special issue: Aging and family caregivers. *Journal of Applied Social Sciences*, 13, 118–41.

Cohen, A., Gjessing, C. C., Fine, L. J., Bernard, B. P., and McGlothlin, J. D. 1997: *Elements of ergonomics programs*, Washington, DC: Department of Health and Human Services, Publication No. 97–117.

Cohen, S., and Herbert, T. 1996: Health psychology: Psychological factors and physical disease from the perspective of human psychoneuroimmunology. *Annual Review of Psychology*, 47, 113–42.

Contrada, R. J., Leventhal, H., and O'Leary, A. 1990: Personality and health. In L. A. Pervin (ed.), *Handbook of personality: Theory and research*, New York: Guilford Press, 638–69.

Cooper, C. L., and Marshall, J. 1976: Occupational sources of stress: A review of the literature relating to coronary heart disease and mental ill health. *Journal of Occupational Psychology*, 49, 11–28.

Fox, M., Dwyer, D., and Ganster, D. 1993: Effects of stressful demands and control on physiological and attitudinal outcomes in a hospital setting. *Academy of Management Journal*, 36, 289–318.

Friedman, H. S., and Booth-Kewley, S. 1987: The "disease-prone personality:" A meta-analytic review of the construct. *American Psychologist*, 42, 539–55.

Friesen, D., and Sarros, J. 1989: Sources of burnout among educators. *Journal of Organizational Behavior*, 10, 179–88.

Ganster, D. C., Fox, M., and Dwyer, D. 1999: Explaining employee health care costs: A prospective examination of stressful job demands, personal control, and physiological reactivity.

Ganster, D. C., and Fusilier, M. R. 1989: Control in the workplace. In C. L. Cooper and I. Roberstson (eds.), *International review of industrial and organizational psychology*, London: Wiley, 235–80.

Ganster, D. C., and Schaubroeck, J. 1991: Work stress and employee health. *Journal of Management*, 17, 235–71.

Gist, M. E., and Mitchell, T. R. 1992: Self-efficacy: A theoretical analysis of its determinants and malleability. *Academy of Management Review*, 17, 183–211.

Grigsby, D., and McKnew, M. 1988: Work-stress burnout among paramedics. *Psychological Reports*, 63, 55–64.

Hurrell, J. J., Jr. 1985: Machine-paced work and the Type A behavior pattern. *Journal of Occupational Psychology*, 58, 15–25.

Ivancevich, J. M., Matteson, M. T., Freedman, S. M., and Phillips, J. S. 1990: Worksite stress management interventions. *American Psychologist*, 45, 252–61.

Jackson, S. E. 1983: Participation in decision making as a strategy for reducing job-related strain. *Journal of Applied Psychology*, 68, 3–19.

Karasek, R. 1979: Job demands, job decision latitude, and mental strain: Implications for job redesign. *Administrative Science Quarterly*, 24, 285–306.

Kasl, S. V. 1978: Epidemiological contributions to the study of work stress. In C. L. Cooper and R. Payne (eds.), *Stress at work*, Chichester: Wiley, 3–48.

Kasl, S. V. 1984: Stress and health. In L. Breslow, J. E. Fielding, and L. B. Lane (eds.), *Annual review of public health*, 5, 319–42.

Lazarus, R. 1991: Psychological stress in the workplace. *Journal of Social Behavior and Personality*, 6 (7), 1–13.

Lim, C., Ong, C., and Phoon, W. 1987: Work stress of firemen as measured by heart rate and catecholamines. *Journal of Human Ergology*, 16, 209–18.

Manning, M. R., Jackson, C. N., and Fusilier, M. R. 1996: Occupational stress, social support, and the costs of health care. *Academy of Management Journal*, 39, 738–50.

Marbury, M. C., Linn, S., Monson, R. R., et al. 1984: Work and pregnancy. *Journal of Occupational Medicine*, 26, 415–21.

Marmot, M., Bosma, H., Hemingway, H., Brunner, E., and Stansfield, S. 1997: Contribution of job control and other risk factors to social variations in coronary heart disease incidence. *The Lancet*, 350 (9073), 235–9.

Marmot, M., Davey Smith, G., Stansfield, S., et al. 1991: Health inequalities among British civil servants: The Whitehall II study. *The Lancet*, 337, 1387–93.

Martin, L. R., Friedman, H. S., Tucker, J. S., Schwartz, J. E., Criqui, M. H., et al. 1995: An archival prospective study of mental health and longevity. *Health Psychology*, 14, 381–7.

McGrath, A., Reid, N., and Boore, J. 1989: Occupational stress in nursing. *International Journal of Nursing Studies*, 26, 343–58.

McGuinnis, J. 1993: 1992 survey of worksite health promotion activities: summary. *American Journal of Health Promotion*, 7, 452–64.

Molleman, E., and Van Kippenberg, A. 1995: Work redesign and the balance of control within a nursing context. *Human Relations*, 48, 795–814.

Murphy, L. R. 1995: Managing job stress: An employee assistance/human resource management partnership. *Personnel Review*, 24, 41–50.

Murphy, L. R. 1996: Stress management in work settings: A critical review of the research literature. *American Journal of Health Promotion*, 11, 112–35.

Mykletun, R. 1984: Teacher stress: Perceived and objective sources, and quality of life. *Scandinavian Journal of Educational Research*, 28, 17–45.

Newman, J. D., and Beehr, T. 1979: Personal and organizational strategies for handling job stress: A review of research and opinion. *Personnel Psychology*, 32, 1–43.

Quinn, R. P., and Staines, G. L. 1979: *The 1977 quality of employment survey: descriptive statistics, with comparison data from the 1969–70 and the 1972–73 survey*, Ann Arbor, MI: Survey Research Center.

Reynolds, S., and Shapiro, D. A. 1991: Stress reduction in transition: Conceptual problems in the design, implementation, and evaluation of worksite stress management interventions. *Human Relations*, 44, 717–33.

Rogers, J., and Dodson, S. 1988: Burnout in occupational therapists. *American Journal of Occupational Therapy*, 42, 787–92.

Ross, C. E., and Mirowsky, J. 1995: Does employment affect health? *Journal of Health and Social Behavior*, 36, 230–43.

Ruchlin, H. S., and Morris, J. N. 1991: Impact of work on the quality of life in community-residing young elderly. *American Journal of Public Health*, 81, 498–500.

Saurel-Cubizolles, M. J., and Kaminski, M. 1986: Work in pregnancy: Its evolving relationship with perinatal outcome (a review). *Social Science and Medicine*, 22, 431–42.

Sauter, S. L., Murphy, L. R., and Hurrell, J. J., Jr. 1990: A national strategy for the prevention of work-related psychological disorders. *American Psychologist*, 45, 1146–58.

Schaubroeck, J., and Ganster, D. C. 1993: Chronic demands and responsivity to challenge. *Journal of Applied Psychology*, 78, 73–85.

Schaubroeck, J., Ganster, D. C., and Fox, M. L. 1992: Dispositional affect and work-related stress. *Journal of Applied Psychology*, 77, 322–35.

Schaubroeck, J., Ganster, D. C., and Jones, J. 1998: Organization and occupation influences in the attraction–selection–attrition process. *Journal of Applied Psychology*, 83, 869–91.

Schaubroeck, J., Ganster, D. C., and Kemmerer, B. E. 1994: Job complexity, Type A behavior, and cardiovascular disorder: A prospective study. *Academy of Management Journal*, 37, 426–39.

Schaubroeck, J., Ganster, D. C., Sime, W., and Dittman, D. 1993: A field experiment testing supervisory role clarification. *Personnel Psychology*, 46, 1–25.

Schaubroeck, J., and Merritt, D. 1997: Divergent effects of job control on coping with work stressors: The key role of self-efficacy. *Academy of Management Journal*, 40, 738–54.

Schnall, P. L., Landsbergis, P. A., and Baker, D. 1994: Job strain and cardiovascular disease. *Annual Review of Public Health*, 15, 381–411.

Selye, H. 1976: *The stress of life*, 2nd edn., New York: McGraw-Hill.

Stoner, C. R., and Fry, F. L. 1983: Developing a corporate policy for managing stress. *Personnel*, May/June, 66–76.

Taylor, S. E., Repetti, R. L., and Seeman, T. 1997: Health psychology: What is an unhealthy environment and how does it get under the skin? *Annual Review of Psychology*, 48, 411–47.

Theorell, T., Tsutsumi, A., Hallquist, J., Reuterwallet, C., et al. 1998: Decision latitude, job strain, and myocardial infarction: A study of working men in Stockholm. *American Journal of Public Health*, 88, 382–8.

Timio, M., and Gentili, S. 1976: Adrenosympathetic overactivity under conditions of work stress. *British Journal of Preventive and Social Medicine*, 30, 262–5.

Timio, M., Gentili, S., and Pede, S. 1979: Free adrenaline and noradrenaline excretion related to occupational stress. *British Heart Journal*, 42, 471–4.

US Department of Labor 1977: *Dictionary of Occupational Titles*, Employment and Training Administration, US Employment Service (4th edn.).

Winslow, R. 1998: Big study shows workers under stress likely to have higher health-care costs. *Wall Street Journal*, October 16, B4.

Wood, R., and Bandura, A. 1989: Impact of conceptions of ability on self-regulatory mechanisms and complex decision making. *Journal of Personality and Social Psychology*, 56, 407–15.

Yancik, R. 1984: Sources of work stress for hospice staff. *Journal of Psychosocial Oncology*, 2, 21–31.

chapter **3**

ADVANCES IN LEADERSHIP TRAINING AND DEVELOPMENT

MARILYN E. GIST AND
DANA McDONALD-MANN

Service industries now dominate the economies of most developed nations, reflecting rapid growth in areas such as health care, high-technology, insurance, delivery, fast food, and consulting. In these industries, both workers and managers need strong interpersonal skills. Workers, for example, have extensive interface with customers; skills such as communications and negotiations are required in many jobs. Managers, on the other hand, find that knowledge workers expect more communication and participation in decision making than was common with factory workers. Workers and managers are both challenged to develop the skills they need to perform effectively with today's organizations.

Accordingly, most organizational training expenditures go for training managers or for training in interpersonal skills. A recent survey of the US training industry (Industry Report, 1997) reported that, of $60 billion spent on organizational training in 1997, approximately two-thirds was spent in these two areas. Given the importance of these areas to organizations, the purpose of this chapter is to report advances in leadership training – with an emphasis on skills involved in managing people.

To understand these advances, some background on leadership training research is needed. Although a full review of the literature is beyond the scope of our chapter, the next section summarizes historically relevant domains of study. Following this, recent advances are presented. These include not only academic studies, but findings from applied research. The chapter concludes by discussing training methods used in organizations. These emphasize skill-based training and feedback for managers and other leaders. Increasingly, these are delivered by distance learning and/or in executive education programs.

■ TRADITIONAL APPROACHES TO LEADERSHIP TRAINING RESEARCH

The scholarly literature on leadership is vast. However, our objective for this chapter requires a focused review of this literature. Given that other sources review the major theories of leadership (for example, Bass and Stogdill, 1990), we concentrated our efforts on studies of leadership, managerial, or supervisory training. Within this domain, we found two types of literature: that concerned with training content and that concerned with training methodology.

Traditional content

Most leadership studies address either the cognitive aspects of leadership, or the motivational and affective concerns of leadership and managerial work (cf. Fiedler and House, 1988). As one might expect, leadership and management training research has tended to do the same.

Traditional cognitive approaches to training often emphasized a specific skill that was relevant to the decision-oriented components of managers' jobs. One such area was performance appraisal training. The 1980s saw an emphasis on training managers to evaluate employees effectively. Although it was generally believed that well-designed rater training could improve managers' performance at employee evaluation (Martin and Bartol, 1986), empirical evidence was quite mixed (Davis and Mount, 1984; Hedge and Kavanagh, 1988). It may be that the environmental and political considerations that managers face when evaluating employees actually undermine the transfer of training in rating accuracy to the job situation (cf. Murphy and Cleveland, 1995).

Another cognitive task that has received research attention is innovative problem solving. Exploring ways of increasing managers' creativity, brainstorming and other approaches to divergent thinking were stressed in early studies (cf. Bobele and Buchanan, 1976). In general, brainstorming was found to be effective so long as group process losses were minimized. Continuing research on divergent thinking, recent evidence showed that cognitive modeling (a process of self-guided statements to facilitate divergent thinking – Gist, 1989) enhanced managers' creativity. Taking a different approach, Basadur et al. (1990) found that trainees' problem-solving style mediated the effect of creativity training on managers' thinking.

In the motivational or affective arena, the literature is dominated by studies of leadership styles. This line of research appears to have roots in situational leadership theory (for example, Fiedler, 1967), and generally explored which leadership style(s) might be "best." Early evidence reported that democratic styles were associated with favorable outcomes, such as commitment, initiative, and motivation (Latona, 1972). Later, Blake and Mouton (1982) explored whether "situationalism" or "one-best style" was preferred, and suggested that one style should be adapted to different situations. Conversely, Hersey et al. (1982) showed that situationalism was quite viable, when four styles (telling, selling, participating, and delegating) were matched to maturity. Other authors have adapted leadership styles to group development (Carew et al., 1986) and to group decision making (Latham, 1987). Similarly, interest grew in whether men and women utilized different styles (Jago and Vroom, 1982) or had different experiences based on inherent style (Wheatley et al., 1991). Staley (1984) reviewed the literature on leadership style and women in mixed groups. Although the topic of leadership styles dominated the training content literature, it has generally not been well validated by empirical work.

Beyond leadership-styles training, a number of specific skills received some attention in the motivational/affective arena. The globalization of business led to an interest in training managers to work in a multicultural environment (Harrison, 1992; Williams et al., 1986). Much of the diversity training of the late 1980s and early 1990s was similarly aimed at managers. Other motivational/affective skills that were commonly trained include assertiveness (Shaw and Rutledge, 1976), listening (Barthakur, 1983), emotional control (Cayer et al., 1988), and managing change (Allen and Nixon, 1988).

In sum, early literature on management training focused on cognitive skills and motivational aspects of leaders' jobs. Cognitive-skills training stressed performance appraisal and innovative problem solving. The motivational training emphasized leadership style, but also explored multicultural issues, diversity, and other emotion-based skills. Later, we will discuss contemporary advances in leadership training research.

Traditional methodology

Although case studies and anecdotal reports characterize the literature on training content, more rigorous work is found in the pedagogical literature. Management training originally utilized mainly lecture, or lecture coupled with role play. One of the significant research contributions of the 1970s and 1980s was the application of social learning theory (SLT – later termed social cognitive theory or SCT) to leadership training. Latham et al. (1975) were among the first to test behavioral observation as an effective training method. Their initial focus was performance evaluation training, but Latham and Saari (1979) later applied behavioral modeling to supervisors' interpersonal skills. In a meta-analysis, Burke and Day (1986) found that behavioral modeling enhanced performance in managerial training, tending to be superior to lecture, or lecture coupled with role play alone. Other scholars explored the social-cognitive mechanisms by which modeling works (Gist et al., 1989; Porras and Hargis, 1982). Basically, modeling demonstrates correct behaviors or performance strategies; these may be learned vicariously. Decker (1986) provided an excellent review of work in behavioral modeling and its application to leadership training.

Another methodology focus in the 1980s involved the use of computers in training programs. In most cases, formats of computer-assisted instruction were varied to assess their effectiveness for delivering training (Davis and Mount, 1984; Gist et al., 1989). Typically, it was found that computer assistance could be an effective tool in training and/or that trained groups outperformed untrained groups. Scholarly findings on microcomputers mirrored the adoption of computer-assisted training in practice (Kearsley and Hillelsohn, 1984; Van-Zwieten, 1984).

Perhaps the greatest emphasis in leadership development has been on assessment centers. Although these serve a variety of purposes (such as selection, promotion, training, and development), early studies addressed validation issues with respect to management tasks. For example, Howard (1983) reported that, within the Bell system, the four factors contributing to managerial advancement needed to be assessed by different techniques. Specifically, cognitive tests were suited to intellectual ability, interpersonal skills were measured best by group exercises, administrative skills were assessed via in-basket, and advancement motivation by interviews, projective tests, and personality measures.

However, challenges were raised about the validity of early assessment center ratings. For example, with ratings involving collective-assessor judgments (such as, group exercises), agreement may be subject to undue influence. Sackett and Wilson (1982) examined the mechanisms behind consensual judgments in assessment center tasks, and found that while middle managers were rather similar in their influence during the consensus-formation process, upper managers varied widely in influence. This raised questions about the generalizability of assessment ratings across raters and potentially across target populations. Sackett and Dreher (1982) also found that assessment ratings often failed to reflect accurately the underlying traits they claim to measure. It appears that assessment centers need to evaluate their measurement approaches quite carefully. Further, predictive validity may be hampered unless the measures are proven to relate to performance in the target organization.

None the less, in practice, assessment center ratings have proven predictive of managerial advancement for men and women (Pelfrey, 1986; Ritchie and Moses, 1983). Subsequent empirical evidence has supported the validity of the assessment approach. For example, a meta-analysis reported that assessment centers showed validity generalization and situational specificity (Gaugler et al., 1987). Also, a four-year study of raters found no differences in the predictive validity of ratings by senior managers versus psychologists as assessors (Tziner et al., 1993).

In sum, training research has emerged gradually as a rigorous field of study. The 1970s and 1980s saw a content emphasis on cognitive skill and leadership style. Concurrently, behavioral modeling was found to be superior to lecture, or lecture plus role play, for training managers. Theoretical connections were shown between modeling and the vicarious-learning principles of social cognitive theory. Computer-assisted instruction and assessment center technologies appeared as "new developments" of the past training era. Each method showed promise and limitations.

ADVANCES IN RESEARCH ON LEADERSHIP TRAINING

Although research on organizational training has intensified over the past decade, empirical evidence on leadership or management training is much more limited. In this section, we review literature on training and report empirical advances in assessment centers and skill-based approaches.

Training research based on leadership theories

Contemporary interest in leadership theory is as strong as that in the past. Newer perspectives have emerged that extend or advance our earlier knowledge. These include theories related to charismatic/transformational/strategic leadership, those related to leader–employee transactions/exchanges, and those related to the cognitive resources of the leader. To some extent, each has been applied to the subject of leader/manager development. We discuss them in turn below.

Charismatic, transformational, and strategic leadership theories

The earliest research on leadership began with the exploration of trait-based differences between leaders and non-leaders. The observation that some "great men" had charisma fueled much of this work. Despite the failure of earlier trait research to explain much that is deemed useful today, the notion of charismatic leadership resurfaced. The contemporary view proposes that charismatic leadership is linked to organizational effectiveness (Conger and Kanungo, 1988; Sashkin, 1988). By defining charismatic leaders in terms of specific behaviors that are known to predict favorable outcomes (most importantly, demonstrating strategic vision, then establishing strong goals, getting people working together, and so on), the contemporary proposition appears to have merit. Still, empirical evidence is needed before we conclude with certainty that charismatic leadership makes a difference in organizational outcomes.

Transformational leadership theory may be a more compelling approach to studying dynamic leaders. Derived in part from studies of the antecedents of charisma (Avolio and Gibbons, 1988), and observations that businesses faced significant changes in the past decade or so (Tichy and Devanna, 1986), transformational leadership theory emphasizes the need for leaders to initiate and manage organizational change in positive ways. Bass (1990; 1997) defined transformational leadership as occurring when leaders stir their employees to look beyond their own self-interest for the good of the group. He distinguished this from leadership that was merely an employment transaction between managers and employees (that is, transactional leadership). Much support for the conceptual, measurement, and evidential bases of the transformational leadership theory has been provided by Bass and Avolio (1993) and Bass (1998).

With respect to transformational leadership training, less research has been done. However, early results are promising. In a study of 550 Israeli military personnel, participants in a three-day course on transformational leadership reported that the transformational message was inspiring and important, and that they would attempt to implement it in their leadership roles (Popper et al., 1992). Another study of 20 managers used strong experimental methodology to assess results of their exposure to transformational leadership training (Barling et al., 1996). Results showed that the training had significant and favorable effects. Training improved subordinates' perceptions of leaders' transformational leadership, subordinates' commitment, and financial performance at the branch level of the organization.

Although further research is needed, these encouraging results suggest that inclusion of transformational leadership principles in management training should be considered. Useful additions to this line of inquiry would be the contributions from recent work on strategic leadership. House and Aditya (1997, p. 445) argued that: "It is possible for managers to be leaders and leaders to be managers. Managers become leaders by providing vision, direction, strategy, and inspiration to their organizational units, and behaving in a manner that reinforces the vision and its inherent values." We note that providing vision and inspiration are quite similar to Bass and colleagues' view of transformational leadership. However, strategic leadership couches transformation in terms of organizational tasks.

"Strategic leadership includes: making strategic decisions concerning the products and services of organizations and markets; selection of key executives; allocation of resources to major organizational components; formulation of organizational goals and strategy; providing direction for the organization with respect to the organization's domain; conceptualizing and installing organizational designs and major infrastructures, such as compensation, information, and control systems; representing the organization to critical constituencies such as representatives of financial institutions, government agencies, customer interest groups, and labor; and negotiating with such constituencies for legitimacy and resources." (House and Aditya, 1997, p. 445)

No studies were found that directly examined strategic-leadership training. However, Finkelstein and Hambrick (1996) focused on top management showing how strategic leadership affected organizational performance, while others (for example, House and Aditya, 1997) defined strategic leadership in ways that characterize many mid-level, as well as senior, managers. We encourage more studies of training that focuses on transformational and strategic leadership.

Transactional versus leader–member exchange (LMX) theories

Given that traditional views of leadership focused partly on exchanges between managers and subordinates (Bass, 1990), then leader–member exchange (LMX) may be viewed as an empirical advance in the transactional tradition. LMX theory has developed over more than 25 years (Graen and Scandura, 1987; Graen and Uhl-Bien, 1998). It is an approach to leadership that characterizes the professional relationship of leader–subordinate dyads. This line of research also may be viewed as an extension of earlier studies of leadership style, because LMX shows that leaders develop different types of relationships (or use different styles) in dealing with different subordinates. Most recently, a study by Liden and Maslyn (1998) found support for four dimensions of LMX: loyalty; affect; professional respect; and contribution. High-quality exchanges have been associated with a number of favorable outcomes for individuals and organizations (Liden et al., 1997).

Although LMX has been conceptually linked to leadership development, Scandura and Lankau (1996) suggested that further research was needed to explore the role that gender and race relations played in the LMX development process. Studies also should integrate LMX principles into leadership development courses and assess post-training outcomes.

Cognitive resource theory

Another contemporary perspective on leadership explored the circumstances under which intelligence or experience best predicts leader effectiveness. Cognitive resource theory (CRT – Fiedler and Garcia, 1987) posits that intellectual abilities are best under low stress conditions, but that prior experience leads to greater effectiveness under conditions of high stress. Although this theory has evident utility for leader selection, it also has been applied to leader training. In a typical study of university students, Murphy et al. (1992) found that leaders' expertise contributed to group effectiveness only if leaders were first trained in task-relevant knowledge and then were directive in their behavior. We note that this is a form of cognitive-skills training, and that it relates to findings from the group decision-making literature. There it was shown that a person's technical expertise facilitates decisions when that person has the most knowledge among group members, and that the group's performance only capitalizes on the knowledge of its "best member" if that person exerts influence (for example, Bottger, 1984; Bottger and Yetton, 1988; Vroom and Jago, 1978).

Performance-based approaches

Although leadership theories provide a framework for understanding leader behavior, ultimately leaders must perform effectively on the job. Thus, contemporary approaches to management development continue to focus on factors that contribute to performance. These may be skill-based (such as, task knowledge, skills, or abilities) or person-based (such as, personality traits, learned interpersonal behaviors, or general emotional competence). As we show below, assessment centers and training programs have explored both types of performance factors. There is also growing recognition that self-awareness plays an important role in management development.

Assessment centers

Research on assessment centers continues, revisiting older issues as well as addressing new ones. With respect to traditional concerns, Campbell and Bray (1993) reviewed their earlier evidence that an assessment center program successfully predicted managerial performance and potential. Other studies showed continuing concern with construct validity. In a study comparing traditional assessment center dimensions with a set of constructs based on the functional nature of managerial work, Joyce et al. (1994) found the evidence to be weak for both types of constructs. By contrast, Russell and Domm (1995) found that assessment ratings showed greater criterion validity for task-based, rather than trait-based, ratings. These studies continue to show a need for assessment center designs to relate to job demands, and for criterion validation of their measures.

Assessment centers appear to offer value to organizations, and some of this potential applies to management development (Howard, 1997). For example, Englebrecht and Fischer (1995) found that a developmental assessment center, designed around behaviorally-anchored rating scales for the managers' jobs, led to superior performance among supervisors who participated in the center when compared to a control group. The fact that the results sustained for three months shows that assessment and feedback can have long lasting effects as development experiences. A different perspective was taken by Jones and Whitmore (1995) who compared assessees with a naturally-occurring control group ten years later. Although no differences were found in career advancement, assessor ratings of career motivation and assessee developmental activity were related to advancement. These studies suggest that, when carefully designed, assessment centers can predict who is likely to advance, and can aid in their development.

Skill-, emotion-, and behavior-based development

In addition to task-relevant training associated with studies of cognitive resource theory, evidence suggests that leaders may benefit from training in task-relevant skills. Although training may be offered in any skill area, several merit attention here. First, employee assistance training has increased in recent years. One empirical test showed that, although some information was lost, training can be an effective way of ensuring that supervisors gain important information about employee support and corrective feedback strategies (Donohoe et al., 1997). We believe that training remains valuable for many cognitive and information-based tasks.

Next, growing interest in emotional development is seen with leadership training, and personal growth programs tend to emphasize this facet of development. These programs may stress risk taking, emotional expressiveness, teamwork, reflection, and/or self-awareness (Conger, 1993). Their main purpose is to challenge leaders to understand their own feelings in different situations and to explore new ways of responding. Despite the popularity of some emotion-based programs (such as wilderness training) little empirical validation exists concerning their effectiveness.

Last, behavioral development is important for managers. Training in interpersonal skills has received much attention in the past decade. Several studies explored how self-regulatory factors influence the acquisition, maintenance, and generalization of these skills (Gist, 1997). Earlier research showed that training methods, such as cognitive or behavioral modeling tend to be superior for managers' initial skill acquisition (Burke and Day, 1986; Latham and Frayne, 1989) because they vicariously present correct learning points. More recent studies showed that training methods can significantly influence self-regulation, thereby influencing behavioral-skills learning. For example, modeling can increase self-efficacy (Gist, 1989; Gist and Mitchell, 1992; Gist et al., 1989). Also, both initial training and booster sessions tend to increase skill acquisition and maintenance of learning when the training sessions have a process orientation (for example, self-management, mastery focused) rather than an outcome orientation (for example, outcome goals; cf. Kanfer and Ackerman, 1989). Process approaches enhance learning through self-efficacy; accordingly, they are best for trainees who are low to moderate in self-efficacy, but may not be effective for those high in self-efficacy (Gist et al., 1991; Stevens and Gist, 1997). Typically, skill generalization to different tasks responds to different training methods than does skill retention (Baldwin, 1992; Schmidt and Bjork, 1992). However, process-training approaches also have been shown to be more effective than outcome training for skill generalization (Gist et al., 1990; Gist and Stevens, 1998).

Self-awareness

Next, research attention has focused on the need for managers to have strong understanding of their strengths and weaknesses. Although self-awareness may or may not be part of a training program, evidence on its importance for leadership development is fairly clear. Further, the growing use of multi-source evaluations (in which performance feedback may be sought from customers, subordinates, and peers as well as supervisors) suggests that not only are senior management's perceptions considered important, but so are the perceptions of others in and/or outside the organization (cf. Church and Bracken, 1997). The idea behind this practice is that, if managers learn more about how their behavior is viewed, they are more likely to capitalize on their strengths and improve their weaknesses. Some support for this can be inferred from an empirical study by Church (1997). He found that high-performing managers were significantly more managerially self-aware when compared to average-performing managers. Relatedly, in a study of 387 mid-level executives, Ashford and Tsui (1991) found that active feedback seeking (particularly when negative feedback was sought) was central to self-regulation for managerial effectiveness. Thus, others' perceptions of performance can be valid for measuring leader effectiveness – most likely because perceptions may capture process-oriented behaviors that affect outcomes of importance to a leader's job. To the extent that perceptual measures can be associated with objective criteria, confidence in their validity appears to be merited.

In sum, strong evidence shows that content training continues, but that it should not be the sole focus of our attention. Training designs themselves affect training outcomes. Designs should reflect the fact that most trainees face novel challenges in training. They may lack confidence in their capabilities, or be intimidated by excessive performance demands in the learning context. Methods that stress mastery of subskills, self-management, and modeling lead to increased learning across individuals. Also, leaders need self-awareness to interact effectively with others. Clearly, leader-training research now emphasizes the interpersonal demands of contemporary managerial work, as well as cognitive knowledge.

■ ADVANCES IN THE PRACTICE OF LEADERSHIP TRAINING

Training and development is an area of constant change and growth. As the workplace grows increasingly complex, there is the ever-present need for more training and development. Management training alone has become a big business with spending increasing from $10 billion in the mid-1980s to $45 billion by the mid-1990s (Fulmer, 1997). Much of the training that takes place uses a variety of platforms and methodologies. This section discusses management training and development including skill-based training, feedback-intensive training, distance learning, and executive education.

Within the arena of management training, there has been increased interest in leadership development. Some have credited this to the rapid changes in technology and global communications and the greater need for leadership versus management in organizations (Cacioppe, 1998; Kotter, 1990). Although numerous approaches to leadership development exist, one model has been posited to present an integrated approach. Cacioppe (1998) suggests that any leadership development program should: (1) articulate strategic imperatives; (2) set objectives for development; (3) improve abilities, skills, and relationships; (4) participate in the changing direction and new culture of business; (5) improve self-development (awareness); and (6) include on the job follow-up. Within this model, multiple training methodologies can be used. This chapter addresses two broad methodologies of skill-based training and feedback-intensive training, both of which can be used in management training. We then discuss popular platforms of distance learning and executive education.

Skill-based training

Skill-based training is defined as a planned event designed to teach the specific knowledge and skills required to enhance performance (Rossett, 1996). In contrast, feedback-intensive programs (to be discussed later) are designed to provide assessment of current skill level, increased self-awareness, perspective change, and values and goals clarification (McDonald-Mann, 1992). Two domains of learning are encompassed by the term skill-based training: knowledge and skills. Knowledge is a cognitive domain of skill-based training (Nadler and Nadler, 1994). But knowledge alone is not sufficient for changing performance. You must know how to do something before you can do it, but knowing how to do something does not ensure that you possess the necessary skills in order to perform effectively.

Skills are an action domain of learning: the ability "to do." Acquiring a skill requires practice and feedback on performance. Thus, skill-based training should be designed to provide participants with a structured environment in which to learn a specified domain of knowledge and to learn and practice a specified set of skills. Typically, the design of an effective skill-based training environment allows the participant: (1) to learn conceptual information and/or necessary behaviors; (2) to practice using the new information and/or behaviors; and (3) to receive feedback on his or her performance.

Below we will discuss the most frequently used training methods: lecture; case study; role play; behavioral-role modeling; and simulation. Later we discuss distance learning, which uses advanced technology to apply some of the classic training methodologies. For example, distance learning often uses video-conferencing to implement a lecture format for learning, or it may use the Internet to allow learners to participate in a case study exercise or simulation.

Lecture

The lecture-oriented training format remains the most common training methodology. Although a traditional lecture uses one-way communication, an interactive lecture facilitates adult learning. An interactive lecture presents content-specific information but also engages participants in discussions and explorations of the information being presented. House (1996) asserts that audience participation is a critical component of training, and an interactive lecture maximizes this by stimulating questions, generating group discussions, and even encouraging open disagreements or debates. An interactive approach will stimulate questions, generate group discussions, and even encourage an open discussion of disagreements (House, 1996).

A lecture efficiently delivers information (that is, declarative knowledge) to a relatively large group of people in a relatively short amount of time. The amount of interaction encouraged affects the extent to which the learner may tailor the information to his or her needs. Although a lecture format can facilitate knowledge acquisition (for example, theories of conflict management styles), it cannot facilitate skill development (for example, using conflict management techniques). None the less, the utility of a lecture format typically ensures that most training (including experiential programs) will use lecture to build declarative knowledge prior to skills practice.

Case study

As an alternative format for skill-based training, case studies present participants with information describing an organization, a situation in the organization, how the situation was handled, and the outcome. Participants analyze the situation and outcome based on their newly developed skills, and they determine if the action taken was appropriate and what could have been done differently (McDonald-Mann, 1992). A case study includes "the description of a complex situation [and] an in-depth historical record of actions taken" (Alden and Kirkhorn, 1996, p. 499). This methodology forces participants to make independent assessments of the appropriateness of actions taken and alternative solutions. The case study method increases participants' awareness of: (1) previously unrecognized issues; (2) their need to learn a new skill; or (3) both (Alden and Kirkhorn, 1996). The most effective use of case studies in skill-based training would be that of providing a practice opportunity. Once participants have the knowledge base necessary, case studies provide opportunities to practice particularly complex skills, such as those necessary for creative thinking and critical evaluation.

Role play

As another option for skill-based management training, role plays are exercises in which "players spontaneously act out characters assigned to them in a scenario" (Thiagarajan, 1996). Thiagarajan notes that both role plays and simulations (which are discussed below) are based on the theories that active experience facilitates learning better than passive techniques. By their design, role plays mirror parts of reality and focus on the responses that evolve during the exercise. Although they do provide some context within which participants can formulate responses, the context is not typically elaborate. The limited details make possible a relatively unlimited array of responses. As a rule, role plays can be especially useful for practicing interpersonal skills (Thiagarajan, 1996). These include conflict management, negotiation, influencing, team building, active listening, giving and receiving feedback, and communication (McDonald-Mann, 1992).

Behavioral role-modeling

An elaboration of role plays is behavioral role-modeling. Behavioral role-modeling is based on social learning theory (Bandura, 1977). Appropriate behavior is first modeled for participants, after which they may role play the behavior and receive feedback on their performance. For example, in learning appropriate negotiation skills, participants may watch live or videotaped examples of people negotiating effectively.

Like role plays, behavioral role-modeling is useful for learning interpersonal skills. Goldstein and Sorcher (1974) popularized the approach as a way to improve interpersonal and managerial skills. Meta-analysis supports behavioral role-modeling as one of the most effective methods of management training (Burke and Day, 1986).

Simulation

An even more elaborate format for skill-based training is a simulation. Similar to role plays, simulations are designed to replicate a work environment with as much realism as possible. Yet simulations provide significantly more detailed information and more structure than role plays (Gist et al., 1998). This makes them effective tools to teach problem solving, interpersonal skills, and analytical thinking skills. For example, one commercially available training simulation provides detailed information about a fictitious company. After reviewing the information, each trainee assumes the role of a manager in the firm and reviews additional information about this manager and his/her role. As a collective, participants then operate the company. At the completion of the simulation, participants give and receive feedback regarding behaviors demonstrated during the exercise. This debriefing phase is critical to the learning process engendered by simulations.

In sum, a number of training methodologies are commonly used for skill-based leadership training. When designing a training program, it is critical that content be matched with appropriate methodologies. Lecture may be most appropriate for conveying large amounts of information and theory. However, interpersonal skills, such as conflict management, are best taught via interactive methods such as role play.

Feedback-intensive training

Another approach to training, specifically management training (such as leadership development), is feedback-intensive training. As discussed previously, skill-based training focuses on teaching and building specific competencies while feedback-intensive training has the broader goal of increasing self-awareness. Feedback-intensive training has several defining features which help to differentiate it from skills training. Feedback programs are typically classroom-based and away from work. The feedback itself is usually derived from multiple sources. It may be based on various psychometric instruments and/or behavioral exercises during an assessment or training program. The feedback focuses on skills, behaviors, values, and preferences, and may be presented throughout the program (Guthrie and Kelly-Radford, 1998).

Due to their length, feedback-intensive programs typically use a variety of training methodologies. They often combine leaderless-group discussions and simulations with group observation, videotaping and facilitated debriefings. A feedback-intensive program often also includes 360-degree feedback, personality measures, and preference assessments (Guthrie and Kelly-Radford, 1998). Throughout all of the methodologies, the program must be designed to provide the support and security necessary to help participants feel comfortable receiving large amounts of new information about themselves. Overall, these programs are designed to achieve a variety of outcomes: knowledge acquisition; self-awareness change; perspective change; goal attainment and reframing; and behavior change.

Distance learning

Although the training platform of distance learning has begun to receive much attention, the concept of distance learning is not new. Correspondence courses which use the mail as the method of communication technically classify as distance learning. However, more recently, the concept of distance learning has received a more complex definition than a correspondence course. "The U.S. Distance Learning Association has defined distance learning as 'the delivery of education or training through electronically mediated instruction including satellite, video, audio, audiographic computer, multimedia technology, and learning at a distance'" (Leonard, 1996, p. 42).

Overall, distance learning is gaining popularity primarily because of its impact on the manner in which organizations conduct business. Specifically, shifting training to a technology-based approach allows more individuals to receive training at a lower cost thus allowing organizations to remain competitive in an environment requiring increased flexibility and responsiveness in all aspects of business. Also, distance learning programs minimize the amount of time employees are away from their jobs thus decreasing "down time" within organizations. Technology allows participants to schedule training around work requirements as well as eliminating time lost in travel to the training site.

As a training platform, distance learning typically utilizes all of the traditional training methodologies discussed earlier (for example, lecture and case study) and more as well as utilizing almost any technology such as the Internet or videoconferencing. When considering the technology to be used, this should be matched with the demands of the training methodology as well as ensuring "a structured two-way communication for learner–trainer interaction" (Abernathy, 1997, p. 39). Abernathy classifies distance learning technologies as interactive and non-interactive. She makes the distinction that interactive technologies have two-way communication built in while non-interactive technologies must be combined with telephone, fax, or an interactive technology such as e-mail to establish two-way communication. Interactive technologies include audioconferencing, videoconferencing, Internet, e-mail, two-way satellite, and one-way satellite with keypad. By contrast, non-interactive techologies include radio, printed materials, audiotape, CD-ROM, videotape, and one-way satellite without keypad.

The emphasis placed here on interactivity has been corroborated by other authors and researchers who note that interactivity is a critical component for the success of most distance learning programs (Webster and Hackley, 1997). In fact, one "rule of thumb" offered is interactive activities every five to seven minutes (Abernathy, 1997). The exception to this rule of thumb, of course, is the need for cultural sensitivity when working globally. Not all interactivity translates across cultures, and in some cultures, "interactivity in the classroom can violate norms for good instruction" (Filipczak, 1997). Other recommendations to enhance the effectiveness of distance-learning programs include using rich medium, fewer participant locations, and instructors with positive attitudes and interactive styles. To increase medium richness, the technology layout should allow the instructor to maintain eye contact with the on-site and remote participant simultaneously. Also the instructor should maximize a multimedia design by using a variety of the technologies and media available (for example, using the Internet during a videoconferencing program – Webster and Hackley, 1997).

Executive education

Executive education is the world where skill-based training, feedback (reminiscent of feedback-intensive training) and distance learning may converge. As noted earlier, management training had grown to a $45 billion enterprise in 1996. Of this, approximately $12 billion was dedicated to executive education (Fulmer and Vicere, 1996). This increase in executive education expenditures is attributed to a resurging interest in leadership development (Bassi et al., 1998; Fulmer and Vicere, 1996).

With the resurgent interest in leadership development, several trends have evolved which shape the definition of executive education programs. Among the more prominent trends Fulmer and Vicere (1996) cite movement toward more customized, shorter and more focused programs that emphasize the strategic needs of the organization. Also, executive education programs using more action-learning processes which require participants to bring real-world business problems to the program. Participants then use these business problems as projects during the course. Finally, executive education programs are now tending to be part of larger-scale, cascading interventions in organizations. Bassi et al. (1998) cite similar trends listing the following changes in program designs:

- the integration of strategy and leadership development;
- fully integrated executive education systems;
- increased focus on individual development;
- leadership as the critical focus for development;
- recognition of the importance of innovation and entrepreneurship;
- action learning as the preferred learning paradigm;
- use of technology.

In order to achieve the far-reaching objectives typically articulated for executive education, these programs usually combine varying training platforms and methodologies. In order to achieve the strategic focus necessary for this type of program, they are typically rich in highly specific content focused in effective management techniques as well as organization specific and industry specific information. Within this context, executive education typically carries a large skill-based training component which often uses lecture and case study training methodologies as well as the more recent technique of action learning. Executive education programs are also starting to include components similar to feedback intensive programs. In addition to the heavy skill-based components, executive education designers are providing participants with opportunities to receive 360-degree feedback from others in their work environment (typically boss, peers, and direct reports). In some instances, participants may also receive peer feedback from fellow participants during the program. Finally, distance learning innovations are beginning to impact on executive education.

Because the executive education process is time consuming and labor intensive, programs are beginning to combine on-site sessions with distance learning methodologies between the on-site sessions. This allows executives to access the development experience with more flexibility. The increasing demands on top-level executives makes extended periods away from the office unmanageable. Combining on-site sessions with distance learning allows executives to minimize the amount of time they are away from the office. It also allows them to access the developmental opportunities and resources more efficiently. Executive education would not lend itself to a complete distance learning design because face-to-face interaction and networking opportunities are critical to the development of top-level executives. However, some use of distance learning technologies can maximize the use of on-site time.

■ CONCLUSION

Research and practice in the field of leadership training and development has shown strong growth over the past 20 years. Organizations expend significant sums to train managers. Scholars have shed substantial light on: (1) the strength and limitations of training in certain cognitive skills (such as performance appraisal, innovative problem solving); (2) the superior effectiveness of certain training methods (such as behavioral modeling, process orientations); and (3) the importance of self-awareness for leaders. Recently, new platforms for leadership training have emerged. These include distance learning and executive education. We hope that advances in empirical knowledge will be incorporated into future training courses, and that scholars will explore questions raised by current advances in practice. In this manner, leaders will best improve their competencies.

REFERENCES

Abernathy, D. 1997: A start-up guide to distance learning. *Training and Development Journal*, 51(12), 39–47.

Alden, J., and Kirkhorn, J. 1996: Case studies. In R. L. Craig (ed.), *The ASTD training and development handbook*, 4th edn., New York: McGraw-Hill.

Allen, R., and Nixon, B. 1988: Developing a new approach to leadership. Special issue: Lessons from success. *Management Education and Development*, 19, 174–86.

Ashford, S. J., and Tsui, A. S. 1991: Self-regulation for managerial effectiveness: The role of active feedback seeking. *Academy of Management Journal*, 34, 251–80.

Avolio, B. J., and Gibbons, T. C. 1988: In J. A. Conger, and R. N. Kanungo (eds.). *Charismatic leadership: The elusive factor in organizational effectiveness*, San Francisco, CA: Jossey-Bass, 276–308.

Baldwin, T. T. 1992: Effects of alternative modeling strategies on outcomes of interpersonal-skills training. *Journal of Applied Psychology*, 77, 147–54.

Bandura, A. 1977: *Social learning theory*. New York: Holt, Rinehart & Winston.

Barling, J., Weber, T., and Kelloway, E. K. 1996: Effects of transformational leadership training on attitudinal and financial outcomes: A field experiment. *Journal of Applied Psychology*, 81, 827–32.

Barthakur, P. K. 1983: Social skills as noise reduction in interpersonal communication: A two-factor model: Some contributions to managerial training. *Abhigyan*, Fall, 67–79.

Basadur, M., Wakabayashi, M., and Graen, G. B. 1990: Individual problem-solving styles and attitudes toward divergent thinking before and after training. *Creativity Research Journal*, 3, 22–32.

Bass, B. M. 1990: From transactional to transformational leadership: Learning to share the vision. *Organizational Dynamics*, 18(3), 19–31.

Bass, B. M. 1997: From transactional to transformational leadership: Learning to share the vision. In R. P. Vecchio (ed.), *Leadership: Understanding the dynamics of power and influence in organizations*, Notre Dame, IN: University of Notre Dame Press, 318–33.

Bass, B. M. 1998: *Transformational leadership: Industrial, military, and educational impact*, Mahway, NJ: Lawrence Erlbaum Associates.

Bass, B. M., and Avolio, B. J. 1993: Transformational leadership: A response to critiques. In M. M. Chemers and A. Roya (eds.), *Leadership theory and research: Perspectives and directions*, San Diego, CA: Academic Press, 49–80.

Bass, B. M., and Stogdill, R. M. 1990: *Bass and Stogdill's handbook of leadership: Theory, research, and managerial applications*, New York: The Free Press.

Bassi, L., Cheney, S., and Lewis, E. 1998: Trends in workplace learning: Supply and demand in interesting times. *Training and Development Journal*, 52(11), 51–75.

Blake, R. R., and Mouton, J. S. 1982: How to choose a leadership style. *Training and Development Journal*, 36(2), 38–47.

Bobele, K. H., and Buchanan, P. J. 1976: Training managers to be better problem-solvers. *Journal of Creative Behavior*, 10(4), 250–5.

Bottger, P. C. 1984: Expertise and air time as bases of actual and perceived influence in problem-solving groups. *Journal of Applied Psychology*, 69, 214–21.

Bottger, P. C., and Yetton, P. W. 1988: An integration of process and decision scheme explanations of group problem solving performance. *Organizational Behavior and Human Decision Processes*, 42, 234–49.

Burke, M. J., and Day, R. R. 1986: A cumulative study of the effectiveness of managerial training. *Journal of Applied Psychology*, 71, 232–45.

Cacioppe, R. 1998: An integrated model and approach for the design of effective leadership development programs. *Leadership and Organizational Development Journal*, 19(1), 44–54.

Campbell, R. J., and Bray, D. W. 1993: Use of an assessment center as an aid in management selection. *Personnel Psychology*, 46, 691–9.

Carew, D. K., Parisi, C. E., and Blanchard, K. H. 1986: Group development and situational leadership: A model for managing groups. *Training and Development Journal*, 40(6), 46–50.

Cayer, M., DiMattia, D. J., Wingrove, J. 1988: Conquering evaluation fear. *Personnel Administrator*, 33, 97–107.

Church, A. H. 1997: Managerial self-awareness in high-performing individuals in organizations. *Journal of Applied Psychology*, 82, 281–92.

Church, A. H., and Bracken, D. W. 1997: Advancing the state of the art of 360-degree feedback – Guest editors' comments on the research and practice of multirater assessment methods. *Group and Organization Management*, 22(2), 149–61.

Conger, J. A. 1993: Personal growth training: Snake oil or pathway to leadership? *Organizational Dynamics*, 22, 19–30.

Conger, J. A., and Kanungo, R. N. 1988: Training charismatic leadership: A risky and critical task. In J. A. Conger, and R. N. Kanungo (eds.), *Charismatic leadership: The elusive factor in organizational effectiveness*, San Francisco, CA: Jossey-Bass, 309–23.

Davis, B. L., and Mount, M. K. 1984: Effectiveness of performance appraisal training using computer assisted instruction and behavior modeling. *Personnel Psychology*, 37, 439–52.

Decker, P. J. 1986: Social learning theory and leadership. *Journal of Management Development*, 5(3), 46–58.

Donohoe, T. L., Johnson, J. T., and Stevens, J. 1997: An analysis of an employee assistance supervisory training program. *Employee Assistance Quarterly*, 12(3), 25–34.

Englebrecht, A. S., and Fischer, A. H. 1995: The managerial performance implications of a developmental assessment center process. *Human Relations*, 48, 387–404.

Fiedler, F. E. 1967: *A theory of leadership effectiveness*, New York: McGraw-Hill.

Fiedler, F. E., and Garcia, J. E. 1987: *New approaches to effective leadership: Cognitive resources and organizational performance*, New York: John Wiley & Sons.

Fiedler, F. E., and House, R. J. 1988: Leadership theory and research: A report of progress. In Cary L. Cooper and Ivan T. Robertson (eds.), *Key reviews in managerial psychology: Concepts and research for practice*, Chichester, UK: John Wiley & Sons, 96–116.

Filipczak, B. 1997: Think locally, train globally: Distance learning across cultures. *Training*, 34(1), 41–8.

Finkelstein, S., and Hambrick, D. 1996: *Strategic leadership: Top executives and their effects on organizations*, St Paul, MN: West Publishing.

Fulmer, R. M. 1997: The evolving paradigm of leadership development. *Organizational Dynamics*, 25(4), 59.

Fulmer, R. M., and Vicere, A. A. 1996: Executive development: An analysis of competitive forces. *Planning Review*, 24(1), 31–6.

Gaugler, B. B., Rosenthal, D. B., Thornton, G. C., and Bentson, C. 1987: Meta-analysis of assessment center validity. *Journal of Applied Psychology*, 72, 493–511.

Gist, M. E. 1989: The influence of training method on self-efficacy and idea generation among managers. *Personnel Psychology*, 42, 787–805.

Gist, M. E. 1997: Training design and pedagogy: Implications for skill acquisition, maintenance, and generalization. In M. Quinones, and A. Ehrenstein (eds.), *Training for a Rapidly Changing Workplace: Applications of Psychological Research*, Washington, DC: American Psychological Association Press, 201–22.

Gist, M. E., Bavetta, A. G., and Stevens, C. K. 1990: Transfer training method: Its influence on skill generalization, effort expenditure, and performance level. *Personnel Psychology*, 43, 501–23.

Gist, M. E., Hopper, H., and Daniels, D. 1998: Behavioral simulation: Application and potential in management research. *Organizational Research Methods*, 1, 251–95.

Gist, M. E., and Mitchell, T. R. 1992: Self-efficacy: A theoretical analysis of its determinants and malleability. *Academy of Management Review*, 17, 183–211.

Gist, M. E., Schwoerer, C. E., and Rosen, B. 1989: Effects of alternative training methods on self-efficacy and performance in computer software training. *Journal of Applied Psychology*, 74, 884–91.

Gist, M. E., and Stevens, C. K. 1998: Effects of practice conditions and supplemental training method on cognitive learning and behavioral skill generalization. *Organizational Behavior and Human Decision Processes*, 75, 142–69.

Gist, M. E., Stevens, C. K., and Bavetta, A. G. 1991: Effects of self-efficacy and post-training intervention on the acquisition and maintenance of complex interpersonal skills. *Personnel Psychology*, 44, 837–61.

Goldstein, A. P., and Sorcher, M. 1974: *Changing supervisor behavior*, New York: Pergamon Press.

Graen, G. B., and Scandura, T. 1987: Toward a psychology of dyadic organizing. In L. Cummings and B. Staw (eds.), *Research in Organizational Behavior*, 9, 175–208.

Graen, G. B., and Uhl-Bien, M. 1998: Relationship-based approach to leadership: Development of Leader–Member Exchange (LMX) theory of leadership over 25 years: Applying a multi-level multi-domain perspective. In F. Dansereau and F. J. Yammarino (eds.), *Leadership: The multiple-level approaches: Contemporary and alternative. Monographs in organizational behavior and industrial relations*, Vol. 24, Part B, Stamford, CT: JAI Press, 103–55.

Guthrie, V. A., and Kelly-Radford, L. 1998: Feedback intensive programs. In C. D. McCauley, R. S. Moxley, and E. Van Velsor (eds.), *The Handbook of Leadership Development*, San Francisco, CA: Jossey-Bass, 66–104.

Harrison, J. K. 1992: Individual and combined effects of behavior modeling and the cultural assimilator in cross-cultural management training. *Journal of Applied Psychology*, 77, 952–62.

Hedge, J. W., and Kavanagh, M. J. 1988: Improving the accuracy of performance evaluations: Comparison of three methods of performance appraiser training. *Journal of Applied Psychology*, 37, 68–73.

Hersey, P., Angelini, A. L., and Carakushansky, S. 1982: The impact of situational leadership and classroom structure on learning effectiveness. *Group and Organization Studies*, 7, 216–24.

House, R. J. 1996: Classroom instruction. In R. L. Craig (ed.), *The ASTD training and development handbook*, 4th edn., New York: McGraw-Hill.

House, R. J., and Aditya, R. N. 1997: The social scientific study of leadership: Quo vadis? *Journal of Management*, 23, 409–74.

Howard, A. 1983: Measuring management abilities and motivation. *New Directions for Testing and Measurement*, 17 (March), 31–44.

Howard, A. 1997: A reassessment of assessment centers: Challenges for the 21st century. *Journal of Social Behavior and Personality*, 12(5), 13–52.

Industry Report 1997: *Training*, 34, 33–4, 36–7.

Jago, A. G., and Vroom, V. H. 1982: Sex differences in the incidence and evaluation of participative leader behavior. *Journal of Applied Psychology*, 67, 776–83.

Jones, R. G., and Whitmore, M. D. 1995: Evaluating developmental assessment centers as interventions. *Personnel Psychology*, 48, 377–88.

Joyce, L. W., Thayer, P. W., and Pond, S. B. 1994: Managerial functions: An alternative to traditional assessment center dimensions? *Personnel Psychology*, 47, 109–21.

Kanfer, R., and Ackerman, P. L. 1989: Motivation and cognitive abilities: An integrative/ aptitude treatment interaction approach to skill acquisition. *Journal of Applied Psychology*, 74, 657–89.

Kearsley, G., and Hillelsohn, M. J. 1984: How and why (and why not) we use computer-based training. *Training and Development Journal*, 38, 21–4.

Kotter, J. 1990: *A force for change: How leadership differs from management*, New York: The Free Press.

Latham, G. P., and Frayne, C. A. 1989: Self-management training for increasing job attendance: A follow-up and a replication. *Journal of Applied Psychology*, 74, 411–16.

Latham, G. P., and Saari, L. M. 1979: Application of social-learning theory to training supervisors through behavioral modeling. *Journal of Applied Psychology*, 64, 239–46.

Latham, G. P., Wexley, K. N., and Pursell-Elliot, D. 1975: Training managers to minimize rating errors in the observation of behavior. *Journal of Applied Psychology*, 60, 550–5.

Latham, V. M. 1987: Task type and group motivations: Implications for a behavioral approach to leadership in small groups. *Small Group Behavior*, 18, 56–71.

Latona, J. C. 1972: Leadership styles and productivity: A review and comparative analysis. *Training and Development Journal*, 26(8), 2–10.

Leonard, B. 1996: Distance learning: Work and training overlap. *HRMagazine*, 41(4), 41–7.

Liden, R. C., and Maslyn, J. M. 1998: Multidimensionality of leader-member exchange: An empirical assessment through scale development. *Journal of Management*, 24, 43–72.

Liden, R. C., Sparrowe, R. T., and Wayne, S. J. 1997: Leader-member exchange theory: The past and potential for the future. In G. R. Ferris et al. (eds.), *Research in Personnel and Human Resources Management*, 15, Greenwich, CT: JAI Press, 47–119.

Martin, D. C., and Bartol, K. M. 1986: Training the raters: A key to effective performance appraisal. *Public Personnel Management*, 15(2), 101–9.

McDonald-Mann, D. 1992: Skill-based training. In C. D. McCauley, R. S. Moxley, and E. Van Velsor (eds.), *Handbook of leadership development*. San Francisco: Josey-Bass.

Murphy, K. R., and Cleveland, J. N. 1995: *Understanding performance appraisal: Social, organizational, and goal-based perspectives*, Thousand Oaks, CA: Sage Publications.

Murphy, S. E., Blyth, D., and Fiedler, F. E. 1992: Cognitive resource theory and the utilization of the leader's and group members' technical competence. *Leadership Quarterly*, 3(3), 237–55.

Nadler, L., and Nadler, Z. 1994: *Designing training programs: The critical events model*, 2nd edn., Houston, TX: Gulf Publishing.

Pelfrey, W. V. 1986: Assessment centers as a management promotion tool. *Federal Probation*, 50, 65–9.

Popper, M., Landau, O., and Gluskinos, U. M. 1992: The Israeli Defence Forces: An example of transformational leadership. *Leadership and Organization Development Journal*, 13, 3–8.

Porras, J. I., and Hargis, K. 1982: Precursors of individual change: Responses to a social learning theory based on organizational intervention. *Human Relations*, 35, 973–90.

Ritchie, R. J., and Moses, J. L. 1983: Assessment center correlates of women's advancement into middle management: A 7-year longitudinal analysis. *Journal of Applied Psychology*, 68, 227–31.

Rossett, A. 1996: Job aids and electronic performance support systems. In R. L. Craig (ed.), *The ASTD training and development handbook*, 4th edn., New York: McGraw-Hill.

Russell, C. J., and Domm, D. R. 1995: *Journal of Occupational and Organizational Psychology*, 68, 25–47.

Sackett, P. R., and Dreher, G. F. 1982: Constructs and assessment center dimensions: Some troubling empirical findings. *Journal of Applied Psychology*, 67, 401–10.

Sackett, P. R., and Wilson, M. A. 1982: Factors affecting the consensus judgment process in managerial assessment centers. *Journal of Applied Psychology*, 67, 10–17.

Sashkin, M. 1988: The visionary leader. In J. A. Conger, and R. N. Kanungo (eds.). *Charismatic leadership: The elusive factor in organizational effectiveness*, San Francisco, CA: Jossey-Bass, 122–60.

Scandura, T. A., and Lankau, M. J. 1996: Developing diverse leaders: A leader-member exchange approach. *Leadership Quarterly*, 7, 243–63.

Schmidt, R. A., and Bjork, R. A. 1992: New conceptualizations of practice: Common principles in three paradigms suggest new concepts for training. *Psychological Science*, 3, 207–17.

Shaw, M. E., and Rutledge, P. 1976: Assertiveness training for managers. *Training and Development Journal*, 30(9), 8–14.

Staley, C. C. 1984: Managerial women in mixed groups: Implications of recent research. *Group and Organization Studies*, 9, 316–32.

Stevens, C. K., and Gist, M. E. 1997: Effects of self-efficacy and goal-orientation training on negotiation-skill maintenance: What are the mechanisms? *Personnel Psychology*, 50, 955–78.

Thiagarajan, S. 1996: Instructional games, simulations, and role-plays. In R. L. Craig (ed.), *The ASTD training and development handbook*, 4th edn., NewYork: McGraw-Hill.

Tichy, N. M., and Devanna, M. A. 1986: The transformational leader. *Training and Development Journal*, 40(7), 27–32.

Tziner, A., Ronen, S., and Hacohen, D. 1993: A four-year validation study of an assessment center in a financial corporation. *Journal of Organizational Behavior*, 14, 225–37.

Van Zwieten, J. 1984: Managers and microcomputers: Getting the right mix. *Training and Development Journal*, 38, 31–6.

Vroom, V. H., and Jago, A. G. 1978: On the validity of the Vroom–Yetton model. *Journal of Applied Psychology*, 63, 151–62.

Webster, J., and Hackley, P. 1997: Teaching effectiveness in technology-mediated distance learning. *Academy of Management Journal*, 40(6), 1282–1309.

Wheatley, W. J., Amin, R. W., and Maddox, E. N. 1991: The effects of gender and leadership styles on problem-solving perceptions: Implications for management training and development. *Organization Development Journal*, 9(3), 51–60.

Williams, E. D., Hayflich, P. F., and Gaston, J. 1986: The challenges of a multi-cultural workforce. *Personnel Journal*, 65, 148–51.

chapter **4**

THE PURSUIT OF ORGANIZATIONAL JUSTICE: FROM CONCEPTUALIZATION TO IMPLICATION TO APPLICATION

JERALD GREENBERG AND E. ALLAN LIND

Moral philosophers, ranging from Aristotle (Ross, 1925) through contemporary theorists (for example, Rawls, 1971), have long been concerned with the question of what constitutes justice (for a review, see Cohen and Greenberg, 1982). Their approach primarily has been prescriptive in nature, specifying what must be done to achieve an objective state of justice. By contrast, social scientists, ourselves included, have been interested less in arguing what justice "really is" than in describing people's individual perceptions of fairness. That is, we have taken a descriptive approach – one oriented toward assessing what people perceive as fair and how they respond when they believe that states of fairness have not been attained (for more on the distinction between prescriptive and descriptive approaches to justice, see Greenberg and Bies, 1992).

Although matters of justice perceptions and people's reactions to them arise, and have been studied, in a wide variety of social settings (Greenberg and Cohen, 1982; Walster et al., 1978), the work context has captured the attention of the greatest number of contemporary justice theorists in recent years (for reviews, see Beugré, 1998; Cropanzano and Greenberg, 1997; Folger and Cropanzano, 1998; Greenberg, 1996). There appear to be two basic reasons for this. First, in organizational settings explicit information often is available about the way various resources are allocated, both tangible (such as pay) and intangible (such as time and status). And, questions of justice are fundamental whenever resources are distributed: "Who gets what, and is it fair?"

Second, because the allocation of resources is central to life in organizations, a venue in which working people spend about half their waking hours, individuals tend to be highly sensitive to issues of fairness on the job. Indeed, matters of justice and injustice in the workplace are not taken lightly. Anyone who doubts this casual observation need simply enter a workplace, ask the employees questions about how fairly they are treated on the job, and watch the spirited discussion that is likely to ensue. Our experiences as organizational practitioners have taught us that their attention is unlikely to be directed to various philosophical abstractions about justice, but rather, to the specific attitudes, emotions, and behaviors that are our stock-in-trade as organizational scientists.

Acknowledging the special importance the concept of justice has taken in organizations, Greenberg (1987) coined the term *organizational justice*, which refers to people's perceptions of fairness in organizations – the topic of the present chapter. More precisely, our focus is not on theoretical developments in the field (many of which have been adequately addressed elsewhere; for example, Folger and Cropanzano, 1998), but rather, applications of such developments, a topic that only recently has gained serious attention (for example, Greenberg and Wiethoff, 2000). In the present chapter, we will discuss the implications of various well-established principles of organizational justice for organizational practice and examine the manner in which these implications actually have been translated into practice. In fact, we will trace these implications and applications for each of nine major areas of organizational functioning. To set the stage for these analyses, we will identify the conceptual bases from which they are derived – that is, various established principles of organizational justice.

Before undertaking this analysis, however, we will begin by introducing a conceptual framework that highlights some of the salient issues involved in moving from implication to application of organizational justice principles. We now will present this framework.

■ THE PRACTICAL VALUE OF ORGANIZATIONAL JUSTICE THEORIES

The conclusion we will reach in this chapter is that there have been only a few organizational justice studies conducted to date whose practical value to organizations has been tested directly. However, because the organizational justice literature is so very rich in implications for potential application, we endeavor to illuminate the path from implication to application.

Varieties of applied research: effects application and theory application

The heart of this issue lies in the fact that even when conducted in work settings, our research is designed primarily to inform theory development, and only secondarily, organizational practice. Not surprisingly, we have seen little, if anything, in the way of traditional applied research – that is, research designed directly and immediately to inform supervisory personnel about best practices by carefully assessing reactions to actual work conditions. Instead, organizational justice researchers, like most organizational behavior scholars, tend to study bits and pieces of phenomena that promise to be pieced together into a meaningful whole. The extent to which this promise is fulfilled, and the value of the resulting product to organizational practitioners, of course, is open to debate.

For the record, we believe that this state of affairs is not a limitation, but a strength, when it comes to developing interventions designed to promote perceptions of fairness in the workplace. We base our argument on the distinction between two major approaches to applicability made by Calder et al. (1981) – effects application and theory application – a distinction to which we now turn.

Effects application

The rationale underlying effects-based research is straightforward: "To obtain findings that can be generalized to a real-world situation of interest" (Calder et al., 1981, p. 198). With this in mind, effects researchers attempt to create research procedures – known as "correspondence procedures" – that come as close as possible to matching the qualities of the particular "real world" of interest to the researchers – in our case, organizations in general. Methodologically, they attempt to do this in four ways:

1. by selecting respondents who are representative of those found in a wide variety of organizations;
2. by operationalizing key variables in ways that parallel those in organizations;
3. by selecting research settings that match the environmental variation present in organizations; and
4. by selecting a research design that provides information directly relevant to making organizational decisions.

Clearly, designing such studies is highly challenging in view of the practical constraints of conducting research. This is the case with respect to organizational justice research, where: (1) respondents tend to be selected from small numbers of organizations selected on a convenience basis; (2) most variables are operationalized in ways that have more conceptual meaning to researchers than hedonic value to respondents; (3) the time frames studied are too limited to capture environmental variation; and (4) the immediate relevance to organizational decision makers is not immediately evident.

This state of affairs is not surprising in a field, such as organizational justice, where the vast majority of studies have been rather limited in the research methods used. Most either have been conducted in the laboratory (for example, Greenberg, 1993a), tapped the attitudes of employees from within a single organization (for example, Skarlicki and Folger, 1997), required students to assume managerial roles (Karambayya et al., 1992), or asked practicing managers to recall past situations of interest to the researcher (for example, Sheppard et al., 1994). In other words, much organizational justice research suffers from artificiality that renders it of limited value when it comes to identifying organizational applications.

We do not mean this as an indictment, insofar as the vast majority of organizational justice studies have not been driven by an interest in application, but in theory development. Most organizational justice research has been theoretically guided – that is, designed to shed light on fundamental psychological processes in organizational settings. However, it would be a grievous error to take this as an indication that organizational justice research has little or no applied value. Indeed, our theoretical inquiries into people's perceptions of fairness in the workplace have considerable practical value – some of which has been realized, with even more potential to be realized. The manner in which the applied value of theory-driven research can be realized has been suggested by Calder et al. (1981).

Theory application

In contrast with effects application, Calder et al. (1981) explain that research designed with theory application in mind is performed to test scientific theories that can be generalized in a manner suggesting viable organizational interventions. Because the goal of such research is to understand behavior in organizations, its concern is with developing generalizable theories instead of identifying generalizable effects.

To be applicable to organizational practice, theoretical research must survive two stages of falsification efforts (Calder et al., 1981). First is *theory falsification* – the process of measuring effects within a context for the purpose of disproving a theory. Here, research context and effects are not the researcher's major interest. Instead, scientists are interested in assessing a theory's adequacy by surviving rigorous attempts at falsification (Popper, 1963).

Only once a theory has withstood such testing, is the stage set for using the scientific explanation of the phenomenon in question as the basis for designing an intervention expected to have a desired organizational effect. This too is a falsification procedure insofar as only interventions that survive these testing procedures (that is, by bringing about the expected results) should be implemented in organizational practice. Moreover, such efforts at falsifying applications also may inform the further revision of theories (which suggest new interventions to be tested, and so on).

Calder et al. (1981) caution that this *intervention falsification* step is crucial and that neither theorists nor practitioners should assume that the same falsification procedures used to test theory are also sufficient to ensure successful application. Rather, accepted theories provide a framework for designing interventions that themselves must be subjected to rigorous efforts at refutation. Calder et al. acknowledge that "the process of translating from theory to intervention is necessarily a creative one" (p. 198) in part because theories generally do not specify how their abstract constructs are embodied in organizations and in part because theories do not address all the variables that are likely to affect behavior in organizations.

To illustrate the interdependence between theory falsification and intervention, Calder et al. (1981) use an example that bears repeating. Various theories of aerodynamics explain the processes underlying flight. Although this knowledge is necessary, it is not sufficient for designing an airplane. For this, additional information about such key variables as stress and material strength also must be ascertained. Only by systematically and repeatedly designing and testing airplanes that succeed and fail in various real flight situations is it possible to expose their weaknesses. And these, once identified, are more informative than successes when it comes to suggesting changes to be made "back at the drawing board."

This example illustrates a key point: even if the application fails (for example, the plane crashes), it does not necessarily mean that the theory is flawed. It only may imply that the intervention itself is in need of reworking. In this connection, theory application lies in sharp contrast with effects application. Whereas effects research is concerned with the generalizability of specific effects observed in research studies, theory research is concerned with the extent to which the theoretical relationship an intervention is presumed to represent may be applied beyond the research setting.

■ THE NATURE OF APPLIED RESEARCH IN ORGANIZATIONAL JUSTICE

For the most part, effects research on organizational justice has not been conducted. This is understandable insofar as the construct of justice may be far too abstract to attract the attention of practitioners as an area of practical application. By contrast, matters of justice have captured the imagination of many contemporary organizational scholars, whose efforts have provided us with a strong conceptual basis for theory development. Indeed, many theories (or, at least, portions thereof) have been tested over the years. These have resulted in several well-established principles that logically may be applied to organizational practice. For the most part, very few of these principles have been put to practical test in any manner that lend themselves to testing for falsification in the manner just described. As such, we are left with far more potential applications than actual applications of organizational justice. Framing this notion differently, we depict organizational justice research in terms of the process outlined in figure 4.1.

Initially, we conducted research designed to test conceptual ideas. Although many of these have implications for organizational practice, or are framed in terms of an organizational problem (such as adverse reactions to downsizing, employee theft, turnover, and the like), the studies are designed essentially with theory building, rather than application, in mind. As such, the most active nod to application in such

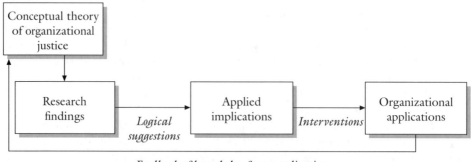

Feedback of knowledge from applications
to theory development

Figure 4.1   The interrelationships between organizational justice theory, research, implications, and applications

work usually comes in the form of passing recommendations for practice tucked away in a journal article's discussion section. We refer to studies of this type as ones that spark ideas for implementation. Most of our studies are of this type. Only rarely, however, do investigations of organizational justice take the next logical step by putting these implications to the test in organizations.

This would involve developing interventions that follow from these implications and directly assessing their impact on organizational functioning over the long term. Doing this promises not only to benefit practitioners, of course, but it also promises to aid further efforts at theory development. After all, information about the impact of organizational interventions may provide vital information that not only informs, but directs, future efforts at theory building. In view of the failure of organizational justice researchers to take the step from implication to application (and then back to theory development), it is difficult for us to point to many successes at justice-based application in this sense.

This is not to say that the many investigations that have studied organizational justice are not valuable from an applied perspective. Indeed, they are critical. Our point simply is that they have not gone far enough in the process. By identifying some of our successes and failures in this regard, we hope to stimulate future organizational researchers and practitioners to make a concerted effort toward developing and testing organizational interventions derived from the growing body of research and theory on organizational justice. Before doing this, however, we will set the stage for this analysis by identifying several of the organizational justice principles that most clearly lend themselves to organizational applications.

■ OVERVIEW OF ORGANIZATIONAL JUSTICE PRINCIPLES

Because there have been so many earlier reviews of organizational justice theories and concepts (see, for example, Beugré, 1998; Cropanzano and Greenberg, 1997; Folger and Cropanzano, 1998; Greenberg, 1996), we will not reiterate this material here. Rather, our goal is to prepare the reader for our analysis of applications by outlining some of the key principles on which these applications are based. These may be thought of as well-researched general ways in which justice may be created in the workplace. Specifically, these principles focus on various well-established tenets of *distributive justice* – the fairness of the way outcomes are distributed – and *procedural justice* – the fairness of the procedures used to determine those distributions (for an elaboration of this distinction, see Greenberg, 1987). We will now outline four such principles.

The equity principle: outcomes should be distributed proportional to contributions

One of the earliest findings in the study of organizational justice is that a principle of "equity" or proportionality defines what is seen as fair in most organizational contexts in which resources are distributed (Adams, 1965; Homans, 1961). Stated in its simplest form, the equity principle says that what people receive from an organization should be proportional to their contributions – or put differently, that people should get what they deserve. In general, research has shown that people attempt to create equitable distributions of rewards in their relationships with others (including employers) and respond negatively when these are not attained (Leventhal, 1976; Walster et al., 1978).

As simple as the equity principle may be to articulate, bringing it to realization can be quite complex. For example, it is not always clear exactly what constitutes an outcome and a contribution (status, for example, falls into this category). We will note some additional complexities in our discussion of the perception principle, below. Before doing so, however, it is essential to mention a few other aspects of how the equity principle plays out in organizations.

In general, people expect that compensation and other trappings of rank will be distributed in accord with the amount of work and the responsibilities they have within a company. In these areas, the proportionality principle constitutes an accepted definition of justice. With respect to other outcomes, however, input concerns are less important when it comes to defining justice. For example, some organizational outcomes, such as medical insurance benefits, are considered fairly distributed when they are shared equally, regardless of the recipient's contributions. Our point is that, although proportionality may be the predominant principle on the outcome side of organizational justice, there are occasions in which attention to outcomes can be overdone, and where other distributive principles (such as equality and need) may prevail (Deutsch, 1985). Despite this, however, a large body of evidence underscores the centrality of the equity principle of justice in the workplace (for a review, see Greenberg, 1982).

The perception principle: justice is in the eye of the beholder

When one tries to be fair, it is crucial to remember that actually being fair (such as by following other established principles of justice) is often less important than doing what is seen as fair (Greenberg, 1990b). Nowhere is this more clear than in attempts to put into practice the proportionality principle just described. A problem that arises in any situation in which "inputs" are not clearly defined is that people will tend to distort their own contributions upward, relative to others.

Consider a situation, for example, where a company has two salespeople, one of whom has a territory that for years has been more profitable than the other. We can expect competing judgments about whether pay should be proportional to sales or scaled somehow relative to historical levels. The salesperson with the historically stronger territory will argue that the better sales were the result of years of hard labor; the salesperson with the weaker territory will argue that there should be some recognition of the "uphill fight" needed to sell there.

We do not mean to suggest that justice is completely subjective. Workers do, in fact, recognize and accept clear, unambiguous differences as just reason for differences in payment. However, when a variety of inputs and outcomes are being compared (such as when some have contributed time and others money, or when some are reimbursed in money and others in prestige), perceptual bias is likely to occur.

Although our discussion thus far has focused on perceptual bias in distributive justice judgments, it is clear that similar biases prevail when it comes to procedural justice judgments. For example, suppose a manager makes a decision, such as implementing a pay freeze, that adversely affects his or her employees. Although employees will not like this decision, the degree to which they accept it will depend on their belief that the manager made the decision fairly (such as by following some of the principles of procedural justice described below). Importantly, this involves not only following such principles, but taking steps to ensure that others become aware of this. In other words, it often is necessary to bring one's actions directly to "the eyes of the beholder."

The voice principle: input into decisions enhances perceptions of fairness

Much of one's sense of fair treatment on the job comes from the procedures one encounters, and research and theory demonstrate the pervasive impact of a particular dimension of process. One of the most widely replicated findings in both laboratory and field studies of organizational justice is the "voice effect" (Folger, 1977; Greenberg and Folger, 1983): when people affected by a decision are given an opportunity to voice their concerns, facts, needs, and options about that decision, they will view that process as fairer than if they are not given such an opportunity (Thibaut and Walker, 1975). The effect appears to be very general and robust. As will become apparent in this chapter, voice effects occur in a wide variety of organizational contexts.

Investigations of the voice effect make it clear that what is involved is *not* that workers must have a veto over decisions, but instead that they feel that their position and concerns are considered (see, for example, Lind et al., 1983; Tyler, 1987). Indeed, providing voice can enhance acceptance of authoritative decisions by making the process fairer (Lind et al., 1993; Tyler et al., 1985). This only works, of course, when employees believe that their voice will be listened to. Indeed, if the granting of voice is seen as a façade or a political ploy, feelings of fair treatment will be even more negative than if no voice were provided at all (Folger et al., 1983).

There are a wide variety of organizational procedures and practices that can enhance feelings of voice (Kim and Mauborgne, 1997), ranging from formal hearing procedures to everyday management practices. For example, voice can be provided by giving each party to a sexual harassment complaint the time and resources needed to present his or her evidence and concerns to an impartial ombudsman. In more mundane contexts, managers who engage in regular "walk-arounds" to talk (and listen!) to subordinates, middle managers who use "skip-level" meetings to hear about what is of current concern to front-line workers, and executives who eat breakfast or lunch with lower-level employees are all likely to enhance feelings of voice. Whether formal or informal, voice seems to work to the greater benefit of the organization, enhancing feelings of fairness and improving the acceptance of decisions and policies (Lind and Tyler, 1988).

It is important to note that the granting of voice is not the only way to promote perceptions of procedural justice in the workplace. In fact, Leventhal et al. (1980) identify several additional criteria whose importance to promoting organizational justice has been established. These include: (1) the *consistency* rule (behaving consistently toward people); (2) the *bias suppression* rule (following procedures that are free of self-interest); (3) the *accuracy* rule (basing decisions on accurate information); (4) the *correctability* rule (allowing for decisions to be corrected, such as appeals in the legal system); (5) the *representativeness* rule (incorporating the interests of all concerned parties); and (6) the *ethicality* rule (following prevailing moral and ethical standards). Although these six procedural rules have not been as carefully researched as the voice principle, their implications for establishing organizational justice are widely recognized (Greenberg, 1987).

The interpersonal justice principle: socially sensitive treatment enhances perceptions of even undesirable outcomes

One of the newer, but most powerful, findings in research on organizational justice is that receiving dignified, respectful treatment has an enormous positive effect on the feeling that one has been treated fairly by one's employer, whereas undignified, disrespectful treatment has equally strong potential to engender feelings of unfairness (Brockner and Wiesenfeld, 1994).

This effect appears to involve two key elements: the amount of information presented about an outcome; and the amount of social sensitivity conveyed about the potentially harmful effects of that outcome (Greenberg, 1994a). Individually and together, each of these factors contribute to the belief that one has acted fairly, and enhances acceptance of the resulting outcomes. As obvious as it may seem, considerate, ethical action is crucial to the feeling that one has been treated fairly. When this piece of the justice puzzle is juxtaposed with the noteworthy consequences of fairness, described in the sections that follow, it becomes clear that some relatively straightforward principles of good managerial behavior can yield a variety of important organizational benefits.

Now that we have identified some of the key principles of organizational justice, we will now turn our attention to ways in which these principles can be, and have been, applied to improving organizational functioning.

▩ IMPLICATIONS AND APPLICATIONS OF ORGANIZATIONAL JUSTICE PRINCIPLES

Some potential implications of justice principles for organizational practice were first identified by Greenberg and Folger (1983; Folger and Greenberg, 1985). From the time these theorists first speculated about ways in which justice concepts may be applied to organizational settings, many researchers explicitly have designed theoretical studies with organizational implications in mind. A much smaller number even have developed research-based applications whose impact as organizational interventions have been tested.

We now will review nine specific areas of organizational functioning in which the implications and applications of organizational justice principles are most clearly illustrated (for overviews of some other areas, see Beugré, 1998; Cropanzano and Greenberg, 1997; Folger and Cropanzano, 1998).

Employee theft

Although experts are uncertain of the exact losses resulting from employee theft, they agree that the figure is considerable (in the billions of dollars annually), and as such, that the phenomenon is worthy of efforts aimed at eliminating, or at least reducing, it (Albrecht et al., 1995). Traditionally, such efforts have been directed at imposing deterrents, such as introducing security cameras and strict financial auditing procedures (Purpura, 1998), and at attempting to screen out prospective employees who are most predisposed to steal (Murphy, 1993). In response to the limited success that these approaches have had in deterring employee theft, more recently, Greenberg (Greenberg, 1990b, 1993a, 1993b, 1997, 1998; Greenberg and Scott, 1996) has examined employee theft in terms of the social dynamics occurring between individuals in the workplace. Specifically, in this connection, Greenberg has established that employees steal in response to perceptions of underpayment inequity.

The notion that underpaid employees may be inclined to steal follows from equity theory's claim (Adams, 1965) that people will experience the distress associated with underpayment inequity when they believe that the rewards they receive (that is, their "outcomes") are inadequate for the work they perform (that is, their "inputs"). People in this state are motivated to redress this inequity so as to alleviate the distress it causes. One way of doing this is by engaging in behavior that raises one's outcomes – which, despite its dubious propriety, is precisely what is accomplished by taking company property.

Greenberg demonstrated this phenomenon in several studies. The first (Greenberg, 1990b) was a quasi-experiment in which employee theft (unexplained losses in inventory known as "shrinkage") was assessed in three manufacturing plants in different locations operated by the same company. In two of the plants (comprising the experimental groups) a financial crisis led company officials to impose a 15 percent cut in pay over a ten-week period for all employees. No changes were made in the case of the third factory (the control group), in which identical work was performed by demographically similar employees. In keeping with equity theory, employees who received pay cuts expressed feelings of underpayment, and in their factories theft rates were significantly higher than in the factory whose employees experienced no pay cut.

Beyond this, Greenberg (1990b) found that the manner in which the pay cut was explained to the employees had a dramatic effect on theft. The employees of one randomly selected experimental plant received an elaborate explanation about the reason underlying the pay cut by a corporate official who showed considerable sensitivity and concern about the effects of this decision. By contrast, the employees of the other plant received limited information about the basis for the pay cut by an official who displayed only superficial expressions of remorse. This difference in the manner in which the pay cut was presented proved to have a striking effect on theft: over twice as much theft occurred in the plant whose employees received a limited explanation by a socially indifferent authority than in the plant whose employees received a thorough explanation presented in a highly sensitive manner. These findings are noteworthy insofar as they illustrate that reactions to underpayment inequity are moderated by interpersonal variables. Although both groups of employees were subjected to the same distributive injustice, their willingness to redress this inequity by stealing depended on the manner in which that injustice was presented to them.

Acknowledging that these findings are limited by a confounding between two variables – the nature of the information presented and the degree of social sensitivity displayed – Greenberg (1993a) attempted to replicate them conceptually in a laboratory study. Specifically, he manipulated these variables independently by informing college students hired to perform a task in different ways that they would be receiving less than the agreed-upon wages for their work ($3, instead of $5, as promised) thereby leading them to experience a state of underpayment inequity. There also was a control condition in which participants received the agreed-upon amount of $5. To see how it affected participants' reactions to this inequity, these announcements were made in a manner that systematically manipulated high and low levels of information (the quality of the information on which the underpayment was based) in conjunction with high and low levels of social sensitivity (that is, remorse and concern about this state of affairs).

After this information was presented, participants were given an opportunity to take their pay from a stack of coins the experimenter hastily threw on a nearby desk. Because it appeared that the researcher did not know how much money he left, participants were led to believe that he would not know how much money they took, thereby allowing them to take more than the $3 permitted without getting caught. In reality, of course, the researcher knew precisely how many coins of each denomination he left, making it possible to determine precisely how much money each participant took. Amounts in excess of $3 were considered theft.

Consistent with equity theory, those participants who were paid the promised amount (that is, those who were equitably paid) did not steal. However, those who were underpaid *did* steal, but the amount they took varied as a function of the way the underpayment inequity was presented. Those who received high amounts of information stole less than those who received low amounts of information, and those who were shown high amounts of social sensitivity stole less than those who were shown low amounts of social sensitivity. Furthermore, these effects combined additively: individuals exposed to high amounts of both variables stole the least, whereas those exposed to low amounts of both variables stole the most. These findings were replicated in another laboratory study (Greenberg, 1994b), supporting their generalizability.

These studies illustrate not only that people steal in response to underpayment inequity but also that the degree to which they do so depends on the manner in which they are treated. Individuals who receive positive interpersonal treatment (thorough explanations presented in a socially sensitive manner) are less inclined to respond to underpayment inequity by stealing than are individuals who receive negative interpersonal treatment (cursory explanations presented in an uncaring manner) in response to the same inequity.

The most obvious applied implication of this finding is straightforward: employee theft may be reduced by avoiding conditions in which people feel underpaid. However, this is far easier said than done. The organizational reality is that some people are likely to feel underpaid for a variety of reasons that may be impractical to control. For this reason, it is useful for practicing managers to take steps to keep employees from responding negatively to any inequities they may experience. In this regard, Greenberg's (1990b, 1993a, 1994b) findings have additional implications. Specifically, they suggest that managers would be wise to explain the decisions they make by providing a great deal of supporting information (suggesting that their decision was not made capriciously) and by demonstrating a great deal of interpersonal concern and sensitivity – particularly when these decisions are expected to have negative effects. These implications are particularly appealing because they are not only simple and inexpensive to follow, but are in keeping with good management practices.

Recently, Greenberg (1999b) tested an organizational intervention derived from these and related findings from the literature on procedural justice. The setting was three discount stores from a chain that was experiencing extremely high levels of internal shrinkage – theft of items from storerooms (a location where employees had routine access, but not customers). Over the years, security cameras proved to have little effect, as did pre-employment screening for honesty. An attitude survey completed company-wide revealed that the employees were highly dissatisfied with management. They expressed feelings of underpayment, dissatisfaction with their jobs, and a lack of commitment to the organization. Employees depicted their managers as being disrespectful, uncaring, insensitive, and generally unconcerned with their welfare. They also reported that supervisory personnel at all levels routinely failed to involve them in decisions, keeping them in the dark about the underlying reasons for various company policies. In short, employees described their managers in a manner that closely matched the low levels of information and social sensitivity manipulated in Greenberg's (1990b, 1993a) experiments.

An intervention was designed to change the managerial style of supervisory personnel in one of the three store locations studied. This consisted of systematically training managers in what Greenberg (1999b) calls *interpersonal justice training* (IJT): techniques of delegation, supportive communication and related topics that correspond to the variables shown by Greenberg (1990b, 1993a) to mitigate theft reactions to inequity. Importantly, so as to avoid biasing efforts at testing the training effectiveness, no mention was made of the relationship of the training to the employee theft problem. The training occurred in one randomly selected store for two hours per week over an eight-week period. It consisted of involving the participants in a variety of role-playing exercises, having them read and analyze several cases, and discussing relevant managerial problems at their stores.

Managers in a second store, selected at random, were trained by the same individual for the same amount of time over the same period, but on an unrelated topic – improving customer service (the unrelated training control group). This group was included in the study to assess the degree to which any training at all may have had an effect. Finally, managers in a third store, also selected at random, received no training at all (the no training control group). The same pre-intervention measures of employee attitude and internal shrinkage were taken at regular intervals during and after the training period.

Greenberg (1999b) found that IJT was effective at improving employees' attitudes – at first only somewhat, but then considerably, after the training was completed. Although these effects dropped somewhat after this initial period, work-related attitudes (such as job satisfaction, commitment, turnover intentions, and so on) remained consistently higher than they were before IJT began. Of greater importance was the fact that theft was reduced by over half in the group receiving IJT (from about 8 percent to less than 4 percent). This effect first emerged two weeks after training was completed and has remained relatively stable for six months afterwards. No appreciable changes in theft were observed in either of the control groups. As one store employee told the researcher in a focus group interview, "[my supervisor] used to be a real SOB, and I hated working from him, so I stole every chance I got. Now, he's so kind to me, I'd feel bad about taking anything." Because this sentiment was expressed by so many employees (in varying degrees, of course), it appears that a prior element of organizational culture that encouraged theft appears to have been alleviated.

It is interesting to note that the theft reductions occurred not as a result of direct training in loss control (the more typical, direct route), but training in interpersonal treatment. This directly establishes the importance of training people in ways that are considered interpersonally fair. Its importance goes beyond the effects of one intervention in one organization at one time. Instead, it represents a huge beginning at developing and testing organizational interventions based on organizational justice research. Before Greenberg's (1990b, 1993a) "theory research" (cf. Calder et al., 1981), it is unlikely that practitioners would have sought to reduce employee theft by training managers in ways of being interpersonally fair. Now, however, interventions based on this research have been developed that have proven useful in reducing theft. Clearly, much more remains to be done in this regard. Questions regarding the relative effectiveness of various techniques are bound to be raised, as are issues of the longevity of their impact. Still, this modest study represents the first step in this direction.

Performance appraisal

It is an unfortunate fact of organizational life that many employees believe the methods used to appraise their job performance are unfair (Levine, 1975). Indeed, evidence suggests that although employees naturally do not like receiving poor evaluations, their concerns about the fairness of these evaluations stems from the nature of the procedures on which they are based (Greenberg, 1986a). Not surprisingly, they sometimes reject appraisal systems they believe measure performance inaccurately and are fraught with bias (Ilgen and Barnes-Farrell, 1984).

This raises a key question: exactly what performance evaluation procedures are believed to be fair? Several studies provide good general answers. For example,

Landy et al. (1978) found that managerial and professional employees' perceptions of the fairness of their performance evaluation system was related to various procedural variables, such as the opportunity to express personal feelings and the frequency of evaluation. Importantly, they replicated these findings even when performance outcomes were held constant (Landy et al., 1980).

In a more general, open-ended study, Greenberg (1986b) asked a group of managers to think of an incident in which they received a particularly fair or unfair performance evaluation and to report exactly what made it so fair or unfair. He then used additional samples to sort these responses into like factors and used these to develop a questionnaire in which the fairness of various factors was assessed. Factor analyzing the results revealed two factors that accounted for most of the variance. This included a procedural justice factor, with significant loadings on five variables: (1) soliciting input prior to evaluation and using it; (2) two-way communication during the interview; (3) ability to challenge/rebut evaluations; (4) rater familiarity with ratee's work; and (5) consistent application of standards. A distributive justice factor also emerged, with significant loadings on two variables: (1) receipt of rating based on performance achieved; and (2) recommendation of salary/promotion based on rating.

These results are important insofar as they closely correspond to various theoretically derived notions of organizational justice. For example, the items on two-way communication and soliciting input correspond closely to Thibaut and Walker's (1975) notion that fairness is enhanced when people have a voice in the decisions affecting them. The other three procedural justice items are consistent with Leventhal et al.'s (1980) rules for creating fair procedures (for example, the item about appeals procedures is an application of their correctability rule). Finally, the distributive justice variables closely correspond to the idea that rewards be proportional to contributions is fundamental to equity theory (Adams, 1965).

Various additional studies confirm the importance of these variables in enhancing perceptions of fairness. For example, in keeping with the fair process effect (Greenberg and Folger, 1983), several studies have found that input into appraisal decisions is a key determinant of the fairness of the resulting judgments (Dipboye and de Pontbraind, 1981; Lissak, 1983). This is also likely to be one reason why performance evaluations that include self-appraisals are better accepted than those that do not include this information (Teel, 1978). In keeping with Leventhal et al.'s (1980) "accuracy rule" of procedural justice, research also has shown that the fairness of performance evaluations is enhanced by the use of procedures, such as diaries, that ensure the accuracy of performance judgments (Greenberg, 1987).

Until recently, research on the fairness of performance appraisals has failed to consider the impact of various interpersonal justice factors, such as the manner in which supervisors treat their employees. Dulebohn and Ferris (1999), however, have filled this void with their recent study of food service workers. Specifically, the fairness of these employees' performance evaluations was significantly related to the extent to which they believed their supervisors treated them in a pleasant manner (such as, by complimenting them, praising them, and offering to help them).

The studies reported thus far have tested practical implications of organizational justice tenets. However, a recent study by Greenberg (1999a) takes this a step further by testing the impact of a performance appraisal intervention based on organizational justice principles. Specifically, Greenberg (1999a) compared employees' reactions to two different performance appraisal systems: a traditional, supervisory rating system in which individual supervisors evaluated their subordinates' performance; and a multi-source performance system in which employees received evaluations not only from their supervisors, but also their same-level peers, external customers, and other individuals from within the company to whom they provided service. These various sources were assumed to promote procedural justice perceptions insofar as their use incorporates several key features of procedural justice identified by Leventhal et al. (1980), and whose role in performance appraisal fairness has been established empirically by Greenberg (1986b). Notably, compared to single-source evaluations, multi-source evaluations are likely to be less subject to bias and to have the capacity to be corrected (insofar as any one ratee's bias can be countered by another's rating) and more likely to be based on accurate information (insofar as different ratees are likely to have different sources of valid performance information). Although practitioners have assumed that subordinates recognize the fairness of multi-source performance evaluations (for example, Tornow and London, 1998), evidence to this effect previously has not been available.

Several key features of the Greenberg (1999a) study make the comparisons meaningful. First, each evaluation system was employed in different locations whose employees had no contact with each other, thereby making contamination resulting from employees' comparisons between the procedures unlikely. Second, both offices were newly opened, and were staffed primarily by employees who had no prior experience with the company, therefore minimizing any expectations they may have about customary procedures. This also ensured that the timing of performance evaluations (and measures of reactions to them) occurred at the same time (after 6 and 12 months of work), thereby minimizing the possibility of history effects as a threat to external validity (Cook and Campbell, 1979). Finally, the average supervisory performance ratings in both locations were not significantly different from each other, discounting the possibility that performance level differences may moderate reactions to various measures.

The key findings of interest are that the employees who were evaluated by multiple sources responded more positively than those who were evaluated only by their supervisors. Specifically, employees who were rated by their supervisors only expressed moderate levels of job satisfaction and organizational commitment. They also believed that the performance evaluation system was moderately fair. These unremarkable reactions stand in sharp contrast with the extremely positive reactions of those who were evaluated by multiple raters. Specifically, these employees not only expressed significantly higher levels of job satisfaction and organizational commitment, but they also recognized that their performance appraisal system was significantly more fair. This pattern of findings occurred during both the six-month and one-year appraisal periods.

There are clearly additional ways in which organizational justice principles can be incorporated into performance appraisal procedures beyond using multiple raters (for suggestions, see Greenberg, 1986c). Still, the Greenberg (1999a) study is instructive insofar as it illustrates one attempt at introducing an organizational intervention designed to enhance employees' reactions to performance evaluations that was derived from the organizational justice literature. This makes it only one of a small number of theory-based studies of organizational justice designed to test an intervention.

Employee discipline

Historically, the practice of employee discipline has been based on reinforcement theory (Skinner, 1953), and as such, has focused more on observable behavior than on internal processes, such as perception. However, the shift toward social cognitive approaches to organizational behavior in recent years (e.g., Martinko, 1995; Sims and Gioia, 1986) has paved the way for broader approaches to employee discipline (Arvey and Jones, 1985), including ones that take into account employees' perceptions of fairness (Ball et al., 1994). Using notions of fairness to help explain people's reactions to discipline is intuitively appealing insofar as justice notions are central to well-established moral principles bearing on discipline, such as doling out a punishment that "fits the crime" (Furby, 1986).

Research has established that matters of fairness play a key role in people's reactions to discipline. We see this, for example, in a laboratory study by Bennett and Cummings (1991) in which the more unfair the procedure was for administering punishment, the less satisfied participants were with that punishment, and the more their task performance suffered. Although such findings are informative from a theoretical perspective, the artificiality of the laboratory setting makes it difficult to capture reactions to punishments that have hedonic relevance to research participants.

In response to this limitation, Ball et al. (1994) conducted a field study in which employees were interviewed about punishments they recently received from their supervisors. The focus was on actual disciplinary events that were earlier identified by the employees' supervisors themselves. The disciplinary episodes covered a wide range of infractions that varied in seriousness. Among the questions asked were ones focusing on the respondents' control over the discipline (for example, input into the disciplinary outcome and the process used to determine it, consideration of the employee's viewpoint) and the harshness of the discipline (for example, too harsh compared to others, too harsh given the infraction).

Each of these variables was predictive of a key organizational outcome. Notably, the subordinates' perceived control was related to their subsequent organizational citizenship behavior (a concept we will describe in more detail in the following section). This is in keeping with the principle of organizational justice established by Thibaut and Walker (1975) according to which people believe that outcomes are fairer when they have had a voice in determining them than when they do not. Ball et al. (1994) also found that subordinates' perceptions of harshness were related to their subsequent job performance (as assessed by their supervisors). Workers who believed that the punishments they received were too harsh for the infractions they committed were unlikely to invest future effort in job performance. This is in keeping with equity theory's claim that people should be rewarded in proportion to the contributions they make (Adams, 1965). As such, individuals who believe they have been harmed too much may redress that perceived inequity by refraining from making further contributions to their jobs.

Given that concerns about fairness are related to key aspects of people's work behavior, it follows that practitioners seeking to change various aspects of work behavior may do so by getting workers to follow key tenets of organizational justice. This was the rationale behind a training program of 71 unionized Canadian supervisors conducted by Cole and Latham (1997). Specifically, the training was conducted in small groups held over five half-days. The sessions consisted of role-playing exercises focusing on six key factors: (1) explanation of the performance problem; (2) the demeanor of the supervisor; (3) subordinates' control over the process; (4) arbitrariness; (5) employee counseling; and (6) privacy. These six training foci were chosen because in an earlier study by Ball (1991) they emerged in a factor analysis of 17 procedural justice characters related to fairness in disciplinary action.

To assess the effectiveness of the training, two groups of judges were asked to evaluate the behavior of the supervisors who role played supervisors administering discipline in each of four different test scenarios. The judges were unionized employees who participated in the role-play tests, and subject matter experts (labor law attorneys, managers, and union officials). After watching video-tapes of the test scenarios, both groups of judges evaluated the trainees on each of 14 procedural justice variables, including the supervisor's counseling efforts, demeanor, arbitrariness, control, and explanation of the behavior on which the punishment was based. Overall, both groups of judges rated the trained group as behaving more fairly than an untrained, control group. The judges also believed that the trained group was going to perform better as supervisors than the control group, a difference that was shared by the trainees themselves.

These findings are important insofar as they suggest that training in key aspects of procedural justice may effectively sensitize supervisors to act in ways that enhance the perceived fairness of the discipline they administer. They also are noteworthy insofar as they demonstrate the effectiveness of an intervention derived from theory-based research. Unfortunately, however, Cole and Latham's (1997) findings do not assess the effectiveness of training on the job, even over the short term. Although they demonstrate that trained supervisors are capable of demonstrating the behaviors in which they are trained in a controlled setting, no measure is provided of the extent to which the desired behaviors are imported into the actual work setting. Indeed, this is the very kind of generalization from supervisory training that is desired in organizations (Camp et al., 1986). In conclusion, although Cole and Latham (1997) have developed the kind of interventions we believe are useful for theory applications, their failure to assess their effectiveness properly needs to be addressed in the future to fully derive the benefits of theory applications in this context.

Organizational citizenship behavior

In recent years, organizational scientists have devoted considerable attention to studying organizational citizenship behavior (OCB) – various informal prosocial acts that go above and beyond the call of duty, such as showing courtesy to others on the job, acting conscientiously about work, being a "good sport," and protecting their organization's best interests (Organ, 1988; Organ and Moorman, 1993).

Because such forms of behavior are informal, workers are likely to have more direct control over them compared to formal job requirements, over which they generally have little discretion. This, together with the reluctance that workers may have to express their feelings of injustice by behaving negatively (for example, withholding performance or being destructive; Giacalone and Greenberg, 1997), has made OCB a dependent variable that is particularly sensitive to perceptions of organizational justice. Not surprisingly, scientists have found that various OCBs are significantly related to employees' perceptions of organizational justice (for reviews, see Greenberg, 1993b; Podsakoff and MacKenzie, 1993).

Unfortunately, a clear picture of the exact nature of the relationship between justice perceptions and OCB has not emerged. Although some studies (for example, Deluga, 1994) have found that general justice perceptions are related to various forms of OCB, others have found that procedural justice is a better predictor than distributive justice (Ball et al., 1994; Konovsky and Folger, 1991). Still other studies have found that the social and interpersonal aspects of justice are better predictors than either the more structural, distributive or procedural factors (Moorman, 1991; Lee, 1995).

Inconsistencies also have arisen regarding which particular forms of OCB are most strongly related to justice perceptions. For example, Moorman (1991) found that although interactional justice predicted altruism, courtesy, sportsmanship and conscientiousness, it did not predict civic virtue. Further complicating things, different patterns have emerged in different nations (Farh et al., 1990) and some studies have found that the effects of justice perceptions on OCB are not direct but, rather, moderated by the effects of a third variable, trust (Konovsky et al., 1995).

Despite these inconsistencies, Skarlicki and Latham (1996) successfully sought to enhance OCBs among a group of union laborers in Canada by training their managers in various aspects of organizational justice. Specifically, managers were trained in four three-hour training sessions held over a three-week period. Training consisted of: lecture; case study; role playing; and group discussions focusing on Leventhal's (1980) various determinants of procedural justice, ways of providing voice, ways to enhance the fairness of the social interaction between labor and management, and the importance of managing impressions of fairness on the job. Importantly, these training foci were derived directly from the various principles of organizational justice identified earlier in this chapter. Three months after training, incidents of OCB were found to be higher among employees of the trained managers than among employees of the untrained ones. These findings are important insofar as they show that OCB can be enhanced directly by training managers to behave fairly toward their employees. As such, this study represents a highly successful intervention of organizational justice principles.

Conflict resolution

The resolution of subordinates' conflicts and complaints is a ubiquitous feature of management at all levels. In fact, there are several indications that managerial conflict resolution is more important than ever. For example, the growing popularity of team-based work structures (Katzenbach and Smith, 1993), which makes workers highly interdependent on each other for outcomes, promises to breed interpersonal frustrations and conflict. And, should team conflict turn from mild disagreement to personal animosity, its productivity is bound to suffer.

In addition, growing governmental regulation of the work environment, with the initiation of many different "causes of action" in the courts and with movement in many Western countries away from an "employment at will" legal doctrine, means that effective conflict resolution methods are critical to controlling litigation costs (Sitkin and Bies, 1994). Whereas a manager in years past may have attempted to resolve conflict between subordinates by firing one or more of the parties, a contemporary manager may refrain from doing so for fear of triggering a lawsuit on such grounds as sexual harassment, employment discrimination, or wrongful termination. In reaction to the regulation of workplace relationships and decisions, many organizations have institutionalized conflict management by creating procedures and positions (for example, ombudsmen and mediation centers) to try to diffuse conflict (and counteract illegal behavior) before the conflict escalates into an agency hearing or a lawsuit.

It could be even argued that the decreasing influence of labor unions in many workplaces has made conflict management skills and procedures all the more important. Although strict rules eliminate many real or potential disputes in unionized work settings, in the absence of a union the freer, more ad hoc allocation of tasks, responsibilities, resources, and rewards can lead to more individual conflicts. Similarly, where in a unionized work setting conflicts about pay, termination, and task are resolved often through union–management negotiations that dispose of whole classes of disputes, in many non-unionized settings each such dispute must be handled and resolved by managers on the site.

These considerations, and the experience of anyone who has had to manage others, make it clear that managing conflicts is critical to the success of any organization. Fortunately, the organizational justice literature, and a related research literature on the role of procedural fairness in resolving disputes in the courts (for a review, see MacCoun et al., 1992), provides some very useful tools for managing organizational conflict. We described above the "voice" effect – the tendency of people to think that procedures are fairer when those affected by the process have been granted an opportunity to express their views, their perspectives, and their concerns. The voice effect was in fact discovered in studies of conflict resolution (Lind et al., 1978; Thibaut and Walker, 1975; Walker et al., 1974), where it was observed that procedures that gave the disputing parties a clear, formal opportunity to present their evidence and arguments were seen as fairer than procedures that did not provide any such opportunities. In the years since, many studies in both laboratory and field settings have shown this same finding (for reviews, see Lind and Tyler, 1988; Tyler and Smith, 1997).

In some respects, the findings on the effect of voice are contrary to conventional wisdom about how disputes should be managed. Many writers in the area of human resource management imply that negotiation and mediation are the best procedures for resolving disputes in organizations. These procedures are better than procedures like arbitration or adjudication (where a third party decides on a resolution to the dispute and has the power to impose that resolution), the argument goes, because in mediation or negotiation the parties can fashion their own solution or have the right to reject resolutions that are not in line with their interests. But this line of reasoning does not take into account the power of voice procedures. There is a substantial set of studies showing that adjudication can be just as acceptable as mediation or negotiation for resolving disputes, provided that the adjudication includes procedures that offer the disputants plenty of voice. As we note below, this is good because there are other reasons to prefer adjudication procedures in many organizational settings.

First, let us consider some research studies that show the acceptability of adjudication procedures in resolving disputes in legal contexts. Then, we will report some findings that show similar patterns of results within an organizational context. Lind et al. (1990) studied disputants' reactions to four court procedures: negotiation; mediation; arbitration; and trial. The research was conducted in state courts in Virginia, Maryland, and Pennsylvania. The negotiation and mediation procedures involved the sort of consensual dispute resolution that is often endorsed for organizational dispute resolution; the arbitration and trial procedures involved the provision of voice to the disputants, but with adjudication of the dispute, that is, with the decision being imposed by a third party. Results of the study showed that the two adjudication procedures were seen as fairer than the two consensual procedures. Further data analysis showed that the adjudication procedures were seen as fairer because disputants who experienced these procedures felt that they had more opportunity to present their views and that they had been treated in a more dignified fashion than disputants who experienced negotiation or mediation.

Two other full-scale studies of court procedures, one conducted in the state of New Jersey (MacCoun et al., 1988) and the other conducted in a US federal district court (Lind, 1990; Lind et al., 1993), give additional evidence of the usefulness of voice-mandating adjudication procedures as tools for conflict management. Both of these studies involved evaluations of what are called "court-annexed arbitration programs." In these programs, disputants must take their conflict to a court-appointed arbitrator, but they do not have to accept the arbitrator's decisions. Because most of the cases referred to arbitration would normally be settled prior to trial, the studies end up comparing arbitration procedures or negotiation procedures, for the most part. In both studies, the researchers assessed such things as whether the arbitration process was seen as fair and whether more cases were resolved before trial, comparing the arbitration program process either to a randomly selected control group of cases (in the Lind, 1990, study) or to cases in other parts of the state (in the MacCoun et al., 1988, study).

Both studies showed that the arbitration procedure was seen as being at least as fair as (and in the case of the Lind study, fairer than) the conventional negotiation/ trial process. Once again, the key factor in the success of both arbitration programs was the fact that disputants felt they had plenty of voice – plenty of opportunity to present their evidence, views, and arguments – in the arbitration procedure. In both studies, the perceived fairness of the arbitration process held whether the disputant won or lost the case. The Lind study, reanalyzed by Lind et al. (1993), took the finding one step further, showing that litigants were more likely to accept the outcome of the arbitration process to the extent that they saw the process as fair, such as when they had voice during the arbitration hearing. These findings held whether the litigants were in court as individuals or as representatives of corporations.

These studies, and others like them (for example, Lind and Shapard, 1981) show that, at least in legal contexts, disputants will endorse adjudicative procedures that allow them a good opportunity to voice their evidence and concerns and that, if voice is provided, the disputants will accept and obey the decision of the arbitrator or judge (Lind et al., 1993). But does this finding hold for disputes inside organizations? There is plenty of evidence that it does. For example, Huo et al. (1996) asked employees of a public university and employees of a German auto manufacturer to describe a recent instance in which they had taken a problem to their supervisor, including instances of conflict with other employees. As was the case with the disputants in legal settings, employees with disputes were willing to accept decisions when they felt they had been given an adequate opportunity for voice.

What does all this mean for the practice of conflict management in organizations? First and foremost, it suggests a procedure, and a style, of intervention that can effectively deal with workplace disputes. Managers can use what might be termed "applied arbitration" to deal with disputes among subordinates. That is, the manager can call in the disputing employees, together or separately, hear what they have to say about the issue in conflict, and then make a judgment that is binding on everyone. If the process includes a clear opportunity for voice, and if the manager makes it evident that he or she is considering each person's views (see, Tyler, 1987, for research showing that to be effective voice must be heard to be considered), then whether or not their position prevails the disputants will feel they have been treated fairly, leaving them inclined to accept the decision.

This "applied arbitration" approach to conflict management has another advantage. Unlike negotiation or mediation of workplace disputes, which place all or part of the control over the outcome in the hands of the disputants, this approach allows the manager to retain control of the outcome and to make sure that the resolution of the dispute fits the goals and policies of the organization. As long as this control is exercised in the context of consideration of the voiced concerns of the disputants, the process will be regarded as fair and the outcome will be accepted as fair.

One final note with respect to the issues raised here. We certainly do not mean to imply that negotiation or mediation are always unfair procedures. Indeed, research (Lind et al., 1994; Lind et al., 1997) shows that negotiation and mediation can be seen as quite fair, as long as the disputants feel that the mediator or the other party is giving them a chance to voice their concerns and considering what they have to say. Thus, as we noted in our discussion of the voice effect, one can achieve the same result either with a procedure (applied arbitration) or with a process (active prompting of voice and consideration) – namely a process and an outcome that are seen as fair.

Reactions to layoffs and terminations

Justice becomes a particularly sensitive issue when bad outcomes have to be delivered (Brockner and Wiesenfeld, 1994), and there are few worse organizational outcomes than the termination of employment. It is not surprising, therefore, that organizational justice researchers have studied how people form fairness judgments, and how these fairness judgments affect behavior, in the context of layoffs and firings. In this connection, there are two lines of work – one on the impact of fairness judgments on those who lose their job (Lind et al., 1998; Youngblood et al., 1992), and another focusing on the impact of fairness judgments of those who survive layoffs (Brockner and Greenberg, 1990; Brockner et al., 1992). Both lines of research show substantial impact of the process by which terminations are managed, and the work on the fairness judgments of those whose jobs are terminated offers some specific indications of precisely what makes for a fair termination process. We now will review both lines of research.

Reactions of terminated workers

In a study analyzing the various reasons people listed for filing wrongful termination claims, Youngblood et al. (1992) found that many such lawsuits were based on the belief that the termination procedures used were believed to be unfair. Following up on this, a more recent study by Lind, Greenberg, Scott, and Welchans (1998) focused on the relationship between people's feelings of unfair treatment at termination and their filing of wrongful termination lawsuits against their former employers. Specifically, these researchers surveyed nearly 1,000 workers who had been fired or laid-off from their jobs. If a significant relationship is found between feelings of unfair treatment and behaviors such as seeking legal advice or filing wrongful termination complaints, the researchers argued, the implications would be meaningful insofar as each wrongful termination lawsuit carries an average cost of more than $80,000, in legal fees and other expenses, win or lose (Dertouzos et al., 1988). Accordingly, if practices could be identified that reduce feelings of unfairness, which thereby reduce the likelihood of lawsuits, the benefits would be remarkable.

The Lind et al. (1998) study did, in fact, find a strong connection between feelings of unfair treatment at termination and the initiation of wrongful termination claims. Figure 4.2 illustrates precisely how strong the relationship is: nearly 15 percent of those who felt they had been treated very unfairly filed claims, whereas less than 1 percent of those who felt they had been treated very fairly filed claims. This translates to a per-employee cost difference of approximately $11,200 attributable to fair or unfair treatment. Clearly, it is worth investing some effort into improving reactions to the termination process.

What factors contribute to these feelings of fairness? Of all the variables examined in this study, feelings of fair treatment at termination were far and away the most powerful factor in determining who would sue and who would not. This result held both for employees who had lost their job in a layoff and those who had been fired. In addition, as can be seen from figure 4.2, the strongest effect was seen among

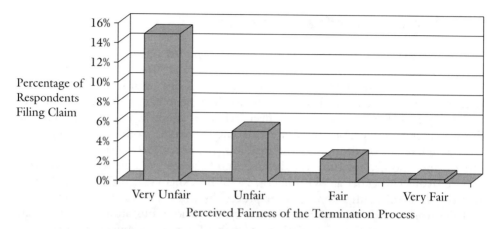

Figure 4.2 The relationship between perceived fair treatment at termination and filing wrongful termination claims (based on data reported by Lind et al., 1998)

people who felt that they had been treated very unfairly. Lind et al. (1998) labeled the especially high claiming rate among these respondents (who composed slightly over a third of the sample) a "vendetta effect," because it appeared that they were so angry about their treatment that they pursued law suits regardless of whether or not they expected to win. They seemed more interested in "making the organization pay" than in whether they actually received a wrongful termination award. Such forms of retaliation in the workplace also have been demonstrated elsewhere (Skarlicki and Folger, 1997).

All of this suggests that we would be well advised to discover precisely what it is that makes people feel more or less fairly treated in the context of a job termination. Fortunately, the Lind et al. (1998) study provides some clear indications. First, unfairness was measured in this study by using questions tapping the extent to which the former employee was treated with dignity and respect and the degree to which he or she believed that an adequate, honest explanation for the termination was provided. Decent, calm treatment of the worker whose job is about to be terminated and personal, sensitive notification of the impending termination are thus key elements of fair process at this difficult time. The study suggests that, even in the context of an unpleasant firing, maintaining decency, while at the same time providing a clear picture of why the termination was occurring, is well worth the effort given its mitigating effects on litigation.

The study asked about a number of employer practices, common at the time of termination, which were found to correlate strongly with feelings of fairness. Specifically, the more notice the worker had of the impending termination and the more help the employer offered in finding new employment, the more fair the termination process was believed to be. For example, about 46 percent of those who received little or no help in finding a new job felt that they had been treated unfairly, whereas only 3 percent of those who received a great deal of help felt this way. The manner in which the termination is announced also mattered greatly. Of those told in person by a manager or owner that they would be losing their jobs, only about

30 percent felt that they had been treated unfairly, whereas among those notified in some other way that they were going to lose their job, over 50% felt they had been treated unfairly.

These dramatic findings suggest that what is needed to instill a feeling of fairness – or at least, to minimize feelings of unfairness – in the context of job termination are such practices as giving personal, early notification of the termination, offering help in finding new employment, and being highly sensitive to the social psychological implications of the termination. Within this last factor, concern with the social and psychological implications of the termination, come through very clearly in the Lind et al. (1998) study. Ironically, the employees who were most likely to show a vendetta effect were those who were, prior to termination, most committed to the organization. If these high commitment employees are treated poorly, their self-identity is likely to be threatened, leading them to find new meaning in their lives by becoming a "professional defendant," by seeking to define themselves by their opposition to their former employer. The message is clear: fair process is critical, especially for those employees who are committed to one's organization.

Survivors' reactions to layoffs

The line of research addressing survivors' reactions to layoffs gives even more sup-port to the importance of fair process in termination activities. The work of Brockner and his colleagues (1994) makes it clear that any appearance of unfairness in the layoff process can have a negative residual impact on the organization, quite apart from the question of litigation by disgruntled former employees. Specifically, this research shows that if survivors have the impression that layoff decisions were made unfairly, they will become less committed to the organization. In fact, to the extent that the survivors identify with the terminated employees this negative effect on commitment is magnified (Brockner et al., 1992).

Presumably, one of the things about which survivors worry as they examine the fairness or unfairness of termination procedures and decisions, is "what will happen to me?". Unfair procedures make people worry more, whereas fair procedures make the workplace more predictable and rational. Returning momentarily to Lind et al.'s (1998) survey of recently terminated employees, one of the interesting findings was that terminated employees accepted the idea that economic and financial factors could cost them their job, without blaming their former employer much for these situation-mandated terminations. What they did insist on, however, was that the translation of business necessity into a lost job be arrived at fairly and that they be dealt with in a dignified and straightforward fashion. That study made it clear that there were some "good guy" employers, who gave considerable notice of layoffs, helped former employees find new jobs, explained why they were laying off workers and treated their departing employees with dignity and respect. There also were "bad guy" employers, who gave little or no notice, offered little help in finding new employment, offered no credible explanations, and made the termination process undignified. The essence of the research is that the "good guys" ended up almost never being sued, whereas the "bad guys" must have had litigation expenses that very nearly offset any financial benefit they realized from the downsizing!

Some practical implications and applications

The clear practical implication of these findings is that it pays to promote fairness while dismissing employees, and that this may be accomplished by showing dignity and respect in the process of communicating the dismissal. Although the injury of the dismissal may not be reduced, adverse reactions to the insult of insensitive treatment may be avoided. Recent research by Skarlicki et al. (1998) indicates that these benefits generalize beyond victims and survivors, to uninvolved observers. These researchers created four different mock newspaper stories reporting the manner in which a local bank handled the layoff of 125 employees. The stories contained high and low amounts of two variables established to promote procedural justice in the workplace – amount of voice given about the layoff and the degree of explanation given about the layoff. As predicted, readers of the stories believed that the bank's actions were fairer when it was depicted as using high, rather than low, levels of each variable. These reactions may be important insofar as they influence the corporate image of the organization in question.

Because the participants in the Skarlicki et al. (1998) study were college students reading mock stories, of course, no reputational damage was created by the unfair accounts. However, the findings of a field experiment by Greenberg (1991) suggest that such damage may, in fact, occur. Participants in this research were employees of an assembly plant who wrote brief narratives describing what it was like to work in their company. They did this twice – the first time being six weeks before layoffs occurred and the second immediately after layoff notices were distributed. The wording of these notices was manipulated in a manner that provided either high or low levels of information about the reason for the layoff decision and high or low levels of sympathy (that is, either sincere expressions of sorrow, or detached statements citing the business necessity of the decision). These statements accompanied notices (which were true, of course) indicating either that they themselves were being laid off, or that other employees were being laid off.

Raters' assessments of the affective tone of the workers' descriptive statements concerning their jobs were carefully analyzed both before and after the layoff notices were given. The results were striking: descriptions of the company became more negative following the layoff, although less so among survivors than victims themselves. However, even among victims, negative reactions were mitigated by the use of statements reflecting high levels of informational and interpersonal justice. (On an ethical note, after data collection, all employees were carefully counseled in person by a company official who provided thorough explanations about the layoffs in a manner demonstrating a high level of interpersonal sensitivity.)

The Greenberg (1991) study demonstrates the successful use of an intervention carefully derived from research and theory on the interpersonal aspects of organizational justice (for a review, see Greenberg, 1993b). It seems safe to say that the negative reactions expressed by employees whose dismissals were unfairly explained to them eventually may have led to wrongful termination suits. Such "bad-mouthing" also may have led to reputational damage, which may take its toll on the success of recruiting efforts, a topic to which we now turn.

Organizational staffing

To industrial/organizational psychologists, the concept of "fairness" traditionally has referred to selection procedures that have sound psychometric properties (such as reliability and validity), a concern that still remains important (Arvey and Sackett, 1993). More recently, however, the notion of selection fairness has been broadened to encompass job applicants' perceptions of the fairness of the procedures used to make selection decisions (Gilliland, 1993; Schuler, 1993).

This attention is warranted by research evidence showing that both current employees and prospective hires respond negatively to unfair selection procedures. For example, Gilliland (1994) found that employees who believed their company used fair selection procedures as the basis for selecting them expressed more positive attitudes toward their work and displayed higher performance than those who believed that unfair selection procedures were used. Unfair procedures also may keep prospective hires from even accepting offers. Specifically, Singer (1992, 1993) found that job applicants were less likely to accept positions with companies they believed were using unfair selection procedures than companies whose procedures they deemed to be fair. Companies that violate procedural rules (especially when the results of such violations disadvantage people) send strong messages that these are undesirable places in which to work (Ployhart and Ryan, 1998).

These findings raise the question: Precisely what selection procedures are believed to be fair and unfair? For one, research has shown that applicants believe unstructured interviews to be fairer than structured interviews (for example, Smither et al., 1993). This is in keeping with the notion that because unstructured interviews are likely to allow considerable opportunities for applicants to explain themselves – thereby providing voice in the decision-making process – they are likely to be considered fair (Thibaut and Walker, 1975).

According to Leventhal et al. (1980), fairness also may be enhanced by the use of procedures that are believed to yield accurate results. With this in mind, it is not surprising that such selection procedures as assessment centers, because they tap a wide variety of work-related skills, are widely regarded as fair (Rynes and Connerley, 1993). By the same token, because they have questionable face validity, questions about the fairness of techniques such as biographical inventories and personality inventories also tend to be raised (Smither et al., 1993). Other procedures, such as screening employees or prospective hires for drug use, may or may not be perceived as fair depending on how accurate the testing procedures are believed to be (Tepper and Braun, 1995). Specifically, the extent to which various procedural justice factors are incorporated into the screening procedure, such as advance notice, justifications, and a system for filing a grievance in response to undesirable results (Cropanzano and Knovsky, 1995) the fairer those procedures are likely to be.

In short, it is clear that matters of fairness are of great importance when it comes to making staffing decisions in organizations. The various selection procedures that applicants believe to be fair are those that incorporate various organizational justice principles. Despite this, we are unaware of any investigations that have specifically sought to promote fairness by intentionally incorporating these principles. That is, no intervention studies have been conducted in this area. This is understandable insofar as the goal of promoting impressions of fairness in selection among prospective employees is relatively new. However, in view of the rich implications that studies of organizational justice have for the practice of organizational staffing and the growing interest in this topic, we would not be surprised to find many such efforts in the future.

Strategic decision making

In a remarkable series of studies, Kim and Mauborgne (1991, 1993, 1995) examined the relationship between various procedural fairness factors and the behavior of managers in multinational corporations. Kim and Mauborgne begin by noting the problem that exists in one form or another in most organizations, particularly global organizations: How can the organization promulgate a strategic vision and plan to the diverse local offices that must implement the policy? The answer, their research shows, is to use decision-making procedures that are procedurally fair.

Kim and Mauborgne (1995), for example, offer striking evidence of the usefulness of procedurally fair processes in knitting together an organization. Specifically, they collected data in 19 multinational corporations, asking subsidiary managers to rate five dimensions of procedural justice: bilateral communication; the capacity of subsidiary units to challenge and refute the strategic views of head office managers; the extent to which head office managers involved in strategic decision making are well informed about the situations faced by local units; and the extent to which head office managers are consistent and non-discriminatory in their decision-making procedures. These dimensions, which were derived from open-ended questions using a method similar to that used by Greenberg (1986b), are quite similar to a number of factors that have been identified as key components of procedural justice in other contexts. For example, their bilateral communication and challenge components look a lot like the concept of "voice" mentioned in many applied studies in this chapter, and the "well-informed" component is likely to be closely tied to the same idea, since head office managers who invite and consider input from subsidiary office managers are likely to be seen as well-informed by those managers. The remaining two dimensions reflected procedural justice components often labeled "explanations" and "neutrality" (Lind and Tyler, 1998).

They also asked head office and subsidiary top managers to rate their last strategic planning process on four additional dimensions, all related to the effectiveness of strategic decision making: global learning; global strategic renewal; speed of global strategic decision making; and balancing global efficiency and local responsiveness. Kim and Mauborgne correlated the procedural justice components with the strategic decision-making measures and found that the fairer the procedures that were used, the more effective the outcomes of these procedures were believed to be. In fact, with the exception of the speed measure, procedural justice accounted for more than half of the variation in the quality of strategic decision making.

Of course, the next step in the application of organizational justice research, given the remarkable demonstration of the power of procedural justice in strategic decision making, is to delineate specific practices and procedures that enhance such things as bilateral communication and the capacity to challenge head office understandings of strategic issues. Then, these practices and procedures will require empirical evaluation. Meanwhile, however, the Kim and Mauborgne studies make it clear that fair process play a key part in enhancing the effectiveness of global strategic decisions.

Organizational change

Change has become such a pervasive and ubiquitous fact of contemporary organizational life that it sometimes fails to capture the attention of workers. Indeed, it frequently is challenging to get workers to pay serious attention to even the most important changes insofar as these may be seen as little more than a passing fad, the "change du jour," if you will (Kissler, 1991). Of course, without widespread acceptance, even the most reasonable change is doomed to failure. Growing evidence suggests that change efforts are likely to be accepted when these are handled in a way that incorporates fair procedures (Cobb et al., 1995; Novelli et al., 1995).

Guidance on precisely how this may be accomplished is provided by several studies. For example, in one of the evaluations of court-annexed arbitration procedures described earlier, Lind (1990) found that both disputants and attorneys were willing to endorse continuation of the new arbitration procedures if they had experienced the process and found it to be fair. Studies in a wide variety of other contexts have established that the explanations used to justify a variety of organizational change have been found to enhance acceptance of those changes as fair. This has been found in such contexts as relocations (Daly and Geyer, 1994), policy changes (Parker et al., 1997), electronic control systems (Kidwell and Bennett, 1994), the introduction of self-managed work teams (Kirkman et al., 1996), and human resource information systems (Eddy et al., 1999).

Because theorists (such as Cobb et al., 1995; Novelli et al., 1995) only recently have identified various potential connections between organizational justice and organizational change, there have not been many intervention studies conducted in this area. However, one study by Greenberg (1994a) falls into this category. Greenberg (1994a) demonstrated the importance of organizational justice in quite another setting. He systematically manipulated the degree to which employees received key information about an impending smoking ban, and the degree to which that information was presented in a socially sensitive fashion. In keeping with basic tenets of interpersonal and informational justice (and his research on employee theft described earlier; Greenberg, 1990b, 1993a), Greenberg (1994a) found that each of these factors contributed significantly to the employees' expressed compliance with the smoking ban – importantly, this even included smokers, who as a group, were most adversely affected.

Areas of potential future applications

It is apparent from the nine application areas we have described thus far that organizational justice principles offer some useful managerial tools – either real or potential.

In our opinion, these domains represent only a few of the most fertile areas for applying organizational justice. Because there are so many areas of organizational functioning in which the core issues are closely linked to trust, compliance, the security of one's position, and the identity of one's corporate affiliation (Huo et al., 1996) – all of which are reactions that are closely tied to organizational justice – it would be surprising if organizational justice concepts did not apply to many other areas as well. In this regard, Beugré (1998) has identified several areas of organizational practice in which potential connections to organizational justice have been underdeveloped. These include promoting customer satisfaction (Tax et al., 1998), developing the global economy (James, 1993), accepting mergers and acquisitions (Citera and Rentsch, 1993), and maintaining the physical environment (Opotow and Clayton, 1994).

■ A CONCLUDING ASSESSMENT: THE CURRENT STATUS OF APPLIED ORGANIZATIONAL JUSTICE

There are several good reasons to believe that the justice-based organizational interventions described here will be well received in organizations if they are attempted. For example, we know that when it comes to selecting social technologies, organizational decision makers are inclined to use techniques whose benefits are immediately obvious (Moore, 1996). These include "ease of use, *perceptions of fairness*, the likelihood of interpersonal conflict or of harm, compatibility with an organization's culture, and the self-interest of the decision makers" (Colarelli, 1998, p. 1047, emphasis added).

The interventions we have identified compare favorably along these criteria. For example, they are generally very easy to use – so much so, in fact, that they may be better identified as "sound managerial practice" than "social technology." Given the widespread research on the principles underlying the interventions, their perceived fairness is not at question, especially insofar as they also appear to help ease interpersonal conflict. Managers who promote the fairness of their actions also are clearly acting in accord with not only their own self-interest (Greenberg, 1990a), but also the culture of organizations in which fairness is a cherished value (Schein, 1985).

We believe that organizations that use justice-based interventions are likely to continue using them, even if the immediate benefits are not realized. As Colarelli (1998) has explained, this often occurs because interventions may have latent, or unobserved, effects that are, themselves, functional. In the case of organizational justice, it is possible that the complexities of the social and technical environments in which organizations operate may render some interventions less than successful. However, in no case are their effects likely to be harmful – and, to our knowledge, no such effects ever have been demonstrated. To the contrary, unexpected, ancillary benefits actually may accrue.

For example, suppose a manager offers an explanation of an undesirable organizational change (such as a layoff, a smoking ban, or a pay cut) that is thorough and well informed, and that is presented in a caring and socially sensitive manner. The research reviewed here suggests that acceptance of these outcomes should be enhanced, thereby discouraging negative reactions (such as theft, aggression, resignations). However, we can envision cases in which these effects might not manifest themselves because of the effects of other, unexpected factors that offset them (for example, change in management policy or the pay system) or perhaps, the idiosyncratic manner in which they are operationalized. Regardless, there is good reason to suspect that even this ostensibly "failed" intervention attempt may be beneficial insofar as it helps promote the impression that the manager and/or the organization itself is concerned about being fair (Greenberg, 1990b).

Why, then, do we not see more organizational justice-based interventions? The most immediate answer to this question is that organizational justice is a relatively new area of study (Greenberg, 1987), one in which applications only recently have been attempted (for a review, see Greenberg and Wiethoff, 2000). As such, the field has not yet captured the attention of practicing managers looking for a new and useful tool to add to their bag of tricks.

Although the field's many scholarly successes may turn this around, this is not necessarily so. The mere fact that a social technology works as intended does not ensure that organizations will "jump on the bandwagon" of adapting it. First, they have to know about it. And, organizational justice scholars have been less than proactive in bringing their work to the attention of the informed managerial public (for a noteworthy recent exception, see Kim and Mauborgne, 1997). Second, organizations tend to select social technologies by imitating the best practices of other organizations (Nelson and Winter, 1982). Again, because reports of successful organizational justice interventions have not yet jumped outside the ivy-covered walls of academia – at least not on any widespread basis – general managerial awareness of the importance of organizational justice remains limited.

From our experience as practitioners, attempting to "sell" organizational justice principles to practicing managers is often challenging. The problem we often confront is that most managers like to believe that they are "already fair," and sometimes resist – if not outright resent – an outsider's efforts to help them in this regard. Explaining the fact that we can show them in precise terms how to cultivate this impression sometimes meets with polite indifference – even if we are attempting to use our technology for critical purposes, such as curtailing employee theft or minimizing the occurrence of wrongful termination lawsuits.

Then, even when we sometimes win arguments and get a foot in the door, we often face difficulties in introducing suitable conditions for testing the effectiveness of our interventions. Indeed, the several intervention studies we have discussed here, in which organizations were willing to test our interventions (for example, Greenberg, 1990b, 1994a), were the exception rather than the rule. Even in these cases, the so-called manipulations were really quite minor in scope – but not in effect!

Finally, as scientist-practitioners, we are obliged to acknowledge the real possibility that tests of organizational justice-based interventions may not be conducted as frequently as may be desirable because of a general bias against applied research in the academic community (Cascio, 1995). As organizational scientists immerse themselves in the everyday challenges of gaining access to research sites, using appropriate measurements, and other scientific-based concerns, they are likely to be self-conscious about what they have to offer the organizational community by way of answers to their questions. Then, when also faced with pressure from colleagues who not-so-subtly describe the stigma against conducting applied research, even the most motivated applied scientist may think twice before moving in this direction.

As difficult as it may be to counter these forces, we hope that the work we have described in this chapter will inspire some organizational justice researchers to take at least a small step in this direction. After all, to fully understand the basic processes underlying perceptions of organizational justice in organizations, we believe it is essential to assess reactions to efforts to create justice in the workplace as we have outlined on these pages. Simply put, when it comes to matters of organizational justice, we echo Kurt Lewin's well known dictim, "There's nothing as practical as a good theory" (in Marrow, 1969). Our theories are good, and we now wait for the practice to follow.

REFERENCES

Adams, J. S. 1965: Inequity in social exchange. In L. Berkowitz (ed.), *Advances in experimental social psychology*, Vol. 2, New York: Academic Press, 267–99.

Albrecht, W. S., Wernz, G. W., and Williams, T. L. 1995: *Fraud: Bringing light to the dark side of business*, Burr Ridge, IL: Irwin.

Arvey, R. D., and Jones, A. P. 1985: The use of discipline in organizational settings: A framework for future research. In L. L. Cummings and B. M. Staw (eds.), *Research in organizational behavior*, Vol. 7, Greenwich, CT: JAI Press, 367–408.

Arvey, R. D., and Sackett, P. R. 1993: Fairness in selection: Current developments and perspectives. In N. Schmitt and W. Borman (eds.), *Personnel selection*, San Francisco: Jossey-Bass, 171–202.

Ball, G. A. 1991: Outcomes of punishment incidents: The role of subordinate perceptions, individual differences, and leader behavior, unpublished doctoral dissertation, Pennsylvania State University.

Ball, G. A., Trevino, L. K., and Sims, H. P. Jr. 1994: Just and unjust punishment: influences on subordinate performance and citizenship. *Academy of Management Journal*, 37, 299–322.

Bennett, R. J., and Cummings, L. L. 1991: The effects of schedule and intensity of aversive outcomes on performance: A multitheoretical perspective. *Human Performance*, 4, 155–69.

Beugré, C. D. 1998: *Managing fairness in organizations*, Westport, CT: Quorum.

Brockner, J., and Greenberg, J. 1990: The impact of layoffs on survivors: An organizational justice perspective. In J. Carroll (ed.), *Applied social psychology and organizational settings*, Hillsdale, NJ: Lawrence Erlbaum Associates, 45–75.

Brockner, J., Konovsky, M., Cooper-Schneider, R., Folger, R., Martin, C., and Bies, R. J. 1994: Interactive effects of procedural justice and outcome negativity on victims and survivors of job loss. *Academy of Management Journal*, 37, 397–409.

Brockner, J., Tyler, T. R., and Cooper-Schneider, R. 1992: The higher they are, the harder they fall: The effects of prior commitment and procedural injustice on subsequent commitment to social institutions. *Administrative Science Quarterly*, 37, 241–61.

Brockner, J., and Wiesenfeld, B. M. 1994: The interactive impact of procedural and outcome fairness on reactions to a decision: The effects of what you do depend on how you do it. *Psychological Bulletin*, 120, 189–208.

Calder, B. J., Phillips, L. W., and Tybout, A. M. 1981: Designing research for application. *Journal of Consumer Research*, 8, 197–207.

Camp, R. R., Blanchard, P. N., and Huszczo, G. E. 1986: *Toward a more organizationally effective training strategy and practice*, Englewood Cliffs, NJ: Prentice-Hall.

Cascio, W. F. 1995: Wither industrial and organizational psychology in a changing world of work? *American Psychologist*, 50, 928–39.

Citera, M., and Rentsch, J. J. 1993: Is there justice in organizational acquisitions? The role of distributive and procedural fairness in corporate acquisitions. In R. Cropanzano (ed.), *Justice in the workplace: Approaching fairness in human resource management*, Hillsdale, NJ: Lawrence Erlbaum Associates, 211–30.

Cobb, A. T., Wooten, K. C., and Folger, R. 1995: Justice in the making: Toward understanding the theory and practice of justice in organizational change and development. In W. A. Pasmore and R. W. Woodman (eds.), *Research in organizational change and development*, Vol. 8, Greenwich, CT: JAI Press, 243–95.

Cohen, R. L., and Greenberg, J. 1982: The justice concept in social psychology. In J. Greenberg and R. L. Cohen (eds.), *Equity and justice in social behavior*, New York: Academic Press, 1–41.

Colarelli, S. M. 1998: Psychological interventions in organizations: An evolutionary perspective. *American Psychologist*, 53, 1044–56.

Cole, N. D., and Latham, G. P. 1997: Effects of training in procedural justice on perceptions of disciplinary fairness by unionized employees and disciplinary subject matter experts. *Journal of Applied Psychology*, 82, 699–705.

Cook, T. D., and Campbell, D. T. 1979: *Quasi-experimentation: Design and analysis issues for field settings*, Chicago: Rand McNally.

Cropanzano, R., and Greenberg, J. 1997: Progress in organizational justice: Tunneling through the maze. In C. L. Cooper and I. T. Robertson (eds.), *International review of industrial and organizational psychology*, Vol. 12, London: Wiley, 317–72.

Cropanzano, R., and Konovsky, M. 1995: Resolving the justice dilemma by improving the outcomes: The case of employee drug screening. *Journal of Business and Psychology*, 10, 221–43.

Daly, J. P., and Geyer, P. D. 1994: The role of fairness in implementing large-scale change: Employee evaluations of process and outcomes in seven facility relocations. *Journal of Organizational Behavior*, 15, 623–38.

Deluga, R. J. 1994: Supervisor trust building, leader-member exchange and organizational citizenship behavior. *Journal of Occupational and Organizational Psychology*, 67, 315–26.

Dertouzos, J., Holland, E., and Ebener, P. 1988: *The legal and economic consequences of wrongful termination*. Santa Monica, CA: Rand Corporation.

Deutsch, M. 1985: *Distributive justice*. New Haven, CT: Yale University Press.

Dipboye, R. L., and de Pontbraind, R. 1981: Correlates of employee reactions to performance appraisals and appraisal systems. *Journal of Applied Psychology*, 66, 248–51.

Dulebohn, J. H., and Ferris, G. R. 1999: The role of influence tactics in perceptions of performance evaluations' fairness. *Academy of Management Journal*, 42, 288–303.

Eddy, E. R., Stone, D. L., and Stone-Romero, E. F. 1999: The effects of information management policies on reactions to human resource information systems: An integration of privacy and procedural justice perspectives. *Personnel Psychology*, 52, 335–58.

Farh, J., Podsakoff, P. M., and Organ, D. W. 1990: Accounting for organizational citizenship behavior: Leader fairness and task scope versus satisfaction. *Journal of Management*, 16, 705–21.

Folger, R. 1977: Distributive and procedural justice: Combined impact of "voice" and improvement of experienced inequity. *Journal of Personality and Social Psychology*, 35, 108–19.

Folger, R., and Cropanzano, R. 1998: *Organizational justice and human resource management*, Thousand Oaks, CA: Sage.

Folger, R., and Greenberg, J. 1985: Procedural justice: An interpretive analysis of personnel systems. In K. Rowland and G. Ferris (eds.), *Research in personnel and human resources management*, Vol. 3, Greenwich, CT: JAI Press, 141–83.

Folger, R., Rosenfield, D., and Robinson, T. 1983: Relative deprivation and procedural justification. *Journal of Personality and Social Psychology*, 45, 268–73.

Furby, L. 1986: Psychology and justice. In R. L. Cohen (ed.), *Justice: Views from the social sciences*, New York: Plenum, 153–203.

Giacalone, R., and Greenberg, J. 1997: *Antisocial behavior in organizations*, Thousand Oaks, CA: Sage.

Gilliland, S. W. 1993: The perceived fairness of selection systems: An organizational justice perspective. *Academy of Management Review*, 18, 694–734.

Gilliland, S. W. 1994: Effects of procedural and distributive justice on reactions to a selection system. *Journal of Applied Psychology*, 79, 691–701.

Greenberg, J. 1982: Approaching equity and avoiding inequity in groups and organizations. In J. Greenberg and R. L. Cohen (eds.), *Equity and justice in social behavior*, New York: Academic Press, 389–435.

Greenberg, J. 1986a: The distributive justice of organizational performance evaluations. In H. W. Bierhoff, R. L. Cohen, and J. Greenberg (eds.), *Justice in social relations*, New York: Plenum, 337–51.

Greenberg, J. 1986b: Determinants of perceived fairness of performance evaluations. *Journal of Applied Psychology*, 71, 340–2.

Greenberg, J. 1986c: Organizational performance appraisal procedures: What makes them fair? In R. J. Lewicki, B. H. Sheppard, and M. H. Bazerman (eds.), *Research on negotiation in organizations*, Vol. 1, Greenwich, CT: JAI Press, 25–41.

Greenberg, J. 1987: A taxonomy of organizational justice theories. *Academy of Management Review*, 12, 9–22.

Greenberg, J. 1990a: Looking fair versus being fair: Managing impressions of organizational justice. In. B. M. Staw and L. L. Cummings (eds.), *Research in organizational behavior*, Vol. 12, Greenwich, CT: JAI Press, 111–57.

Greenberg, J. 1990b: Employee theft as a reaction to underpayment inequity: The hidden costs of pay cuts. *Journal of Applied Psychology*, 72, 55–61.

Greenberg, J. 1991: Social fairness and employees' reactions to layoffs, unpublished manuscript, The Ohio State University, Columbus.

Greenberg, J. 1993a: Stealing in the name of justice: Informational and interpersonal moderators of theft reactions to underpayment inequity. *Organizational Behavior and Human Decision Processes*, 54, 81–103.

Greenberg, J. 1993b: Justice and organizational citizenship: A commentary on the state of the science. *Employee Responsibilities and Rights Journal*, 6, 227–34.

Greenberg, J. 1994a: Using socially fair treatment to promote acceptance of a work site smoking ban. *Journal of Applied Psychology*, 79, 288–97.

Greenberg, J. 1994b: Restitution and retaliation as explanations for employee theft, unpublished manuscript, The Ohio State University, Columbus.

Greenberg, J. 1996: *The quest for justice on the job*. Thousand Oaks, CA: Sage.

Greenberg, J. 1997: A social influence model of employee theft: Beyond the fraud triangle. In R. J. Lewicki, R. J. Bies, and B. H. Sheppard (eds.), *Research on negotiation in organizations*, Vol. 6, Greenwich, CT: JAI Press, 29–52.

Greenberg, J. 1998: The cognitive geometry of employee theft: Negotiating "the line" between taking and stealing. In R. W. Griffin, A. O'Leary-Kelly, and J. M. Collins (eds.), *Dysfunctional behavior in organizations: Non-violent dysfunctional behavior*, Stamford, CT: JAI Press, 147–94.

Greenberg, J. 1999a: Comparing the fairness of single-source and multi-source performance evaluations, unpublished data. The Ohio State University, Columbus.

Greenberg, J. 1999b: Interpersonal justice training (IJT) for reducing employee theft: Some preliminary results, unpublished data. The Ohio State University, Columbus.

Greenberg, J., and Bies, R. J. 1992: Establishing the role of empirical studies of organizational justice in philosophical inquiries into business ethics. *Journal of Business Ethics*, 11, 433–44.

Greenberg, J., and Cohen, R. L. 1982: *Equity and justice in social behavior*. New York: Academic Press.

Greenberg, J., and Folger, R. 1983: Procedural justice, participation, and the fair process effect in groups and organizations. In P. B. Paulus (ed.), *Basic group processes*, New York: Springer-Verlag, 235–56.

Greenberg, J., and Scott, K. S. 1996: Why do employees bite the hands that feed them? Employee theft as a social exchange process. In. B. M. Staw, and L. L. Cummings (eds.), *Research in organizational behavior*, Vol. 18, Greenwich, CT: JAI Press, 111–56.

Greenberg, J., and Wiethoff, C., 2000: Organizational justice as cause and consequence: Implications for application. In R. Cropanzano (ed.), *Justice in the workplace*, Vol. 2: *From theory to practice*, Mahwah, NJ: Lawrence Erlbaum and Associates.

Homans, G. C. 1961: *Social behavior: Its elementary forms*, New York: Harcourt, Brace, and World.

Huo, Y. J., Smith, H., Tyler, T. R., and Lind, E. A. 1996: Superordinate identification, subgroup identification, and justice concerns: Is separatism the problem; is assimilation the answer? *Psychological Science*, 7, 40–5.

Ilgen, D. R., and Barnes-Farrell, J. L. 1984: *Performance planning and evaluation*, Chicago: SRA.

James, K. 1993: The social context of organizational justice: Cultural, intergroup, and structural effects on justice behaviors and perceptions. In R. Cropanzano (ed.), *Justice in the workplace: Approaching fairness in human resource management*, Hillsdale, NJ: Erlbaum, 21–50.

Karambayya, R., Brett, J. M., and Lytle, A. 1992: Effects of formal authority and experience on third-party roles, outcomes, and perceptions of fairness. *Academy of Management Journal*, 35, 426–38.

Katzenbach, J. R., and Smith, D. K. 1993: *The wisdom of teams*, Boston, MA: Harvard Business School.

Kidwell, R. E., and Bennett, N. 1994: Employee reactions to electronic systems. *Group and Organization Management*, 19, 203–18.

Kim, W. C., and Mauborgne, R. A. 1991: Implementing global strategies: The role of procedural justice. *Strategic Management Journal*, 12, 125–43.

Kim, W. C., and Mauborgne, R. A. 1993: Procedural justice, attitudes, and subsidiary management compliance with multinationals' corporate strategic decisions. *Academy of Management Journal*, 36, 502–26.

Kim, W. C., and Mauborgne, R. A. 1995: A procedural justice model of strategic decision making: Strategy content implications in the multinational. *Organizational Science*, 6, 44–61.

Kim, W. C., and Mauborgne, R. 1997: Fair process: Managing in the knowledge economy. *Harvard Business Review*, 75(4), 65–75.

Kirkman, B. L., Shapiro, D. L., Novelli, L., Jr., and Brett, J., 1996: Employee concerns regarding self-managing work teams: A multidimensional justice perspective. *Social Justice Research*, 9, 47–67.

Kissler, G. D. 1991: *The change riders*, Reading, MA: Addison-Wesley.

Konovsky, M. A., Elliott, J., and Pugh, S. D. 1995: *The dispositional and contextual predictors of citizenship behavior in Mexico*. Paper presented at the annual meeting of the Academy of Management, Vancouver, BC, Canada, August.

Konovsky, M., and Folger, R. 1991: *The effects of procedural and distributive justice on organizational citizenship behavior*. Paper presented at the annual meeting of the Academy of Management, Miami Beach, FL, August.

Landy, F. J., Barnes, J. L., and Murphy, K. R. 1978: Correlates of perceived fairness and accuracy of performance evaluation. *Journal of Applied Psychology*, 63, 751–4.

Landy, F. J., Barnes-Farrell, J., and Cleveland, J. 1980: Correlates of perceived fairness and accuracy of performance evaluation: A follow-up. *Journal of Applied Psychology*, 65, 355–6.

Lee, C. 1995: Prosocial organizational behaviors: The roles of workplace justice, achievement striving, and pay satisfaction. *Journal of Business and Psychology*, 10, 197–206.

Leventhal, G. S. 1976: The distribution of rewards and resources in groups and organizations. In L. Berkowitz and E. Walster (eds.), *Advances in experimental social psychology*, Vol. 9, New York: Academic Press, 91–131.

Leventhal, G. S. 1980: What should be done with equity theory? In K. J. Gergen, M. S. Greenberg, and R. H. Willis (eds.), *Social exchange: Advances in theory and research*, New York: Plenum, 27–55.

Leventhal, G. S., Karuza, J., and Fry, W. R. 1980: Beyond fairness: A theory of allocation preferences. In G. Mikula (ed.), *Justice and social interaction*, New York: Springer-Verlag, 167–218.

Levine, M. M. 1975: *Comparative labor relations law*, Morristown, NJ: General Learning Press.

Lind, E. A. 1990: *Arbitrating high-stakes cases: An evaluation of court-annexed arbitration in a United States district court*, Santa Monica, CA: Rand Corporation.

Lind, E. A., Erickson, B. E., Friedland, N., and Dickenberger, M. 1978: Reactions to procedural models for adjudicative conflict resolution: A cross-national study. *Journal of Conflict Resolution*, 22, 318–41.

Lind, E. A., Greenberg, J., Scott, K. S., and Welchans, T. D. 1998: *The winding road from employee to complainant: Situational and psychological determinants of wrongful termination lawsuits*. Paper presented at the annual meeting of the Academy of Management, San Diego, CA, August.

Lind, E. A., Huo, Y. J., and Tyler, T. R. 1994: . . . And justice for all: Ethnicity, gender, and preferences for dispute resolution procedures. *Law and Human Behavior*, 18, 269–90.

Lind, E. A., Kulik, C., Ambrose, M., and Park, M. 1993: Individual and corporate dispute resolution: Using procedural fairness as a decision heuristic. *Administrative Science Quarterly*, 38, 224–51.

Lind, E. A., Lissak, R. I., and Conlon, D. E. 1983: Decision control and process control effects on procedural fairness judgments. *Journal of Applied Social Psychology*, 4, 338–50.

Lind, E. A., MacCoun, R. J., Ebener, P. E., Felstiner, W. L. F., Hensler, D. R., Resnik, J., and Tyler, T. R. 1990: In the eye of the beholder: Tort litigants' evaluations of their experiences in the civil justice system. *Law and Society Review*, 24, 953–96.

Lind, E. A., and Shapard, J. E. 1981: *Evaluation of court-annexed arbitration in three federal district courts*, Washington, DC: Federal Judicial Center.

Lind, E. A., and Tyler, T. R. 1988: *The social psychology of procedural justice*, New York: Plenum.

Lind, E. A., Tyler, T. R., and Huo, Y. 1997: Procedural context and culture: Variation in the antecedents of procedural justice judgments. *Journal of Personality and Social Psychology*, 73, 767–80.

Lissak, R. I. 1983: Procedural fairness: How employees evaluate procedures, unpublished doctoral dissertation, University of Illinois, Urbana-Champaign.

MacCoun, R. J., Lind, E. A., and Tyler, T. R. 1992: Alternative dispute resolution in the courts. In D. Kagehiro and W. Laufer (eds.), *The handbook of law and psychology*, New York: Springer-Verlag, 95–118.

MacCoun, R. J., Lind, E. A., Hensler, D. R., Bryant, D. L., and Ebener, P. A. 1988: *Alternative adjudication: An evaluation of the New Jersey automobile arbitration program*, Santa Monica, CA: Rand Corporation.

Marrow, A. F. 1969: *The practical theorist: The life and work of Kurt Lewin*, New York: Basic Books.

Martinko, M. J. 1995: *Attribution theory: An organizational perspective*, Delray Beach, FL: St. Lucie Press.

Moore, R. F. 1996: Caring for identified versus statistical lives: An evolutionary view of medical distributive justice. *Ethnology and Sociobiology*, 17, 329–401.

Moorman, R. H. 1991: Relationship between organizational justice and organizational citizenship behaviors: Do fairness perceptions influence employee citizenship? *Journal of Applied Psychology*, 76, 845–55.

Murphy, K. R. 1993: *Honesty in the workplace*, Pacific Grove, CA: Brooks/Cole.

Nelson, R. R., and Winter, S. G. 1982: *An evolutionary theory of economic change*, Cambridge, MA: Belknap.

Novelli, L., Jr., Kirkman, B. L., and Shapiro, D. L. 1995: Effective implementation of organizational change: An organizational justice perspective. In C. L. Cooper and D. M. Rousseau (eds.), *Trends in organizational behavior*, Vol. 2, New York: Wiley, 15–36.

Opotow, S., and Clayton, S. 1994: Green justice: Conceptions of fairness and the natural world. *Journal of Social Issues*, 50, 1–11.

Organ, D. W. 1988: *Organizational citizenship behavior: The good soldier syndrome*, Lexington, MA: Lexington Books.

Organ, W. W., and Moorman, R. J. 1993: Fairness and organizational citizenship behavior: What are the connections? *Social Justice Research*, 6, 5–18.

Parker, C. P., Bales, B. B., and Christensen, N. D. 1997: Support for affirmative action, justice perceptions, and work attitudes: A study of gender and racial-ethnic group differences. *Journal of Applied Psychology*, 82, 376–89.

Ployhart, R. E., and Ryan, A. M. 1998: Applicants' reactions to the fairness of selection procedures: The effects of positive rule violations and time of measurement. *Journal of Applied Psychology*, 83, 3–16.

Podsakoff, P. M., and MacKenzie, S. B. 1993: Citizenship behavior and fairness in organizations: Issues and directions for future research. *Employee Responsibilities and Rights Journal*, 6, 235–47.

Popper, K. 1963: *Conjectures and refutations*, New York: Harper Torchbooks.

Purpura, P. P. 1998: *Security and loss prevention*, 3rd edn., Boston: Butterworth-Heinemann.

Rawls, J. 1971: *A theory of justice*, Cambridge, MA: Harvard University Press.

Ross, W. D. (ed.) 1925: *The Oxford translation of Aristotle*, Vol. IX: *The Nicomachean Ethics*, London: Oxford University Press.

Rynes, S. L., and Connerly, M. L. 1993: Applicant reactions to alternative selection procedures. *Journal of Business and Psychology*, 7, 261–77.

Schein, E. H. 1985: *Leadership and organizational culture*, San Francisco: Jossey-Bass.

Schuler, H. 1993: Social validity of selection situations: A concept and some empirical results. In H. Schuler, J. L. Farr, and M. Smith (eds.), *Personnel selection and assessment: Individual and organizational perspectives*, Hillsdale, NJ: Lawrence Erlbaum Associates, 11–26.

Sheppard, B. H., Blumenfeld-Jones, K., Minton, W. J., and Hyder, E. 1994: Informal conflict intervention: Advice and dissent. *Employee Responsibilities and Rights Journal*, 7, 53–72.

Sims, H. P., Jr., and Gioia., D. A. 1986: *The thinking organization*. San Francisco: Jossey-Bass.

Singer, M. S. 1992: Procedural justice in management selection: Identification of fairness determinants and associations of fairness perceptions. *Social Justice Research*, 5, 49–70.

Singer, M. S. 1993: *Fairness in personnel selection*, Aldershot, New Zealand: Avebury.

Sitkin, S. B., and Bies, R. J. 1994: *The legalistic organization*, Thousand Oaks, CA: Sage.

Skarlicki, D. P., Ellard, J. H., and Kelln, B. R. C. 1998: Third-party perceptions of a layoff: Procedural, derogation, and retributive aspects of justice. *Journal of Applied Psychology*, 83, 119–27.

Skarlicki, D. P., and Folger, R. 1997: Retaliation in the workplace: The role of distributive, procedural, and interactional justice. *Journal of Applied Psychology*, 82, 434–43.

Skarlicki, D. P., and Latham, G. P. 1996: Increasing citizenship behavior within a labor union: A test of organizational justice theory. *Journal of Applied Psychology*, 81, 161–9.

Skinner, B. F. 1953: *Science and human behavior*, New York: Macmillan.

Smither, J. W., Reilly, R. R., Milsap, R. E., Pearlman, K., and Stoffey, R. W. 1993: Applicants' reactions to selection procedures. *Personnel Psychology*, 46, 49–75.

Tax, S. S., Brown, S. W., and Chandrashekaran, M. 1998: Customer evaluations of service complaint experiences: Implications for relationship marketing. *Journal of Marketing*, 62, 60–76.

Teel, K. S. 1978: Self-appraisal revisited. *Personnel Journal*, 57, 364–7.

Tepper, B. J., and Braun, C. K. 1995: Does the experience of organizational justice mitigate the invasion of privacy engendered by random drug testing? An empirical investigation. *Basic and Applied Social Psychology*, 16, 211–25.

Thibaut, J., and Walker, L. 1975: *Procedural justice: A psychological analysis*, Hillsdale, NJ: Erlbaum Lawrence Associates.

Tornow, W. W., and London, M. 1998: *Maximizing the value of 360-degree feedback*, San Francisco: Jossey-Bass.

Tyler, T. R. 1987: Conditions leading to value expressive effects in judgments of procedural justice: A test of four models. *Journal of Personality and Social Psychology*, 52, 333–44.

Tyler, T. R., Rasinski, K., and Spodick, N. 1985: The influence of voice on satisfaction with leaders: Exploring the meaning of process control. *Journal of Personality and Social Psychology*, 48, 72–81.

Tyler, T. R., and Smith, H. J. 1997: Social justice and social movements. In D. Gilbert, S. T. Fiske, and G. Lindzey (eds.), *Handbook of social psychology*, Vol. 4, New York: McGraw-Hill, 595–629.

Walker, L., LaTour, S., Lind, E. A., and Thibaut, J. 1974: Reactions of participants and observers to modes of adjudication. *Journal of Applied Social Psychology*, 4, 295–310.

Walster, E., Walster, G. W., and Berscheid, E. 1978: *Equity: Theory and research*, Boston: Allyn and Bacon.

Youngblood, S. A., Trevino, L. K., and Favia, M. 1992: Reactions to unjust dismissal and third-party dispute resolution: A justice framework. *Employee Responsibilities and Rights Journal*, 5, 283–307.

chapter 5

TEAM EFFECTIVENESS IN THEORY AND IN PRACTICE

J. RICHARD HACKMAN, RUTH WAGEMAN, THOMAS M. RUDDY AND CHARLES L. RAY

■ TEAM EFFECTIVENESS IN THEORY

Kurt Lewin's oft-quoted statement that there is nothing so practical as a good theory is comforting to those of us who seek to do scholarly work that can make a constructive difference in the world. Yet his statement is agnostic about the *kind* of theory that is most useful in guiding practice. Our research on work team performance suggests that actionable theory may have to be quite different from what scholars usually produce in the course of their research.

Normal social science focuses on cause–effect relationships among variables that are of interest to researchers, and eventually results in empirical generalizations that summarize what scholars have learned about those relationships. Implications for action follow naturally from those generalizations: If *x* has been found to cause *y*, then actors who seek the latter should do everything they can to promote the former. In small group research, the basis for developing those kinds of implications for action was established decades ago in books by McGrath and Altman (1966) and by Hare (1976). Both of these works are carefully compiled and indexed summaries of the relationships among variables of interest to group researchers, and both provide excellent summaries of the state of knowledge about group behavior and performance as of the time they were written. As informative as these compilations were, however, we see no evidence that they have made much of a difference in how work teams actually are designed, supported, and led in organizations.

Why not? One possibility is that the knowledge about how to create effective work groups is indeed available, sound, and applicable, but practitioners are unable to surmount what Pfeffer and Sutton (1999) call the "knowing–doing" problem – an inability to actually use in practice what one knows to be the proper course of action. The power of the knowing–doing problem is seen in the decades-long series of action research projects by Argyris (1985, 1993). In those studies, managers learned in training sessions how to behave more authentically in work relationships (that is, in ways that foster two-way exchange of task-relevant thoughts and feelings), and they had ample opportunity to practice and internalize their new behaviors.

Yet many participants found themselves unable to sustain those behaviors in the back-home setting, especially when dealing with highly consequential and emotionally charged issues, the ones for which valid data are most needed.

As pervasive and pernicious as the knowing–doing problem is, the difficulty of actually using in practice research findings about influences on group performance runs much deeper. The root of the problem, we believe, lies in the very nature of cause–effect models of group behavior and performance. It would be lovely if research had identified a handful of powerful and direct causes of team effectiveness, because then actors could simply manipulate those factors knowing that, if they succeeded, performance improvements certainly would result. For example, if research had established that performance is a direct positive function of the heterogeneity of membership, then managers could compose groups to maximize the diversity within the group. Or, if research had established that a "democratic" leadership style fostered excellent performance, then managers could be confident that the more democratically they behaved, the better their groups would perform. But influences on group performance are almost never so simple and straightforward. Heterogeneous groups do sometimes perform better than homogeneous groups – but sometimes they do not. Democratic leadership works better in some situations, but not in others. The list of exceptions to main-effect generalizations goes on, and it is long.

Those exceptions invariably prompt researchers to develop "contingency" models that specify the circumstances under which causal variables, such as heterogeneous composition or democratic leadership, do and do not result in performance improvements. Once contingency thinking takes hold, researchers tend to suggest more and more distinctions and to add ever more qualifications to simple causal propositions (Hackman, 1985). Eventually, the point of diminishing returns is reached, with improvements in explanatory power lagging behind increases in model complexity. Moreover, research in cognitive psychology raises doubts about actors' ability to process multiple contingencies in deciding how to behave (Slovic, 1981), further limiting the usefulness of such models in guiding the behavior of those who design and lead groups.

Our research on group behavior and performance has gradually led us to the conclusion that models that are useful to, and useable by, organizational actors must be of a wholly different kind than standard cause–effect and contingency models. We describe below the properties of one such model, lay out its conceptual propositions, and discuss its implications for action. Then we relinquish the word processor to our colleagues from the world of practice, who provide their perspectives on what *actually* is required to promote team effectiveness in work organizations.

Approach

We seek to identify the conditions that, when present, increase the likelihood that organizational work teams will perform effectively. The first order of business, therefore, must be to be explicit about our domain (what a "work team" is) and our criteria (how we construe "team effectiveness").

Our domain is work teams in organizations. Such teams have three features. First, they are *real* groups – intact social systems, complete with boundaries, interdependence among members, and differentiated member roles (Alderfer, 1977). Second, they have one or more *group tasks* to perform, producing some outcome for which members bear collective responsibility and whose acceptability potentially can be assessed. Finally, such teams operate in an *organizational context*. This means that the group, as a collective, manages its relations with other individuals or groups in the larger social system in which it operates. We are concerned only with teams for which all three attributes are present – that is, real groups that perform team tasks in organizational contexts.

All teams that fall within our domain have the authority to manage their own internal processes. The authority of some teams does not extend beyond that basic level, whereas others also have the right to alter their own structures, or even to change their composition or their purposes (for details, see Hackman, 1986). Level of authority, in itself, does not determine how well a team is likely to perform; it does, however, signal whether interventions aimed at helping a team do well would be better directed to teams themselves (appropriate for those that have substantial authority to manage their own affairs) or to team managers (for teams that do not).

When anyone – a researcher, a manager, or a team member – points to some measure as a sign of how "effective" a work team is, that person implicitly is making a statement of what he or she values. Our values are reflected in a three-dimensional conception of effectiveness, and we do not count as effective any team that fails on any of the three dimensions. First, the productive output of the team (that is, its product, service, or decision) meets or exceeds the standards of quantity, quality, and timeliness of the team's clients – that is, the people who receive, review, and/or use the output. It is the client's standards and assessments that count. Not those of the team itself, except in those rare cases when the team is the client of its own work. Not those of outside researchers or evaluators, except when they are engaged to do an assessment by those who *do* have legitimacy as reviewers. And not even those of the team's manager, who only rarely is the person who actually receives and uses a team's output. Good teams meet their clients' expectations.

Second, the social processes the team uses in carrying out the work enhance the members' capability to work together interdependently in the future. Effective teams operate in ways that build shared commitment, collective skills, and task-appropriate coordination strategies – not mutual antagonisms and trails of failures from which little is learned. They become adept at detecting and correcting errors before serious damage is done and at noticing and exploiting emerging opportunities. And they periodically review how they have been operating, milking their experiences for whatever learning can be had from them. An effective team is a more capable performing unit when its work is finished than it was when work began.

Third, the team experience, on balance, contributes positively to the learning and personal well-being of individual team members. Teams can be wonderful sites for learning – for expanding one's knowledge, acquiring new skills, and exploring perspectives on the world that differ from one's own. Teamwork also can engender feelings of belonging, providing members with a secure sense of their place in the social world. While not denying the inevitability of rough spots in the life of any group, we none the less do not count as effective any team for which the impact of the group experience on members' learning and well-being is substantially more negative than positive. If the group compromises members' personal learning or if their main reactions to the group experience are frustration and disillusionment, then the costs of generating the group product were too high.

Our model of team effectiveness seeks to specify the organizational conditions and leader behaviors that increase the likelihood that a work team will meet the three criteria just described. The aspiration is a model that is useful to practitioners as they create and support work teams and that also is inviting of empirical assessment and correction by researchers. As will be seen, our approach is neither to specify the main "causes" of group performance nor to provide a long list of specific variables that can be manipulated, like the levers on a mechanical device, to increase team effectiveness. Instead, we posit a small number of organizational conditions that, when in place, increase the likelihood (but by no means guarantee) that the team members will develop into an effective performing unit.

Specifying the conditions under which groups can effectively chart their own courses is very different from conventional scholarly models (in which the attempt is to link causes tightly to effects) as well as from action strategies that derive from those models (in which practitioners attempt to manage team processes more-or-less continuously in real time). As a metaphor, consider two alternative strategies that could be used by a pilot landing an aircraft. One strategy is to "fly the airplane down," continuously adjusting heading, sink rate, and airspeed with the objective of arriving at the runway threshold just above stall speed, ready to flare the aircraft and touch down smoothly. A second strategy is to get the aircraft stabilized on approach while still far from the field, making small corrections as needed to heading, power, or aircraft configuration to keep the plane "in the groove." The safer strategy is the second one; indeed, when a pilot finds that he or she is in the first situation the prudent action is to go around and try the approach again. To be stabilized on approach is to have the basic conditions established such that the natural course of events leads to the desired outcome – in this case, a good landing. We seek to apply this same way of thinking to how work teams are structured, supported, and led.

Conditions that foster team effectiveness

To perform well, a team must surmount three hurdles. It must: (1) exert sufficient effort to get the task accomplished at an acceptable level of performance; (2) bring adequate knowledge and skill to bear on the work; and (3) employ task performance strategies that are appropriate to the work and to the setting in which it is being performed (Hackman and Morris, 1975). We refer to these three hurdles as *process criteria* of effectiveness. They are not the ultimate test of how well a group has performed (see above for our views about that), but they turn out to be useful both for assessing how a group is doing as it proceeds with its work and for diagnosing the nature of the problem if things are not going well. One can readily ask, for example, whether a group is having difficulties because of an effort problem, a talent problem, or a strategy problem, and then target remedial interventions on the appropriate features of the group's structure or context.

A high standing on the process criteria cannot be achieved through exhortation or by instructions to group members. Instead, it is the presence of four organizational conditions that increase the likelihood that a group's work will be characterized by sufficient effort, ample task-relevant knowledge and skill, and task-appropriate performance strategies. These four conditions are: (1) clear, engaging direction; (2) an enabling team structure; (3) a supportive organizational context; and (4) available, expert coaching.

Clear, engaging direction

The "direction" of a group is the specification of its overall purposes. Direction is critical in energizing the team, in getting it properly oriented toward its major objectives, and in engaging the full range of members' talents. Our research suggests that a good direction for a team is simultaneously challenging, clear, and consequential.

1.   *Challenging.* The performance target set for a team must be neither too demanding (and therefore beyond the team's reach) nor too easy (and therefore not a challenge). Too great a stretch, and people do not even bother to try; too small a stretch, and they do not *need* to try. Research by Atkinson (1958) and others has shown that individual motivation is greatest when the person has about a 50–50 chance of succeeding on a task; we see no reason to doubt that the same is true for work teams.

Also critical in energizing a work team is whether its direction focuses mainly on the end-states to be achieved or on the means by which the team is to proceed with its work. Those who create work teams should be insistent and unapologetic about exercising their authority to specify end-states, but equally insistent about not specifying the details of the means by which the team is to pursue those ends. That state of affairs, shown in the upper right quadrant of table 5.1, fosters energetic, task-focused work (in the jargon of the day, team "empowerment"). Specifying both ends and means (lower right quadrant) mitigates the challenge to team members and, at the same time, under-uses the full complement of team members' resources; specifying neither (upper left quadrant) invites anarchy rather than focused, purposive team work; and specifying means but not ends (lower left quadrant) is the worst of all possible cases.

2.   *Consequential.* When a piece of work has clear consequences for team members or for the well-being of other people, members are more likely to engage the full range of their talents in executing the work than they are when group purposes are viewed as of little real consequence. For consequential work, there is little likelihood that a team will fall victim to the "free rider" problem in using member talents (that is, people not contributing what they know, or what they know how to do, to the team's work). At the same time, the chances increase that the team will weight members' contributions in accord with their actual expertise rather than use some task-irrelevant criterion such as status, gender, or equality of workload in deciding how to deploy member talents. When it is the championship game, the team cannot afford to let everybody play – even if that means that less talented or experienced members have to remain on the bench. If winning is important enough, second-tier players willingly sit on the bench for the good of the team.

Table 5.1 Setting direction about means versus ends

		Specify *ends*?	
		No	Yes
Specify *means*?	No	Anarchy	Engaged, goal-directed work
	Yes	Turn-off (Worst of all)	Wasted human resources

Managers sometimes use rhetorical devices to try to make a team's direction seem more consequential than it really is (this is akin to the motivational ploy of convincing brick carriers that they actually are building a cathedral). If such devices work at all, their effect is temporary because it becomes clear soon enough that what one *really* is doing, day after day, is carrying bricks. It is impossible to generate a statement of direction that engages the full range and depth of members' talents for work that is essentially trivial.

3. *Clear.* A work team's purposes must be clear as well as challenging. A clear direction orients the team toward its objective, and is invaluable to members as they weigh alternative strategies for proceeding with the work. As a metaphor, consider a mountain-climbing team that has encountered a fork in the trail. Absent a clear and shared understanding of which peak is the team's objective, members may waste considerable time and fall into unnecessary conflict as they debate which way to go. The same is true for work teams. There are numerous choices to be made in the course of work on almost any task, and decision making about such matters is almost always facilitated by a clear and concrete statement of direction. To have a purpose of "serving customers" or "creating value for the firm," for example, is to have no real purpose at all, and to implicitly invite team members to spend excessive time wandering about trying to figure out what they are really supposed to do.

There is a twist, however, in that statements of direction sometimes can be *too* clear. When a team's purposes are spelled out explicitly and completely, there is little room for members to add their own shades of meaning to those purposes, to make sense of them in their own, idiosyncratic ways. Such sense-making processes are an essential part of coming to "own" a piece of work, and an overly explicit statement of direction can pre-empt them. Moreover, if a team's direction is clear, specific, *and* of great consequence for team members (for example, if their jobs or a significant bonus hangs in the balance), then there is a real risk that the team will be tempted to engage in inappropriate behaviors (such as fudging numbers) to ensure their success (Corn, 1998), or that they will focus too intently on the measures used to gauge their success, at the expense of the real purposes of their work (Kerr, 1975). Good direction for a work team is clear, it is palpable – and it is incomplete.

In sum, good direction for work teams is challenging (which *energizes* members), it is clear (which *orients* them to their main purposes) and it is consequential (which *engages* the full range of their talents). Direction comes first, because everything else depends upon it – how the team is structured, the kinds of organizational supports that are provided, and the character of leaders' hands-on coaching.

An enabling team structure

Some teams have difficulty accomplishing their work because they were not set up right in the first place. They may have to contend with overly elaborate structures that get in the way of getting anything done, or they may have the opposite problem of insufficient structure (this is not uncommon for self-managing teams whose creators think that teams can work everything out on their own). Our research has identified three structural features as key in fostering competent team work.

1. *Task design.* The team task should be well-aligned with the team's purpose and high on what Hackman and Oldham (1980) call "motivating potential." This means that the team task is a whole and meaningful piece of work for which members share responsibility and accountability, and that is structured so that members receive regular and trustworthy data about how they are doing. Well-designed group tasks foster high, task-focused effort by team members.

2. *Team composition.* The team should be as small as possible given the work to be accomplished, and should include members with ample skills in both the task and interpersonal domains. Moreover, the team should have a good *mix* of members – people who are neither so similar to one another that they are like peas from the same pod nor so different that they risk having difficulty communicating and coordinating with one another. A well-composed team ensures that members have, and can use, the full complement of knowledge and skills that is required to achieve the team's purposes.

3. *Core norms of conduct.* A team should have established early in its life clear and explicit specification of the basic norms of conduct for member behavior. Expectations about acceptable behavior tend either to be "imported" to the group by members or established very early in its life (Bettenhausen and Murnighan, 1985; Gersick, 1988). Moreover, core norms tend to remain in place until and unless something fairly dramatic occurs to force a rethinking about what behaviors are and are not appropriate (Gersick and Hackman, 1990). Up-front norms of conduct should actively promote continuous scanning of the performance situation and pro-active planning of group performance strategies, and they should specify the kinds of behaviors that are "out of bounds" for the team. Clear specification of core norms frees members from spending excessive time discussing what behaviors are and are not acceptable in the group, and facilitates the development of task performance strategies that are appropriate to the team's task and situation.

A supportive organizational context

The structures and systems of many organizations have evolved over the years to provide good support for work that is performed by *individual* organization members. Work teams in such organizations may find it difficult or impossible to obtain the kinds of support that they require, the special resources that teams need but that individual performers may not. Our research has identified three features of the organizational context that appear to be especially consequential for work team effectiveness.

1.   The reward system should provide recognition and other positive consequences for excellent *team* performance. Rewards to individuals should never provide disincentives for task-oriented collaboration among team members, which is a common (if unintended) feature of traditional, individual-focused appraisal and compensation systems.

2.   The educational system should make available to the team, at the team's initiative, technical or educational assistance for any aspects of the work for which members are not already knowledgeable, skilled, or experienced – including, if necessary, the honing of members' skills in working together on collective tasks.

3.   The information system should provide the team with whatever data and projections members need as they select or invent task- and situation-appropriate strategies for carrying out the team's work.

It is no small undertaking to provide these supports to teams, especially in established organizations whose support systems are professionally designed and administered. State-of-the-art performance appraisal systems, for example, may provide reliable and valid measures of individual contributions but be wholly inappropriate for assessing and rewarding work done by teams. Compensation policies may make no provision for rewarding excellent collective performance and, indeed, may explicitly prohibit financial awards to teams. Human resource departments may be expert in identifying individuals' training needs and in providing courses to meet those needs, but training in team skills may not be available at all. To align existing organizational systems with the needs of task-performing teams can be a major challenge, one that requires the exercise of influence both upward in the organization and laterally across functional boundaries. The challenge is worth taking on, however, because an unsupportive organizational context can undermine even teams that are otherwise quite well directed and well structured.

Available, expert coaching

It is not always easy for a team to take advantage of positive performance conditions, particularly if members have relatively little (and/or relatively negative) experience in teamwork. A leader can do much to promote team effectiveness by helping team members learn how to work interdependently. The role of the help provider is not, of course, to dictate to group members the one best way to proceed with their collaborative work. It is, instead, to help members learn how to minimize the "process losses" that invariably occur in groups (Steiner, 1972), and to consider how they might work together to generate synergistic process gains. Specific kinds of help that leaders can provide for each of the three process criteria of effectiveness include the following:

1.   *For effort*. Helping members minimize coordination and motivation problems (process losses that can waste effort), and helping them build commitment to the group and its task (a process gain that can increase effort).

2.   *For knowledge and skill.* Helping members avoid inappropriate weighting of different individuals' ideas and contributions (a process loss), and helping them learn how to share their expertise to build the group's repertoire of skills (a process gain).

3.   *For performance strategies.* Helping members avoid failures in implementing their performance plans (a process loss), and helping them develop creative new ways of proceeding with the work (a process gain).

Such coaching can, of course, be provided at any point in the course of a team's work, but there are three times in a team's life when members are likely to be especially open to particular coaching interventions: (1) at the beginning, when a group is just starting its work, it is especially open to interventions that focus on the effort members will apply to their work; (2) at the midpoint, when the group has completed about half its work (or half the allotted time has elapsed), it is especially open to interventions that help members reflect on their performance strategies; and (3) at the end, when the work is finished, the team is ready to entertain interventions aimed at helping members learn from their experiences (for details, see Hackman and Wageman, 1999).

Summary

Table 5.2 summarizes our discussion of the enabling performance conditions. It relates the three process criteria of effectiveness to the conditions that may help a group score well on them. For each of the process criteria, some aspect of the team's direction, some structural feature, some aspect of the organizational context, and some type of process assistance are identified as particularly inviting points of intervention.

For a team displaying problems in members' effort levels, one would focus on the level of challenge in the team's direction, on the motivational properties of the group task, on the reward system of the organization, and on group dynamics having to do with motivation and commitment. For a team with talent-related problems, one would focus on the consequentiality of the team's direction, on the composition of the team, on the educational system of the organization, and on group dynamics having to do with how members weight each other's contributions and how they learn from one another. For teams with strategy-related issues, one would focus on the clarity of the team's direction, on group norms about the management of performance processes, on the information system of the organization, and on group processes having to do with the invention and implementation of new ways of proceeding with the work.

Each of the four conditions we have just discussed – direction, structure, context, and coaching – has within it subconditions that are the operationalization of that condition at the next-lower level of analysis. Each of those subconditions, in turn, has subconditions of its own. It is something like a set of Russian dolls, each of which has other, smaller dolls within it. Although the basic conditions that foster team effectiveness are few in number, simple, and easy to remember, the amount of learning that can be done about them is without limit.

Table 5.2 Points of leverage for creating conditions that enhance team effectiveness

| | Points of leverage | | | |
Process criteria	Direction	Structure	Context	Coaching
Ample effort	Challenging	Motivational structure of group task	Reward system	Remedying coordination problems; building commitment
Sufficient knowledge and skill	Consequential	Team composition	Education system	Remedying inappropriate "weighting" of inputs; fostering cross-training
Task-appropriate performance strategies	Clear	Core norms of conduct	Information system	Remedying implementation problems; fostering innovation in strategy development

Implications for team leadership

The four conditions that foster team effectiveness are conceptually straightforward and would seem relatively simple for a leader to establish. Provide teams with direction that is challenging, consequential, and clear. Create a structure – task, composition, and norms – that promotes competent teamwork. Tune the organizational reward, educational, and informational systems so that they support teams in their work. And provide hands-on coaching that helps teams take advantage of their favorable performance circumstances. In this way of thinking, leaders have two primary responsibilities. First, is to get the team set up right and launched on a good trajectory, and second, is to manage "at the margins," making small interventions as needed to help members learn how to exploit the opportunities and solve the problems that they encounter.

The order in which the four conditions are listed is significant. Direction comes first, because how one would structure a team depends most of all upon what its main purposes are. Structure comes next, because if a team's structure is flawed (that is, if its task, composition, or norms are badly off the mark) then a supportive organizational context will be of little help. Coaching comes last, because even highly competent coaching is unlikely to make much of a difference if the basic features of the performance situation are inimical to competent teamwork.

These implications were empirically supported in a study by Wageman (1999) of self-managing service teams at the Xerox Corporation (the home organization of our co-authors on this chapter). Wageman found that a team leader's influence comes mostly from his or her design choices, with coaching activities making a difference only secondarily, through small adjustments in what is an already well-determined trajectory. Coaching helped well-designed teams exploit their favorable circumstances, but even competent coaching made little difference in the effectiveness of poorly designed teams. Poor coaching (for example, identifying a team's problems and telling members how they should solve them), on the other hand, was much more deleterious for poorly designed teams than for those that had an engaging direction, a good structure, and solid contextual supports.

The good news of this part of the chapter is that the basic conditions that we have been discussing appear, based on research findings thus far, to provide a relatively high and sturdy platform on which a work team can operate with good prospects for success. The bad news is that these four conditions, as simple and straightforward as they are, can be devilishly difficult to implement, especially in organizations that have been "tuned" over the years to support work by individual performers rather than by teams. We leave it to our practitioner colleagues to tell us why this should be so, and to advise us what, if anything, can be done about it.

■ TEAM EFFECTIVENESS IN PRACTICE

The journey from theory to practical application can be a long and winding road – with many detours before reaching the final destination, but also with many opportunities for learning. The 15-year journey of Xerox's customer services organization toward empowered teams began with the success Japanese firms were enjoying in driving products up-market during the early 1980s. Japan's success was in traditional American strongholds such as the auto industry, steel, and copiers. Xerox's competitive benchmarking noted significant improvement by Japanese team-based organizations in customer satisfaction and productivity. To compete, Xerox Service needed to significantly increase responsiveness to its customers while reducing operating costs. An analysis using queuing theory showed that, relative to individual technicians with assigned customers, work groups of service technicians (small groups of four to seven task-interdependent people with shared responsibility for a set of customers) could improve response time to customer calls. Because response time is a major customer satisfier, the work groups' better response time had the potential to significantly improve customer satisfaction. We therefore undertook an intervention to change the structure, deployment, and management of Xerox's 13,000 US field service employees.

We initially developed a simple model for work teams based mainly on practical experience with successful groups. This model had the following key elements: (1) application of queuing theory to field service dispatch processes – that is, changing from a one-technician-per-customer model to groups of individuals sharing responsibility for a set of customers; (2) increased employee involvement in day-to-day decision making to meet customer requirements; (3) refocusing management on customer satisfaction and on supporting the work groups rather than coordinating individuals; and (4) inversion of the traditional management triangle (see figure 5.1).

Underlying this model was our belief that customer satisfaction was the most important outcome for the organization, and that the people closest to the customer know better than anyone else how to meet customer requirements. We defined management's role as supporting teams' needs and ensuring the consistent and competitive delivery of customer satisfaction.

Operationalizing our model required a full year of sustained effort. Specifically, the transition to teams involved the four key elements: (1) establishing a vision of where the organization was heading, and of how teams would know when that destination had been reached; (2) structuring teams of individuals with shared responsibilities;

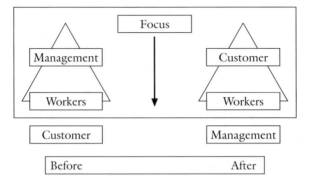

Figure 5.1   Inversion of traditional management triangle

(3) providing management and staff support in the form of education, training, communications, reward systems, and operating information; and (4) developing coaches who had expertise in the design, development, and deployment of teams. These elements closely parallel those described earlier in this chapter by Hackman and Wageman.

We now have implemented teams throughout the worldwide service community in over 35 countries, and these key elements prevail as the most important operational actions that must be taken by management. As simple as it may seem to implement these elements, each intervention has surfaced a new twist as we moved from theory to reality. In the following pages we describe the lessons we learned as we expanded our work group strategy globally. We describe our journey in the context of Hackman and Wageman's four conditions that foster team effectiveness: (1) clear, engaging direction; (2) enabling team structure; (3) supportive organizational context; and (4) available, expert coaching. Our journey had many unexpected turns, which sometimes required us to turn back and rethink our choices. As we gradually learned the lessons summarized below, however, we found ourselves able to act ever more effectively in creating team-based environments within Xerox customer services around the world.

Lessons about establishing clear and engaging direction

Most managers agree that teams need clear direction to function effectively. However, actually establishing direction can be difficult for many reasons. First, different managers appear to want different outcomes from teams. For example, service managers at Xerox communicated a wide range of reasons for why teams were being created. Outcomes included better territory coverage, reduction in the number of managers, additional learning, increased employee satisfaction, improved customer satisfaction, and lower costs. Although teams *can* achieve all of these things, stating them all as objectives can be confusing to employees and can result in competing goals.

When our "vital few" objectives for empowered teams became a list of 15 different items, each driven by a different layer of management, senior management had to take action to regain focus. Senior managers accomplished this by linking the work group strategy's key objectives to the service representatives' performance appraisals. These appraisals included four key elements: customer satisfaction; service cost (productivity); employee satisfaction; and quality process improvement. Appraisals were conducted at the work-group level to ensure that all team members were held jointly responsible for delivering business results. This approach helped to align the members of individual work groups around a common set of goals and objectives.

✳ *Lesson learned:* Senior management must understand that too many directions can result in no direction at all.

It is very difficult to align a large number of people to the same direction. How do you get 35 Vice Presidents of Customer Services Operations, over 100 Service Directors, 1,000 first-line managers, and 24,000 employees all buying into and acting upon the same general direction? On one occasion, the Vice President of Service for United States Operations communicated a vision and performance objectives for teams to 35 Service Directors as part of the "Managing for Results Process" (a policy deployment process within Xerox). The Service Directors then put their spin on this direction, based upon their local market environment, and communicated it to over 600 first-line managers. The first-line managers also modified the message based on the contexts of their local teams and their local performance targets, and communicated it to over 13,000 employees. This trickle-down method had the advantage of customizing the message and goals to specific local team environments. However, it also watered down the global organizational direction, resulting in several hundred teams moving in different directions that were at times in conflict with each other. One of our solutions to this problem was to split performance appraisals between "team level results" and "individual behaviors." By focusing all work groups on a common set of team-level metrics (specifically, customer satisfaction, response time, and expense management) senior management found an effective method to reinforce the group message. Goals and feedback about individual behaviors, on the other hand, provided some local flexibility in setting behavioral expectations.

✳ *Lesson learned:* Organizational direction often gets lost in the downward cascade.

Sent messages often are not the received messages. No matter how many times and in how many different formats one communicates direction, people tend to hear what they want to hear. The Canadian Service operation communicated its team vision and objectives for 1995 using multiple channels – videotapes, newsletters, general communication meetings, work group meetings, fliers in employees' paychecks, training courses, and one-on-one discussions. A follow-up survey several months later asked employees to state the direction in which the company was moving, and to explain why teams were a central part of that direction. Only 50 percent of the people could articulate the direction in words that closely resembled senior management's intended message. This result – despite the thoroughness of Canadian Service's communication program – raised the question of whether the problem with communicating clear direction was on the senders' side or the receivers' side.

Lesson learned: Direction cannot be over-communicated. Received messages must be constantly checked and the intended message reinforced.

Organizational direction changes rapidly in a dynamic business environment. Managers sometimes communicate the importance of empowerment one minute, and then dictate actions the next minute to accommodate changing business needs. For example, when launching empowered teams in a large European country, service representatives were told that being members of such teams would enable them to take on more decision-making authority and more responsibility for running their business. Three months after the launch of the teams, management froze all spending, travel, and new programs due to a downturn in sales and a devaluation of the country's currency. Many team members perceived these changes as a lack of commitment to real empowerment.

* *Lesson learned:* Rapidly changing business environments can undo efforts to maintain a clear, consistent direction.

Even senior managers can be uncertain about direction. While launching empowered teams in a South American country, the Service Director brought the Vice President of Operations to a meeting to address a group of first-line managers who had just completed team start-up training. Even though the Vice President had agreed to begin the team effort in his country, he still had lingering doubts regarding the amount of effort and change that would be required. On the drive to the meeting site, the Vice President told the Service Director, "I'm not sure that this team effort is best thing for the organization. We are under a lot of pressure for short-term results, and this could derail our performance this year." The Service Director pulled the car over in very heavy traffic and told the Vice President, "If you are going to talk this way to the managers, I am not taking you to the meeting. You will set the wrong direction from the start and we will never be successful in changing our people's behavior." After a long debate they continued on to the meeting. The Vice President listened to the first-line managers discuss what they had learned from the training. He was so impressed with their maturity and their commitment to the team strategy that he gave a highly motivating speech about how teams were critical to the future of the service business.

Lesson learned: Those responsible for articulating direction are themselves sometimes unsure what that direction should be. They "get it" in different ways, at different times, and from different sources. Exposure to successful teams, in particular, can reinforce managers' own commitment to the collective direction that they are supposed to be advocating.

Lessons about creating an enabling team structure

Most managers understand that teams must be designed properly in terms of size, skill mix, interdependence, and stability to ensure team effectiveness. However, they commonly encounter real world forces that compromise the implementation of these principles.

Team size

We found that determining the proper team size is a balancing act between having enough members to get the work done and few enough for effective coordination and decision making. Our experience suggested that teams of 10–12 people had excellent flexibility in back-up and coverage (improved call queuing times, reduced impact of vacations and absences), but that they struggled to make real-time consensus decisions. Moreover, large teams often developed so much internal conflict that members had to form mini-teams to get the team's work accomplished. As a member of a 12-person team told us, "In the two years that we were together, the only decision that we agreed to as a group was the need to break up and split into two smaller groups." Teams of four to seven people provided for us an optimal balance between the ability to back each other up and effective decision making and coordination.

Lesson learned: It is often tempting – but a mistake – to overemphasize the performance benefits of large teams and ignore their coordination costs.

Team skills

In an organization in which all members work in teams, composing a team requires a juggling act to balance skills within teams with the maintenance of performance across teams. Our managers often struggled between having several well-balanced work teams that required intensive coaching and having some high-performing teams rich with talent but others that required concentrated managerial time and attention. To cope with this dilemma, managers tried several different strategies. One was to break up a high-performing team and spread around the talent to several teams in the hope that cross-fertilization would result in several high-performing teams. Unfortunately, this approach often resulted in several poor- to average-performing teams. A second strategy was to concentrate all "low skill" people into one team where they could be tightly managed. A third was to create a dichotomy within each team of the skills and motivational levels of team members – in the hope that the good performers would mentor the low-performing employees. This strategy often resulted in the high performers ignoring other team members and working independently, poor performers expecting the good performers to pick up their work, and heated conflicts between the two subgroups.

We now coach managers to take a more differentiated view of "skill levels." Some service representatives deemed "low skill" may be technically deficient but superb as process facilitators. Teams need a range of skills, and managers who take that fact into account can create a balance and a diversity of talents in each of their teams.

Lesson learned: Creating a balance of technical skills across multiple teams can suboptimize the technical performance of some teams. But taking a differentiated view of skill levels in composing a team offers the opportunity to find useful and productive roles even for those individuals who are technically less than proficient.

Task design

Ensuring that a team has a high level of task interdependence is critical to its effectiveness. One way to increase task interdependence is to provide cross-training so that team members can back each other up. Cross-training helps teams to share responsibility for customers, engage in collective decision making, and even conduct effective meetings, since all members have similar knowledge. Service teams whose members were not cross-trained often wound up with a few people who had similar skill sets working closely together, another subset of people backing each other up, and one person serving as a generalist, "floating" around where needed. Such a configuration can be technically effective, but it undermines interdependence, close cooperation, and collective decision making. Managers often object to cross-training, however. They cite the high cost of training, the loss of productivity due to time away from work, the need for back-up to allow people to be trained, concerns about over-training people with skills that they seldom use, and the belief that training members to be generalists results in average skills in all areas, limited depth in any given skill, and reduced performance in unusual troubleshooting situations.

Lesson learned: Cross-training increases task interdependence, cooperation, and team effectiveness, but often is prohibitively expensive and resisted by line managers.

Team stability

Most of our managers now acknowledge that teams need to stay together to be effective. However, organizational pressures, such as discontinued products, outsourcing services to lower cost providers, retirements, and changing sales markets, still make it difficult to keep teams intact. In one European country, for example, managers sought to increase communication between the sales and service forces to better serve the needs of the customers. To realign the service representatives to specific sales market segments (such as schools, law offices, and banks), all teams were broken up and reorganized by markets. Service team members still were required to get back-up from their previous team members, however, because they had the requisite skills. The result of this mass team break-up was lost time in new team start-up, confusion, conflicting goals, time lost in travel, and lost productivity.

Lesson learned: Team stability is critical to team effectiveness, but market pressures, new strategies, and other competing goals can make team stability a low priority for managers.

Norm development

Operating norms and work processes are critical to team performance, but take time to develop, internalize, and enforce. At Xerox, we found that team success could be enhanced by creating start-up guides for new members, to help them become quickly acclimated to team expectations. For example, a team in Mexico called the "Fatboys" developed a videotape that showed a day in the life of a team member, illustrating through real day-to-day behavioral examples the team's values and expectations. The start-up guides, which generally address the team's mission, goals, norms, and work processes, often are borrowed from especially effective teams and then customized to fit with a given team's purposes and preferences.

Lesson learned: Teams can make good use of quick start-up tools to help establish norms and work processes.

Lessons about creating a supportive organizational context for teams

We believe that a systemic approach, in which all elements of the organizational context (for example, training, performance feedback, recognition and rewards, technology) are integrated, is critical in creating successful teams. For example, an organization's reward system should be tied to its objectives, and performance on those objectives monitored and tracked by a team-level information system. However, many barriers exist in aligning various organizational systems. The following section describes the lessons we learned as we sought to integrate team support structures at Xerox.

Team rewards

The key barriers to implementing team-based recognition and reward systems are two closely related factors: (1) generating sufficient funding for rewards that motivate employees; and (2) maintaining a balance between the organization's goals and outcomes that teams themselves can achieve. Most recognition and reward programs in Xerox are now under the control of the local units, which was not the case when work teams were first implemented. The decentralization of reward system design means that local organizations must use their own budgets and profits to fund reward and recognition programs, and local managers are appropriately concerned about the return on their investment in rewards to overall business unit results. When they put money on the table, local management's biggest worries are about the political consequences of paying out large sums of money to a few high-performing teams if the performance of the overall organization is poor. The majority of programs end up being one of three types: (1) open-ended programs in which multiple teams can win, but the payouts are so small that they do not motivate team members; (2) closed-ended programs in which only the "top teams" can earn large prizes, which motivate only a small percentage of the teams; or (3) gainsharing-like programs that combine team-level performance measures with organization-level performance thresholds. With these programs, there often is little that teams can do to achieve the organization-level targets, or the programs are so complex that team members cannot figure out what behaviors will generate a payout.

Still, some managers have recognized the motivational leverage that well-designed team reward systems can provide and have found ways to create systems that avoid the pitfalls described above. For example, one location in the Midwest has a gain-sharing system with clear links to team- and organization-level performance, and exceptional payouts for both over-achievement of targets and for significant performance improvements. The best programs tend to be open-ended, clearly focused on team rather than individual outcomes, generous in payout size, and reinforcing of both high-level performance and continuous improvement. In a decentralized organization such as Xerox, it is essential that technical expertise in developing effective reward and recognition programs exist at the local level, and developing such expertise also is a significant implementation challenge.

Lesson learned: It is difficult to implement a high-quality team-based reward and recognition system. Local managers may need help devising open-ended programs that tie rewards to team-level performance, provide meaningful payouts, and reinforce both superb performance and continuous improvement.

Training

The major barrier to providing adequate training for teams is time. It takes time for people to gain new knowledge and skill, and that disrupts day-to-day workflows. In addition, downsizing at Xerox over the last five years has resulted in more being asked of fewer people, which has limited the time available for "off-the-street" activities. To address the time problem, a large proportion of Xerox Service training is now computer-based, self-administered training that employees are expected to complete when customer call rates are low or on their personal time. On-the-job training is also becoming the norm, with experienced employees training other employees during the natural course of work.

Another barrier to providing adequate training is anticipating what specific skills will be needed in the future and how many people will need these skills. The skyrocketing cost of training makes over-training a very costly mistake for an organization. Moreover, if employees are not able to apply these skills right away, they often lose them. In the United States, employee training by "inoculation" was the initial approach. People were brought into a room for several days and told everything they needed to know about being teams. This approach was not very successful, since much of the learning was lost because team members had no real experience working together. In Brazil, by contrast, senior management formed intact groups and broke the training into four-hour modules that were delivered over an eight- to ten-week period. This approach allowed work groups to learn specific skills, such as developing team decision processes, and then go out and immediately apply those skills in their work environments.

Lesson learned: Training intact teams is crucial, with learning experiences spread out over several weeks or months to enable the teams to apply their newly learned skills.

Information systems

Information systems that provide teams with real-time information are essential, but it takes a great deal of time to develop and maintain these systems. Xerox teams too often were asked to take responsibility for business decisions without having access to the real-time data that were needed to evaluate alternative courses of action. We are now on our third team-based information system in the last five years. The current system supplies teams with all relevant performance metrics and provides access to detailed data about each of those metrics. However, even this system needs to be constantly updated and modified as organizational priorities and goals change. Local teams and managers must monitor and maintain, and not merely use, their organizational information systems.

Lesson learned: Team-level performance information systems are critical. These systems can never be started too soon, and they must be constantly assessed and modified as teams' objectives and priorities change.

Even with the best team-based information systems, poor-performing teams that could benefit most from data-based problem-solving often do not have the time to do so. A frequently heard story from members of poor-performing teams is that they do not have the time to conduct meetings or to use problem-solving processes because they can barely keep up with their daily workload. This kind of thinking often leads teams into downward performance spirals because they never take the time to change the work processes that are undermining their performance.

Lesson learned: Teams must take time to actually *use* information systems in solving problems and refining work processes.

Lessons about providing expert coaching

Teams – especially new teams – need expert coaching. Yet we found that managers who had been assigned coaching responsibilities often did not themselves have experience working in teams, and therefore were not viewed as knowledgeable and credible coaches by team members. Moreover, reductions in the number of managers sometimes resulted in spans of control that were too large to allow managers to engage in extensive coaching. Two stories highlight these points.

When we began creating teams in the United States, initial training, support, and attention were concentrated on the front-line team members. Their managers were not formed into teams and most had limited experience working with teams. As the work teams developed, the managers were left far behind. Team members would come to managers with team-related problems that the managers could not help resolve. Eventually, mature teams stopped going to their managers for support and the managers then struggled to develop the poor-performing teams without access to the team practices that had been developed by the high-functioning teams. Much later, in Brazil, the opposite approach was taken. Managers were formed into teams four to six months before employee work teams were created, which provided managers ample opportunity for learning and development before they began working with front-line teams. Work teams in Brazil benefited greatly from the experience and learning of these management teams.

Lesson learned: Allowing managers to experience working in teams themselves before asking them to work with other teams increases their coaching capabilities.

Many team-based organizations seek to reduce management costs and increase spans of control by pushing decision-making authority down to front-line teams. However, this approach can go too far, such as when so many managers are removed that those remaining have insufficient time to work with their teams. In Canada, management increased the span of control from approximately 15:1 to 50:1 over a two-year period. The result was a decrease in employee satisfaction, customer satisfaction, and business results. By contrast, the span of control in Brazil was gradually increased from 12:1 to approximately 20:1 over a one-year period. As their span of control increased, managers realized that they had no choice but to change the focus of their coaching activities from individuals to teams as intact units. With the benefit of this team-focused coaching, teams in Brazil eventually generated significant improvements in employee satisfaction, in customer satisfaction, and in business results.

Lesson learned: Managers *can* be encouraged to manage teams rather than individuals by increasing their spans of control, but this process can go too far. The ideal span of control is three to four teams, depending on the teams' level of maturity and performance effectiveness.

Summary

We have described here a few of the lessons we learned from Xerox's 15-year journey in developing empowered work teams. In the words of the late musician Jerry Garcia: "What a long strange trip it's been." The concepts about team effectiveness that Hackman and Wageman discuss in the theoretical section of this chapter closely parallel those that we encountered in our work with service teams at Xerox. Understanding those concepts, however, was but the first step toward implementing them. There were structures, systems, habits, attitudes, assumptions, and emotions that we also needed to understand, act on, and learn from in the process of turning the concepts into reality. We made mistakes, we constantly revised our course of action, and occasionally we were lucky.

Today, we continue to make mistakes, and to learn, as we address new obstacles brought by new developments in the technological, cultural, market, and organizational contexts. Especially challenging these days is finding ways to maintain teams in a constantly changing organizational structure that requires flexible and fluid teams with rotating and evolving team membership. This kind of organizational design does not allow for team stability and may call into question several of the key lessons we learned. It will be interesting to see how well the theoretical and experiential lessons we have learned so far will hold up as we take teams into this new environment.

REFERENCES

Alderfer, C. P. 1977: Group and intergroup relations. In J. R. Hackman and J. L. Suttle (eds.), *Improving life at work*, Santa Monica, CA: Goodyear.

Argyris, C. 1985: *Strategy, change and defensive routines*, Boston: Pitman.

Argyris, C. 1993: *Knowledge for action*, San Francisco: Jossey-Bass.

Atkinson, J. W. 1958: Towards experimental analysis of human motivation in terms of motives, expectancies, and incentives. In J. W. Atkinson (ed.), *Motives in fantasy, action, and society*, Princeton: Van Nostrand.

Bettenhausen, K., and Murnighan, J. K. 1985: The emergence of norms in competitive decision-making groups. *Administrative Science Quarterly*, 30, 350–72.

Corn, R. I. 1998: The influence of treatment style and gender on occupational misconduct. Unpublished manuscript, Department of Psychology, Harvard University.

Gersick, C. J. G. 1988: Time and transition in work teams: Toward a new model of group development. *Academy of Management Journal*, 31, 9–41.

Gersick, C. J. G., and Hackman, J. R. 1990: Habitual routines in task-performing teams. *Organizational Behavior and Human Decision Processes*, 47, 65–97.

Hackman, J. R. 1985: Doing research that makes a difference. In E. E. Lawler, A. M. Mohrman, S. A. Mohrman, G. E. Ledford, and T. G. Cummings (eds.), *Doing research that is useful for theory and practice*, San Francisco: Jossey-Bass.

Hackman, J. R. 1986: The psychology of self-management in organizations. In M. S. Pallak and R. O. Perloff (eds.), *Psychology and work: Productivity, change, and employment*, Washington, DC: American Psychological Association.

Hackman, J. R., and Morris, C. G. 1975: Group tasks, group interaction process, and group performance effectiveness: A review and proposed integration. In L. Berkowitz (ed.), *Advances in experimental social psychology*, Vol. 9, New York: Academic Press.

Hackman, J. R., and Oldham, G. R. 1980: *Work redesign*, Reading, MA: Addison-Wesley.

Hackman, J. R., and Wageman, R. 1999: Toward a theory of team coaching. Unpublished manuscript, Department of Psychology, Harvard University.

Hare, A. P. 1976: *Handbook of small group research*, 2nd edn., New York: Free Press.

Kerr, S. 1975: On the folly of rewarding A while hoping for B. *Academy of Management Journal*, 18, 769–83.

McGrath, J. E., and Altman, I. 1966: *Small group research: A synthesis and critique of the field*, New York: Holt.

Pfeffer, J., and Sutton, R. I. 1999: *Turning knowledge into action: The organizational knowing-doing problem*, Boston: Harvard Business School Press.

Slovic, P. 1981: Toward understanding and improving decisions. In E. A. Fleishman (ed.), *Human performance and productivity*, Hillsdale, NJ: Erlbaum.

Steiner, I. D. 1972: *Group process and productivity*, New York: Academic Press.

Wageman, R. 1999: How leaders foster self-managing team effectiveness: Design choices versus hands-on coaching. Unpublished manuscript, Graduate School of Business, Columbia University.

chapter **6**

THEORY AND PRACTICE OF LEADERSHIP: INTO THE NEW MILLENNIUM

RAM N. ADITYA, ROBERT J. HOUSE, AND STEVEN KERR

▨ INTRODUCTION

In the approximately seven decades that leadership has been addressed as a topic of study, much water has flowed under the bridge. Numerous theories of leadership have been developed, some of which have passed into oblivion while others have survived the tides of scientific inquiry. However, as Bass (1990) has noted, the practice of leadership dates back in history well before its evolution as a field of study. In this chapter we explore the theoretical developments in leadership, the cumulative knowledge they have generated, and the questions they have left un-answered with regard to the practice of leadership. We also look at leadership as it is enacted in industry, the problems it presents for scientific investigation, and the interface between theory and practice that defines our current state of knowledge about the leadership phenomenon. Broadly, the first part of the chapter sets out the theoretical models, and the second part brings comments on these theories from a practitioner's perspective. Because the two sections approach the issue of leadership from different professions, no attempt has been made to ensure consistency in the narrative across sections: we believe the value of the chapter is realized in the differences, wherever they arise, between the academic approach and the practical viewpoint expressed in the refreshingly candid but expert comments.

A classification of the over 3,000 studies listed by Bass (1990) would actually yield no more than a handful of basic models. Most of these address primarily the leader–follower relationship in isolation, neglecting the environment external to this relationship that includes the organizational and societal cultures in which the leaders function, the powers-that-be to whom leaders themselves have to report, and situational factors that influence the leader–follower relationship. In fact, it may be argued that the early theories were not really theories of leadership, but rather theories of supervision or, at best, theories of management. However, we review these as they formed the foundations of leadership research in organizational behavior.

■ TRAIT THEORIES: LEADERSHIP AS LEADER

The initial studies of leadership, starting from the 1930s and going into the 1950s, treated leadership and leader as synonymous. With no theoretical foundations on which to base ideas, early investigators focused on the personality and physical characteristics of leaders: appearance, energy level, height, and gender on the physical side; and authoritarianism, intelligence, need for achievement, and need for power on the psychological side. Individual studies produced large effect sizes (in the order of $r = 0.50$) but failed to replicate. Several scholars have reviewed the literature on empirical studies of leadership traits (for example, Gibb, 1947; Jenkins, 1947; Stogdill, 1948). The overall consensus that emerged from these reviews was that this was not a promising track of inquiry, and the concept of universal traits was not useful in explaining leadership.

As we shall see later, the failure of these theories to produce empirical replications was not so much due to the inappropriateness of the constructs as unreliability of measurement. Personality traits were themselves in an early stage of theoretical evolution. Measurement theory was also in its infancy. Different studies operationalized personality traits differently, and psychometric properties were not established. Furthermore, empirical studies were mostly based on student and adolescent samples, or else on organizational employees and supervisors at lower organizational levels rather than people in prominently leading positions. Whatever the causes of failure, in the midst of this pessimism about leadership traits, Stogdill (1948) held that rather than discarding the trait idea altogether, it might be fruitful to consider the interaction of personality attributes with environmental factors.

It was unfortunate for leadership research that Stogdill was interpreted as recommending the abandoning of traits altogether whereas he actually recommended studying traits in interaction with situational variables. This misinterpretation persisted well into the 1960s, and was to have a profound influence on the course of developments in leadership theory. It focused attention on the search for other influential variables while fostering almost complete abandonment of the notion of personal traits as explanatory factors.

■ THE BEHAVIORAL SCHOOL

With the horizon looking bleak for leadership traits, scholars turned to the idea of leader behavior as a viable alternative. Optimism in this arena was fueled by the reasoning that, unlike the personality variables, leader behaviors were directly observable; therefore, if there were universally effective leader behaviors, it should be possible to discover these by either observing leaders in action in a laboratory setting, or by asking subordinates about the behavior of their immediate superiors. Three influential programs of research developed at Harvard, Ohio State University and the University of Michigan over the next three decades, and collectively came to be known as the behavioral school of leadership. Bales and his associates at Harvard uncovered, through laboratory studies, three classes of leader behavior central to leader effectiveness: person-oriented behaviors; task-oriented behaviors; and individual prominence inducing behaviors (Bales, 1954). Factor analytic studies conducted by Stogdill and his associates (for example, Stogdill and Coons, 1957) at the Ohio State University and interviews conducted by members of the Institute for Social Research at the University of Michigan (for example, Kahn and Katz, 1953; Likert, 1961; Mann, 1965) supported the influence of person-oriented and task-oriented behaviors. Behaviors relating to individual prominence did not get much attention from these studies, and disappeared from the literature. The person- and task-oriented behaviors that drew most attention were the factor-analyzed constructs of *consideration* and *initiating structure*, so labeled by the researchers at the Ohio State University.[1] Consideration (C) referred to leader behaviors that were aimed at maintaining close social relationships with subordinates. Initiating structure (IS) referred to leader behaviors aimed at creating a structured working environment in which role ambiguity and conflict could be minimized. However, the relationship between these leader behaviors and subordinates' satisfaction or other criteria of managerial effectiveness did not prove to be stable across studies (House, 1971; Larson et al., 1974). Like the research on traits, the studies were conducted primarily on student samples in the laboratory, or were based on field observations of lower level supervisors and managers rather than on leaders at high levels. Of course, an argument could be made that these were really studies of management, not leadership – that distinction was to crystallize in the literature only much later, with the work of such scholars as Zaleznik (1977). In any case, there were other shortcomings of the behavioral studies that stemmed from methodological considerations. Measures of leader behavior were often obtained through questionnaires that asked for respondents' recall of their superiors' behavior. The leadership constructs of Initiating Structure and Consideration originally labeled and advanced by the Ohio State team were measured through several different scales that were created in the 1950s under the same labels. These various instruments were subsequently shown to measure substantially different specific leader behaviors. It is not surprising that these scales produced different correlations, in some cases even opposite in direction, with measures of leader effectiveness (Schriesheim et al., 1976). In any case, attention now shifted to situational factors that could moderate the relationship between leader behaviors and effectiveness.

▪ CONTINGENCY THEORIES

The 1970s brought refinements in systematic treatment of the leadership phenomenon. Finding personal dispositions and behaviors inadequate, scholars invoked context and leader–follower relationships to explain leadership effectiveness. Such models came to be referred to as 'contingency' models or theories of leadership, following Fiedler's (1967, 1971) introduction of contingency theory.

Contingency theory

Fiedler's theory addressed the relationship between leadership style and group performance (also taken as leader effectiveness) under the moderating influence of situational favorableness. Leadership style was measured by a scale that asked respondents to rate their least preferred co-worker (LPC) on 16 to 24 different attributes such as friendliness and cooperativeness. High scores anchored the positive side of each attribute. The resulting "LPC" score was taken as representing the extent to which a leader was motivated by consideration of tasks (low LPC score) as opposed to consideration of relationships with followers (high LPC score). Fiedler (1971, p. 129) cautioned against this rather simplistic interpretation of the LPC score, noting that the above interpretation was only valid in stressful situations. He further noted evidence that the LPC score may be associated with cognitive complexity, with high LPC leaders tending to be more complex in their thinking about groups.

The construct that moderates the relationship between LPC scores and group performance (in other words, between leadership style and effectiveness) is termed situational favorableness.[2] This construct has three dimensions: the extent to which the situation is conducive to the leader's use of power and influence; the extent to which the task is structured; and the quality of relations between leader and followers. To the extent that the leader is in a position to use influence, has good relations with subordinates, and has a structured task, the situational favorableness is said to be high. Conceptualizing each of the three component dimensions as dichotomous variables produces $2 \times 2 \times 2 = 8$ levels of situational favorableness, visualized in three dimensions as eight octants. The contingency model addresses the question of which leadership style might be best suited to various types of situations. Specifically, it states that task-oriented (low LPC) leaders will be more effective in very favorable or very unfavorable situations, while relationship-oriented (high LPC) leaders will be more effective in moderate situations.

The contingency model has been criticized for conceptual reasons (Schriesheim and Kerr, 1977).[3] Earlier, Ashour (1973) had noted that the empirical findings are inconsistent and do not account for much of the variance in group performance.[4] However, in two separate meta-analyses of empirical findings, Peters et al. (1985) and Strube and Garcia (1981) concluded that there was substantial support for certain aspects of Fiedler's model.[5]

Strube and Garcia found overall support for the Contingency Theory based on 33 tests that were used by Fiedler (1967) to develop the model and 145 subsequent tests of the validity of the model. Controlling for the possibility that this support might arise predominantly from the studies conducted by Fiedler and his associates, Strube and Garcia tested and established that the model was equally well supported by studies in which Fiedler and his associates were not involved. However, the meta-analysis failed to support some of the octant-specific predictions.

Peters et al. (1985) meta-analyzed the empirical data relevant to the Contingency Theory using data from studies based on within-octant interacting groups. They found that laboratory studies showed overall support for the model with the exception of one octant, and that field studies fell short of supporting the overall model and predictions for five of the eight octants. The combination of inconsistent findings, frequent lack of support for hypothesized results, and inadequate accounting for variance in the dependent variables proved unsatisfactory to many, and the search for a better theory continued.

Path–goal theory

Another theoretical development formulated in an attempt to reconcile the inconsistencies observed in task and person-oriented leader behavior was the path–goal theory (House, 1971; House and Mitchell, 1974). Path–goal theory specifies the interaction of four leader behaviors (initiating structure, consideration, participative behaviors, and achievement-oriented behaviors[6]), a number of situational moderators (task structure, role ambiguity, job autonomy, job scope, task interdependence), follower traits (dependence, authoritarianism, ability, locus of control), and other variables (follower expectancies, valences, and path instrumentalities) in explaining two measures of leader effectivness: follower satisfaction and follower performance.

Wofford and Liska (1993) meta-analyzed some 120 tests of various hypotheses generated by the path–goal theory. Their analyses indicated support for 12 of the 26 hypotheses relevant to the theory. Interestingly, all four of their hypotheses regarding differences in measuring instruments used for leader behaviors were supported, indicating the sensitivity of statistical results to the measuring instruments used.[7] The implication was that the choice of measuring instrument determined the support found for the theory. Additionally, several scholars note that the complexity of the model and the resulting profusion of hypotheses make the existing studies inadequate for testing the model overall (Evans, 1996; Schriesheim and Nieder, 1996; Yukl, 1993). As in the case of contingency theory, the combination of inconsistent findings, frequent lack of support for hypothesized results, and inadequate explanatory power of the theoretical model caused dissatisfaction with the path–goal theory and a continued search for a better explanation.

In a later refinement of the model, House (1996) recognized a boundary condition for the path–goal theory: the assumption of rationality in follower cognition. Specifically, followers must be confident and accurate in their estimates of probabilities associated with goal accomplishment and with the receipt of extrinsic rewards contingent on performance. Both uncertainty and stress would influence these estimates, and would serve to invalidate the model.

Decision process model

Vroom and Yetton (1973) proposed a decision model based on contingency variables that could be used by leaders to make organizational decisions. The model is seen as an aid to determining economically and technically sound solutions to problems. The potential level of acceptance of the solution by the subordinates is an important influence on the successful implementation of the solution.

The model is operationalized in the form of a decision tree. The decision rules, recast as seven questions answered sequentially, are designed to help managers determine appropriate decision processes. In order, they are: (1) Is decision quality (that is, economic and technical appropriateness) an issue for consideration?; (2) Is there sufficient information for a high-quality decision?; (3) Is the problem structured?; (4) Is subordinate acceptance of the decision crucial to effective implementation?;

(5) If the decision were to be taken by the leader alone, is there reasonable certainty that the subordinates will accept it?; (6) Are the organizational goals relevant to the problem shared by subordinates?; and (7) Is the solution likely to lead to conflict among subordinates? The path from statement of the problem to the decision mode is in the form of a decision tree, and the answers to the questions determine the route to a "feasible set" of decision modes. Fourteen possible feasible sets are specified, referred to as *problem types* by Vroom and Yetton (1973). The feasible sets include between one and five types of decisions.

The model describes seven decision-making methods that are believed to have different outcomes under different situations. These methods range from autocratic through democratic decision processes. Five methods are relevant to *group* decision making, and include two authoritarian processes (denoted AI and AII); two consultative processes: consultation with subordinates individually (CI) and consultation with subordinates as a group (CII); and a group process of joint decision making (GII). Of these, three (AI, AII and CI) are also relevant to *individual* decision making, as are two additional methods: GI, joint decision making by superior and subordinate, and DI, delegation of the decision.

Further, Vroom and Yetton list seven problem attributes indicated by prior research to be relevant to decision making. The combination of five decision processes, seven problem attributes, and seven decision rules constitutes the variables in the original normative theory. A series of relationships among these variables represented by Boolean algebraic equations make up the theory.

Partial support for the model comes from a few empirical studies. In one study, Margerison and Glube (1979) asked 47 owner-operators of cleaning franchises in the USA and Canada to respond to vignettes of problems presented to them by indicating the decision processes they would use to solve the problems. Respondents who conformed most closely to the Vroom–Yetton model were found to have more profitable operations and more satisfied employees. Four other studies (Bhohnisch et al., 1987; Tjosvold et al., 1986; Vroom and Jago, 1988; Zimmer, 1978) involved field observation of decision processes. Managers were asked to recall past problems, various problem attributes, and decision outcomes. The median proportion of successful decisions reported in the four studies was 67 percent of all decisions by managers whose decision processes were consistent with the model's prescriptions, and 33 percent for managers who used decision processes inconsistent with that suggested by the theory. These figures imply that managers can double the success rate of their decisions by following the prescriptions of the model.[8]

Field (1982) examined the theory in a laboratory setting using a sample of 276 business school students formed into groups to solve experimentally manipulated problems. Field found that only four of the seven rules had the predicted effect. Specifically, decisions made through processes consistent with the model (that is, within the feasible set) had a higher effectiveness rating than decisions made outside the feasible set, but the effect size was small (Cohen's $d = 0.30$). Stated differently, 49 percent of decisions made by processes in the feasible set and 34 percent of those by processes outside the feasible set were effective. However, after controlling for group membership and problem difficulty, decision processes were found to account for only 2 percent of the variance in decision effectiveness.

In another laboratory study, reported in Vroom and Jago (1988, p. 80), it was found that 54 percent of effective decisions were in the feasible set, and 29 percent were outside the feasible set. These figures, however, are not corrected for group differences and problem difficulty and, in view of Field's (1982) finding, may greatly overestimate the effect of decision processes on decision effectiveness.

Overall, the decision process theory is supported better in field studies than in laboratory studies. It may be argued that the laboratory studies were limited in that they offered no real consequence to the participants. This would serve to make the experimental manipulation of goal congruence or the need for subordinate acceptance less effective. On the other hand, the field study results suffer from at least three confounds that tend to yield overestimation of effects. First, there is the bias from correlated observations, as all the variables involved had been measured using reports from the same managers in the sample. Secondly, the effects observed in the field studies were not corrected for the effects of other moderating variables, such as leader and follower stress levels, problem difficulty, or leader and follower intelligence and experience. These variables, when controlled for, had resulted in a substantial reduction in the effect of decision processes on effectiveness in other studies (for example, Fiedler and Garcia, 1987; Field, 1982). Finally, the field studies used managers' self-reports. Self-report data have been shown in prior research to differ from data based on direct observations (Bass, 1957; Besco and Lawshe, 1959; Campbell, 1956; and Graham and Gleno, 1970). Given the fact that (1) the Vroom–Yetton theory is a highly rational theory, and (2) managers in the field studies can be expected to present themselves as highly rational, a strong rationality bias based on social desirability may be expected in the results, tending to overestimate the effects. The validity of this argument has been demonstrated in a subsequent study by Field and House (1990), in which responses were solicited from both decision makers and subordinates. While the data from the managers supported the model, those obtained from the subordinates did not. The opposing results were primarily due to differences in ratings of decision effectiveness and ratings of the acceptance requirement by subordinates. Subordinates generally rated decisions as less effective and having higher acceptance requirements than did the decision makers (managers).

Heilman et al. (1984) demonstrated the same phenomenon in a laboratory setting. Subjects were assigned to subordinate and manager roles. Subordinates' ratings of decision effectiveness disconfirmed the model, while managers' ratings tended to confirm it. Similar results were obtained for ratings of subordinate commitment.

A decade and a half after its initial formulation, the decision process theory was modified (Vroom and Jago, 1988) by adding a number of problem attributes and decision rules as well as a new criterion variable called "overall effectiveness." The effectiveness variable was composed of decision quality, decision commitment (which replaced decision acceptance) and two additional criteria of decision effectiveness: (1) the effect of the decision process on subordinate development; and (2) decision costs, measured by the time available to make the decision. The decision criteria in the modified theory were expressed as mathematical functions of decision process and problem attributes.

The reformulated theory has 12 problem attributes, 12 decision rules and eight problem types, each representing one of the eight combinations of individual and group decision outcome criteria: decision quality; decision commitment; minimum time required; and maximum subordinate development. There is one normative model (that is, one set of questions) for each decision criterion. Thus, the number of possible combinations of problem attributes, desired criteria and decision rules is very large, an aspect that makes practical application unwieldy. Therefore, the models have been computerized into a kind of "expert" system.

The validity of two of the models (the decision quality and decision acceptance models) has been assessed in a study by Jago et al. (1985; reported in Vroom and Jago, 1988, p. 179). In this study, the investigators obtained correlation coefficients between the predictions of the models and the actual outcomes resulting from 80 decisions as follows: 0.38 for decision quality, 0.84 for subordinate's commitment, and 0.68 for decision effectiveness (quality multiplied by acceptance). These results indicate strong support for parts of the model. However, their study employed no controls for group differences or problem difficulty; therefore, in view of Field's (1982) observations stated earlier, it is likely that their obtained results overestimate support for the model.

In sum, it appears that the decision process theory is yet to be empirically demonstrated through rigorous research, and many of the early criticisms of it still hold. Field (1979) had observed that: (1) the theory assumes congruence between the decision makers' goals and organizational goals; (2) assuming it is valid, its application still requires training, limiting its scope to those who can afford the time and expense; (3) the theory ignores other skills required for participative/democratic decision styles; and (4) the model is excessively complex.[9]

While the computerization of the reformulated model addresses the second limitation listed above, the complexity of the model, making it untestable, remains an issue. There is a need to simplify the model. Especially since it forms the basis for a commercialized training program, empirical substantiation of the models' predictions is desirable. Field suggests that a model with four situation attributes instead of seven, and two decision processes rather than five will equally protect decision quality and acceptance. His model is summarized briefly in the following set of decision rules, using terms found in Vroom and Jago (1988):

> If acceptance of the decision by subordinates is critical to effective implementation and it is not reasonably certain that subordinates would accept an autocratic decision, but they share organizational goals (or decision quality is not important) use GII; otherwise, use CII.

While lauding the parsimony of this simplified model, we would draw attention to certain results from investigations of other theories that might enhance the decision process model. Findings by Fiedler and Garcia (1987) in testing their cognitive resource theory, described further on, suggest that leader/follower stress, intelligence and experience significantly influence decision effectiveness. It may be worthwhile to study the roles of these variables in the decision process model.

Situational leadership theory

Hersey and Blanchard (1982) developed a situational theory of leadership involving four leadership styles: telling, selling, participating, and delegating. The variable that is believed to determine the appropriateness of one or another style of leadership is the subordinates' "maturity" level, or "the degree to which followers are ready and willing to tackle the task facing the group." According to Hersey and Blanchard, just as the parent gradually relinquishes control of the child as it matures, managers would move from a "telling" to a "delegating" style as the followers "mature." This model has a high degree of face validity and is the foundation for a commercial management training program sold by Hersey and Blanchard. To our knowledge, there have been few empirical tests of the theory. Vecchio (1987) found in one empirical investigation involving 303 teachers in high schools that the theoretical predictions are supported mainly for recent employees, who needed and appreciated task structuring from their leader. Another study by Pascarella and Lunenburg (1988) purported to test the situational leadership theory using elementary school principals from two school districts, but actually only tested the effectiveness of the training program based on the model. The authors found neither a significant increase in leader effectiveness following the training period, nor any increase in the range of leadership styles. In the absence of variation in the independent variable (leadership style range) there is no test of the theory of leadership, only of training effectiveness. However, given the practical implications of the theory, especially in light of Vecchio's (1987) findings, and the fact that it is the foundation of a commercially distributed training program, it seems to us that it is professionally incumbent on the authors to provide evidence relevant to the validity of the model.

It is noteworthy that Hersey and Blanchard's theory, although proposed as a situational theory of leadership, really addresses a core aspect of dyadic relationships between leaders and followers. An implication of this theory is that, due to expected individual differences in "maturity" level of followers, different leader behaviors are called for with each subordinate.

Cognitive resource theory

Fiedler's investigations into the interplay between dispositional and situational factors in the search for a better understanding of leadership led to the formulation of the cognitive resource theory (CRT) of leadership (Fiedler and Garcia, 1987; Fiedler, 1995). One of the most important findings of Fiedler and his associates is that, under low stress, intelligence is positively correlated, and experience negatively correlated, with performance. In contrast, under high stress intelligence is negatively correlated with performance, and experience positively correlated. In other terms, under conditions of high job- or boss-related stress, intelligent leaders perform worse than less intelligent but more experienced people. These findings are interesting in their counter-intuitive implications. However, they are empirically supported through field and laboratory studies (Fiedler, 1995).

Fiedler (1996, p. 247) states that:

"An oversimplified explanation of this interference effect is that we cannot think logically and analytically while at the same time reacting to emergencies and stress on the basis of over-learned previous knowledge and behavior, i.e., experience. Nor can a team carefully consider all the options and alternatives to solving a problem when their highly experienced leader tells them that 'we have gone over all of these arguments before and don't need still another study.'"

Other scholars, too, have noted the influencing qualities of stress. Simon (1987) has described stress as the "enemy of rationality." It is believed to narrow one's focus of attention and search for alternatives, to cause rigidity (Staw et al., 1981), and to lead to authoritarian decision making, as well as increasing desire for and dependence on authoritarian leaders (Sales, 1972).

It is well acknowledged that both participative and authoritarian leadership styles can be effective depending on the circumstances. A central question in leadership research involves the conditions under which one or the other style is more effective. Much research has gone into this issue (Tannenbaum and Schmidt, 1973; Vroom and Yetton, 1973; see also Filley et al., 1976, and Vroom and Jago, 1988, for reviews). Cognitive resource theory provides one answer. It suggests that, in general, authoritarian leadership will be more effective than participative leadership when leader–subordinate relationships are poor, but leaders have control over the followers' behavior; participative leadership works better when relationships are good but leaders do not have control over their subordinates' behavior. However, in the first case, under conditions of stress, leaders would do better to rely on their experience rather than their intelligence, whereas under relatively stress-free conditions they may do better to use their intelligence. In the second case (for participative leadership style) a similar argument can be made, but primarily with regard to intelligence and experience of the follower group rather than that of the leader. Of course, when both follower–leader relations are poor and the leader has no control over the followers, neither style of leadership is likely to be effective.

Fiedler (1996, p. 248), on the basis of the cognitive resource theory, recommends a two-pronged strategy to develop good leaders. The first is to recruit individuals with required intellectual abilities, experience, and job-relevant knowledge. The second is to provide working environments that allow leaders to make effective use of the cognitive resources for which they were hired. In one study, Fiedler (1996) found that a stress reduction program improved the scores of officer candidates on an in-basket management simulation task that required intelligence rather than experience for effective performance.

The cognitive resource theory has occupational ramifications as well. Some occupations, such as those of fighter pilots and firefighters, are inherently stressful. For such occupations, over-learning is recommended. On the other hand, certain other occupations draw heavily on intelligence, such as research and development, or software development. For these occupations, where reliance on past experience may prove to be suboptimal, stress reduction measures are likely to enhance performance.

The revised path–goal theory

While the cognitive resource theory was the outcome of efforts by Fiedler to improve on his contingency theory of leadership,[10] the original path–goal theory was revised by House in 1996 to specify boundary conditions, in terms of situational contingencies, for specific hypotheses concerning eight classes of leader behaviors and their relationship to work unit effectiveness (House, 1996). The tenets of the 1996 path–goal theory, while based on empirical findings from all extant theories, are yet to be empirically tested in their revised form.

■ REVIVAL OF TRAIT THEORIES: NEW AND IMPROVED

Lessons from the past

In the early 1970s, interest in leadership traits re-emerged due to substantial advancements in theory and measurement of personality. At the same time, scholars drew attention to hitherto unrecognized yield from early trait research. House and Baetz (1979), for instance, pointed out that when studies of adolescents and children were omitted from Stogdill's (1948) review, the results showed a rather consistent set of relationships between some traits, followers' perceptions and indicators of leadership, with many correlations ranging from 0.40 to 0.50. The traits identified by House and Baetz were intelligence, prosocial assertiveness (or dominance, as measured by the California Personality Inventory), self-confidence, energy-activity, and task-relevant knowledge.

Stogdill (1974), updating his 1948 review of the trait literature in the light of studies conducted between 1949 and 1970, concluded that he had undermined the universality of certain traits in leadership. Lord et al. (1986) conducted a meta-analysis of 35 of the early studies dealing with six leader traits. Focusing on follower perceptions rather than the leaders themselves, they found that intelligence, dominance, masculinity and, to some extent, adjustment, were all perceived as important characteristics of leaders.

Critics of trait theories argue that traits must be stable, and that they must predict behavior over the long term in a variety of situations (Davis-Blake and Pfeffer, 1988). Schneider (1983) has observed that many traits manifest themselves primarily in those situations that provide arousal for those traits. Thus, the difference in behavior between aggressive individuals and passive individuals is likely to be witnessed only in aggression-provoking situations. House et al. (1996) have observed that individual dispositions may be stable over extended periods of time but not necessarily for life. Traits may predict behavior only in the short term, but in leadership, even short-term behavior often has long-term consequences.

Mischel (1973) has introduced a contingency into the trait models, suggesting that the environment determines the extent to which individual dispositions influence behavior. He makes a distinction between "strong" and "weak" situations. Strong situations are those in which there are norms, with incentive and disincentive systems in place to guide behavior. In highly formalized organizations there is less opportunity for free expression of dispositional tendencies, while informal work environments allow more flexibility. Mischel's argument has been supported in one laboratory study (Monson et al., 1982), and two field studies (Barrick and Mount, 1993; Lee et al., 1990).

These findings, while showing that the study of leader traits has considerable promise, provide no explanation for the associations between the traits and leader effectiveness. A number of newly sprung theories seek to do just that.

Achievement motivation

A trait theoretically identified in the 1940s that was to have much influence on the study of leadership was McClelland's (1961) "achievement motivation." Achievement motivation is defined as an unconscious concern for achieving excellence in accomplishments through one's *individual* efforts (McClelland et al., 1958). Individuals high in achievement motivation set challenging goals for themselves, assume personal responsibility for goal accomplishment, are highly persistent in the pursuit of goals, take calculated risks to achieve goals and actively collect and use information for feedback purposes (McClelland, 1985). They tend toward these behaviors even in the absence of external stimuli or incentives; and in the presence of achievement-arousing stimuli, they exhibit these behaviors more strongly than do individuals low in achievement motivation.

Achievement motivation is theoretically predicted to contribute to effective entrepreneurship (McClelland, 1985) and effective leadership of small task-oriented groups (House et al., 1991). High achievement-oriented individuals are able to direct their own behavior toward desired objectives with little formal training or direction from other agencies. Litwin and Stringer (1968) demonstrated experimentally that small groups managed by individuals who enacted achievement-oriented and achievement-arousing behaviors were more effective than groups with managers who did not engage in such behaviors.

Spangler's (1992) meta-analysis of 115 studies demonstrated overall support for the theory. Spangler also found differences between thematic apperception test (TAT) measures of unconscious achievement motivation (nAch) and questionnaire measures of conscious achievement orientation; and differences in the relationships of the two measures with other variables, and in the influence of different moderators on these measures. His findings are consistent with the assertion of the theory (McClelland, 1985) that conscious and unconscious motivations are qualitatively different. Collins et al. (1999), meta-analyzed 36 studies that addressed entrepreneurial performance at the individual level of analysis and provided information useful for the examination of potential moderating variables. They found overall support for McClelland's theory that need for achievement was significantly related to entrepreneurial action. Specifically, they also found significant relationships of nAch with both components of entrepreneurial activity – career choice and entrepreneurial performance. They observed combined effect sizes in the region of 0.20 to 0.25 between nAch and entrepreneurship (choice and performance), using either of two random effects procedures, after excluding a single anomalous result in the selection of studies that showed a distinctly strong correlation of 0.49. These results are encouraging, considering that performance is influenced by a host of other factors, such as role clarity, ability, and environmental sources of resistance and support.

However, achievement orientation is not always a positive influence on outcomes. House et al. (1991) found achievement motivation of US presidents was inversely related to archival measures of presidential effectiveness. They argued that the relevant motive for effective political behavior is the power motive, and that achievement motivation is likely to interfere with the effectiveness of political behavior. More recently, House et al. (1997) found that achievement motivation reflected in interviews with chief executives is strongly associated with indicators of organizational effectiveness in entrepreneurial firms. In contrast, achievement motivation reflected in interviews with heads of divisions of large and more bureaucratic firms, was not associated with indicators of organizational effectiveness. Presumably, individuals high in achievement motivation identify too personally with the task to delegate effectively. Consequently, they are more successful in small organizations, where the personal involvement required of a leader is proportionally much higher than it is in large organizations.

Power and affiliation motives

Logically extending the observation that management involves influencing other people, and thus revolves around power, scholars have hypothesized the need for power as a motivating force in effective leadership (McClelland, 1975; Winter, 1973). McClelland's (1975) leader motive profile (LMP) theory suggests that effective leaders will have a high level of power motivation that is (1) accompanied by a concern for the moral use of power, and (2) greater than affiliative motivation (a motive that facilitates close personal relationships with others).

These hypothesized relationships have found support in a number of laboratory studies (reviewed by House and Baetz, 1979) and several field studies (McClelland and Boyatzis, 1982; Miner and Dachler, 1973; Spangler and House, 1991; Winter, 1978, 1991). For instance, Winter (1978) found a significant association between LMP and career success of entry level managers in non-technical positions over an eight-year interval. Using data from AT&T over a 16-year interval, similar results were obtained by McClelland and Boyatzis (1982) and Winter (1991), in separate analyses with different operationalizations of LMP. McClelland and Burnham (1976) found that work units of high LMP managers had employees with a greater sense of responsibility and team spirit, and perceived more clarity of organizational demands than did work units of low LMP managers.

The condition relating to moral concerns is important. It is only when leaders have a high concern for morality in the exercise of power that they will use it constructively for the social welfare of the followers (Winter and Barenbaum, 1985).

It must be noted that LMP theory addresses leadership effectiveness primarily for medium-to-large organizations. In cases where the boundary condition of medium and large organizations does not hold – that is, in small organizational contexts – the power motive should be less relevant than the achievement motive, described earlier. Interestingly, however, House et al. (1997) found that LMP theory was most predictive of chief executive charismatic leader behavior in small entrepreneurial organizations. This finding is inconsistent with the boundary conditions specified for LMP theory (that is, large complex non-technical organizations) but consistent with Mischel's argument that dispositions are most likely enacted under weak psychological conditions. In entrepreneurial organizations, chief executives are less constrained by formal organizational rules and policies than are their counterparts in large organizations.

House et al.'s (1997) study also contributed to an understanding of some leader behaviors associated with LMP. It was found that LMP is rather strongly associated with follower reports of their superiors as being charismatic, displaying integrity, and being supportive.

Charismatic leadership theory

The 1976 theory of charismatic leadership (House, 1977) has enjoyed support from both laboratory and field studies (Yukl, 1993). Charismatic leaders are hypothesized to be self-confident, with a strong need for power, conviction in the moral correctness of their beliefs, and a willingness to take risks and persevere in the face of opposition.

More recently, LMP has been theorized as an antecedent to charismatic leadership emergence and effectiveness (House et al., 1997). Charismatic theory has been considerably broadened in scope and is now referred to as value-based leadership theory (House et al., 1997), discussed further on.

Leader flexibility and social sensitivity

Studies by Kenny and his associates (Kenny and Hallmark, 1992; Kenny and Zaccaro, 1983; Zaccaro et al., 1991) have demonstrated the importance, for the emergence of leadership, of what they call leadership flexibility and social sensitivity. Social sensitivity refers to the ability to perceive as well as anticipate variations in constituent group situations and the environment. Flexibility refers to the ability to modify one's own behavior in response to these perceptions and anticipations. Kenny and Zaccaro (1983) derived these constructs from a re-analysis of data reported by Barnlund (1962). Barnlund's study concerned the emergence of leaders who had supervised multiple groups over an extended period of time. The tasks of these groups varied so that each one required a different constellation of skills. Kenny and Zaccaro found that a substantial proportion of the variance in leadership emergence could be explained by what they could only interpret as behavioral flexibility and social sensitivity. This speculation received support in a subsequent study by Zaccaro et al. (1991). The notion of flexibility was also substantiated in a historical study of US presidents by Simonton (1987).

■ CONTEMPORARY THEORIES OF LEADERSHIP

The last two decades have seen the emergence of a number of new theories that take fresh perspectives on the leadership phenomenon.

Leader–member exchange theory

Whereas scholars hitherto had looked at leader traits, leader behavior, and situational contingencies, the issue of evolving relationships between leaders and followers had not been given much attention. The vertical dyadic linkage (VDL) model was the first to explicitly address this aspect. The VDL model (Dansereau et al., 1975; Graen and Cashman, 1975) introduced the notion of differentiated dyadic relationships between leaders and their followers. While previous models treated all followers as one group, the VDL model recognized the formation of two kinds of relationships between leader and followers. Some followers develop close working relationships with their leader and become part of a trusted "in-group." Others who do not develop such relationships with the leader form the "out-group." The VDL model has since evolved into the leader–member exchange (LMX) theory of leadership, focusing more on the quality of dyadic relationships and its effects on organizational outcomes (Graen and Uhl-Bien, 1995).

The proclaimed domain of LMX theory covers such questions as the relational characteristics optimal for desired outcomes, the conditions and behaviors necessary for such characteristics to be developed, and the effects of such characteristics on subsequent leader and follower behavior and performance. Intuitive answers to these questions may not always be correct. For instance, it might seem reasonable to expect that followers would seek to build high-quality relationships with their leaders, characterized in LMX as being built on mutual trust, respect, and obligation between subordinates, with wider latitude and discretion given to favored subordinates. Graen et al. (1986) found that leader behaviors designed by training to improve LMX relationships had positive effects on only those subordinates whose growth need strength was high.

Much of the empirical research on LMX is plagued by biases due to common sources, reported elsewhere.[11] However, some results from the better controlled studies are worth noting. Kinicki and Vecchio (1994) found a modest correlation of LMX with locus of control ($r = 0.32$) and a larger correlation of LMX with supervisors' perceived time pressure ($r = 0.48$). These variables were hypothesized as conditions leading to high-quality LMX. Although the correlational design of the study does not permit causal inference, the results provide some indication of possible factors involved. There is some support also for a positive association between LMX and citizenship behaviors (Deluga, 1994; Manogran and Conlon, 1993; Wayne and Green, 1993; Yammarino and Dubinsky, 1992).

Studies addressing the relationship between LMX and employee turnover have yielded correlations ranging from 0.02 to −0.44 (Ferris, 1985; Graen et al., 1982; Vecchio, 1985; Vecchio et al., 1986; Vecchio and Norris, 1996). Similarly, correlations between LMX and performance are unreliable, ranging from 0.02 to 0.33.

Many of the studies use subjective reports of perceived performance. When objective measures of performance are used, however, the correlations are small, ranging from $r = 0.07$ (Duarte et al., 1993) to $r = 0.25$ (Vecchio and Gobdel, 1984).

Implicit leadership theory

Another fresh perspective on leadership was offered by the implicit leadership theory (ILT) advanced by Robert Lord and his associates (Lord et al., 1978, 1984, 1986; Lord and Maher, 1991). In contrast to other theories, ILT focuses on followers' perceptions of leaders. Lord and Maher (1991, p. 11) define leadership as the process of being perceived by others as a leader. Taking a categorization theory perspective, they argue that perceptions of leadership can take place through either consciously inferential or spontaneous recognition processes. These perceptions form hierarchically ordered cognitive categories in followers' minds. Each of the categories is represented by a prototype (or mental image) of a leader that is based on prior knowledge about human behavior and perceived underlying traits of a leader. The prototypes constitute a follower's implicit theory of leadership. Lord et al. (1984) established the existence of leader prototypes through a series of laboratory studies.

The main contribution of ILT, however, lies in its focus on follower expectations, although later developments (for example, distributed leadership) move away from the ILT perspective. Leader conformity to the expectations of subordinates can be readily appreciated as being relevant to effective leadership. Empirical tests also support the idea that implicit leadership theories influence the exercise of leadership (Hanges et al., 1997; Sipe and Hanges, 1997). Results from the GLOBE study (House et al., 1999) support the notion of culturally endorsed implicit leadership theories in follower perceptions.

Neo-charismatic theories – the new genre

In the mid-1970s, there evolved a new set of theories that went beyond simple notions of trait, behaviors, and contingencies to more abstract phenomena revolving around the concept of charisma. The 1976 theory of charismatic leadership (House, 1977), transformational leadership (Bass, 1985; Burns, 1978), the attributional theory of charismatic leadership (Conger and Kanungo, 1987), visionary theories (Bennis and Nanus, 1985; Kouzes and Posner, 1987; Nanus, 1992; Sashkin, 1988) all come under the rubric of what Bryman (1993) categorizes as the new leadership theories. They are classified under one roof because of certain common characteristics (for an integration of these theories, see House and Shamir, 1993). They focus on organizational leadership at the top, and on achievement of extraordinary levels of organizational performance in the face of environmental obstacles, primarily through follower motivation, commitment, loyalty, and respect. In doing this, the theories address leader attributes and behaviors at a symbolic and emotional level rather than at the physical level.

House and Shamir (1993) assert that certain leader behaviors, particularly visionary, empowering, role-modeling, image building, and risk-taking behaviors constitute the charismatic leadership syndrome. Support for the influence of these behaviors on overall performance of organizations and political administrations has been obtained in several studies (Curphy, 1990; Hater and Bass, 1988; House et al., 1991; Howell and Frost, 1989; Howell and Higgins, 1990; Koene et al., 1993; Koh et al., 1991; Pareira, 1987; Pillai and Meindl, 1991; Roberts, 1985; Simonton, 1987; Trice and Beyer, 1986; Waldman et al., 1996). The samples contributing to these findings have been drawn from a variety of sources: informal leaders of task groups; educational administrators; military officers; supervisors, middle managers, and high-level executives in business organizations and government agencies; and data on US presidents.

The available evidence reflects the wide applicability of charismatic behaviors in the US. There is some evidence that this might be the case in other cultures as well. The instrument most widely used in studies of charismatic leadership is the multifactor leadership questionnaire (MLQ) (Bass and Avolio, 1989).[12]

In a meta-analysis of 32 results, Lowe et al. (1996) found a mean corrected correlation of 0.35 between MLQ measures of leader charisma and independent ratings of leader effectiveness. A second analysis using subordinate rather than independent ratings of leader effectiveness yielded a corrected correlation of 0.81.[13]

In response to Lindholm's (1990) contention that "charisma" refers primarily to socially undesirable and destructive leadership traits, Howell and House (1992) distinguish between two kinds of charismatic leadership: personalized and socialized leadership. Personalized charismatic leadership is self-aggrandizing, exploitative, and authoritarian, exemplified in its worst form in Hitler's rule over Germany. However, the more common form of charismatic leadership is socialized to be altruistic, collectivist, and egalitarian. Such leadership can be observed across political, public service, and corporate domains. House and Shamir (1993) have observed that charismatic, transformational, and visionary leadership theories all contain the same essential ingredients – a focus on affective states of followers, and leader behavior that is symbolic and emotionally arousing.

Value-based leadership

The most recent theory of the neocharismatic school is an extension of the 1976 theory of charismatic leadership (House et al., 1996), called the value-based theory of leadership. This theory specifies the leader motive profile and leaders' self-confidence and conviction as predictors of charismatic behaviors. It also predicts that the emergence and effectiveness of value-based leaders will be facilitated by the following factors: environmental stress and uncertainty; opportunity for moral considerations; lack of goal clarity; and weak linkages between performance and reward. Specifically, according to the theory, value-based leadership is facilitated when goals cannot be easily specified or measured, and rewards cannot be linked directly to individual performance; when the task is consistent with dominant societal values and moral considerations; and finally, when there is a high level of stress and uncertainty in the environment. Of these factors, the moderating effect of uncertainty has been empirically established (Pillai and Meindl, 1991; Waldman et al., 1996; Waldman et al., 1996) while the other effects are yet to be tested.

Other neocharismatic theories also offer scope for further investigation. In visionary theories of leadership (Bennis and Nanus, 1985; Kouzes and Posner, 1995; Nanus, 1992; Sashkin, 1988), the theoretical link between specified leader behaviors (for example, communication of a vision) and follower performance is not well explicated. In the attributional theory of charisma advanced by Conger and Kanungo (1987), the specific theoretical attribution processes invoked are not clear. The self-concept and motive-arousal processes described by House and Shamir (1993) as the basis for value-based leadership theory are yet to be verified empirically. Transformational leadership theory asserts that leaders who enact the theoretical transformational leader behaviors of charisma, individualized consideration, and intellectual stimulation will: (1) cause major positive transformations of organizations; (b) cause followers to have a higher level of needs as specified in Maslow's need theory; and (3) stimulate followers to rise to higher levels of principled morality (Bass, 1985; Burns, 1978). To date there is no empirical evidence of such effects of the specified transformational leader behaviors on organizations or followers. It may be that scholars who are enthused about the "new leadership theories" of the neocharismatic leadership paradigm are romanticizing this new genre of leadership and attributing to "transformational" and "charismatic" leaders more than can be reasonably expected of any leader. Further empirical inquiry is needed to resolve this issue.

▉ LEADERSHIP VERSUS MANAGEMENT

In spite of the fact that several thousand empirical studies exist on leadership, they appear to be lost to the literature on management. House and Aditya (1997, p. 444) note that practical discussions of leadership in the media failed to even mention any part of this vast literature base.

Several factors may account for this apparently paradoxical state of affairs. In 1977, Abraham Zaleznik brought to the fore a number of distinctions between managers and leaders. Although an individual may be called upon to be both a manager and a leader, the two roles, he argued, were very different in nature. Managers primarily concerned themselves with the organization of tasks. Leaders, by comparison, concerned themselves with developing people. Yukl (1994, p. 4) sums up the issue well by noting that ". . . managers are oriented toward stability and leaders are oriented toward innovation; managers get people to do things more efficiently whereas leaders get people to agree about what things should be done."

For decades, however, management scholars have been treating the two terms synonymously. It is possible, therefore, that both practitioners and politicians might have seen this literature as inapplicable to their domains. Even within the purview of management, scholars of leadership have often used the concepts of management and supervision interchangeably. Thus, many studies of leadership have drawn their samples from front-line supervisors in corporations. House (1996) has argued for the usefulness of distinguishing between management, supervision, and strategic leadership. Some of the recent theories (such as Bass, 1985; Bennis and Nanus, 1985; Conger and Kanungo, 1998; Sashkin, 1987) do explicitly recognize these distinctions. Interviews and focus group research conducted in 38 countries as part of the GLOBE project (House et al., 1999) reveals a view of leadership as involving the communication of an organizational vision, the inspiring of followers, the generation of follower self-confidence, and coping with environmental uncertainty. In contrast, management has been viewed primarily as the process of implementing a leader's vision, and maintaining organizational infrastructures while facilitating organizational change.

Strategic leadership

The distinction between leadership and management or supervision is highlighted by recent references to the term "strategic" leadership (Finkelstein and Hambrick, 1996), to distinguish it from the supervisory leadership that has been the subject matter of much of the organizational leadership literature. Strategic leadership focuses on organizational responses to industrial and economic conditions in the environment, and is concerned with the leadership of entire organizations.

House and Aditya (1997, p. 446) observe that strategic management has been a prominent part of the curriculum in the earliest business schools in the US. However, strategic leadership has only recently received attention.[14] The findings emerging from five empirical studies concerning the effects that CEOs have on organizational performance (House et al., 1991; Smith et al., 1984; Thomas, 1988; Waldman et al., 1996; Waldman et al., 1996) is that strategic leaders do have significant influence on the overall performance of their organizations. A number of studies (reviewed by House and Singh, 1987) also show that executive succession has substantial effects on organizational performance.

▪ RECENT ADVANCEMENTS: DISTRIBUTED LEADERSHIP REVISITED

Classical management theory emphasized a unitary chain of command (Fayol, 1949), and much of the study of leadership has adhered to the notion of a single leader with a group of followers achieving a common goal. Recent conceptualizations of leadership from the Dwight D. Eisenhower Leadership Development Program, echoing ideas earlier articulated by Bales (1954), and Bowers and Seashore (1966), suggest that the distribution of leadership among two or more individuals may be optimal and more effective for organizational performance in at least certain types of environments. The tenets of this view (Eisenhower Leadership Group, 1996) best summed up in Astin and Astin (1996, p. 16) runs counter to those of implicit leadership theory in that a leader need not necessarily be one who is perceived as a leader.

Three forms of distributed leadership are described in the literature. In *delegated leadership*, two or more individuals at the top are accorded specialized functional roles that represent generic leadership functions within the organization. Practical applications of this concept have been documented, for instance, by Elderkin and Bartlett (1993) and by Schlender (1995). *Co-leadership*, first proposed by Bales (1954, p. 320) distinguishes between task and social roles, and is based on the observation that the individual who emerges as the task leader is not always the best liked. Task leaders who do not also perform socially-oriented roles are likely to lose the acceptance and cooperation of their group members. The group usually accords the social role to another individual. Organizational performance is most effective when the task leader and social leader recognize each other's roles and work together. Finally, *peer leadership* entails the distribution of generic leadership functions among several individuals so that they would enact *the same* specific leader behaviors contemporaneously. Bowers and Seashore (1966) have documented the significant association of peer leadership with organizational performance in a leading life insurance company. Measuring the extent to which both peers and superiors engaged in supportive leadership, goal emphasis, work facilitation, and interaction facilitation, they found that peer leadership often had a higher correlation with agency performance than leadership exercised by the formal manager of the agency.

■ LEADERSHIP THEORY IN PRACTICE: AN EXECUTIVE COMMENTARY

The "gap" between theory and practice is a topic of much conversation and popular writing on management. In fact, however, the issue is not one of a gap, but of a two-way causal relationship between theory and practice. Much of social scientific inquiry is based on observation. The theoretical generalizations resulting from such observation then influence practice by either promoting or inhibiting certain behaviors. The following sections represent a practitioner's perspective on the roles that various theories of leadership have played in the corporate world.[15]

Trait theories

This chapter correctly notes that to those interested in empirical replication, a historical weakness of trait theories has been their unreliability of measurement. In the world of practice, however, that is virtually no impediment at all. This is because (1) practitioners are far more likely than researchers to take the position that "we'll know it when we see it," and (2) many of the yardsticks practitioners use are physically observable so they can be reliably measured (for example, height, gender, composure).

However, two things about traits are of great concern to practitioners: (1) the legal risks of relying on them; and (2) the fact that they are hard to change. With respect to performance appraisal, for example, a working rule in many corporations is that when you criticize something about someone, you should also provide suggestions as to how they might do better next time. If the perceived problem is that they are short, or female, ideas for improvement are likely to be limited. In General Electric, I am happy to say, we do not use height or gender as yardsticks of performance. We do, however, maintain that one of the four keys to effective leadership is personal energy, and this is used as a screen to govern recruitment and promotion. It is true that, for the most part, we know it when we see it. When we don't see it, however, it is not clear what to tell someone to do about it.

The behavioral school

In general, practitioners are favorably disposed toward behavioral theories of leadership. First, compared to traits, behaviors are easier to change, which makes for more constructive appraisal and feedback sessions. Second (as is also the case with traits), the behavioral school supports the notion that leadership is portable. In General Electric (GE), for example, a typical path for a highly regarded leader is to go from a short-cycle consumer business (lighting) to a long-cycle defense business (aircraft engines), or from plastics to medical systems, or from GE Capital to NBC. If leadership effectiveness depends on traits, or on ideal ways of behaving, then placing leaders in very different situations should be no cause for concern.

Most practitioners do not much worry about whether data come from students, or supervisors, as opposed to executives. They don't read that literature anyway, and the behaviors they look for in their recruitment and promotional screens derive more from the norms and belief systems of the enterprise than from empirical research. GE, for example, believes that one of the four keys to effective leadership is "energizability" – the ability to move, inspire, and energize other people. (It might be argued that this is more an *outcome* of particular leader behaviors than a behavior itself; however, we label it a behavior, assume that other desirable behaviors derive from it, and use it as a screen for selection, promotion, and distribution of rewards.)

With respect to the relative importance of (person-oriented) Consideration and (task-oriented) Initiating Structure, there is not a great deal of consensus among practitioners. General Electric worries less about Consideration than about Initiating Structure. We'll take both when we can get both, but we're not at all confident that the dimensions are independent. It seems to us that sometimes you have to give up Consideration to get Structure, and sometimes you have to use Structure to get Consideration. To illustrate this paradox, when GE's CEO Jack Welch initiated Work-Out (the employee empowerment program), and made it mandatory, the *Wall Street Journal* headlined: "No more autocratic leadership, Welch decrees!"

When questioned about the seeming inconsistency of pushing so hard for employee empowerment, yet making many of the GE initiatives mandatory, the Chairman of GE responded:

> "Take our new Six Sigma initiative as an example. I'm only a few years from retirement, and I'd just as soon not have to learn a whole new language and way of behaving. But I'm convinced that Six Sigma will totally delight our customers, and make a fortune for our shareholders. So what right have I to make it voluntary? I don't have the option not to learn it, and I don't have the option of saying to my people, 'this will be hugely beneficial to our customers and shareholders, but it's up to you'. It's not up to you. What's up to you is whether you learn Six Sigma, or work somewhere else."

Fiedler's contingency theory

As opposed to what usually occurs, in the case of Fiedler it is the academics who have, for 30 years, been fascinated by a black box (LPC) that offers prediction without much understanding, while most practitioners have shied away. Fiedler undeniably deserves a huge amount of credit for helping to popularize the concept of contingency models in general. His own theory, however, and the training program it spawned (Leader Match) have not had influence in many practitioner organizations, and have played no role in the development of leaders at Crotonville or elsewhere in GE.

Vroom and Yetton's decision process model

Although not without shortcomings, this model is well respected by practitioners and is widely used in corporate leadership development centers, including Crotonville. To the extent that any one concept can be said to guide an organization as large and as diverse as GE, the formula that undergirds Vroom and Yetton's model,

Quality × Acceptance = Effectiveness

is that concept. That formula, first used to great advantage by Norman Maier and also by Tannenbaum and Schmidt, is the intellectual driver for the work Jack Welch has done in General Electric. During the first eight years that Welch served as CEO (1981–8), he worked on such "IQ" activities as downsizing, delayering, and divestiture of unprofitable businesses. It was during this phase that Welch declared that GE's businesses would be #1 or #2 in any market they were in, or he would "fix, sell, or close." (It was also during this phase that he acquired the nickname "Neutron Jack," named after the bomb that took out people but left the buildings standing.) Beginning in 1989, Welch consciously turned his attention to such high "A" initiatives as Work-Out, an employee empowerment effort that Fortune labeled "the most significant culture change program in the history of corporate America."

Through the eyes of practitioners, one of the most useful aspects of the Vroom–Yetton model is that it legitimates both autocratic and democratic leader behavior, maintaining that each is appropriate in particular situations. The model is therefore a wonderful battering ram that can be used to break down dictatorial cultures, where any show of empowerment is seen as a weakness, and is also effective in "touchy-feely" organizations that regard any act of leadership as unbridled fascism. The model also provides information about when to use group as opposed to individual decision making, which is a thorny puzzle in many firms. Furthermore, by taking into account time availability as well as the importance of subordinate development, the revised version of the model adds another layer of credibility, since every practitioner knows that time pressure is the enemy of participation, and developing subordinates often requires giving them enough autonomy to make, and hopefully learn from, mistakes.

As previously noted, the model does have some shortcomings. This chapter has already pointed out a number of these. From a practitioner's point of view, I would add the following:

1. While the model permits and legitimates democratic leadership, it is always *the leader* who decides which style to use in each situation. In the early days of Work-Out, I never met a GE leader who didn't believe that, in theory,

employee empowerment was a good thing. I did meet several, however, who never (until the day of their dismissal) were able to actually empower anyone, because their subordinates were too new, or time was too scarce, or the cost of being wrong was too high, or for some other reason.

2. The model has no memory. It considers each decision in terms of its situational characteristics, but does not factor in what the leader did last time or the time before. Thus, without intention or even awareness, Vroom–Yetton (and other contingency theories) tends to recommend rather drastic swings from autocratic to democratic leadership. However, most leaders have learned that if their behavior does vary so drastically, they will be perceived as acting inconsistently and unpredictably. Therefore, it is not surprising that when Vroom first compared the behaviors his model recommends to the behaviors of actual leaders, he found that a "striking difference between the behavior of the model and of the typical manager lies in the fact that the former shows far greater variance with the situation. If a typical manager voluntarily used the model as the basis for choosing . . . he would become both more autocratic and more participative" (Vroom, 1974).

Hersey and Blanchard's situational leadership theory

This approach to leadership has been around for a long time, but had a rebirth in some practitioner organizations after Blanchard wrote *The One Minute Manager*. The model is not employed at Crotonville, where it is considered to be an under-researched, over-simplified version of Vroom–Yetton. (It can be argued that the Hersey–Blanchard construct "maturity level" is implicit in several of Vroom and Yetton's questions.)

While Hersey–Blanchard does not enjoy Vroom and Yetton's popularity, it does share most of the shortcomings. Particularly troublesome is the model's reliance on the leader's judgment regarding which style to use in a given situation. While subordinate maturity is considered to be a critically important variable, leader maturity is assumed to be constant, that is, high. The possibility that followers may be immature is factored into the equation; that leaders may be immature is not even considered. If it is true, as Hersey and Blanchard suggest, that mature people are self-confident and feel good about themselves, then immature people – even immature leaders – probably lack self-confidence and don't feel good about themselves. How likely is it that such people can and will engage in the flexible, adaptive behaviors required by the Hersey–Blanchard model (and by other contingency theories, for that matter)? Aren't they more likely to hoard rather than share power, and protect rather than delegate authority, regardless of situational contingencies?

Cognitive resource theory

To summarize a key learning point from cognitive resource theory, House cites Herb Simon's remark that "stress is the enemy of rationality." Now most of us practitioners "don't know nothin'" about this Simon fellow, but we're certainly familiar with the American philosopher Mike Tyson, who once observed that "everybody has a strategy until they get hit in the mouth" (which shows that great minds really do think alike).

Although not many practitioner organizations make use of cognitive resource theory, most organizations do worry about the interplay of the variables the theory articulates. Most practitioners would also agree with the conclusion that, under stress, people tend to act very differently from their behavior otherwise. Earlier, I made reference to some GE leaders who were psychologically unable to engage in participative, empowering behavior. Far more common were leaders who did permit participation by subordinates – except in cases when time was short, decisions were important, and circumstances were stressful. When those circumstances were perceived to exist, it was back to (top–down) business as usual.

From a practitioner perspective, probably the most significant drawback to cognitive resource theory is the inclusion of intelligence as an important variable. In today's United States there are some things that are dangerous even to think about, and career-ending to employ as independent or moderating variables. Most practitioners would put intelligence at the top of the list.

Achievement motivation

Since need for achievement is a trait, it is subject to all the criticisms of trait theories that were previously voiced. Nevertheless, from a practitioner standpoint, the achievement motivation literature constitutes a wonderful body of theory, research, and practice. While the writings of McClelland and Atkinson are not exactly required reading in GE, the company has, albeit intuitively, created systems of goal setting, appraisal, feedback and reward that are prototypical of a high "nAch" organization: challenging ("stretch") goals; personal responsibility for goal attainment and rewards based on goal attainment; moderate, calculated risk taking; and quick, clear, continual feedback. General Electric is today the only surviving member of the original Dow Jones organizations, and few insiders would quibble with the notion that these aspects of GE's culture have played a huge role in the success the firm has enjoyed.

As an interesting sidelight, Jack Welch maintains that GE's success stems from its continual reinvention of itself – that even though it is one of the world's largest organizations, its systems, structures, norms and processes enable it to "walk, talk, move and think like a small firm." With this comment in mind, remember House and Aditya's (1997) observation that achievement motivation is usually associated with organizational effectiveness in entrepreneurial firms, but not in large, bureaucratic organizations. GE's experience suggests that maybe it is not that achievement motivation cannot lead to effectiveness in large organizations, but rather that most large organizations fail to instill the essential attributes of achievement motivation into their norms, systems and structures.

Charismatic leadership theory

House and Aditya's (1997) characterization of charismatic leaders as "self-confident, with a strong need for power, conviction in the moral correctness of their beliefs, and a willingness to take risks and persevere in the face of opposition," is a dead-on description of the Chairman of General Electric. While the benefits to any organization of having a Jack Welch are undeniable, charismatic leadership is not without its risks and costs. One of the most important ways we can benefit from future research pertains to the question of effective leader succession. When John Kennedy and Martin Luther King were killed, for example, the social movements they spawned lost energy and power that was never recaptured. Welch is scheduled to retire from GE at the end of the year 2000. Between now and then his task, and ours, is to institutionalize the forces that seemingly flow so effortlessly from him, and to depersonalize the cues, stimuli, and incentives that cause people to pursue and care about organizational objectives.

Leader–member exchange theory

Since the initial explication of the vertical dyadic linkage model in the 1970s, the corporate world has been subjected to an incredible amount of downsizing, delayering, outsourcing, globalization, and wave after wave of mergers, acquisitions, joint ventures and a host of non-traditional organizational forms and structures. In the wake of all this, leader–member exchange probably strikes most practitioners as something of an anachronism. In the "boundaryless" world of GE, for example, work teams are unstable, temporary organizations abound, most "leaders" don't have surbordinates, and "in-groups" and "out-groups" are nearly impossible to distinguish. In this environment, "the quality of dyadic relationships" is not foremost in most people's minds. (Incidentally, because of this environment, among the most popular GE courses are those that offer guidelines about peer leadership and "influence without authority;" the interested reader should see the discussion of "distributed leadership revisited" earlier in this chapter.)

Leadership versus management

Long before the academic literature stopped treating leaders and managers synonymously, corporations were providing sharply differentiated rewards to the two populations, and educating them differently as well. This emphasis on executive education did not happen because the practitioner community had insights the academics lacked. It happened because organizations such as Crotonville have always, like the Watergate investigators, "followed the money." While most academic researchers were learning that supervisors are easier than executives to access, and samples are larger, most corporate trainers were discovering that money is more readily available for executive education than for supervisory training. With more money to spend, corporate trainers were able to introduce executives to a variety of "strategic leadership experiences" that were unavailable to managers at lower levels, including international trips and bubble assignments; outward bound experiences; action learning projects; 360-degree feedback and executive assessments; and multi-week courses at first-rate universities. Of course, I am speaking here about the form of executive education; with respect to content, corporate trainers share with academics the disadvantage created by the fact that until recently, not much research existed, so not much was known about "strategic leadership" *per se*.

A final note on the search for universal leadership attributes

Some years ago, while I was at USC and consulting to GE, I was asked to conduct Work-Outs (in which employees are encouraged to speak openly and critically to their senior management) in Taiwan and Japan. I conferred with some colleagues who are far more sophisticated about global matters than I, and got an earful about the absurdity of undertaking such an American-style intervention in two Asian cultures. They scared me enough to enlist the support of local nationals from the two countries, who convinced me to scrub most of my design in favor of something they recommended, and both sessions were successful.

What I think I learned from experiences such as this is that nearly everything we think we know about human nature is country- and culture-specific. Nearly everything – but not everything. I have written elsewhere that:

> "For organization members to maximize organizational and personal outcomes, they must be able to obtain both guidance and good feelings from their work settings. Guidance is usually offered in the form of role or task structuring, while good feelings may stem from 'stroking' behaviors, or may be derived from intrinsic satisfaction associated with the task itself. The research literature does not suggest that guidance and good feelings must be provided by the hierarchical superior; it is only necessary that they somehow be provided." (Kerr, 1978)

To me, one of the most useful formulas in the world is:

Ability × Motivation = Performance

It serves as a reminder that, if you want someone to do something they're not doing now, you've got to make them able (guidance), and make them want to (good feelings). To me, this is as close as we are likely to get to any universal truth about leadership. While it is not necessary for a leader to *personally* provide for the ability and motivation of his or her followers, it is the leader's role to see to it that, one way or another, irrespective of country or culture, these things are provided.

▪ SUMMARY AND CONCLUSION

In this chapter, we have attempted to outline the major theories of leadership and some emerging trends in the development of leadership research. We have tried to document the accumulation of knowledge on the subject by tracing the evolution of leadership research from its beginning several decades ago. At this juncture, it is useful to take stock of the limitations of extant research, which in themselves provide scope for further study.

First, it is well known that much of leadership theory has been developed in the United States. Given the diversity of cultural norms around the globe, the question of whether these theories are applicable in other cultures is a legitimate concern, voiced by a number of scholars, notably Hofstede (1980a, 1980b). Even within the confines of theoretical postulations, the introduction of cultural diversity as a variable may influence the predictions that can be made (see, for example, Aditya, 1994). However, the foregoing arguments do not mean that the search for universally effective leadership traits and behaviors need be futile. Commonalities in the problems faced by organizations worldwide, such as the need to ensure task performance and collaboration among organizational members, invoke the possibility that there may be universal solutions, or at least universal aspects of the solutions. On a speculative note, the disposition to influence others, as noted by House and Baetz (1979) may well be a universal requirement of leaders. Ironically enough, issues of power and influence in organizations (for example, Kipnis, 1976, 1984; Kipnis et al., 1980, 1984; Xin and Tsui, 1996; Yukl, 1994) were traditionally not part of the organizational leadership literature until McClelland's (1975) invocation of the need for power in the LMP model. Based on subsequent work linking leadership and power (for example, House, 1988, 1991), House and Aditya (1997, p. 455) suggest an outline for a theory of political leadership that may serve to advance our understanding of this aspect of the leadership phenomenon.

The little empirical evidence that does exist for universal leadership attributes is worth noting. Bass et al. (1979) found that managers in 12 countries all indicated the desirability of getting work done with less authority. Smith and Peterson's (1994) study of managers in 25 countries suggested that delegation may be a universally desired leadership behavior. Finally, qualitative research conducted as part of the GLOBE project in 38 countries of widely differing cultures suggests that certain behaviors – such as communication of an organizational vision, providing inspiration, instilling confidence in followers, introducing organizational change, and showing the way to cope with highly stressful environmental conditions – may be universally endorsed leadership traits. However, the manifestation of these behaviors employed in the different countries may vary.

Leadership and cultural diversity

It was mentioned earlier that much of leadership theory has been developed in the United States. There is increasing recognition of the fact that the underlying assumptions in these theories may not generalize across cultures. Further, as observed by Chen and Van Velsor (1996, p. 292), the knowledge base regarding leadership behaviors of non-traditional and non-Western leaders is very limited. As corporate environments become increasingly global, corporate leaders, like political leaders, cannot afford to ignore the influence of cultural diversity on the phenomenon of leadership. It is evident from a growing number of sources (for example, Chemers et al., 1995; Loden and Loeser, 1991; Morrison, 1992; Triandis et al., 1994), that the issue of leading diverse individuals and groups requires substantial theoretical development and empirical research. At the present time the literature on this issue is largely speculative and anecdotal.

Perhaps, as Chen and Velsor (1996, p. 290) note, a starting point for research into the effects of cultural diversity on leadership is to be found at the dyadic level of analysis. Thus, LMX theory and the 1971 version of path–goal theory would appear to provide a base for such investigation. The problem with directly applying these theories, however, is that in their current form, they reflect dominant Western values such as individualistic orientation; emphasis on rationality rather than on tradition or spirituality; and a focus on the short term rather than the long run. For instance, in order to effectively apply LMX theory it is necessary to understand what constitutes desired, acceptable, and effective relationships between superiors and subordinates. In collectivistic societies, group identification often defines individual self-concept (Markus and Kitayama, 1991; Triandis, 1995). Differences in interpretation of specific behaviors across cultures can lead to deviations from the predicted course of LMX development in multicultural environments (Aditya, 1994), restricting its applicability. A foundational framework for a theory of cross-cultural leadership has been advanced by House et al. (1997).

NOTES

1. For a good summary of the conceptualizations of leader behaviors in various studies, see Bowers and Seashore (1966).
2. Later renamed "situational control."
3. See also Fiedler (1977) for a rejoinder to this critique.
4. See also Fiedler's (1973) reply to Ashour.
5. For arguments on the validity of Strube and Garcia's findings, see Vecchio (1983) and Strube and Garcia's (1983) rejoinder.
6. Participative and achievement oriented behaviors were added to the original 1971 theory by House and Mitchell (1974). Much of the research on path–goal theory, however, has focused only on the first two leader behaviors, namely consideration and initiating structure.
7. Schriesheim et al. (1976) have observed that two instruments used to measure initiating structure and consideration – the Supervisor Behavior Description Questionnaire (SBDQ) and Leadership Opinion Questionnaire LOQ – included punitive and autocratic leader behaviors and were thus not appropriate for use in testing the path–goal theory. Earlier versions of the Leader Behavior Description Questionnaire (LBDQ) also suffer from the same shortcomings. Only form XII of the LBDQ is found to be appropriate.
8. It is important to recognize, however, that the studies do not establish the probability of a particular decision in the feasible set being successful, or the probability of a particular manager being successful by always following the prescriptions of the model.
9. Vroom and Jago (1988, p. 179) have acknowledged that the model involves over a million and a half combinations of problem attributes. Testing the model in entirety is practically impossible under these circumstances.
10. The details of this development are set out in House and Aditya (1997, pp. 429–30).
11. For a detailed critique of the LMX theory and the empirical support for it, see House and Aditya, 1997, pp. 430–7.
12. MLQ includes three subscales to measure transformational leadership: charisma, individualized consideration, and intellectual stimulation. Although the subscales have acceptable psychometric properties, the factor structure congruence with theorized transformational leadership dimensions remains unclear (Curphy, 1990; Howell and Avolio, 1993). House and Aditya (1997, p. 442) explain, however, that the charisma subscale is quite appropriate for measuring overall charismatic leadership, although not appropriate for measuring specific charismatic leadership behaviors.

13. The question of whether "corrections" (for example, Hunter and Schmidt, 1991) are appropriate in meta-analysis is debatable (Rosenthal, 1991); corrected correlations usually result in inflated effect sizes, but their usefulness in extending our understanding of relationships as they exist in real life is not clear.
14. A review of theoretical discourses on this subject is provided by Jackson and Ruderman (1995). A comprehensive summary of empirical research on strategic leadership is available in Finkelstein and Hambrick (1996).
15. The practitioner, Steve Kerr (co-author of this chapter), is Executive Vice President of Leadership Development at General Electric, and Director of the GE Crotonville Institute for Leadership Development.

REFERENCES

Aditya, R. N. 1994: Managing the multinational sales force: Cross-cultural exchange in the dyad. *Proceedings of the American Marketing Association Summer Educators' Conference*, San Francisco, CA: American Marketing Association.

Ashour, A. S. 1973: Further discussion of Fiedler's contingency model of leadership effectiveness: An evaluation. *Organizational Behavior and Human Performance*, 9, 339–55.

Astin, H. S., and Astin, A. W. 1996: *A social change model of leadership development guidebook, version 3*, Los Angeles, CA: Higher Education Research Institute, University of California.

Bales, R. F. 1954: In conference. *Harvard Business Review*, 32(2), 44–50.

Barnlund, D. C. 1962: Consistency of emergent leadership in groups with changing tasks and members. *Speech Monographs*, 29, 45–52.

Barrick, M. R., and Mount, M. K. 1993: Autonomy as a moderator of the relationships between the Big Five personality dimensions and job performance. *Journal of Applied Psychology*, 78(1), 111–18.

Bass, B. M. 1957: Leadership opinions and related characteristics of salesmen and sales supervisors. In R. M. Stogdill and A. E. Coons (eds.), *Leader behavior: Its description and measurement*. Research Monograph No. 88, Bureau of Business Research, Ohio State University.

Bass, B. M. 1985: *Leadership and performance beyond expectations*, New York: Free Press.

Bass, B. M. 1990: *Handbook of leadership: A survey of theory and research*, New York: Free Press.

Bass, B. M., and Avolio, B. J. 1989: *Manual: The multifactor leadership questionnaire*, Palo Alto, CA: Consulting Psychologists Press.

Bass, B. M., Burger, P. C., Doktor, R., and Barrett, G. V. 1979: *Assessment of managers: An international comparison*, New York: Free Press.

Bennis, W., and Nanus, B. 1985: *Leaders: The strategies for taking charge*. New York: Harper & Row.

Besco, R. O., and Lawshe, C. H. 1959: Foreman leadership as perceived by superiors and subordinates. *Personnel Psychology*, 12, 573–82.

Bhohnisch, W., Jago, A. G., and Reber, G. 1987: Predicting Austrian leader behavior from a US measure of behavioral intent: A cross-cultural replication. In V. H. Vroom and A. G. Jago. 1988: *The new leadership: Managing participation in organizations*, Englewood Cliffs, NJ: Prentice-Hall.

Bowers D. G., and Seashore, S. E. 1966: Predicting organizational effectiveness with a four-factor theory of Leadership. *Administrative Science Quarterly*, 11, 238–63.

Bryman, A. 1993: Charismatic leadership in business organizations: Some neglected issues. *Leadership Quarterly*, 4(3/4), 289–304.

Burns, J. M. 1978: *Leadership*. New York: Harper & Row.

Campbell, D. C. 1956: *Leadership and its effects on the group*. Monograph No. 83, Bureau of Business Research, Ohio State University.

Chemers, M. M., Oskamp, S., and Costanzo, M. A. 1995: *Diversity in organizations*, Thousand Oaks, CA: Sage.

Chen, C. C., and Van Velsor, E. 1996: New directions for research and practice in diversity leadership. *Leadership Quarterly*, 7(2), 285–302.

Collins, C. J., Hanges, P. J., and Locke, E. A. 1999: The relationship of need for achievement to individual entrepreneurship: A meta-analysis. Manuscript under review.

Conger, J. A., and Kanungo, R. A. 1987: Toward a behavioral theory of charismatic leadership in organizational settings. *Academy of Management Review*, 12, 637–47.

Conger, J. A., and Kanungo, R. A. 1998: *Charismatic leadership in organizations*, New York: Sage.

Cronshaw, S. F., and Lord, G. R. 1987: Effects of categorization, attribution, and encoding processes on leadership perceptions. *Journal of Applied Psychology*, 72, 97–106.

Curphy, G. J. 1990: An empirical evaluation of Bass' (1985) theory of transformational transactional leadership. Unpublished Doctoral Dissertation, University of Minnesota.

Dansereau, F., Graen, G. B., and Haga, W. 1975: A vertical dyad linkage approach to leadership in formal organizations. *Organizational Behavior and Human Performance*, 13, 46–78.

Davis-Blake, A., and Pfeffer, J. 1988: Just a mirage: The search for dispositional effects in organizational research. *Academy of Management Review*, 14(3), 385–400.

Deluga, R. J. 1994: Supervisor trust building, leader–member exchange and organizational citizenship behavior. *Journal of Occupational and Organizational Psychology*, 67, 315–26.

Duarte, N. T., Goodson, J. R., and Klich, N. R. 1993: How do I like thee? Let me appraise the ways. *Journal of Organizational Behavior*, 14, 239–49.

Eisenhower Leadership Group 1996: *Democracy at risk: How schools can lead*, Washington DC: United States Department of Education.

Elderkin, K. W., and Bartlett, C. A. 1993: *General Electric: Jack Welch's second wave* (A). Harvard Business School, case number: 9-391-248.

Evans, M. G. 1996: R. J. House's path-goal theory of leader effectiveness. *The Leadership Quarterly*, 7(3), 305–9.

Fayol, H. 1949: *General and industrial management*, London: Isaac Pitman.

Ferris, G. R. 1985: Role of leadership in the employee withdrawal process: A constructive replication. *Journal of Applied Psychology*, 70(4), 777–81.

Fiedler, F. E. 1967: *A theory of leadership effectiveness*, New York: McGraw-Hill.

Fiedler, F. E. 1971: Validation and extention of the contingency model of leadership effectiveness: A review of empirical findings. *Psychological Bulletin*, 76, 128–48.

Fiedler, F. E. 1973: The contingency model: A reply to Ashour. *Organizational Behavior and Human Performance*, 9, 356–68.

Fiedler, F. E. 1977: A rejoinder to Schriesheim and Kerr's premature obituary of the contingency model. In J. G. Hunt and L. L. Larson (eds.), *Leadership: The cutting edge*. Carbondale, IL: Southern Illinois University Press.

Fiedler, F. E. 1995: Cognitive resources and leadership performance. *Applied Psychology – An International Review*, 44, 5–28.

Fiedler, F. E. 1996: Research on leadership selection and training: One view of the future. *Administrative Science Quarterly*, 41, 241–50.

Fiedler, F. E., and Garcia, J. E. 1987: *New approaches to effective leadership: Cognitive resources and organizational performance*, New York: Wiley.

Field, R. H. G. 1979: A critique of the Vroom–Yetton contingency model of leadership behavior. *Academy of Management Review*, 4, 249–57.

Field, R. H. G. 1982: A test of the Vroom–Yetton normative model of leadership. *Journal of Applied Psychology*, 67, 523–32.

Field, R. H. G., and House, R. J. 1990: A test of the Vroom–Yetton model using manager and subordinate reports. *Journal of Applied Psychology*, 75(3), 362–6.

Filley, A. C., House, R. J., and Kerr, S. 1976: *Managerial process and organizational behavior*, Glenview, IL: Scott, Foresman & Co.

Finkelstein, S., and Hambrick, D. 1996: *Strategic leadership: Top executives and their effects on organizations*, St. Paul, MN: West Publishing.

Gibb, C. A. 1947: The principles and traits of leadership. *Journal of Abnormal and Social Psychology*, 42, 267–84.

Graen, G., and Cashman, J. F. 1975: A role-making model of leadership in formal organizations: A developmental approach. In J. G. Hunt, and L. L. Larson (eds.), *Leadership frontiers*, Kent, OH: Kent State University Press, 143–65.

Graen, G. B., and Uhl-Bien, M. 1995: Relationship-based approach to leadership: Development of leader–member exchange (LMX) theory of leadership over 25 years: Applying a multi-level multi-domain perspective. *Leadership Quarterly*, 6(2), 219–47.

Graen, G. B., Liden, R. C., and Hoel, W. 1982: Short notes: Role of leadership in employee withdrawal process. *Journal of Applied Psychology*, 67(6), 868–72.

Graen, G. B., Scandura, T., and Graen, M. R. 1986: A field experimental test of the moderating effects of growth need strength on productivity. *Journal of Applied Psychology*, 71, 484–91.

Graham, W. K., and Gleno, T. 1970: Perception of leader behavior and evaluation of leaders across organizational levels. *Experimental Publication System*, Ms. 144A, Issue 4.

Hanges, P. J., Lord, R. G., Day, D. V., Sipe, W. P., Smith, W. C., and Brown, D. J. 1997: Leadership and gender bias: Dynamic measures and nonlinear modeling. In R. G. Lord (Chair), *Dynamic systems, leadership perceptions, and gender effects*. Symposium presented at the Twelfth Annual Conference of the Society for Industrial and Organizational Psychology.

Hater, J. J., and Bass, B. M. 1988: Supervisor's evaluations and subordinates' perceptions of transformational leadership. *Journal of Applied Psychology*, 73, 695–702.

Heilman, M. E., Hornstein, H. A., Cage, H. H., and Herschlag, J. K. 1984: Reactions to prescribed leader behavior as a function of role-perspective: The case of the Vroom–Yetton model. *Journal of Applied Science*, 69, 50–60.

Hersey, P., and Blanchard, K. 1982: *Management of organizational behavior: Utilizing human resources*, Englewood Cliffs, NJ: Prentice-Hall.

Hofstede, G. 1980a: *Culture's consequences: International differences in work related values*, Beverly Hills, CA: Sage.

Hofstede, G. 1980b: Motivation, leadership and organization: Do American theories apply abroad? *Organizational Dynamics*, 9(1), 42–63.

House, R. J. 1971: A path-goal theory of leader effectiveness. *Administrative Science Quarterly*, 16, 321–38.

House, R. J. 1977: A 1976 theory of charismatic leadership. In J. G. Hunt and L. L. Larson (eds.), *Leadership: The cutting edge*, Carbondale, IL: Southern Illinois University Press, 189–207.

House, R. J. 1988: Power and personality in complex organizations. *Research in Organizational Behavior*, 10, 305–57.

House, R. J. 1991: The distribution and exercise of power in complex organizations: A MESO-theory. *Leadership Quarterly*, 2(1), 23–58.

House, R. J. 1996: Path–goal theory of leadership: Lessons, legacy and a reformulated theory. *The Leadership Quarterly*, 7(3), 323–52.

House, R. J., and Aditya, R. N. 1997: The social scientific study of leadership: Quo vadis? *Journal of Management*, 23(3), 409–73.

House, R. J., and Baetz, M. L. 1979: Leadership: Some empirical generalizations and new research directions. *Research in Organizational Behavior*, 1, 341–423.

House, R. J., Delbecq, A. L., and Taris, T. 1997: Value-based leadership: A theory and an empirical test. Working paper, Reginald H. Jones Center for Strategic Management, Wharton School of Management.

House, R. J., Hanges, P. J., Ruiz-Quintanilla, S. A., Dorfman, P. W., Javidan, M., Dickson, M., Gupta, V., and 159 authors. 1999: Cultural influences on leadership and organizations: Project GLOBE. In W. H. Mobley (ed.), *Advances in global leadership*. JAI Press.

House, R. J., and Mitchell, T. R. 1974: Path–goal theory of leadership. *Journal of Contemporary Business*, 3, 81–97.

House, R. J., and Shamir, B. 1993: Towards the integration of transformational, charismatic and visionary theories. In M. M. Chemers, and R. Ayman (eds.), *Leadership theory and research: Perspectives and directions*. San Diego, CA: Academic Press, Inc.

House, R. J., Shane, S., and Herold, D. 1996: Rumors of the death of dispositional theory and research in organizational behavior are greatly exaggerated. *Academy of Management Review*, 21(1), 203–24.

House, R. J., and Singh, J. V. 1987: Organizational behavior: Some new directions for I/O psychology. *Annual Review of Psychology*, 38, 669–718.

House, R. J., Spangler, D., and Woycke, J. 1991: Personality and charisma in the US presidency: A psychological theory of leadership effectiveness. *Administrative Science Quarterly*, 36, 364–96.

House, R. J., Wright, N., and Aditya, R. N. 1997: Cross-cultural research on organizational leadership: A critical analysis and a proposed theory. In C. Earley and M. Erez (eds.), *New frontier series of the Society for Industrial and Organizational Psychology*, Hillsdale, NJ: Lawrence Erlbaum.

Howell, J., and Avolio, B. J. 1993: Transformational leadership, transactional leadership, locus of control, and support for innovation: Key predictors of consolidated-business-unit performance. *Journal of Applied Psychology*, 78, 891–902.

Howell, J. M., and Frost, P. J. 1989: A laboratory study of charismatic leadership. *Organizational Behavior and Human Decision Processes*, 43(2), 243–69.

Howell, J. M., and Higgins, C. 1990: Champions of technological innovation. *Administrative Science Quarterly*, 35, 317–41.

Howell, J. M., and House, R. J. 1992: Socialized and personalized charisma: An essay on the bright and dark sides of leadership. Unpublished manuscript, School of Business Administration, The University of Western Ontario.

Hunter, J. E., and Schmidt, F. L. 1991: Correcting for sources of artificial variation across studies. In H. Cooper and L. V. Hedges (eds.), *The handbook of research synthesis*, New York: Sage.

Jackson, S. E., and Ruderman, M. N. (eds.) 1995: *Diversity in work teams*. Washington, DC: American Psychological Association.

Jenkins, W. O. 1947: A review of leadership studies with particular reference to military problems. *Psychological Bulletin*, 44, 54–79.

Kahn, R. L., and Katz, D. 1953: Leadership practices in relation to productivity and morale. In D. Cartwright and A. Zander (eds.), *Group dynamics*. New York: Harper & Row.

Kerr, S. 1978: Substitutes for leadership: Their meaning and measurement. *Organizational Behavior and Human Performance*, 22, 375–403.

Kenny, D. A., and Hallmark, B. W. 1992: Rotation designs in leadership research. *Leadership Quarterly*, 3(1), 25–41.

Kenny, D. A., and Zaccaro, S. J. 1983: An estimate of the variance due to traits in leadership. *Journal of Applied Psychology*, 68, 678–85.

Kinicki, A. J., and Vecchio, R. P. 1994: Influences on the quality of supervisor–subordinate relations: The role of time-pressure, organizational commitment, and locus of control. *Journal of Organizational Behavior*, 15, 75–82.

Kipnis, D. 1976: *The powerholders*, Chicago: University of Chicago Press.

Kipnis, D. 1984: The use of power in organizations and in interpersonal settings. In S. Oskamp (ed.), *Applied social psychology annual* 5, Beverly Hills: Sage, 172–210.

Kipnis, D., Schmidt, S. M., Swaffin-Smith, C., and Wilkinson, I. 1984: Patterns of managerial influence: Shotgun managers, tacticians and bystanders. *Organizational Dynamics*, 12(3), 58–67.

Kipnis, D., Schmidt, S., and Wilkinson, I. 1980: Intraorganizational influence tactics. *Journal of Applied Psychology*, 65, 440–52.

Koene, H., Pennings, H., and Schreuder, M. 1993: Leadership, culture, and organizational effectiveness. In K. E. Clark and M. B. Clark (eds.), *The impact of leadership*, Greensboro NC: The Center for Creative Leadership.

Koh, W. L., Terborg, J. R., and Steers, R. M. 1991: The impact of transformational leadership on organizational commitment: Organizational citizenship behavior teacher satisfaction and student performance in Singapore. Paper presented at the Academy of Management, Fontenbleu, FL.

Kouzes, J. M., and Posner, B. Z. 1987: *The leadership challenge: How to get extraordinary things done in organizations*, San Francisco, CA: Jossey-Bass.

Kouzes, J. M., and Posner, B. Z. 1995: *The leadership challenge: How to keep getting extraordinary things done in organizations*, 2nd edn., San Francisco, CA: Jossey-Bass.

Larson, L. L., Hunt, J. G., and Osborn, R. N. 1974: Correlates of leadership and demographic variables in three organizational settings. *Journal of Business Research*, 2, 335–47.

Lee, C., Ashford, S. J., and Philip, B. 1990: Interactive effects of "type A" behavior and perceived control on worker performance, job satisfaction, and somatic complaints. *Academy of Management Journal*, 33, 870–81.

Likert, R. 1961: *New patterns of management*, New York: McGraw-Hill.

Lindholm, C. 1990: *Charisma*, Cambridge, MA: Basil Blackwell.

Litwin, G. H., and Stringer, R. A., Jr. 1968: *Motivation and organizational climate*, Boston: Harvard Business School Press.

Loden, M., and Loeser, R. H. 1991: Working diversity: Managing the differences. *Bureaucrat*, 20(1), 21–25.

Lord, R. G., Binning, J. F., Rush, M. C., and Thomas, J. C. 1978: The effects of performance cues and leader behavior on questionnaire ratings of leadership behavior. *Organizational Behavior and Human Performance*, 21(1), 27–39.

Lord, R. G., De Vader, C. L., and Alliger, G. M. 1986: A meta-analysis of the relation between personality traits and leadership perceptions: An application of validity generalizations procedures. *Journal of Applied Psychology*, 71(3), 402–10.

Lord, R. G., Foti, R., and De Vader, C. 1984: A test of leadership categorization theory: Internal structure, information processing, and leadership perceptions. *Organizational Behavior and Human Performance*, 34, 343–78.

Lord, R. G., and Maher, K. J. 1991: *Leadership and information processing: Linking perception and performance*, Boston: Unwin Hyman.

Lowe, K. B., Kroeck, K. G., and Sivasubramaniam, N. 1996: Effectiveness correlates of transformational and transactional leadership: A meta-analytic review of the MLQ literature. *Leadership Quarterly*, 7(3), 385–425.

Mann, F. C. 1965: Toward an understanding of the leadership role in formal organization. In R. Dublin (ed.), *Leadership and productivity*, San Francisco: Chandler.

Manogran, P., and Conlon, E. J. 1993: A leader–member exchange approach to explaining organizational citizenship behavior. *Proceedings of the Annual Meeting of Academy of Management*, Atlanta: GA, 249–53.

Margerison, C., and Glube, R. 1979: Leadership decision-making: An empirical test of the Vroom and Yetton Model. *Journal of Management Studies*, 16, 45–55.

Markus, H., and Kitayama, S. 1991: Culture and the self: Implications for cognition, emotion and motivation. *Psychological Review*, 98, 224–53.

McClelland, D. C. 1961: *The achieving society*, New York: Van Nostrand Reinhold.

McClelland, D. C. 1975: *Power: The inner experience*, New York: Irvington.

McClelland, D. C. 1985: *Human motivation*, Glenview, IL: Scott, Foresman.

McClelland, D. C., Atkinson, J. W., Clark, R. A., and Lowell, E. L. 1958: *The achievement motive*, New York: Appleton-Century-Crofts. (Reissued with new introduction by John W. Atkinson, New York: Irvington, 1976.)

McClelland, D. C., and Boyatzis, R. E. 1982: Leadership motive pattern and long-term success in management. *Journal of Applied Psychology*, 67, 737–43.

McClelland, D. C., and Burnham, D. H. 1976: Power is the great motivator. *Harvard Business Review*, 54(2), 100–10.

Miner, J. B., and Dachler, H. P. 1973: Personnel attitudes and motivations. *Annual Review of Psychology*, 24, 379–402.

Mischel, W. 1973: Toward a cognitive social learning reconceptualization of personality. *Psychological Review*, 80, 252–83.

Monson, T. C., Hesley, J. W., and Chernick, L. 1982: Specifying when personality traits can and cannot predict behavior: An alternative to abandoning the attempt to predict single act criteria. *Journal of Personality and Social Psychology*, 3, 385–499.

Morrison, A. M. 1992: Developing diversity and organization. *Business Quarterly*, 57(1), 42–8.

Nanus, B. 1992: *Visionary leadership: Creating a compelling sense of direction for your organization*. San Francisco: Jossey-Bass.

Pascarella, S. V., and Lunenburg, F. C. 1988: A field test of Hersey and Blanchard's situational leadership theory in a school setting. *College Student Journal*, 22(1), 33–7.

Pereira, D. 1987: Factors associated with transformational leadership in an Indian engineering firm. Paper presented at Administrative Science Association of Canada, Vancouver.

Peters, L. H., Hartke, D. D., and Pohlman, J. T. 1985: Fiedler's contingency model of leadership: An application of the meta-analysis procedure of Schmidt and Hunter. *Psychological Bulletin*, 97, 274–85.

Pillai, R., and Meindl, J. R. 1991: The effects of a crisis on the emergence of charismatic leadership: A laboratory study. Best Paper Proceedings, Annual Meeting of the Academy of Management, Miami, 420–5.

Roberts, N. C. 1985: Transforming leadership: A process of collective action. *Human Relations*, 38, 1023–46.

Rosenthal, R. 1991: *Meta-analytic procedures for social sciences*, Newbury Park, CA: Sage.

Sales, S. 1972: Authoritarianism: But as for me, give me liberty, or give me maybe, a great big, strong, powerful leader I can honor, admire, respect and obey. *Psychology Today*, 94–8, 140–3.

Sashkin, M. 1988: The visionary leader. In J. A. Conger and R. A. Kanungo (eds.), *Charismatic leadership: The elusive factor in organizational effectiveness*, San Francisco: Jossey-Bass, 122–60.

Schlender, B. 1995: What Bill Gates really wants. *Fortune Magazine*, 131(1), 34–6.

Schneider, B. 1983: Interactional psychology and organizational behavior. In L. L. Cummings and B. M. Staw (eds.), *Research in organizational behavior*, Vol. 5, Greenwich: JAI Press, 1–31.

Schriesheim, C., House, R. J., and Kerr, S. 1976: Leader initiating structure: A reconciliation of discrepant research results and some empirical tests. *Organizational Behavior and Human Performance*, 15(2), 297–321.

Schriesheim, C., and Kerr. S. 1977: Theories and measures of leadership: A critical appraisal of present and future directions. In J. C. Hunt and L. L. Larson (eds.), *Leadership: The cutting edge*, Carbondale, IL: Southern Illinois University Press.

Schriesheim, C., and Neider, L. L. 1996: Path–goal leadership theory: The long and winding road. *Leadership Quarterly*, 7(3), 317–21.

Simon, H. A. 1987: Making management decisions: The role of intuition and emotion, *Academy of Management Executive*, 1, 57–64.

Simonton, D. K. 1987: Presidential inflexibility and veto behavior: Two individual-situational interactions. *Journal of Personality*, 55(1), 1–18.

Sipe, W. P., and Hanges, P. J. 1997: Reframing the glass ceiling: A catastrophe model of changes in the perception of women as leaders. In R. G. Lord (Chair), *Dynamic systems, leadership perceptions, and gender effects*. Symposium presented at the Twelfth Annual Conference of the Society for Industrial and Organizational Psychology.

Smith, J. E., Carson, K. P., and Alexander, R. A. 1984: Leadership: It can make a difference. *Academy of Management Journal*, 27, 765–76.

Smith, P. B., and Peterson, M. F. 1994: Leadership as event management: A cross-cultural survey based on managers from 25 nations. Paper presented at the International Congress of Psychology, Madrid.

Spangler, W. D. 1992: The validity of questionnaire and TAT measures of need for achievement: Two meta-analyses. *Psychological Bulletin*, 112(1), 140–54.

Spangler, W. D., and House, R. J., 1991: Presidential effectiveness and the leadership motive profile. *Journal of Personality and Social Psychology*, 60(3), 439–55.

Staw, B. M., Sandelands, L. E., and Dutton, J. E. 1981: Threat-rigidity effects in organizational behavior: A multilevel analysis. *Administrative Science Quarterly*, 26, 501–24.

Stogdill, R. M. 1948: Personal factors associated with leadership: A survey of the literature. *Journal of Psychology*, 25, 35–71.

Stogdill, R. M. 1974: *Handbook of leadership: A survey of theory and research*, New York: Free Press.

Stogdill, R. M., and Coons, A. E. 1957: *Leader behavior: Its description and measurement*, Columbus, OH: Bureau of Business Research.

Strube, M. J., and Garcia, J. E. 1981: A meta-analytical investigation of Fiedler's contingency model of leadership effectiveness. *Psychological Bulletin*, 90, 307–21.

Strube, M. J., and Garcia, J. E. 1983: On the proper interpretation of empirical findings: Strube and Garcia (1981) revisited. *Psychological Bulletin*, 93(3), 600–3.

Tannenbaum, R., and Schmidt, W. H. 1973: How to choose a leadership pattern. *Harvard Business Review*, 51, 162–80.

Thomas, A. B. 1988: Does leadership make a difference to organizational performance? *Administrative Science Quarterly*, 33, 388–400.

Tjosvold, D., Wedley, W. C., and Field, R. H. G. 1986: Constructive controversy, the Vroom–Yetton model, and managerial decision-making. *Journal of Occupational Behavior*, 7, 125–38.

Triandis, H. C. 1995: *Individualism and collectivism*, Boulder, CO: Westview Press.

Triandis, H. C., Dunnette, M. D., and Hough, L. M. (eds.) 1994: *Handbook of industrial and organizational psychology*, 2nd edn., Vol. 4, Palo Alto, CA: Consulting Psychologists Press, Inc.

Trice, H. M., and Beyer, J. M. 1986: Charisma and its routinization in two social movement organizations. In B. M. Staw and L. L. Cummings (eds.), *Research in organizational behavior*, Vol. 8, Greenwich, CT: JAI Press, 113–64.

Vecchio, R. P. 1983: Assessing the validity of Fiedler's contingency model of leader effectiveness: A closer look at Strube and Garcia. *Psychological Bulletin*, 93(2), 404–8.

Vecchio, R. P. 1985: Predicting employee turnover from leader–member exchange: A failure to replicate. *Academy of Management Journal*, 28(2), 478–85.

Vecchio, R. P. 1987: Situational leadership theory: An examination of a prescriptive theory. *Journal of Applied Psychology*, 72(3), 444–51.

Vecchio, R. P., and Gobdel, B. C. 1984: The vertical dyad linage model of leadership: problems and prospects. *Organizational Behavior and Human Performance*, 34, 5–20.

Vecchio, R. P., Griffeth, R. W., and Hom, P. W. 1986: The predictive utility of the vertical dyad linkage approach. *Journal of Social Psychology*, 126, 617–25.

Vecchio, R. P., and Norris, W. R. 1996: Predicting employee turnover from performance, satisfaction and leader–member exchange. *Journal of Business and Psychology*, 49, 436–58.

Vroom, V. H. 1974: *Leadership revisited*. Technical Report No. 7, School of Organization and Management, Yale University.

Vroom, V. H., and Jago, A. G. 1988: *The new leadership: Managing participation in organizations*, Englewood Cliffs, NJ: Prentice-Hall.

Vroom, V. H., and Yetton, P. W. 1973: *Leadership and decision-making*, Pittsburgh: University of Pittsburgh Press.

Wahba, M., and Bridwell, L. 1975: Maslow reconsidered: A review of the need hierarchy theory. *Organizational Behavior and Human Performance*, 15(2), 212–40.

Waldman, D., House, R. J., and Ramirez, G. 1996: A replication of the effects of US CEO charismatic leadership on firm profitability under conditions of certainty and uncertainty based on Canadian executives. Unpublished manuscript, the Wharton School of Management, University of Pennsylvania.

Waldman, D., Ramirez, G., House, R. J., and Purnam, P. 1996: The effects of US CEO leader behavior on firm profits under conditions of environmental certainty and uncertainty: A longitudinal investigation. Working paper, Reginal Jones Center for Strategic Management, Wharton School of Management.

Wayne, S. J., and Green, S. A. 1993: The effects of leader–member exchange on employee citizenship and impression management behavior. *Human Relations*, 46, 1431–40.

Winter, D. G. 1973: *The power motive*, New York: Free Press.

Winter, D. G. 1978: *Navy leadership and management competencies: Convergence among tests, interviews, and performance ratings*, Boston: McBer and Company.

Winter, D. G. 1991: A motivational model of leadership: Predicting long-term management success from TAT measures of power motivation and responsibility. *Leadership Quarterly*, 2(2), 67–80.

Winter, D. G., and Barenbaum, N. B. 1985: Responsibility and the power motive in women and men. *Journal of Personality*, 53, 335–55. Reprinted in A. J. Stewart and M. B. Lykes (eds.), *Gender and personality*, Durham, North Carolina: Duke University Press, 247–67.

Wofford, J. C., and Liska, L. Z. 1993: Path–goal theories of leadership: A meta-analysis. *Journal of Management*, 19, 857–76.

Xin, K. R., and Tsui, A. S. 1996: Different strokes for different folks? Influence tactics by Asian-American and Caucasian-American managers. *Leadership Quarterly*, 7(1), 109–32.

Yammarino, F. J., and Dubinsky, A. J. 1992: Superior–subordinate relationships: A multiple level of analysis approach. *Human Relations*, 45, 575–600.

Yukl, G. 1993: A retrospective on Robert House's 1976 theory of charismatic leadership and recent revisions, *Leadership Quarterly*, 4(3/4), 367–73.

Yukl, G. 1994: *Leadership in organizations*, 3rd edn., Englewood Cliffs, NJ: Prentice-Hall.

Yukl, G., Falbe, C. M., and Youn, J. Y. 1993: Patterns of influence behavior for managers. *Group and Organization Management*, 18, 5–24.

Zaccaro, S. J., Foti, R. J., and Kenny, D. A. 1991: Self-monitoring and trait-based variance in leadership: An investigation of leader flexibility across multiple group situations. *Journal of Applied Psychology*, 76, 308–15.

Zaleznik, A. 1977: Managers and leaders: Are they different? *Harvard Business Review*, 55(3), 67–78.

Zimmer, R. J. 1978: Validating the Vroom–Yetton normative model of leader behavior in field sales force management and measuring the training effects of TELOS on the leader behavior of district managers. Doctoral dissertation, Virginia Polytechnical Institute and State University.

chapter 7
JOB SATISFACTION:
RESEARCH AND PRACTICE
TIMOTHY A. JUDGE AND ALLAN H. CHURCH

It is probably a truism – something so obvious that it need not be proven – that morale matters. It was Napoleon who remarked, "An army's effectiveness depends on its size, training, experience, and morale, and morale is worth more than all the other factors combined." In this century, the advent of the human relations movement is credited with emphasizing the importance of workplace attitudes. Indeed, a casual perusal of works emanating from the human relations movement – starting with Roethlisberger and Dickson (1939), and culminating in Likert (1967), Maslow (1965), McCregor (1966) – readily reveals the emphasis that organizational psychology placed on workplace morale. Although since that time the literature on job satisfaction has had its ebbs and flows, and concomitant identity crises, research on job satisfaction shows no signs of abating. In his 1976 landmark review, Locke estimated that over 3,300 studies on job satisfaction had been conducted up to 1973. Using the PSYCHINFO database, we were able to find references to another 7,856 studies on job satisfaction published since 1973. Job satisfaction may be the most widely studied topic in all of industrial/organizational psychology.

The purpose of this chapter is to describe the topic of job satisfaction as it is researched and practiced. Specifically, we will describe what we know about the nature, causes, and consequences of job satisfaction from previous research. In the next section of the paper, we will describe practical issues that concern how job satisfaction is treated in organizations. In this section we consider why job satisfaction is important to organizations, how it is considered and treated in organizations, and how job satisfaction research and practice can be better integrated in the future.

■ RESEARCH ON JOB SATISFACTION

What is job satisfaction?

The most popular – and we believe the best – single definition of job satisfaction was supplied by Locke (1976), who defined job satisfaction as "a pleasurable or positive emotional state resulting from the appraisal of one's job or job experiences" (p. 1304). Implicit in Locke's definition is the importance of affect and cognition. Hulin (1991) appears to agree with Locke. While Hulin's review places considerable emphasis on cognitive processes that determine job satisfaction, he refers to the outcome of these processes as *work role affect*, implicitly recognizing the interplay between perception, evaluation, and affect in judgments of job satisfaction.

Surprisingly, this view has not gone unchallenged. Some researchers have argued that job satisfaction reflects more cognitive than affective components (Organ and Near, 1985). Brief (1998) readily agrees, noting that "organizational scientists often have been taping the cognitive dimension while slighting or even excluding the affective one" (p. 87). In support of his argument, Brief uses an earlier study (Brief and Roberson, 1989) which shows that cognitions correlate more strongly (ave. $r = 0.70$) with job satisfaction than does affect (ave. $r = 0.43$). The limitation with this study exposes the problem with the entire argument – it seems likely that job beliefs (cognitions) are as influenced by affect as is job satisfaction itself. (Imagine evaluating your supervisor as untrustworthy and mean-spirited, and having no feelings about it.) It is also important to note that this study, as well as others (Weiss et al., 1999), clearly show that *both* cognition and affect contribute to job satisfaction.

Thus, in evaluating our jobs, as when we think about most anything consequential, both cognition and affect are involved. When we think, we have feelings about what we think. When we have feelings, we think about what we feel. Cognition and affect are thus inextricably related, in our psychology and even in our psychobiology. Evidence indicates that when individuals perform specific mental operations, a reciprocal relationship exists between cerebral areas specialized for processing emotions and those specific for cognitive processes (Drevets and Raichle, 1998). There are cognitive theories of emotion (Reisenzein and Schoenpflug, 1992), and emotional theories of cognition (Smith-Lovin, 1991).

We are not suggesting that the dual roles of affect and cognition should not be studied in the context of job satisfaction. What we are objecting to is (1) the characterization of measures of job satisfaction as either cognitive or affective, and (2) the need to develop new, affectively-laden measures of job satisfaction, or to replace measures of job satisfaction with "work affect" measures. Cognition and affect can help us better understand the nature of job satisfaction, but they are not substitutes for job satisfaction any more than the accumulated body parts of a cadaver substitute for a living human.

Theories of job satisfaction

There are many theories of job satisfaction. A review of all these theories cannot be provided here. Rather, the most popular and heavily researched theories are reviewed below.

Two-factor theory

One of the earliest theories of job satisfaction is Frederick Herzberg's two-factor theory (Herzberg, 1967). Herzberg argued that the factors that lead to satisfaction are often different from those that lead to dissatisfaction. Herzberg based this conclusion on a series of interviews of workers. When asked to consider factors connected to a time when they felt satisfied with their jobs, individuals generally talked about intrinsic factors, such as the work itself, responsibilities, and achievements (Herzberg termed these "motivators"). Conversely, when workers were asked to consider factors that lead to dissatisfaction, most individuals discussed extrinsic factors such as company policies, working conditions, and pay (Herzberg termed these "hygienes"). Herzberg further found that intrinsic factors were more strongly correlated with satisfaction while extrinsic factors were more strongly correlated with dissatisfaction. Based on these findings, Herzberg argued that elimination of the dissatisfiers (hygiene factors) could only remove dissatisfaction, but not bring satisfaction. To cause individuals to be satisfied with their jobs, then, the organization must focus on motivator factors, such as making the work more interesting, challenging, and personally rewarding.

Despite its intuitive appeal, the two-factor theory has been roundly criticized by researchers. There are many logical problems with the theory, and many flaws in Herzberg's methodology (see Locke, 1969). Numerous empirical studies have attempted to replicate and test Herzberg's findings with independent methods, with little success (for example, Hulin and Smith, 1967). Contrary to Herzberg's claim, research has consistently shown that intrinsic and extrinsic factors contribute to both satisfaction and dissatisfaction (Wernimont, 1966). As Carroll (1973) concluded, "Most of [the] evidence revolves around the fact that both hygienes and motivators can cause either satisfaction or dissatisfaction with the motivators being the more potent variables in most cases" (p. 5). Thus, though the theory continues to be advocated by Herzberg and recommended for further study by others (Brief, 1998), these attempts at resurrecting the theory run against considerable scientific evidence. As Korman (1971) noted, disconfirming evidence has "effectively laid the Herzberg theory to rest" (p. 179). Given the virtual absence of tests of the two-factor theory since 1971, we find Korman's comment a suitable epitaph.

Value-percept theory

Following his definition of values as that which one desires or considers important, Locke (1976) argued that individuals' values would determine what satisfied them on the job. Only the unfulfilled job values that were valued by the individual would be dissatisfying. Accordingly, Locke's value-percept theory expresses job satisfaction as follows:

$$S = (V_c - P) \times V_i, \text{ or}$$

Satisfaction = (want − have) × importance

Where S is satisfaction, V_c is value content (amount wanted), P is the perceived amount of the value provided by the job, and V_i is the importance of the value to the individual. Thus, value-percept theory predicts that discrepancies between what is desired and received are dissatisfying only if the job facet is important to the individual. Individuals consider multiple facets when evaluating their job satisfaction, so the satisfaction calculus is repeated for each job facet.

One potential problem with the value-percept theory is that what one desires (V_c or want) and what one considers important (V_i or importance) are likely to be highly correlated. Though in theory these concepts are separable, in practice many people will find it difficult to distinguish the two. For example, why should I desire a great deal of pay if pay is not important to me? Despite this limitation, research on Locke's theory has been supportive (Rice et al., 1990). One study (Rice et al., 1991) found that facet importance moderates the relationship between facet amount and facet satisfaction, but facet importance does not moderate the relationship between facet satisfaction and overall job satisfaction. This is exactly what Locke predicted in his theory, as he argued that facet satisfactions should additively predict overall satisfaction because facet importance was already reflected in each facet satisfaction score.

Cornell integrative model

Hulin et al. (1985) and Hulin (1991) provide a model of job satisfaction that attempts to integrate previous theories of attitude formation. The model proposes that job satisfaction is a function of the balance between role inputs – what the individual puts into the work role (such as training, experience, time, and effort) – compared to role outcomes – what is received (pay, status, working conditions, and intrinsic factors). The more outcomes received relative to inputs invested, the higher work role satisfaction will be, all else being equal. The Hulin model further proposed that the individual's opportunity costs exert a significant effect on job satisfaction. In periods of labor oversupply (that is, high unemployment), the individual will perceive their inputs as less valuable because of the high competition for few alternative positions, and the opportunity cost of their work role declines (that is, work role membership is less costly relative to other opportunities). Therefore, as unemployment rises, the subjective utility of inputs falls – making perceived value of inputs less relative to outcomes – thus increasing satisfaction. Finally, the Hulin model argues that an individual's frames of reference, which they define as past experience with outcomes, influence how individuals perceive current outcomes received. The fewer, or less valued, the outcomes received in the past and as current employment opportunities erode, the same outcomes per inputs will increase job satisfaction (that is, more was received than had been in the past). Again, the reverse scenario is also true. Although the breadth and integration of the Hulin model is impressive, direct tests of the model are lacking. One partial test (Judge, 1990) of the model was not particularly supportive.

Job characteristics model

The job characteristics model (JCM) argues that job enrichment is the core underlying factor in making employees satisfied with their jobs. The model, introduced by Hackman and Oldham (1976), focuses on five core job characteristics to make one's work challenging and fulfilling: (1) *task identity*, or the degree to which one can see one's work from beginning to end; (2) *task significance*, or the degree to which one's work is seen as important and significant; (3) *skill variety*, or the extent to which the job allows employees to do different tasks; (4) *autonomy*, or the degree to which employees have control and discretion regarding the conduct of their job; and (5) *feedback*, or the degree to which the work itself provides feedback for how the employee is performing the job. According to the theory, jobs that are enriched to provide these core characteristics are likely to be more satisfying and motivating than jobs that do not provide these characteristics.

There are several indirect pieces of evidence supporting Hackman and Oldham's emphasis of intrinsic job characteristics. First, when individuals are asked to evaluate different facets of work such as pay, promotion opportunities, co-workers, and so forth, the nature of the work itself consistently emerges as the most important job facet (Jurgensen, 1978). Second, of the major job satisfaction facets – pay, promotion opportunities, co-workers, supervision, and the work itself – satisfaction with the work itself is almost always the facet most strongly correlated with overall job satisfaction (for example, Rentsch and Steel, 1992). Thus, if we are interested in understanding what causes people to be satisfied with their jobs, the nature of the work (intrinsic job characteristics) is the first place to start.

Research directly testing the relationship between workers' reports of job characteristics and job satisfaction has produced consistently positive results. There have been several quantitative reviews of the literature indicating positive results (Fried and Ferris, 1987; Loher et al., 1985). Recently, Frye (1996) provided an update and reports a true score correlation of 0.50 between job characteristics and job satisfaction. Most of the studies have used self-reports of job characteristics, which has garnered its share of criticisms (Roberts and Glick, 1981). It is true that subjective reports of job characteristics correlate more strongly with job satisfaction than do objective reports. However, objective reports, even with all of their measurement imperfections, still show consistently positive correlations with job satisfaction (Glick et al., 1986). Though the theory has its imperfections, the empirical data suggest that intrinsic job characteristics are the most consistent situational predictor of job satisfaction. The implication is that if organizations are interested in satisfying their employees, they should consider situational interventions that will increase the perception of intrinsic job characteristics. Two methods of accomplishing this are job rotation (employees alternate performing different jobs) and job enlargement (jobs are redesigned to expand the number of tasks associated with a particular job).

Dispositional approaches

Though researchers have long recognized that there are individual differences in job satisfaction, only in the last 15 years has a dispositional approach to job satisfaction become prominent. Staw and Ross (1985) demonstrated that job satisfaction scores demonstrate stability over time, even when individuals' jobs change. Another provocative study by Staw and colleagues revealed that childhood assessments of affective temperament were correlated with adult job satisfaction up to 40 years later (Staw et al., 1986). Evidence even indicates that the job satisfaction of identical twins reared apart is similar (see Arvey et al., 1991). Although this literature has had its critics (for example, Davis-Blake and Pfeffer, 1989), an accumulating body of evidence indicates that variance in job satisfaction across individuals can be traced to measures of affective temperament (House et al., 1996).

Despite its contributions to our understanding of job satisfaction, one of the limitations in this literature is that it has not been informative as to *how* dispositions might affect job satisfaction. As recently as five years ago, the literature was compared to a "black box" – evidence suggests that something works, but we have little idea of what is inside the box (Erez, 1994). More recently, researchers have begun to explore the psychological processes that might underlie dispositional sources of job satisfaction. For example, Weiss and Cropanzano (1996) suggest that affective temperament may influence the experience of emotionally significant events at work, which in turn influence job satisfaction. Similarly, both Brief (1998) and Motowidlo (1996) recently have offered theoretical models in an attempt to illuminate the relationship between dispositions and job satisfaction.

Continuing this theoretical development, Judge et al. (1998a) have found that core self-evaluations, a broad personality trait composed of self-esteem, generalized self-efficacy, internal locus of control, and low neuroticism, is correlated with job satisfaction. Judge et al. (1998a) found that one of the primary causal mechanisms was through the perception of intrinsic job characteristics. Thus, Judge et al. argue that the most important situational variable affecting job satisfaction, intrinsic job characteristics, is linked to what may be the most important dispositional predictor, core self-evaluations. Judge and Bono (in press) have shown that core self-evaluation is correlated with job satisfaction across occupations. Their best estimate of the overall relationship between core self-evaluations and job satisfaction was 0.37.

The researchers investigating the dispositional source of job satisfaction have their differences. Brief, George, and colleagues focus on mood at work and have used positive and negative affectivity as dispositional constructs (for example, Brief, 1998). Weiss, Cropanzano, and colleagues emphasize affective events at work and the emotions and cognitions these events produce (for example, Weiss and Cropanzano, 1996). Judge, Locke, Erez, and colleagues focus on core self-evaluations (Judge et al., 1998). The differences in these approaches are important. However, we should not assume that they are oriented toward different objectives – all seek to better understand the dispositional source of job attitudes. The approaches may not even be competitors. We view these different approaches are signs of a healthy area of scientific inquiry.

Summary and integration

Of the job satisfaction theories that have been put forth, it appears that three have garnered the most research support: Locke's value-percept theory, the job characteristics model, and the dispositional approach. It is interesting to note that one of these theories is, essentially, a situational theory (job characteristics model), another is a person theory (dispositional approach), and another is a person–situation interactional theory (value-percept model). Although this may lead one to assume that these theories are competing or incompatible explanations of job satisfaction, this is not the case. Judge et al. (1997), in seeking to explain how core self-evaluations would be related to job satisfaction, proposed that intrinsic job characteristics would mediate the relationship. Indeed, Judge et al. (1998a) showed that individuals with positive core self-evaluations perceived more intrinsic value in their work. Judge et al. (in press) showed that the link between core self-evaluations and intrinsic job characteristics was not solely a perceptual process – core self-evaluations were related to the actual attainment of complex jobs. Since job complexity is synonymous with intrinsic job characteristics, this shows that part of the reason why individuals with positive core self-evaluations perceived more challenging jobs and reported higher levels of job satisfaction is that they actually have obtained more complex (and thus challenging and intrinsically enriching) jobs. The work of Judge and colleagues thus shows that dispositional approaches and the job characteristics model are quite compatible with one another.

What about the relationship between the job characteristics model and value-percept theory? If most individuals value the nature of the work itself more than other job facets, and evidence indicates that they do (Jurgensen, 1978), then Locke's theory would predict that increasing the level of intrinsic job characteristics (thus reducing the have–want discrepancy with respect to intrinsic characteristics) would be the most effective means of raising employees' job satisfaction. Thus, although the job characteristic model and Locke's value-percept model present different perspectives on job satisfaction, their implications may be the same – as long as employees value intrinsic job characteristics (which they appear to), both would suggest that, for most people, the most effective way to increase job satisfaction would be to increase intrinsic job characteristics.

Measurement of job satisfaction

Perhaps the two most extensively validated measures are the Job Descriptive Index (JDI; Smith et al., 1969) and the Minnesota Satisfaction Questionnaire (MSQ; Weiss et al., 1967). The JDI assesses satisfaction with five different job facets: pay; promotion; co-workers; supervision; and the work itself. The JDI is reliable and has an impressive array of validation evidence behind it. The MSQ has the advantage of versatility – long and short forms are available, and faceted and overall measures are available. There are additional measures that have been widely used in research, though these measures do not carry with them validation evidence as impressive as the JDI or MSQ.

There are two additional relevant issues. First, some measures of job satisfaction, such as the JDI, are faceted, while others are global. If a measure is facet-based, overall job satisfaction is typically defined as a sum of the facets. Scarpello and Campbell (1983) found that individual questions about various aspects of the job did not correlate well with a global measure of overall job satisfaction. Based on these results, the authors argued that faceted and global measures do not measure the same construct. In other words, the whole is not the same as the sum of the parts. Scarpello and Campbell conclude, "The results of the present study argue against the common practice of using the sum of facet satisfaction as the measure of overall job satisfaction" (p. 595). This conclusion is probably premature. Individual items generally do not correlate highly with independent measures of the same construct.

If one uses job satisfaction *facets* (as opposed to individual job satisfaction *items*) to predict an independent measure of overall job satisfaction, the correlation is considerably higher. For example, using data that one of the authors has collected, if one uses the JDI facets to predict a measure of overall job satisfaction, the combined multiple correlation is 0.87.

Second, while most job satisfaction researchers have assumed that single-item measures are unreliable and therefore should not be used, this view has not gone unchallenged. Wanous et al. (1997) found that the reliability of single-item measures of job satisfaction is 0.68. Though this is a respectable level of reliability, it is important to keep in mind that this is lower than most multiple-item measures of job satisfaction. For example, Judge et al. (1994) used a three-item measure of job satisfaction that was reliable ($\alpha = 0.85$). The items in this measure were:

1. All things considered, are you satisfied with your present job (circle one)? YES NO
2. How satisfied are you with your job in general (circle one)?

1	2	3	4	5
Very Dissatisfied	Somewhat Dissatisfied	Neutral	Somewhat Satisfied	Very Satisfied

3. Below, please write down your best estimates on the percent time you feel satisfied, dissatisfied, and neutral about your present job on average. The three figures should add up to equal 100%. ON THE AVERAGE:

The percent of time I feel satisfied with my present job _____%   (*note*: only this response is scored)

The percent of time I feel dissatisfied with my present job _____%

The percent of time I feel neutral about my present job _____%

TOTAL _____%

When used in practice, these items need to be standardized before summing. Although this measure is no substitute for the richness of detail provided in a faceted measure of job satisfaction, we do believe it is a reasonably valid measure of overall job satisfaction.

Outcomes of job satisfaction

Given the centrality of the construct to industrial/organizational psychology, job satisfaction has been correlated with many outcome variables. The relationship of job satisfaction to the most frequently investigated and important outcome variables are reviewed below.

Life satisfaction

Researchers have speculated that there are three possible forms of the relationship between job and life satisfaction: (1) spillover, where job experiences spill over into the life, and vice-versa; (2) segmentation, where job and life experiences are balkanized and have little to do with one another; and (3) compensation, where an individual seeks to compensate for a dissatisfying job by seeking fulfillment and happiness in his or her non-work life, and vice versa. Judge and Watanabe (1994) argued that these different models may exist for different individuals and were able to classify individuals into the three groups. On the basis of a national stratified random sample of workers, they found that 68 percent of workers could be classified as falling into the spillover group, 20 percent of individuals fell into the segmentation group, and 12 percent fell into the compensation group. Thus, the spillover model appears to characterize most individuals.

Consistent with the spillover model, a quantitative review of the literature indicated that job and life satisfaction are moderately strongly correlated – a meta-analysis revealed the average "true score" correlation of +0.44 (Tait et al., 1989). Since the job is a significant part of life, the correlation between job and life satisfaction makes sense – one's job experiences spill over onto life. However, it also seems possible that the causality could go the other way – a happy non-work life spills over onto job experiences and evaluations. In fact, research suggests that the relationship between job and life satisfaction is reciprocal – job satisfaction does affect life satisfaction, but life satisfaction also affects job satisfaction (Judge and Watanabe, 1993).

Job performance

The relationship between job satisfaction and performance has an interesting history. The Hawthorne studies are credited with making researchers aware of the effect of attitudes on performance. Shortly after the Hawthorne studies, researchers began taking a critical look at the hypothesis that a happy worker is a productive one. Most of the qualitative reviews of the literature suggested a weak, positive, and somewhat inconsistent relationship among the constructs. In 1985, a quantitative review of the literature suggested that the true correlation between job satisfaction and performance was 0.17 (Iaffaldano and Muchinsky, 1985). These authors concluded that the presumed relationship among the constructs was a "management fad" and that the correlation was "illusory." This study has had an important impact on researchers. Most industrial/organizational psychologists who write on the topic conclude that the relationship among the constructs is trivial. Relying on Iaffaldano and Muchinsky, the satisfaction–performance relationship has been described as "meager" (Brief, 1998, p. 42), "negligible" (Weiss and Cropanzano, 1996, p. 51), and "bordering on the trivial" (Landy, 1989, p. 481).

Not everyone agrees with this conclusion. Organ (1988) suggests that the failure to find a relationship between job satisfaction and performance is due to the narrow means that is often used to define job performance. Organ argued that when performance is construed to include many constructive behaviors not generally reflected in a performance appraisal instrument, such as organizational citizenship behaviors, its correlation with job satisfaction will improve. Research tends to support Organ's proposition in that job satisfaction correlates reliably with organizational citizenship behaviors (Organ and Ryan, 1995).

There is another perspective. Perhaps researchers have been wrong to dismiss the relationship between job satisfaction and performance. We have completed a study that represents a much more comprehensive review of the literature than has been the case in previous research, identifying 295 studies (Judge et al., 1998). When the correlations are corrected for the effects of sampling error and measurement error (based on inter-rater reliability for job performance and composite reliability for job satisfaction), the average true score correlation between overall job satisfaction and job performance is 0.30. The correlation between job satisfaction and performance was considerably higher for complex jobs than for less complex jobs, indicating complex jobs may afford greater autonomy, thus giving individuals greater latitudes to act on their satisfaction (or dissatisfaction). Thus, contrary to previous reviews, it does appear that job satisfaction is moderately correlated with performance. It also appears that the relationship between satisfaction and performance generalizes to the organizational level of analysis (Harter and Creglow, 1998).

Withdrawal behaviors

Job satisfaction displays relatively consistent, negative, and weak correlations with absenteeism and turnover. The average correlation is generally in the –0.25 range. Job dissatisfaction appears to display weak, negative – but significant – correlations with other specific withdrawal behaviors, including unionization, lateness, drug abuse, and retirement. Hulin et al. (1985) have argued that these individual behaviors are manifestations of the underlying construct of job adaptation. Hulin et al. proposed that these individual behaviors can be grouped together as manifestations of job adaptive proclivities. Because the base rate of occurrence of most single withdrawal behaviors is quite low, aggregating across a variety of adaptive behaviors, as Hulin (1991) demonstrated, improves both the distribution and the theoretical basis of the withdrawal construct. Rather than predicting isolated behaviors, withdrawal research would do better, as this model suggests, to consider individual behaviors as manifestations of an underlying adaptive construct. Several studies have been supportive of Hulin's approach, finding that isolated withdrawal behaviors can be grouped into one or more behavioral families, and job satisfaction better predicts these behavioral families than the individual behaviors comprising these families.

■ HOW JOB SATISFACTION IS VIEWED AND TREATED IN ORGANIZATIONS

Overview

Despite the media attention regarding generally positive economic trends and unprecedented growth in certain business sectors such as the Internet over the last several years (for example, Useem, 1999), from a practitioner perspective it would be a fair statement to say that employees are less than completely satisfied with their present jobs. A common theme given the business climate of the early 1990s, it seems the only real element that has changed in industry today is the level of concerted attention to the construct of satisfaction itself. Perhaps this is due to the fact that while unemployment is at an all-time low and e-commerce is booming, the average employee in an organization must more than ever accept the continued and frequent possibility of large-scale downsizing, restructuring, or merger situations in any given organization or industry. Micklethwait and Wooldridge (1996) noted, for example, that despite the strong economy, a survey of 1,200 US companies conducted by the American Management Association indicated that more than 40 percent were intending to eliminate jobs in the coming year in conjunction with ongoing organizational restructuring initiatives. Mike Moore (1996) has termed this situation the American *Bad* Dream: "If you work hard, and the company prospers – you lose your job!" (p. 11). Given such conditions, it should be no wonder that cynical cartoon strips such as *Dilbert* (Adams, 1996) that lampoon organizations, leadership and management, and employee's quality of worklife, have become so popular.

Cynicism is not the only indicator or outcome of job satisfaction related concerns, however. The field of consulting plays an important part here as well. The management consulting profession, for example, has proven to be extremely financially successful, with estimated annual revenues close to $40 billion (Micklethwait and Wooldridge, 1996). Moreover, the area of organization change and development has seen a significant rise at almost all levels as well. In fact, consulting efforts of this type have reached the point where Organization Development (OD) and Human Resource Development (HRD) practitioners often find themselves entering mid-stream (Burke et al., 1997) into a variety of pre-existing initiatives and interventions where they can be treated as interchangeable vendors rather than content experts (Church and Waclawski, 1998a). Despite this growth, however, consulting work in this area still typically focuses on morale, communications, leadership motivation, and management development – all of which relate to issues of job satisfaction in one form or another. Unfortunately, many other and often competing initiatives and interventions pursued by other types of consultants are either aimed specifically at or result in significant restructuring and/or downsizing efforts wherein employees are left feeling confused, powerless, and dehumanized – the very same outcomes proffered by Bellah et al. (1985) in their description of the inevitable devaluing of humanity and community in modern organizational life. Needless to say, these types of outcomes make it difficult for individuals to feel satisfied with their jobs.

One might expect the notion of job satisfaction to be in the forefront of employers' minds. Interestingly enough, however, the extent to which organizations have adopted the term and institutionalized interventions based on job satisfaction related theory and research is considerably more mixed. Job satisfaction, for example, is rarely included as part of an organization's key values, basic beliefs, core competencies or guiding principles, nor is the topic given much direct exposure in popular business books. Rather, the idea of having satisfied employees is more likely to be considered some form of outcome or end-state, which occurs as a result of adherence to some more proactively typically action oriented set of factors, behaviors or set of interventions (for example, Church, 1995; Neuman et al., 1989; Wagner, 1994).

Generally speaking, attention to job satisfaction related issues seems to range anywhere from complete repression of the term to fully integrated measurement and evaluation tools, such as annual organization culture surveys (for example, Church and Waclawski, 1998b; Kraut, 1996), multi-rater feedback methodologies (such as Bracken, 1996; Tornow, 1993), or the Balanced Scorecard approach (Kaplan and Norton, 1992). Even in those organizations where job satisfaction issues are addressed directly through formal institutional systems and policies, the conceptualization tends to be more outcome oriented, such as morale, commitment, or even turnover. Thus, while these areas are entirely different psychological constructs in the literature, managers and practitioners often use the terms interchangeably when working with and responding to these types of issues. This blurring of the construct itself and intermittent level of implementation raises some important issues for researchers and theorists working in the area of job satisfaction, as well as for the practitioners who must work within and manage such complex boundaries.

The purpose of the following section is to explore in more detail the conceptualization and utilization of job satisfaction related issues in organizational settings as well as some of the complexities for practitioners in these environments. First, the importance of job satisfaction for practitioners will be discussed. Next, various approaches to understanding, measuring and utilizing job satisfaction in organizations will be covered. The final section will include barriers and areas for future research. These issues will be addressed through a combination of organization and consulting experience and the use of a series of short interviews conducted with senior I/O, OD, and HR individuals in various organizational settings. These data were collected from 17 individuals across a number of organizations representing different industries and sizes including government, electronics, pharmaceuticals, food service, professional services, educational assessment, I/O consulting, financial services, transportation, aerospace, OD consulting, and petroleum. All individuals were asked to respond to the same set of six questions regarding the understanding and use of job satisfaction related research and constructs in their organization (see the Appendix for a detailed list of questions and a list of contributors).

Who is responsible for job satisfaction?

Although the content domain of job satisfaction has traditionally been associated with I/O theory and research, the applied aspects of working with satisfaction related issues and interventions in organizations are by no means confined to I/O psychologists. OD and HRD practitioners are also often engaged in working with these types of issues, particularly with respect to change management and leadership development related processes. Further, the group of professionals most associated with job satisfaction related issues in an organization might be under an entirely different name or function altogether. Some of these other possibilities include Personnel Research – which was the case, for example, at IBM in the early 1990s – Performance Improvement, Organization Effectiveness, and even Executive and Management Development such as at Microsoft (Church et al., 1998). Thus, it is quite common to have individuals with I/O psychology backgrounds employed in functions whose names and/or objectives more closely mirror these other areas. In addition to these functional groups and the three major types of practitioners mentioned above, there is an increasing emphasis for more traditional HR professionals to move their skill sets in this direction (Robinson and Robinson, 1996). Thus, the practitioner responsible for job satisfaction related concerns could be located almost anywhere in the organization.

Regardless of nomenclature, however, from a systemic view of the organization as a series of sub-processes and role-sets (Katz and Kahn, 1978) I/O, OD, and HRD practitioners share a common focus on the interplay between people, the nature of their jobs, and the organization as a whole. In essence, this focus on employee quality of worklife and employee satisfaction both serves a needed function for the organization, and provides a value-added contribution for the I/O, OD, HRD professional. The management subsystem, on the other hand, is concerned with the process of converting inputs to outputs. Thus, while some managers and executives might indeed be concerned with having motivated, satisfied and hard working employees, the task of diagnosing, monitoring and affecting change in these areas is principally the realm of the I/O, OD, HRD or related functions. This is not always an easy assignment, as some organizations have had entire functions dedicated just to the measurement of employee perceptions while others may have only a single individual responsible for these types of issues. None the less, the I/O, OD, and HRD practitioner represents the primary repository of such expertise and indeed to some extent the conscience in these areas. Moreover, this trend continues to be true today in many organizations despite the emphasis in the business literature over the last decade on moving some of the relationship oriented and retention related practices and decisions to line management (for example, Block, 1993).

Why job satisfaction is important to practitioners and organizations

Although one could argue that job satisfaction might be an inherently important topic, there are several more compelling reasons for practitioners, managers, and executives to be concerned with such an issue. These include the importance of the job to self-identity, the changing nature of work, the potential impact of attitudes on individual and organizational performance, and the potential impact of job attitudes on organizational change. Each of these is described briefly below.

Importance of the job to self-identity

Several decades ago the French sociologist Jacques Ellul (1964) argued in his book, *The Technological Society*, that "work is an expression of life . . . to assert that the individual expresses his personality and cultivates himself in the course of his leisure is to accept the suppression of half the human personality" (p. 399). Although Ellul's comments reflect the concerns of his generation regarding the substitution of workers with machines and the subsequent devolution of the human experience, his message concerning the importance of people's jobs in defining "who we are" is still highly relevant if Peter Senge's (1990) comments in the enormously popular *The Fifth Discipline* are any indication: "We are trained to be loyal to our jobs – so much so that we confuse them with our own identities" (p. 18). Clearly, for many individuals, personal notions of self-image and self-worth are inextricably connected to the role or job they hold in their organization (Bellah et al., 1985; Zedeck, 1992). Perhaps it should not be surprising, then, that items reflecting the employees' attitudes toward the work they do are quite often some of the highest rated items in organization culture survey efforts. In short, an individual's feelings and satisfaction with his or her job are extremely important to personal well-being. From this perspective alone, job satisfaction *should be* an important agenda and metric, at least for practitioners in the psychological, behavioral, and human sciences such as I/O, OD, and HRD.

The changing nature of work

The central nature of jobs and job satisfaction also presents somewhat of a problem for practitioners and organizations interested in individual effectiveness and retention, given the nature of today's global and rapidly changing business environment. More specifically, as anyone who has worked in, studied, or consulted with organizations over the last decade knows, the form and function of these social systems and what has traditionally been known as "work" and "jobs" have experienced what amounts to a paradigm shift (Church et al., 1996; Howard, 1995; Kraut and Korman, 1999). Aside from the issues of global competition and changing workforce demographics, these conceptual changes in the nature of work are largely due to the fact that many organizational changes and initiatives – for example, restructuring, re-engineering, downsizing, process improvement methodology, network organizations, and strategic alliances – are now directed at altering the nature of people's jobs substantially and/or eliminating them altogether. The prevalence of these approaches in industry today, along with continued enhancements in information technology, has prompted some I/O practitioners to suggest that the notion of a job as traditionally defined is no longer a viable construct. Howard (1995) concludes, for example, that "the job is, after all, an artifact of the industrial age, created to package work in factories and bureaucratic organizations. [It] is disappearing in favor of an amorphous collection of work" (pp. 520, 523). As these changes occur, however, greater instability and ambiguity result, which consequently place more pressure on practitioners, managers, and executives to respond to satisfaction related concerns among employees.

Does this then mean that job satisfaction is no longer an important issue as well? Although the answer is most certainly an unqualified "no," the shift in organizational structures and the nature of work does suggest that practitioners, managers, and executives may need to concern themselves more with the larger construct of employee satisfaction than job satisfaction. There is another implication here for practitioners as well. The more jobs become less stable entities, the more I/O practitioners in particular may need to shift their skillsets to the organizational domain of the field (and therefore more in alignment with some of their OD and HRD counterparts), such as organizational culture, leadership, group processes, mission and strategy, values, and transformational change. Of course, many practitioners are already engaging in these areas.

The potential impact of attitudes on individual and organizational performance

There are additional reasons for practitioner and organizational interest in job satisfaction as an outcome. Varying levels of employee satisfaction, quality of work-life (QWL), and organizational commitment, for example, have been linked to reductions in performance, product quality and customer responsiveness, as well as increases in turnover (for example, Cohen, 1993; Golembiewski and Sun, 1990; Harter and Creglow, 1998; Schneider and Bowen, 1985; Ulrich et al., 1991). Job related attitudes and perceptions are also central features in several diagnostic and prescriptive organizational models (for example, Bray, 1994; Burke and Litwin, 1992; Nadler and Gerstein, 1992). Given the potentially negative effects of such outcomes on both organizational effectiveness and on people's lives, it is imperative that I/O, OD, and HRD practitioners – as well as managers and executives – have a clearer understanding of the relationships and constructs involved so that decisions can be affected. While arguably a concern for all types of settings, the problem is enhanced for those organizations whose employees are either sales driven or customer service oriented (Schneider and Bowen, 1985). A firm whose work force is primarily sales or service based is likely to suffer considerable training and development costs as well as damaged client relationships if negative attitudes among their employees are conveyed directly to clients or result in greater employee turnover.

The potential impact of job attitudes on organizational change

While the types of relationships described above are certainly important, there is another type of outcome with respect to job satisfaction related interventions that has not yet been mentioned and that many managers, and executives fail to fully appreciate – the success or failure of other change initiatives. In short, employee related issues of this type are a critical yet under-acknowledged component of effective change management initiatives. Even though the organization consulting profession continues to experience significant growth year after year (Micklethwait and Wooldridge, 1996), mounting evidence suggests that the majority of these large-scale interventions either fail completely or have little to no impact on the client organization. A survey of 300 electronics companies in 1992, for example, indicated that 63 percent of those organizations implementing total quality management (TQM) efforts had failed to yield improvements in their level of product defects (Schaffer and Thompson, 1992). Other studies and practitioners have noted similar types of results for other large-scale interventions such as re-engineering, business process improvement, and culture change efforts (such as Kotter, 1995; Spector and Beer, 1994; Trahant and Burke, 1996). While there are certainly a variety of individual and organizational factors that influence the success or failure of a given change effort, more and more practitioners are citing inattention to process or people related issues (for example, Champy, 1995; Kotter, 1995; Siegal et al., 1996) as the primary source almost regardless of the nature of the intervention. These process issues include, among other things, a focus on the attitudes, perceptions, and reactions of the people being affected by the change effort, which, of course, is directly related to their level of satisfaction. Even if this cause–effect relationship is somewhat overstated, from a financial perspective alone (given the billions of dollars spent annually on implementing and maintaining change efforts), it seems hard to argue that organizations should not be concerned with the importance of job satisfaction theory, measurement, and research.

Working with job satisfaction in organizations

Given the arguments made above regarding the importance of job satisfaction for I/O, OD, and HRD practitioners as well as organizational leadership, one might expect job satisfaction and related issues to have a central focus in organizations. In fact, however, there is considerable variability in the levels of formal emphasis, understanding, and intervention placed on the topic. In fact, it is safe to say that the state of job satisfaction as a construct and formal target in organizations for policy and intervention by practitioners appears to be almost as divergent as the theories and research in the field. The following section will examine the manner in which job satisfaction theory and research is actually conceptualized, measured, and utilized in organizations in more detail based in large part on the practitioner interview data described earlier. Topics to be covered include levels of importance and understanding, levels of integration and intervention, and barriers and challenges for practitioners and organizations.

Levels of importance and understanding

Although job satisfaction is a common topic in most I/O and OB text books for students (such as Landy, 1989) and is certainly a primary area of concern for practitioners in these areas as well, a review of the subject indices for the majority of management books, including many best sellers, reveals that job satisfaction *per se* is not a particularly compelling topic from the executive and management perspective, and therefore not often included. Consulting experience at both the more systemic corporate levels as well as in executive coaching sessions with middle level managers and service professionals also tends to support this notion. In other words, while management in organizations would probably not disagree with a general statement regarding the relevance of job satisfaction, in practice this is not likely to be one of the areas that generates much enthusiasm or interest.

When practitioners were asked about the general perception of job satisfaction, its relative importance, and the use of the term in their organizations, responses generally mirrored the observations above. Although all of the interviewees were quite familiar with the concepts themselves, the extent to which others in their organization shared a similar understanding was extremely limited. For example, about half of the respondents indicated that job satisfaction as a term and singular construct was rarely if ever mentioned or considered in their organizations:

- "Job satisfaction is virtually never discussed in the senior staff meetings I attend within our business unit."

- "It's never mentioned."

- "I don't find many of the practitioners I come into contact with using the phrase job satisfaction. It is hardly ever mentioned as a separate construct, although I don't doubt that many would subscribe to such a notion."

- "Job satisfaction is important in my organization although it is not in any way defined specifically or measured."

- "The term job satisfaction is not used here."

- "I think the term is generally considered as a measure of emotional state in relation to work and impacting on motivation to work – and emotional state seems to be viewed by the senior leadership as something that committed employees should not have time to even consider."

- "At town meetings with the President or others, questions or comments that even come close to issues affecting job satisfaction are not addressed. It has had zero importance in the 4.5 years I have been here."

- "The topic is a foreign substance."

- "Job satisfaction is implicit. We don't discuss it in the boardroom and I've never seen it as a topic on any agenda. People do not use the term, nor is it even given lip service. Job satisfaction is implicit because we're a family owned organization and it is assumed that everyone is happy because we offer them such a great deal."

- "People derived satisfaction because they were able to add value at all levels due in part to our flat structure and team oriented approach, but we never called it job satisfaction."

- "Since we're in a manufacturing/engineering business, people principles (soft-side) are typically secondary – though we'd never admit that."

Even for those individuals who noted that their organizations did make use of the construct, it was apparent that other terms were often substituted instead:

- "Job satisfaction is an infrequently used term here; instead the term is employee satisfaction or enthusiasm or commitment."

- "People use the terms satisfaction, satisfied employees, job satisfaction, motivated employees somewhat interchangeably."

- "More often, individuals are likely to use the term morale."

- "We don't use the term job satisfaction, but use the term employee satisfaction."

- "Job satisfaction (as a subset of employee satisfaction) typically includes such issues as job challenge, job autonomy, job variety, job meaningfulness, and job closure (feedback)."

While there are certainly conceptual similarities between the constructs of organizational commitment, morale, enthusiasm, motivation, and even the broader employee satisfaction, clearly from a theoretical and research perspective these practitioner waters are already looking rather muddy. Unfortunately, the situation does not improve with respect to implementation.

When asked next about the utilization of current theory and research on job satisfaction, the result here was far from surprising. More specifically, while a number of individuals commented that satisfaction related issues and concerns were indeed important in their organization, relatively few indicated a wide level of understanding of the theoretical concepts and current research in their organization. Most of the comments in this regard were direct and unequivocal:

- "Traditional theoretical concepts are not considered."

- "Job satisfaction is understood as defined by whoever is talking about it at the time."

- "There is wide variation in how well these concepts are understood by management because we are not strong at selecting and developing managers in these areas. Consequently, even where the concepts are understood, the management culture and reward systems are at best irrelevant to progressive people practices."

- "Job satisfaction theories are simply too mechanistic."

- "I doubt anyone knows about the theories or work in this area – or cares!"

- "I don't find that much of the theoretical discussion surrounding job satisfaction is widely understood in the private sector."

- "The concepts are not used here."

- "Pop business books drive a great deal of our thinking on corporate strategy/programs."

- "Little to no understanding of the theoretical concepts and little to no research."

Among the few divergent responses on this topic, it appears as though the strength and credibility of the internal I/O, OD, or HRD function may be largely responsible:

- "In terms of research and thinking our organization really looks to us for guidance and to make sure we are up-to-date. Our job is to help translate what will work best for us in this culture, at this time and in alignment with our core values."

- "That group is led by an I/O psychologist who understands the theoretical concepts very well and applies these concepts as they perform their work. For example, they used current research when they developed our climate survey."

- "It is a serious topic here for discussion and management. HR professionals readily make the connections between employee satisfaction and other things (for example, retention of "best" people, recruitment and selection, client satisfaction and retention)."

Given some of the typical associations and connotations in the field of consulting in general, not to mention psychology as a science (for example, Adams, 1996; Mickleth-wait and Wooldridge, 1996; Waclawski, 1998), such a relationship between a strong function and the ability to make use of current theory and research would indeed argue for the importance of defining the parameters and raising awareness in general of I/O psychology as a field, as has been argued elsewhere (for example, Church et al., 1997). Moreover, the importance of this relationship also reinforces the need to actively market these types of services and expertise in organizational settings, as some authors have discussed (such as Engdahl et al., 1991; Gilley and Eggland, 1992).

Finally, in terms of whether the importance placed on job satisfaction related concerns was increasing or decreasing, the vast majority of responses indicated that, if anything, the salience of the topic in their organization was on the decline, compared with management agenda in the early 1990s. Interestingly enough, two of the four individuals who indicated an increasing level of importance were both from organizations that were currently undergoing significant changes in structure and senior management. This trend seems to parallel consulting experience as well. Organization assessment and culture surveys as a technique, which often includes a specific satisfaction related component (Burke and Jackson, 1991; Johnson, 1996), were extremely popular in the late 1980s and early 1990s. However, many practi-tioners today would probably agree that from both an external as well as an internal resource perspective these interventions have been largely overcome by a greater interest in multi-rater or 360-degree feedback (Bracken, 1996; Church and Bracken, 1997; Tornow, 1993) and executive coaching-based initiatives (for example, Good-stone and Diamante, 1998; Waclawski and Church, 1999), which tend to focus on perceptions of an individual rather than the attitudes about the job and the organiza-tion. Both sets of tools are still used by some organizations to address satisfaction related concerns and both do indeed measure individual perceptions and attitudes.

Levels of integration and intervention

Based on the description above of the extent to which job satisfaction theory and research are understood in organizations, it should come as no surprise that the levels reported by these practitioners of integration and intervention in this area varied considerably as well. While few organizations have gone to great lengths to incorporate the term job satisfaction at the largest strategic or systems level of the organization (such as, via a statement of values, principles, competencies, or beliefs), the importance of attitudes and perceptions about work in general are also clearly at the forefront of the agenda of many practitioners and some senior executives. Two practitioners, for example, made specific comments about their senior executives in this regard, although these differ in tone considerably:

- "Our CEO even writes working on employee pride (part of which is related to job satisfaction) into his annual goals for the corporation."

- "The only manager I occasionally hear referencing job satisfaction is the CEO. He considers the concept in staffing decisions but business imperatives generally win out."

In general, however, the response to job satisfaction concerns tends to be more systemic. Taken as a whole, there appear to be three levels of integration and subsequent intervention of I/O, OD, and HRD practitioner related policies, programs and interventions: systemic institutionalization, project or initiative based, and minimalization by outcome. Each of these is described briefly below.

Clearly, some organizations and practitioner groups appear to have made a concerted effort to conceptualize, measure, and initiate policies and programs in response to satisfaction related concerns among their employees. Not unlike some of the work occurring in Sears, Roebuck and Company (Rucci et al., 1998), these organizations with systemic institutionalization approaches here have adopted a number of different measurement and information systems (including surveys, multi-rater feedback, and interviews) to provide input about employee satisfaction for management and personnel related decisions. In some of these organizations, for example, the outcome of satisfaction related opinion survey data is even used as part of the formal performance assessment and objective setting processes, via the Balanced Scorecard (Kaplan and Norton, 1992) or similar method:

- "Surveys, 360-feedback, one-on-ones, focus groups – we have lots of listening posts directed at gaining insight into our employees' thoughts, feelings, and opinions. We were really built on the strength of innovative employees and people tend not to innovate when unhappy, so a significant part of the culture especially for HR is to minimize distractions so that employees can concentrate on what they do best."

- "We now take into consideration preferences when assigning new employees to work locations. Also, we have recently implemented a competency-based promotional assessment system for filling supervisory and managerial vacancies. We provide candidates with comprehensive diagnostic feedback. Satisfaction with the previous promotional system was low because candidates never learned why they were not selected for a specific vacancy. Now candidates receive this information, and satisfaction with this component of the job has increased."

- "On an annual basis, the Partner Development Program has taken the 360-degree feedback data partners receive in the course and looks at the direct report ratings as a measure of job satisfaction. The CARE process was also developed by internal HR professionals in response to the 1994 Worldwide employee satisfaction survey and includes four integrated components (Annual Review Process, Performance Review Process, Upward Feedback, and Mentoring)."

Of course, high levels of integration do not guarantee a favorable result, as one practitioner noted:

"We have been using surveys to measure employee satisfaction for some time, though recent global surveys may replace existing regional or business unit ones. These results have been given too much attention, in my opinion, as an end on a balanced scorecard with unrealistic targets, for example, greater than 90% favorable on a question such as 'how satisfied are you with your job?' Too much emphasis on single survey measures can be frustrating."

Other practitioners described a more targeted, bounded, and perhaps less systemic approach to working with and responding to job satisfaction related concerns. These interventions typically focus on specific initiatives, objectives, or task forces that concern satisfaction, morale, motivation, or related types of employee attitudinal issues. The majority of examples given by practitioners reflected this type of approach:

- "We recently created a 'Sustainment' group whose responsibilities include dealing with issues of job satisfaction in the workforce, retaining good employees, running the Employee Assistance Program, and conducting orientation for new employees."

- "The main intervention here is to provide in-house and external staff development and training/growth opportunities for lower level staff to develop new skills."

- "Creating a productive work environment is one of the fundamental components of our Leadership Model and the cornerstone of our HR practices. It is reinforced through training, performance management, diversity, rewards/recognition, and other HR initiatives."

- "Employee satisfaction is given more than lip service, but employee satisfaction tends to be managed through initiatives, some of which are not well integrated into the way we do business."

As noted above, survey feedback represents an important tool for collecting attitudinal and satisfaction related data in organizations. Several practitioners also mentioned the use of organizational climate or culture surveys and/or 360-degree or multi-rater assessments as part of their approach. Although these measures were not typically as fully integrated with formal performance management systems as in the examples given above, practitioners did describe linkages with other types of information as well as utilizing targeted reports for employee satisfaction related organizational change and development initiatives:

- "We are now conducting a climate survey and each organizational component will receive feedback outlining its employees' perceptions. Some organizational components, I am certain, will choose to use this as an outcome measure when future policies and procedures are considered or implemented."

- "We have been conducting research analyses that link employee job satisfaction with client satisfaction and business performance. Preliminary results of these studies have been passed on to senior management for their consideration. Global HR also used the data from the 1997 worldwide survey to look for connections between employee satisfaction, client satisfaction, and a number of other performance measures. In addition they looked for what are the critical few actions that should be taken to make a significant positive impact on employee satisfaction."

- "Employee satisfaction surveys and research based on the survey results will continue on a regular basis as well as interventions designed to further improve employees' satisfaction."

- "We currently use 360 in our leadership training programs and are in the process of conducting a global organization assessment for some of our HR practices (performance management, rewards/recognition, employee development, and leadership training)."

- "There has been discussion of implementing a 360-feedback process, growing out of a organizational effectiveness study that our organization did in 1997."

Of course, this reliance on survey data should not be surprising given the prevalence of survey methodology in organizations (Church and Waclawski, 1998b; Kraut, 1996; Rogelberg and Luong, 1998). Traditionally, this type of large-scale opinion survey has been one of the primary means by which practitioners have been able to assess employee attitudes en masse and provide leadership and management with data for use in decision-making efforts and has a long history in I/O, OD, and HRD practice (for example, Burke et al., 1996; Nadler, 1977). One of the typical concerns, however, with any survey effort is the potential lack of integration and coordinated effort with other initiatives and systems. Two practitioners described such a scenario:

- "Employee surveys, focus groups, benchmarking, team building, communications plans, job reclassifications, competency-based assessment system and leadership development, some 360-feedback. You name it, we do it at least somewhere in the company. While all of this produces some constructive activity, there is little integration. *Kind of like a fibrillating heart – lots of muscular activity but little blood getting pumped* (emphasis added)."

- "The perception here is that survey reports are produced so that managers can say 'see the departmental problems aren't my fault.' "

Often, such an initiative, if not well managed and coordinated, can do more damage than good and may contribute to negative response tendencies and increased cynicism in the future (Church and Waclawski, 1998b; McClough et al., 1998). One might argue that some attention devoted to these issues in an organization is probably better than none, but that is debatable.

The third type of response to job satisfaction related concerns was to downplay the entire notion by treating it primarily as an indicator – that is, a minimalization by outcome approach – or not at all. Practitioners noted examples here that ranged from outright resistance to nominal interest in the issues.

- "For example, in a recent discussion centering on the issue of overtime pay for engineers, someone commented that some engineers were upset that they were not compensated for overtime and other engineers were. The response was that if they had time to worry about such things when we are under pressure to get systems developed that something was wrong with them."

- "Job satisfaction is not measured. Because this is Wall Street, money talks. If people weren't happy, they could have moved their whole team elsewhere."

- "Job satisfaction is not measured or considered at all."

- "We did a series of culture focus groups a couple of years ago and as a result have an annual employee appreciation day now. The results of the survey were never discussed openly with the employee population. Some people view employee appreciation day as a nice thing, others are more cynical (or realistic) and say we should worry about employee morale on days other than employee appreciation day."

- "Only ad hoc attempts if the current situation warrants it and if someone in a decision making position sponsors it. Even then, usually nothing is really done about it."

In some situations the lack of senior manager attention to and perceived credibility of job satisfaction related issues is clearly evident as a source of the problem. Several practitioners provided examples of this situation:

- "Management here doesn't understand assessment tools (for example, surveys, 360), doesn't want to, and won't even try to understand them."

- "Employee satisfaction is not yet a performance metric; however, I have provided benchmarking information to our senior leaders regarding how other companies utilize such metrics in managing their business and performance culture. Seems like the interest is there; but is there the courage and leadership?"

- "Employee satisfaction is considered by management to be a 'soft' measure."

- "Our management strategy is 'top line' oriented and job satisfaction is either assumed or worked on in some ad hoc manner. It is not measured at all."

- "The key barrier is that top management only does what they think is important. We are not a learning organization nor do we share best practices well enough."

- "Few here have a perspective that lasts over 5–10 years, those that do end up leaving due to frustration or medical reasons (peptic ulcers, heart attacks, etc.)."

Others described a process of assessment vis-à-vis what one individual mentioned as the "employee satisfaction as retention paradigm," which in some ways amounts to a dismissal of the issue entirely. Although retention is certainly likely to be related to job satisfaction as an outcome, the variable itself provides absolutely no diagnostic information or guidance for improving working conditions for employees.

- "Bottom line, job satisfaction will be measured by retention rates during the next year."

- "The real question becomes how do we keep and more importantly recommit and reenergize the key players in the organization?"

Clearly, some organizations appear to be quite successful at assessing and integrating job satisfaction related issues into their performance management systems via a variety of methods, many of which are well known to I/O, OD, and HRD professionals. Interestingly enough, however, none of the individuals in this group mentioned the use of some of the more traditional standardized measures such as the Job Descriptive Index (Smith et al., 1969). Moreover, the majority of practitioners, at least in the present sample, were engaged in more of the mid-level approaches, which may be due at least in part to a combination of (1) senior management interest, and (2) the relative size and perceived credibility of the function or department responsible. Given that past research has demonstrated that OD and HRD functions are not all that well perceived in certain industries and types of organizations (for example, Church and McMahan, 1996; McMahan and Woodman, 1992), the fact that many organizations are at least attempting to collect and/or make use of such information is a positive finding.

Barriers and challenges for practitioners and organizations

While the focus on employee quality of worklife and employee satisfaction serves a needed function for the organization as noted above, it also presents the internal practitioner with a variety of personal and professional challenges. The final set of themes in the comments received from the present sample of professionals reflects more specifically some of the barriers and challenges presented by the current state of job satisfaction in organizations. Although some of these have already been alluded to above, there were a number of specific comments and potential areas for future research raised by respondents that are deserving of further consideration.

The first and perhaps most important barrier reflects the issue of priority and the perceived importance of job satisfaction concerns by senior and middle management. While it is probably unrealistic to expect individuals (other than I/O, OD, and HRD practitioners) in organizations to embrace current research and thinking about any topic including job satisfaction, it was somewhat disconcerting to realize that in many large, well known, and financially successful companies job-related attitudes and perceptions are given only intermittent or passing attention at the strategic and executive levels:

- "OD could have a great impact on our organization, but the social sciences don't have a seat at our corporate table."

- "Given that many executives come from the line side of management there is a negative mentality toward 'personnel issues' being perpetuated, and job satisfaction is one of these."

- "Two of our biggest challenges are consistency in application and helping people to see a direct correlation between a productive work environment and the business results."

Integration with other internal systems and adequate follow-through were also cited as problems:

- "Integration of our initiative with one another and with how we do business and with how managers/execs are compensated."

- "Inconsistent follow-through."

Further, while many organizations engage in satisfaction-related assessments through annual survey or multi-rater assessment processes, far fewer appear to fully utilize this information in policy, program, or change initiatives. Regardless of the reason cited – whether competing pressures on time, resources, or attention – there is a clear trend toward lack of appreciation in many organizations for the impact of satisfaction-related issues on employee and subsequently organizational performance. This issue came up several times in the discussion of barriers with practitioners:

- "There is some questioning of whether job satisfaction is desirable anyway."

- "Lack of time to pay attention, a general aversion to anything empirical (managers generally think they know what the issues are even though their views of reality differ among them), a sense of being at war on a business level coupled with an implicit view that concerns about job satisfaction are luxuries we can't afford."

- "Many feel that there are more serious, real issues to address."

- "Time and money – so many good ideas, all of which require time and money while we are in business environment that requires speed and is very competitive – which requires carefully managing costs. It is really in trying to prioritize among all the different ideas people think would improve things and making sure it aligns both philosophically and practically with the business goals. Making the best use of the resources we have and explaining why we are doing which."

- "Our employees are very busy, we have grown considerably during the last few years and have a relatively inexperienced workforce, our organization is quite decentralized, and there can be a lack of resources. All of these make it difficult to address job satisfaction issues as extensively as we would like to."

- "Simply understanding the importance of job satisfaction for their long-term viability. Certainly getting the research on job satisfaction in hands of practitioners would help. I also believe that most organizations don't feel they have the time to do job satisfaction assessments well and on a regular basis"

- "Timeframes – no CEO here dares to initiate a project with a 2–3 year or longer return on investment time frame."

A related concern is the need for more studies linking satisfaction to real, quantifiable outcomes, such as in the Sears example (Rucci et al., 1998). The issue of developing and articulating relatively straightforward and accessible business interventions and solutions for address satisfaction related issues was also mentioned – an area in which traditional, and even some applied research papers, is often lacking. In this regard, the comments from practitioners were extremely consistent – much more so than the field itself:

- "Knowledge of what job satisfaction and the behavioral sciences can contribute to organizational success."

- "Convincing leadership at all levels that job satisfaction does impact the bottom line. Convincing senior management and leadership at other levels that interventions to increase employee satisfaction need not be huge, elaborate, laborious, and unpleasant."

- "Linkages between people-practices, measured employee satisfaction, and work unit performance. Not just one-to-one linkages but analyses of configural antecedents/determinants."

- "Articles that tangibly demonstrate relationships between satisfaction and profitability. What good studies do you know of that demonstrate this relationship, especially across various industries?"

- "Demonstrating the relationship between organizational productivity (broadly defined) and job satisfaction."

- "A compilation of best practices that have been found to be successful for increasing satisfaction with various components of the job and the research that supports the use of these best practices would be very helpful to us. Consistent with this, a summary of path analytic research conducted on the components of job satisfaction and the organizational outcome measures affected by each component would help to clarify the impact of addressing job satisfaction issues on the organization's bottom line."

- "We need more empirical research in organizational economics that ties job satisfaction to the bottom line."

- "How job satisfaction impacts business performance."

While the issue of the perceived importance of job satisfaction related factors represents an important barrier which the field must overcome if current research and literature are to be used effectively to drive organizational decision making, there is a second issue inherent in the I/O, OD, and HRD role in organizations that contributes to this situation – that is, translation. This is a common concern for many practitioners and professional organizations as well. For example, the Research Committee of the American Society for Training and Development has published a series of guidebooks in order to address these types of issues among their corporate membership (for example, Bassi and Russ-Eft, 1997). Similarly, this same argument was the impetus for the development of the *Academy of Management Executive*, as the very first editor noted (Burke, 1987). Even the academically-oriented but highly regarded publication *Personnel Psychology* has recently introduced a section of articles for just this type of work (Hollenbeck and Smither, 1998).

Despite these attempts, however, there is still a real need to reconcile the frequent disconnect between carefully constructed theory and empirical research as published in the literature and the resulting translation of the key messages in that material (whether by the practitioner himself or herself or from some other source) to interventions, policies, and practices which must ultimately be approved and acted upon by leadership and management. Of course, this can present a problem, given some of the more negative connotations associated with I/O and related professionals in organizations (Adams, 1996; Micklethwait and Wooldridge, 1996). Even without these attributions, some executives are likely to listen to peers rather than an expert in the area. As one individual commented, for example:

"CEOs listen to CEOs. In privately held organizations such as ours, our CEO would have to be introduced to the power of job satisfaction work, via an example at another CEO's organization."

Simply getting the importance of the message across, however, is not enough. Although some organizations may be receptive to current thinking in the field, the challenges associated with designing and implementing a new process can be so overwhelming that practitioners are often forced to abandon important elements for the sake of getting something in place, much like any political process. Unfortunately, these types of compromises made on the application side increase the potential for (1) less effective interventions, and (2) less controlled results. While the former outcome has certain cost implications for the organization, the size of which depends on the level of the effort and the degree to which it has been constrained, the latter situation often contributes further to the schism between the science and practice of I/O, OD, and HRD once the inadequacies of a given application are realized. In short, this situation represents one of the fundamental paradoxes of the applied behavioral sciences.

The third and final issue inherent in the application of job satisfaction related interventions in organizations is one of competing values. Related to the issue above regarding constraints, many I/O, OD, and HRD practitioners in organizations (not to mention those consulting externally) must continually find ways to balance the demand for demonstrable immediate business results of any given intervention – for example, whether related to job satisfaction or some other objective – and the positivistic concerns that are part and parcel of these fields. Although this set of tensions has often been raised as an agenda for the more humanistically oriented practice of OD (for example, Church et al., 1994; Greiner, 1980; Margulies and Raia, 1990), the ethics and values of I/O practice have recently begun to receive direct attention as well (for example, Church et al., 1994; Lowman, 1998). At the broadest level the issue is simple, but the decisions are not. What happens, for example, when a practitioner faced with job satisfaction related HR policy decisions (such as downsizing, compensation, promotion) must choose between an intervention or process that has positive political and career implications but a more negative impact on employee morale, and one that may be more career limited (or otherwise personally difficult) but is significantly more likely to affect positive change in people's lives on a day-to-day basis? Though the average person's response to this situation is likely to be normally distributed, I/O, OD, and HRD practitioners are more likely to find such scenarios morally challenging. While there are no simple solutions here, these issues do need to be recognized as they ultimately impact the credibility, viability and ultimately the very essence of the field itself.

ACKNOWLEDGMENTS

The authors wish to thank the following individuals for contributing their thoughts and opinions on the topic of job satisfaction: Susan E. Bumpus, Wayne Camera, Rod Freudenberg, Robert T. Golembiewski, Kenneth D. Hall, David A. Jones, Bill Kohley, Jerry F. Luebke, William Macey, Anne Moeller, Jay Morris, Karen Paul, David M. Pollack, Carol W. Timmreck, Mark Van Buren, William M. Verdi, and Wendy Weidenbaum.

REFERENCES

Adams, S. 1996: *Dogbert's top secret guide to management handbook*, New York, NY: Harper Business.

Arvey, R. D., Carter, G. W., and Buerkley, D. K. 1991: Job satisfaction: Dispositional and situational influences. *International Review of Industrial and Organizational Psychology*, 6, 359–83.

Bassi, L. J., and Russ-Eft, D. (eds.) 1997: *What works: Assessment, development, and measurement*, Alexandria, VA: American Society for Training and Development.

Bellah, R. N., Madsen, R., Sullivan, W. M., Swidler, A., and Tipton, S. M. 1985: *Habits of the heart: Individualism and commitment in American life*, New York: Harper & Row.

Block, P. 1993: *Stewardship: Choosing service over self-interest*, San Francisco, CA: Berrett-Koehler.

Bracken, D. W. 1996: Multisource (360-degree) feedback: Surveys for individual and organizational development. In A. I. Kraut (ed.), *Organizational surveys: Tools for assessment and change*, San Francisco, CA: Jossey-Bass, 117–43.

Bray, D. W. 1994: Personnel-centered organizational diagnosis. In A. Howard and Associates (eds.), *Diagnosis for organizational change: Methods and models*, New York: Guilford, 152–71.

Brief, A. P. 1998: *Attitudes in and around organizations*, Thousand Oaks, CA: Sage.

Brief, A. P., and Roberson, L. 1989: Job attitude organization: An exploratory study. *Journal of Applied Social Psychology*, 19, 717–27.

Burke, W. W. 1987: From the editor. *Academy of Management Executive*, 1, 5.

Burke, W. W., Coruzzi, C. A., and Church, A. H. 1996: The organizational survey as an intervention for change. In A. I. Kraut (ed.), *Organizational surveys: Tools for assessment and change*, San Francisco, CA: Jossey-Bass, 41–66.

Burke, W. W., and Jackson, P. 1991: Making the SmithKline Beecham merger work. *Human Resource Management*, 30, 69–87.

Burke, W. W., Javitch, M. J., Waclawski, J., and Church, A. H. 1997: The dynamics of midstream consulting. *Consulting Psychology Journal: Practice and Research*, 49, 83–95.

Burke, W. W., and Litwin, G. H. 1992: A causal model for organizational performance and change. *Journal of Management*, 18, 532–45.

Carroll, B. 1973: *Job satisfaction: A review of the literature*, Ithaca, NY: New York State School of Industrial and Labor Relations, Cornell University.

Champy, J. S. 1995: *Reengineering management: The mandate for new leadership*, New York, NY: HarperBusiness.

Church, A. H. 1995: Managerial behaviors and work group climate as predictors of employee outcomes. *Human Resource Development Quarterly*, 6, 173–205.

Church, A. H., Boehm, V. R., and Gellerman, W. 1994: From both sides now: Ethical dilemmas in I/O Psychology. *The Industrial-Organizational Psychologist*, 31, 67–74.

Church, A. H., and Bracken, D. W. 1997: Advancing the state of the art of 360-degree feedback: Special issue editors' comments on the research and practice of multi-rater assessment methods. *Group and Organization Management*, 22, 149–61.

Church, A. H., Burke, W. W., and Van Eynde, D. F. 1994: Values, motives, and interventions of organization development practitioners. *Group and Organization Management*, 19, 5–50.

Church, A. H., Crosby, M. M., Davis, D. D., Mohrman, S., and Pearlman, K. 1996: From both sides now: The changing of the job. *The Industrial-Organizational Psychologist*, 33, 57–64.

Church, A. H., Judge, T., Klimoski, R. J., and Latham, G. 1997: From both sides now: The impact of I/O psychology. *The Industrial-Organizational Psychologist*, 35, 103–13.

Church, A. H., and McMahan, G. C. 1996: The practice of organization and human resource development in America's fastest growing firms. *Leadership and Organization Development Journal*, 17, 17–33.

Church, A. H., and Waclawski, J. 1998a: *Designing and using organizational surveys*, Aldershot, England: Gower.

Church, A. H., and Waclawski, J. 1998b: The vendor mind-set: The devolution from organizational consultant to street peddler. *Consulting Psychology Journal: Practice and Research*, 5, 87–100.

Church, A. H., Waclawski, J., McHenry, J., and McKenna, D. 1998: Organization development in high performing companies: An in-depth look at the role of OD in Microsoft. *Organization Development Journal*, 16, 51–64.

Cohen, A. 1993: Organizational commitment and turnover: A meta-analysis. *Academy of Managment Journal*, 36, 1140–57.

Cranny, C. J., Smith, P. C., and Stone, E. F. (eds.) 1992: *Job satisfaction: How people feel about their jobs and how it affects their performance*, New York: Lexington Books.

Davis-Blake, A., and Pfeffer, J. 1989: Just a mirage: The search for dispositional effects in organizational research. *Academy of Management Review*, 14, 385–400.

Drevets, W. C., and Raichle, M. E. 1998: Reciprocal suppression of regional cerebral blood flow during emotional versus higher cognitive processes: Implications for interactions between emotion and cognition. *Cognition and Emotion*, 12, 353–85.

Ellul, J. 1964: *The technological society*, New York: Vintage Books.

Engdahl, R. A., Howe, V., and Cole, D. C. 1991: Marketing OD: What now works and what does not. *Organization Development Journal*, 9, 32–40.

Erez, A. 1994: Effects of self-deception on judgements of subjective well-being and job satisfaction. Unpublished masters thesis, Cornell University.

Fried, Y., and Ferris, G. R. 1987: The validity of the job characteristics model: A review and meta-analysis. *Personnel Psychology*, 40, 287–322.

Frye, C. M. 1996: *New evidence for the Job Characteristics Model: A meta-analysis of the job characteristics-job satisfaction relationship using composite correlations.* Paper presented at the Eleventh Annual Meeting of the Society for Industrial and Organizational Psychology, San Diego, CA.

Gilley, J. W., and Eggland, S. A. 1992: *Marketing HRD within organizations*, San Fransciso: Jossey-Bass.

Glick, W. H., Jenkins, G. D., and Gupta, N. 1986: Method versus substance: How strong are underlying relationships between job characteristics and attitudinal outcomes? *Academy of Management Journal*, 29, 441–64.

Golembiewski, R. T., and Sun, B. 1990: QWL improves worksite quality: Success rates in a large pool of studies. *Human Resource Development Quarterly*, 1, 35–43.

Goodstone, M. S., and Diamante, T. 1998: Organizational use of therapeutic change: Strengthening multisource feedback systems through interdisciplinary coaching. *Consulting Psychology Journal: Practice and Research*, 50, 152–63.

Greiner, L. 1980: OD values and the "bottom line". In W. W. Burke and L. D. Goodstein (eds.), *Trends and issues in organization development*, San Diego: University Associates, 319–32.

Hackman, J. R., and Oldham, G. R. 1976: Motivation through the design of work: Test of a theory. *Organizational Behavior and Human Performance*, 16, 250–79.

Harter, J. K., and Creglow, A. 1998: A meta-analysis and utility analysis of the relationship between core GWA employee perceptions and business outcomes. Working paper 2.0, The Gallup Organization.

Herzberg, F. 1967: *Work and the nature of man*, Cleveland, OH: World Books.

Hollenbeck, J. R., and Smither, J. W. 1998: A letter from the Editor and Associate Editor of Personnel Psychology. *The Industrial-Organizational Psychologist*, 36, 107–11.

House, R. J., Shane, S. A., and Herold, D. M. 1996: Rumors of the death of dispositional research are vastly exaggerated. *Academy of Management Review*, 21, 203–24.

Howard, A. (ed.) 1995: *The changing nature of work*. San Francisco: Jossey-Bass.

Hulin, C. L. 1991: Adaptation, persistence, and commitment in organizations. In M. D. Dunnette and L. M. Hough (eds.), *Handbook of industrial and organizational psychology*, Vol. 2, Palo Alto, CA: Consulting Psychologists Press, 455–505.

Hulin, C. L., Roznowski, M., and Hachiya, D. 1985: Alternative opportunities and withdrawal decisions: Empirical and theoretical discrepancies and an integration. *Psychological Bulletin*, 97, 233–50.

Hulin, C. L., and Smith, P. C. 1967: An empirical investigation of two implications of the two factor theory of job satisfaction. *Journal of Applied Psychology*, 51, 396–402.

Iaffaldano, M. R., and Muchinsky, P. M. 1985: Job satisfaction and job performance: A meta-analysis. *Psychological Bulletin*, 97, 251–73.

Johnson, R. H. 1996: Life in the Consortium: The Mayflower Group. In A. I. Kraut (ed.), *Organizational surveys: Tools for assessment and change*, San Francisco: Jossey-Bass, 285–309.

Judge, T. A. 1990: Job satisfaction as a reflection of disposition: Investigating the relationship and its effects on employee adaptive behaviors. Unpublished doctoral dissertation, University of Illinois.

Judge, T. A., and Bono, J. E. (in press): Relationship of core self-evaluations traits – self-esteem, generalized self-efficacy, locus of control, and emotional stability – with job satisfaction and job performance: A meta-analysis. *Journal of Applied Psychology*.

Judge, T. A., Bono, J. E., and Locke, E. A. (in press): Personality and job satisfaction: The mediating role of job characteristics. *Journal of Applied Psychology*.

Judge, T. A., Boudreau, J. W., and Bretz, R. D. 1994: Job and life attitudes of male executives. *Journal of Applied Psychology*, 79, 767–82.

Judge, T. A., Locke, E. A., and Durham, C. C. 1997: The dispositional causes of job satisfaction: A core evaluations approach. *Research in Organizational Behavior*, 19, 151–88.

Judge, T. A., Locke, E. A., Durham, C. C., and Kluger, A. N. 1998: Dispositional effects on job and life satisfaction: The role of core evaluations. *Journal of Applied Psychology*, 83, 17–34.

Judge, T. A., Thoresen, C. J., Bono, J. E., and Patton, G. K. 1998: *The job satisfaction–job performance relationship: 1939–98*. Paper presented at the Academy of Management National Meeting, San Diego, CA.

Judge, T. A., and Watanabe, S. 1993: Another look at the job satisfaction–life satisfaction relationship. *Journal of Applied Psychology*, 78, 939–48.

Judge, T. A., and Watanabe, S. 1994: Individual differences in the nature of the relationship between job and life satisfaction. *Journal of Occupational and Organizational Psychology*, 67, 101–7.

Jurgensen, C. E. 1978: Job preferences (What makes a job good or bad?). *Journal of Applied Psychology*, 50, 479–87.

Kaplan, R. S., and Norton, D. P. 1992: The balanced scorecard – measures that drive performance. *Harvard Business Review*, January–February, 71–9.

Katz, D., and Kahn, R. L. 1978: *The social psychology of organizations*, 2nd edn., New York: Wiley.

Korman, A. K. 1971: *Industrial and organizational psychology*, Englewood Cliffs, NJ: Prentice-Hall.

Kotter, J. P. 1995: Leading change: Why transformation efforts fail. *Harvard Business Review*, 73, 59–67.

Kraut, A. I. 1996: An overview of organizational surveys. In A. I. Kraut (ed.), *Organizational surveys: Tools for assessment and change*, San Francisco: Jossey-Bass, 1–14.

Kraut, A. I., and Korman, A. K. 1999: The "delta forces" causing change in human resource management. In A. I. Kraut and A. K. Korman (eds.), *Evolving practices in human resource management: Responses to a changing world of work*, San Francisco: Jossey-Bass, 3–22.

Landy, F. J. 1989: *Psychology of work behavior*, Pacific Grove, CA: Brooks/Cole.

Likert, R. 1967: *The human organization*, New York: McGraw-Hill.

Locke, E. A. 1969: What is job satisfaction? *Organizational Behavior and Human Performance*, 4, 309–36.

Locke, E. A. 1976: The nature and causes of job satisfaction. In M. D. Dunnette (ed.), *Handbook of industrial and organizational psychology*, Chicago: Rand McNally, 1297–343.

Loher, B. T., Noe, R. A., Moeller, N. L., and Fitzgerald, M. P. 1985: A meta-analysis of the relation of job characteristics to job satisfaction. *Journal of Applied Psychology*, 70, 280–9.

Lowman, R. L. (ed.) 1998: *The ethical practice of psychology in organizations*, Washington, DC: APA and Bowling Green, OH: SIOP.

Margulies, N., and Raia, A. 1990: The significance of core values on the theory and practice of organization development. In F. Massarik (ed.), *Advances in organization development*, Vol. 1, Norwood, NJ: Ablex Publishing Co, 27–41.

Maslow, A. H. 1965: *Eupsychian management*, Homewood, IL: Irwin.

McClough, A. C., Rogelberg, S. G., Fisher, G. G., and Bachiochi, P. D. 1998: Cynicism and the quality of an individual's contribution to an organizational diagnostic survey. *Organization Development Journal*, 16, 31–41.

McGregor, D. M. 1966: *Leadership and motivation*, Cambridge, MA: MIT Press.

McMahan, G. C., and Woodman, R.W. 1992: The current practice of organization development within the firm: A survey of large industrial corporations. *Group and Organization Management*, 17, 117–34.

Micklethwait, J., and Wooldridge, A. 1996: *The witch doctors: Making sense of the management gurus*, New York: Times Business.

Moore, M. 1996: *Downsize this! Random threats from an unarmed American*, New York: Crown Publishers.

Motowidlo, S. J. 1996: Orientation toward the job and organization: A theory of individual differences in job satisfaction. In K. R. Murphy (ed.), *Individual differences and behavior in organizations*, San Francisco: Jossey-Bass, 175–208.

Nadler, D. A. 1977: *Feedback and organization development: Using data based methods*. Reading, MA: Addision-Wesley.

Nadler, D. A., and Gerstein, M. S. 1992: Designing high-performance work systems: Organizing people, work, technology and information. In D. A. Nadler, M. S. Gerstein, and R. B. Shaw (eds.), *Organizational architecture: Designs for changing organizations*, San Francisco: Jossey-Bass, 110–32.

Neuman, G. A., Edwards, J. E., and Raju, N. S. 1989: Organizational development interventions: A meta-analysis of their effects on satisfaction and other attitudes. *Personnel Psychology*, 42, 461–89.

Organ, D. W. 1988: A restatement of the satisfaction–performance hypothesis. *Journal of Management*, 14, 547–57.

Organ, D. W., and Near, J. P. 1985: Cognition versus affect in measures of job satisfaction. *International Journal of Psychology*, 20, 241–53.

Organ, D. W., and Ryan, K. 1995: A meta-analytic review of attitudinal and dispositional predictors of organizational citizenship behavior. *Personnel Psychology*, 48, 775–802.

Reisenzein, R., and Schoenpflug, W. 1992: Stumpf's cognitive-evaluative theory of emotion. *American Psychologist*, 47, 34–45.

Rentsch, J. R., and Steel, R. P. 1992: Construct and concurrent validation of the Andrews and Withey job satisfaction questionnaire. *Educational and Psychological Measurement*, 52, 357–67.

Rice, R. W., Gentile, D. A., and McFarlin, D. B. 1991: Facet importance and job satisfaction. *Journal of Applied Psychology*, 76, 31–9.

Rice, R. W., Phillips, S. M., and McFarlin, D. B. 1990: Multiple discrepancies and pay satisfaction. *Journal of Applied Psychology*, 75, 386–93.

Roberts, K. H., and Glick, W. 1981: The job characteristics approach to task design: A critical review. *Journal of Applied Psychology*, 66, 193–217.

Robinson, D. G., and Robinson, J. C. 1996: *Performance consulting: Moving beyond training*, San Francisco: Berrett-Koehler.

Roethlisberger, F. J., and Dickson, W. J. 1939: *Management and the worker*, New York: Wiley.

Rogelberg, S. G., and Luong, A. 1998: Nonresponse to mailed surveys: A review and guide. *Current Directions in Psychological Science*, 7, 60–5.

Rucci, A. J., Kirn, S. P., and Quinn, R. T. 1998: The employee–customer profit chain at Sears. *Harvard Business Review*, 76, 83–97.

Scarpello, V., and Campbell, J. P. 1983: Job satisfaction: Are all the parts there? *Personnel Psychology*, 36, 577–600.

Schaffer, R. H., and Thomson, H. A. 1992: Successful change programs begin with results. *Harvard Business Review*, 70, 80–9.

Schneider, B., and Bowen, D. E. 1985: Employee and customer perceptions of service in banks: Replication and extension. *Journal of Applied Psychology*, 60, 318–28.

Senge, P. M. 1990: *The fifth discipline: The art and practice of the learning organization*, New York: Doubleday.

Siegal, W., Church, A. H., Javitch, M., Waclawski, J., Burd, S., Bazigos, M., Yang, T., Andersen-Rudolph, K., and Burke, W. W. 1996: Understanding the management of change: An overview of managers' perspectives and assumptions in the '90s. *Journal of Organizational Change Management*, 9, 54–80.

Smith, P. C., Kendall, L. M., and Hulin, C. L. 1969: *The measurement of satisfaction in work and retirement*, Chicago: Rand McNally.

Smith-Lovin, L. 1991: An affect control view of cognition and emotion. In J. A. Howard and P. L. Callero (eds.), *The self-society dynamic: Cognition, emotion, and action*, New York: Cambridge University Press, 143–69.

Spector, B., and Beer, M. 1994: Beyond TQM programmes. *Journal of Organizational Change Management*, 7, 63–70.

Staw, B. M., and Ross, J. 1985: Stability in the midst of change: A dispositional approach to job attitudes. *Journal of Applied Psychology*, 70, 469–80.

Staw, B. M., Bell, N. E., and Clausen, J. A. 1986: The dispositional approach to job attitudes: A lifetime longitudinal test. *Administrative Science Quarterly*, 31, 437–53.

Tait, M., Padgett, M. Y., and Baldwin, T. T. 1989: Job and life satisfaction: A re-evaluation of the strength of the relationship and gender effects as a function of the date of the study. *Journal of Applied Psychology*, 74, 502–7.

Tornow, W. W. 1993: Editor's note: Introduction to special issue of 360-degree feedback. *Human Resource Management*, 32, 211–19.

Trahant, B., and Burke, W. W. 1996: Creating a change reaction: How understanding organizational dynamics can ease re-engineering. *National Productivity Review*, Autumn, 37–46.

Ulrich, D., Halbrook, R., Meder, D., Stuchlik, M., and Thorpe, S. 1991: Employee and customer attachment: Synergies for competitive advantage. *Human Resource Planning*, 14, 89–103.

Useem, J. 1999: This economy brought to you by the letter 'e'. *Fortune*, 139, 192.

Waclawski, J. 1998: The real world: Psychologists on celluloid and Pulp Fiction "shrinks." *The Industrial-Organizational Psychologist*, 36, 51–60.

Waclawski, J., and Church, A. H. 1999: Four easy steps to performance coaching. *Performance in Practice*, Autumn, 4–5.

Wagner, J. A., III. 1994: Participation's effects on performance and satisfaction: A reconsideration of research evidence. *Academy of Management Review*, 19, 312–30.

Wanous, J. P., Reichers, A. E., and Hudy, M. J. 1997: Overall job satisfaction: How good are single-item measures? *Journal of Applied Psychology*, 82, 247–52.

Weiss, D. J., Dawis, R. V., England, G. W., and Lofquist, L. H. 1967: *Manual for the Minnesota Satisfaction Questionnaire*, Minneapolis: Industrial Relations Center, University of Minnesota.

Weiss, H. M., and Cropanzano, R. 1996: Affective events theory: A theoretical discussion of the structure, causes, and consequences of affective experiences at work. *Research in Organizational Behavior*, 18, 1–74.

Weiss, H. M., Nicholas, J. P., and Daus, C. S. 1999: An examination of the joint effects of affective experiences and job beliefs on job satisfaction and variations in affective experiences over time. *Organizational Behavior and Human Decision Processes*, 78, 1–24.

Wernimont, P. F. 1966: Intrinsic and extrinsic factors in job satisfaction. *Journal of Applied Psychology*, 50, 41–50.

Zedeck, S. 1992: Introduction: Exploring the domain of work and family concerns. In S. Zedeck (ed.), *Work, families, and organizations*, San Francisco: Jossey-Bass, 1–32.

APPENDIX

INTERVIEW QUESTIONS

1. What is the general perception of job satisfaction as a construct in your organization? Do people use the term? Is it given lip service only or is it actually a serious topic for management and/or OD or Personnel Research related interventions? How is it generally defined? Do you feel its importance is increasing, decreasing or remaining constant?

2. How well are the traditional theoretical concepts understood? To what extent (if any) is current research and/or thinking considered or utilized?

3. Is the concept of job satisfaction at all integrated in management strategies and systems? Is it treated as some form of outcome measure at all?

4. What types of interventions, policies, programs, or research efforts (for example, surveys, 360-degree feedback) are currently in place that attempt to address (even if tangentially) job satisfaction related concerns in your organization?

5. What are the key barriers, problems or challenges with respect to addressing job satisfaction related concerns and issues in your organization?

6. What type of research is needed in the future that would be helpful or meaningful to job satisfaction related interventions, policies or programs in your organization?

chapter **8**

Overlooking Theory and Research in Performance Appraisal at One's Peril: Much Done, More to Do

Gary Latham and Soosan (Daghighi) Latham

The primary purpose of performance appraisal is developmental. It is to inculcate in people the desire for continuous improvement (Latham and Wexley, 1994). Secondary reasons are administrative in nature; appraisals provide a basis for determining who should receive a bonus, an increase in salary, a promotion, demotion, termination, and so on. Despite these laudatory objectives, a seminal study (Meyer et al., 1965) conducted at the General Electric Company (GE) showed that appraisals can have a deleterious effect on an employee's performance. Moreover, this decrease in performance may last up to 12–13 weeks subsequent to the appraisal.

The purposes of this chapter are threefold. First, we show myriad ways that research and theory inform practice so that what occurred at GE need not occur elsewhere. Implicit in this discussion is how appraisals can have a deleterious effect on an organization when theory and research are ignored. Second, in a discussion by the second author in her role as Vice President of Human Resources, J.P. Morgan, Canada, specific applications of theory and research are pointed out. Finally, suggestions are made for further research to inform practice.

THEORY AND RESEARCH

Milestones

At GE, Meyer et al. (1965) showed that as a result of appraisals, people often become defensive. In doing so they attack the appraisal instrument by asserting that they are appraised on the wrong things. They attack the appraiser by pointing out that the boss is either too biased to evaluate them accurately, or because the boss only has a limited opportunity to observe them and thus he or she has a distorted perspective of their performance. Consequently, research has been conducted on ways to improve the appraisal instrument as well as the objectivity of the people who use it.

Appraisal instrument

Appraisal instruments generally fall into one or more of the following four categories: a blank sheet of paper; trait scales; outcome measures; or behavioral criteria. A simulation, involving Domtar Company's paper products managers in Canada and the United States, revealed that perceptions of fairness regarding assessments by their peers was as high when a blank sheet of paper served as the appraisal instrument as was the case when the instrument consisted of behavioral criteria. Moreover, the perceptions were higher in the blank sheet condition than it was in the condition where trait scales were used as the instrument for assessing performance (Latham and Seijts, 1997).

Despite this finding, the problems with a blank sheet of paper serving as an appraisal instrument are at least fourfold. First, a blank sheet facilitates errors in observation such as first impressions and recency effects. Second, it increases the probability of feedback that is not based on the knowledge, skills, or abilities (KSAs) that are determined through a job analysis as critical to effective performance. Thus, the feedback may contain irrelevant or erroneous advice. Third, inter-observer reliability is apt to be low. As the Conference Board in the United States pointed out a quarter of a century ago: "A system that is not standardized in its administration, that uses different forms or procedures from place to place or time to time, raises the probability that at least some difference in the performance measure of different employees are in fact the result of the appraisal system and its administration, rather than real differences in employee performance" (Lazer and Wikstrom, 1977, p. 5). Finally, the courts have developed a deep skepticism of appraisals that are subjectively worded. A blank sheet of paper invites such wording.

Many organizations use trait scales to evaluate employees. Traits are generally expressed in terms of personality predispositions. Examples include "conscientiousness," "shows initiative," and "courteous." The traits are considered desirable across jobs throughout the organization. In this vein, trait scales are the forerunner of core competencies.

The drawbacks of using trait scales are at least threefold. First, they are perceived by employees as too subjective (Latham and Seijts, 1997). Second, the courts in North America have pointed out correctly that traits are often so poorly defined that appraisals reflect little more than the caprice of the appraiser. Third, they provide little information on what the person must start doing, stop doing, or consider doing differently. And as Drucker (1973) noted a quarter of a century ago: "An employer has no business with a man's personality . . . An employee owes no 'loyalty', he owes no 'love' and no 'attitudes' – he owes performance and nothing else. Management and manager development should concern themselves with changes in behavior likely to make a man more effective" (pp. 424–5).

Drucker's emphasis on behavior went largely unheeded as practitioners abandoned trait scales in a desire to minimize litigation with disgruntled employees. Instead of focusing on behavior, management by objectives (MBO) was embraced with an emphasis on "bottom line" easily countable measures. The relevance of such measures to an organization's effectiveness is largely unassailable, but in a seminal book their value for appraisal purposes was exposed as nearly useless. Campbell et al. (1970) cogently pointed out that hard criteria or cost-related measures (for example, cars sold divided by hours worked, error free words typed per minute) are often excessive in that they are affected by factors beyond a person's control. For example, the value of the dollar to the yen can result in a Weyerhaeuser Company executive receiving a large bonus when it is undeserved, or being penalized inappropriately, for log exports to countries such as Japan. In addition, cost-related measures are often deficient in that they exclude factors for which a person should be held accountable. For example, focusing primarily on dollars generated by a managing partner at PricewaterhouseCoopers fails to take into account the behaviors necessary to attract, develop, and retain staff by that manager. Moreover, measuring only dollars generated fails to assess the behaviors necessary to attract new business from new customers, or to increase revenue from present customers. Further, Latham and Wexley (1994) noted that a primary focus on bottom-line measures can encourage a "results-at-all-costs" mentality. And, as is the case with trait scales, such measures in and of themselves do not indicate what a person must start doing, stop doing or consider doing differently to influence the organization's bottom line positively. At most, they reveal "the score."

Three milestones in research provided solutions to this problem (Dunnette, 1976). The first is a job analysis developed by Flanagan (1954), namely, the critical incident technique (CIT). It enables researchers and practitioners to identify the behaviors critical for influencing desired performance outcomes. Job analysis requires systematic data collection from subject matter experts, namely job incumbents, supervisors, peers, subordinates, and customers.

The second milestone is a technical report by Wherry that appeared nearly a decade later in a journal (Wherry and Bartlett, 1982). In brief, Wherry proposed a theory of rating that takes into account the performance of the ratee, observation of that performance by the rater, and the recall of those observations by the rater. Among his theorems and corollaries for controlling bias in ratings were: rating scale items which refer to easily observed behavior categories will result in more accurate ratings than will those which refer to hard-to-observe behaviors; the rater will make more accurate ratings when he has been forewarned as to the types of behaviors to be rated; the rater should be given an easily accessible checklist of observer cues for the evaluation of performance; the keeping of a written record between rating periods of specifically observed critical incidents will improve objectivity; and behavior items that are readily classified by the rater as referring to a given area of behavior will result in less overall bias than will items that suggest a complex pattern of behavior to the rater.

The third milestone is behavioral expectation scales (BES) (Smith and Kendall, 1963). A derivation of which are behavioral observation scales (BOS) (Latham and Wexley, 1977, 1994). BES use a Thurstone scale with Gutman scale properties, BOS are simply algebraically summated Likert scales that are either item or factor analyzed. Both are developed from the CIT and Wherry's theory. These appraisal instruments mitigate occurrences similar to those in General Electric where employees claimed that they were assessed on the "wrong things." Behavioral criteria derived from a job analysis are developed by the people for the people. The process emphasizes employee participation in decisions that will affect them.

Additional advantages of behavioral measures is that they facilitate coaching of self and colleagues. They define traits as well as core competencies such as "team playing" in terms of observable, hence verifiable, behavior. They make clear what a person must start doing, stop doing, or be doing differently to enhance an organization's effectiveness, to implement its strategy with excellence. And when based on Wherry's theory, they minimize rating biases.

A series of studies conducted by the American Pulpwood Association showed empirically that there is a direct relationship between what people do (behavior) and the attainment of the organization's strategic goals to increase the productivity of loggers, increase their attendance, and decrease the injury rate (Latham and Wexley, 1977; Latham et al., 1975b; Ronan and Latham, 1974). In 1997, as a member of the Board of the Directors of UNICON, the worldwide association of Assistant Deans and Directors of University Executive Education, and as the Chair of the Research Committee, the second author initiated a study conducted by the first author that showed that there is also a high correlation between what the Executive Education staff do and the attainment of four of the business school's strategic objectives, namely to increase revenue, generate repeat business, achieve organizational sponsor satisfaction, as well as increase the individual participant's satisfaction (Latham, 1998). The product was a behavioral checklist that member business schools can use for self-appraisal. The self-appraisal instrument makes clear what executive education staff must do to attain these four strategic objectives.

The practicality of using BOS was investigated by Wiersma and Latham (1986). Managers, computer programmers, and attorneys for SIAC evaluated BOS, BES, and trait appraisals on seven criteria concerning administrative and motivational aspects of appraisal: ability to give feedback; ability to differentiate among employees; objectivity; position differences; ability to provide training; setting corporate-wide standards; and overall ease of use. These criteria were developed to address complaints that the company's senior management had with the existing appraisal instrument, and by reviewing literature that defined criteria for acceptable appraisal instruments. The results showed that BOS were preferred to BES on each of the seven criteria; BOS were preferred to trait scales on five of the seven criteria. There were no significant differences between BOS and trait scales on the remaining two criteria, namely, ease of use and position differences. BES and trait scales were perceived as relatively the same on most of these criteria. These findings corroborated the results of a laboratory experiment (Fay and Latham, 1982) that found BOS were considered more practical than BES, but that BES and trait scales did not differ significantly on perceptions of practicality.

In a subsequent study (Wiersma et al., 1995), managers and computer programmers in the Netherlands appraised the performance of a subordinate or peer, using BOS, BES, and trait scales. They then evaluated the three appraisal instruments on their ability to give feedback, ability to differentiate, objectivity, position differences, ability to provide training, setting corporate-wide standards, ability to set goals, and overall ease of use. Users preferred the trait scale to the BES on two criteria, namely, ease of use and position differences, and considered the BES and trait scale equivalent on the remaining criteria. However, similar to what was found in the United States, they preferred the BOS to BES on seven criteria, and to the trait scale on all but two criteria.

Rater training

An appraisal instrument is only as good as the appraisers who use it. Few things undermine the effectiveness of an appraisal more than perceptions that the person who is using it is inaccurate. Inaccuracy can occur unintentionally or unconsciously through rating errors such as halo, leniency, stereotyping, and contrast effects. Working with supervisors, Levine and Butler (1952) found that no observable behavior change occurred as a result of a lecture on ways to increase objectivity. People in low level jobs, for the most part, were given low ratings while those in high level jobs received high ratings. Wexley et al. (1973) obtained similar disappointing findings in a laboratory setting regarding contrast effects. Making raters aware of the error did not change their behavior. Even worse, Bernardin (Bernardin and Pence, 1980; Bernardin and Buckley, 1981) showed that blind adherence to a heuristic (for example, don't give a person the same rating on each criterion) leads to a decrease rather than an increase in rating accuracy. He labeled this inappropriate attempt to improve accuracy "rating error training."

The above mis-steps led to the development of effective training programs (for example, Latham et al., 1975a; Bernardin and Buckley, 1981; Sulsky and Day, 1992) that do in fact increase the appraiser's objectivity through the minimization of psychometric rating errors. Regardless of the label or title given to this training by different researchers, the content is essentially the same. Participants in a workshop are given a series of job descriptions. After discussing a given job description, the participants as a group observe an employee on videotape, they rate the employee, and they provide a written justification for their rating. The trainer then informs the participants of the correct rating and generates group discussion on ways to increase observer objectivity (for example, define criteria behaviorally, use multiple observers, record observed behaviors). Through active participation, knowledge of results, and practice, the training has been shown to increase rating accuracy.

In a laboratory experiment, Fay and Latham (1982) found that in the absence of this training, rating errors occur regardless of whether the appraisal instrument consists of traits or observable behaviors. Subsequent to training, however, there were no appreciable differences between BOS and BES with regard to rating error; both were superior to trait scales.

Pursell et al. (1980) found that the validity coefficients involving supervisors' observations were significant only after they had received this training. Noonan and Sulsky (1996), in a study involving the Canadian Armed Forces, found that this training improved the accuracy of officer performance ratings of non-command personnel.

Cognitive processing

Strong methodological skills coupled with a strong research focus is sometimes a two-edged sword. Most I/O psychologists are strong quantitatively, especially relative to many clinical-counseling psychologists. Thus, in response to Thorndike's (1949) seminal book that discussed criteria for criteria, they focused on the psychometric properties of appraisal instruments, namely, validity, reliability, and freedom from bias rather than on practical ways to counsel and develop employees.

A major paradigm shift occurred in 1980, when Landy and Farr attacked the search for the ideal appraisal instrument. They argued that this research emphasis ignored the other half of the equation, namely, the cognitive properties of the rater who uses the appraisal instrument. They pointed out that the rater is an information processor; hence the quality of performance evaluations should be enhanced if I/O psychologists built upon the experimental psychology literature. The result was a plethora of studies conducted for more than a decade on the cognitive processes of raters. The results, unfortunately, are among the few instances where research on performance appraisal failed to inform practice (Banks and Murphy, 1985; Ilgen et al., 1993; Latham, 1986; Latham et al., 1994). The key to developing effective appraisals that inculcate a desire for continuous learning on the part of the people who are being appraised was not to be found in the cognitive processes of appraisers, but rather in the motivation of both them and the people whom they were appraising.

Appraiser motivation

Despite the effectiveness of training programs for increasing the objectivity of appraisers, appraisers who have been trained sometimes continue to distort appraisals. Occam's razor, however, requires science to eschew the complex in favor of the most straightforward explanation of a phenomenon. With regard to rating inaccuracy, this was accomplished by Longnecker et al. (1987). In a cogent essay, they identified political factors in organizations that can induce appraisers to knowingly give incorrect evaluations of employees.

In a similar vein, Napier and Latham (1986) drew upon social cognitive theory (Bandura, 1986) to explain this phenomenon. In an empirical study of appraisers in two disparate industries, newsprint and banking, self-efficacy in conducting appraisals was found to be high among managers in both organizations. In the former industry, however, the performance appraisal was viewed as not affecting a subordinate's status in any way regardless of whether the appraisal was positive or negative; and, similarly the appraisers anticipated neither positive nor negative outcomes for themselves for conducting appraisals. Performance appraisal was viewed as a "non-event." In the second organization, appraisers feared the organizational consequences of "making waves" with their subordinates. Their expected outcome of recording behaviors to document an unfavorable appraisal was a decrease in the probability of they themselves being promoted. Consistent with social cognitive theory, conditions that result in perceptions of high self-efficacy and low outcome expectancies caused resentment. Appraisers who believed that they could make accurate appraisals stopped doing so.

In summary, research shows that regardless of the appraisal instrument and the training that is given to the appraisers who use it, performance appraisal accuracy can be affected adversely by an appraiser's negative outcome expectancies and perceptions of the organization's politics. Consequently, Tziner et al. (1996) developed a 30-item questionnaire that assesses the extent to which organizational politics affect appraisals (for example, give high ratings to avoid negative interactions). The questionnaire was shown to have internal consistency, test–retest reliability and convergent and discriminant validity.

Related to organization politics are perceptions by employees of justice in the workplace. In what is likely to become a seminal article in the appraisal literature, Folger et al. (1992) stated that the dependent variable of primary interest should be the perceived fairness of the appraisal process. Drawing upon organizational justice theory (Greenberg, 1986), they argued that of the variables that influence perceptions of fairness, the actual outcome of an appraisal or performance rating is the least important factor (distributive justice). Of far more importance is an understanding of the appraisal process (procedural justice), the perceived logic and sincerity of the appraiser (interactive justice) and the extent to which the people who are being appraised perceive that their views are taken into account (voice).

Motivating employees

With regard to coaching, goal-setting theory (Locke and Latham, 1990) has been used more than any other as a framework to motivate employees to improve their performance. The early work of Maier (1958) and Meyer et al. (1965) emphasized goal setting in the appraisal process. In a study involving BOS as the dependent variables, Latham et al. (1978) found strong support for the practical use of this theory. Consistent with the theory's predictions, appraisal feedback had no effect on subsequent behavior in the absence of setting specific difficult goals. Employee participation in setting the goals resulted in higher performance than assigning them, not because of greater goal commitment, but rather due to high goals being set. Engineers/scientists, in discussion with their respective supervisors at Weyerhaeuser, set higher goals than was the case where their supervisors set them unilaterally. Consistent with the theory, the higher the goal the higher the performance. Similar results were obtained with Weyerhaeuser's word processing employees (Dossett et al., 1979).

The importance of the appraisal instrument to the goal-setting process has been shown in a series of studies by Tziner and his colleagues. Ten managers and their 62 subordinates at the Israel Airport Authority participated in a field experiment that analyzed the effects of performance appraisal feedback using either BOS or a graphic rating scale (GRS) (Tziner and Kopelman, 1988). Goal clarity and goal commitment was significantly higher when BOS rather than GRS were used. This is because the use of BOS provides a systemic, enduring, built-in vehicle for influencing an employee's performance. BOS provide a comprehensive list of explicit and specific behaviors to be performed. Goal setting derived from the GRS-based performance feedback, however, required that generic performance dimensions be translated into specific behaviors. Many managers were either unwilling or unable to do this.

In a follow-up study at the Israel Airport Authority (Tziner and Latham, 1989), 20 managers received intensive training in giving performance feedback and setting specific goals when conducting appraisals of 125 subordinates. The use of BOS-based appraisals increased work satisfaction significantly more than the use of a GRS-based appraisal. Feedback followed by goal-setting resulted in significantly higher work satisfaction and organizational commitment than feedback alone. Moreover, the combination of BOS-based appraisal, feedback, and goal-setting led to significantly higher work satisfaction than in the GRS conditions.

Tziner et al. (1993) hypothesized that the BOS process, compared with a GRS process, yields higher levels of: (1) goal clarity, acceptance, and commitment; (2) appraisal process satisfaction; and (3) improvement in job performance. A field experiment involving 16 nurse-managers and 115 nurse-subordinates supported these hypotheses.

Finally, Tziner and Kopelman (1998) hypothesized that in comparison to a GRS-based performance appraisal, BOS generate superior goal properties, better goal characteristics, and more favorable user reactions. Data from a field experiment involving 46 police sergeants and their 152 subordinates supported their prediction.

In summary, at least three theories inform performance appraisal in practice. Social cognitive theory explains the necessity of ensuring high self-efficacy on the part of appraisers, namely, their strong belief or conviction that they can indeed evaluate an employee's performance and coach that person effectively. Empirical research suggests that appraisers have high self-efficacy. In addition, appraisers must have high outcome expectancies; they must see the relationship between what they do as appraisers and outcomes that they desire. Empirical research suggests that their perceived outcomes are either neutral or negative.

Organizational justice theory provides guidelines for ensuring that the appraisal process is perceived as fair. Empirical research suggests that organizational politics can negate perceptions of fairness as well as the effect of training programs that increase observer objectivity.

Goal-setting theory provides a motivational technique for employees to improve their performance based on the feedback that they receive in the appraisal process. BOS, derived from the critical incident technique, that take into account Wherry's principles facilitates the goal-setting process.

■ INFORMED PRACTICE: MUCH DONE, MORE TO DO

Much research done: a practitioner's view

The influence of theory and research is evident in the practice of performance appraisal at J.P. Morgan. Morgan, like most organizations, spends considerable time on the performance appraisal process. Historically, this process was often implemented in isolation from other inter-related systems, in particular the organization's strategic plan. Often appraisals were used primarily as an aid to compensation decisions and human resource record keeping. Consequently, the strategic plan document disappeared into employees' bottom desk drawers so that people could continue to pursue "business as usual." This occurred because little or no time was spent on considering what employees must do to implement the strategic plan with zeal. No consideration was given to using performance management systems to evaluate the employees' contribution to the achievement of the organization's strategic goals. Few people realized that much can be done to facilitate and accelerate the implementation of the business plan through effective performance management processes. This is no longer true in Morgan where practice is informed by theory and research.

Appraisal instrument

The late Mason Haire is often quoted for the truism: "that which gets measured gets done." At J.P. Morgan, performance appraisal is a threefold process. Individuals are evaluated against: (1) global core competencies (observable behaviors) thus ensuring a sustainable enduring corporate culture; (2) business criteria that are directly linked to the company's multi-year business strategy; and (3) their own individual performance objectives. The latter are intended to increase the individual's knowledge, skills, and abilities in ways that will enhance both the individual's and Morgan's effectiveness in implementing the organization's strategy. They are set jointly by the appraisee and the appraiser during a year-end performance discussion, adjusted during the year as necessary, and formally reviewed in mid-year. For example, an individual is evaluated against a core competency, leadership, business criteria of revenue generated from new as well as present clients, and a developmental objective of increasing his/her communication skills that will facilitate the attainment of the former two criteria. The respective behavioral definitions of the relevant assessment criteria are provided to employees in the form of a Role Skill Grid. The appraisers and appraisees use the grid as a point of reference in rating self as well as another individual's performance. Consequently, few people at J.P. Morgan dare state that the appraisal instrument assesses them on the wrong criteria or that there is ambiguity in the appraisal instrument. Few people dare to ignore Morgan's business strategy as everyone is measured on the extent to which it is implemented. The individual at J.P. Morgan is the unit of analysis, and the strategic plan provides the basis for developing the appraisal instrument for the assessment of an individual's behavior. Adherence to the strategic plan is the ultimate core competency at Morgan.

Rater objectivity

In practice, appraiser objectivity appears to be the most elusive element of performance management, regardless of the instrument used or the extent of appraiser training provided. Four steps have been taken by J.P. Morgan to maximize appraisal objectivity and accuracy. First, as noted above, the criteria are established at the beginning of the performance management process in terms of verifiable employee behavior. Second, the appraisees are asked to evaluate their performance on an on-going basis against those criteria as well as the goals established for the year. Third, 360-degree feedback is sought from peers, direct reports, and managers. They are asked to evaluate the performance of an appraisee independently. Their feedback must be based on incidents that they have observed during the previous 12 months. The training program described earlier in this chapter is used to minimize such errors as stereotyping and halo from previous performance periods, as well as to increase inter-observer reliability. The fourth and final step is a group appraisal, whereby senior management meet together to evaluate an individual's performance against his/her peers using the same established criteria. The use of multiple appraisers ensures that Morgan has a complete picture of the employee's performance. Divergence in conclusions among populations of appraisers is used to develop the individual's contributions to the organization. A person may be seen as loyal to her boss, committed to her subordinates, and hated by her peers. Behavioral criteria provide the explanation. She is a superb subordinate, a phenomenal boss, coach and facilitator, and a terrible teamplayer who protects turf and builds walls within the organization. Behavioral goals are subsequently set and on-going coaching is given to increase skill and positive outcome expectancies regarding being and being seen as a teamplayer.

Organizational justice

Strouse (1998) described J. P. Morgan, the company's founder, as so convinced of his own rectitude that he seldom courted public favor, and he never explained a decision. After a dinner in his honor in Chicago, *The Tribune* ran the headline, "Money talks, But Morgan Doesn't." On the mantel in his private study, there was a white enamel plaque, "pense moult, parle peu, ecris rien" (think a lot, say little, write nothing). The outcome of his behavior was long-standing distrust by the media and public who were constantly on the look-out for abusers of corporate power. In a letter to his brother-in-law regarding Morgan, T. Roosevelt wrote that people "have passed thru the period of unreasoning trust and optimism into unreasoning distrust and pessimism" (Strouse, 1998, p. 75).

Today, principles of organizational justice are practiced at J.P. Morgan. Appraisal processes are in place. Transparency is emphasized. The logic or rationale underlying appraisal processes are explained. Procedural justice is evident in 360-degree team reviews where the manager and the employee jointly select the appraisers who will provide feedback. Reviewers are encouraged not only to share their feedback with the appraisee, but to suggest developmental opportunities. Distributive justice manifests itself in how people are compensated, promoted, rewarded and recognized based on these evaluations. Voice and interactive justice principles are emphasized through the discussion between the manager and the appraisee where both parties come to an agreement regarding the appraisee's performance and sign the performance document to that effect.

Employee motivation

The primary outcome of an appraisal meeting is goal setting. On-going performance management is used to identify and coach high potential employees whom the company is intent on retaining as a result of their attainment of high goals. These people are consistently given challenging goals that will enable them to achieve the next level in career development. At all stages during the performance management period, appraisers as well as the appraisee, are asked to provide developmental feedback. During the formal performance review discussion with the manager, these goals are examined as to whether they are realistic, "stretch" and hence motivational versus unattainable. Subsequently, the appraisee and the manager jointly agree on 3–5 goals which become the criteria against which the employee is evaluated during the following year. There is an up-front agreement on performance objectives and evaluation criteria. Through this process, as well as adherence to principles of organizational justice, 360-degree feedback, and behavioral appraisals tied directly to the strategic plan, dysfunctional organizational politics that affect appraisals adversely are minimized. Thus it is rare that people leave Morgan because of disagreement with the appraisal that they received.

The findings of I/O psychologists in the performance appraisal management domain have indeed informed practice and influenced organizational decision making at J.P. Morgan. Yet most organization decision makers are unaware that what they do is a result of theories developed and research conducted by I/O psychologists. This may be because organizations such as Morgan tend to have access to and adapt findings from practitioner literature as opposed to academic journals. It may also be due to the fact that many I/O psychologists fail to move beyond their piecemeal research. Consequently, there is as yet no "big bang."

More research to do

Treatment packages

Where is the study that shows organizations the beneficial effects of a treatment package? Recent advances in medicine show that a combination of drugs is necessary to cure various cancers. Similarly, I/O psychologists need to show the overall effect on an organization of: (1) training appraisers (a) in ways to increase their objectivity, (b) to set specific high performance goals, and (c) to practice principles of organizational justice using (2) behaviorally-based appraisal forms derived from the organization's strategy in (3) a climate where the outcome expectations for conducting appraisals are high and positive and (4) dysfunctional organizational politics have been minimized.

Coaching

Many organizations have embraced the 360-degree review process for performance appraisal. Human resource managers know from personal experience that appraisals given annually or even quarterly are not as effective in bringing about an enduring positive change in behavior as is coaching employees on a daily basis. Hence the shift in emphasis from performance appraisal to performance management. Where are the data that can be presented in a convincing way to line managers that taking

the time to do on-going coaching will be as beneficial to their respective department's "score" as it is to their score on the tennis court? For performance management to be linked to business strategy, line managers, rather than HR, must drive
the day-to-day, week-to-week performance management process. The HR manager's role should be limited to working strategically to align employee performance
criteria with the organization's strategy, to train appraiser/coaches in ways to be
objective, to teach legal and organizational implications of lack of objectivity in performance evaluation, and to provide guidelines for ensuring confidentiality, honesty,
and transparency in feedback.

In practice, it remains rare for an individual to rate a fellow team member low,
unless there is significant impact on the performance of the group, and negative consequences to the rater for positive leniency error. In the interests of efficiency and
expediency, appraisers are often asked to pre-rate the candidates prior to a group
meeting. This practice provides opportunities for the appraisers to create coalitions
and to later influence the overall group's decision through peer pressure and/or
hierarchy. There are significant opportunities for I/O psychologists to assist human
resource managers in creating a climate as well as systems to maintain it that enable
employees to provide candid feedback, and to do so without fear of repercussion.

Learning to learn from criticism

An overlooked phenomenon in organizations is that many people do everything in
their power to prevent appraisers from providing them with critical comments. They
even seek ways to punish the appraiser for providing this information.

Training programs that teach appraisers to focus primarily on the behavior rather
than the person, to focus on the desired behavior rather than undesired behavior,
and to focus primarily on the future rather than the past need to be evaluated on
their effectiveness in bringing about an enduring behavioral change. Training programs are similarly needed to teach employees to encourage appraisers to speak
freely to them. Such programs should also teach employees ways to deal effectively
with comments that are critical and unanticipated. Programs that focus on the
acquisition of functional self-talk that increase the employee's self-efficacy may prove
effective in this domain.

Virtual relationships

With the advent of technology enabling instant worldwide communication, direct
face-to-face interactions will become increasingly rare in global organizations such
as Morgan. One or more people in Singapore may report directly to a person in
London who in turn reports directly to a person in New York. The employees may
never meet their respective bosses. Such relationships defy boss–subordinate use of
behavioral observation scales in that the boss will increasingly need to depend on the
observation of others within and outside a team for performance measurement. Any
360-degree feedback that excludes the boss may lend itself to virtual performance
management if it is used as a way to collect behavioral observations. But on what

basis can the superior ensure that the selection of peers, subordinates, and customers whose feedback is solicited is objective and not biased by regional loyalties and friendships? To what extent should the performance criteria be consistent as opposed to a reflection of cultural and geographical differences? Will the accommodation of differences enhance or violate perceptions of organizational justice? How do behavior observation criteria change when communication is primarily, if not totally, through e-mails, voice-mail and video-conferences? Increasingly, an individual will be assigned to a virtual team where the members never meet one another due to geographical distance, yet each of them will be accountable for the team's performance. If the focus of an appraisal is "bottom line" results, the problems noted earlier in this chapter regarding excessiveness and deficiency are encountered. Regardless of the appraisal instrument used, how will perceptions of organizational justice be fostered? How can coaching occur in a practical yet significant way? Collaborative work between HR managers and I/O psychologists is much needed in this area.

Organizational savvy

There is little or no research on the effect of a person's "organizational savvy" on performance evaluation. Organizational savvy performers build a network to effectively enhance perceptions of their performance; performers who view such activity disdainfully as office politics are often seen to be mediocre performers. Where is the truth? When all aspects of performance appraisal are taken into consideration, HR managers are aware that "politics" influence outcomes regarding promotion, rewards, recognition, and compensation. This outcome can greatly undermine the perceived fairness of the performance appraisal process if the individual is rated relatively low despite high objective performance measures, or if the individual is rated high despite relatively low performance measures. Is 360-degree feedback an effective impediment to false positives and negatives? Or, can most people be fooled most of the time by people who, at best, are savvy politically? To what extent are organizational citizenship behaviors, tacit knowledge and organizational savviness inter-related?

Integration

We need a theory of integration regarding human resource management systems. How do the various systems connect with one another? A theory would provide a framework that would allow human resource managers to think across these systems in their daily practice. It is likely that such a theory would magnify the utility of performance appraisal in terms of performance management. Performance appraisals provide the criteria against which selection systems should be validated. Is the person who scored high on the selection test the same person who subsequently performed well on the job? Performance appraisals also identify not only who is in need of training, but the content of training programs. For example, if the process of performance appraisal identifies that conflict resolution skills are needed on the part of numerous managers, this will suggest training content. People whose skill levels are high and highly displayed on the job should be compensated accordingly.

The integration of these human resource systems, and an understanding of the reciprocal effects among them, would facilitate performance management.

SUMMARY AND CONCLUSIONS

As the twentieth century has come to a close, the gap between research on and the practice of performance management/appraisal has narrowed appreciably. Organizational decision makers who ignore this research now do so at their peril. This is because the body of research in this domain for the most part has both practical and theoretical significance. Findings from field research have been subjected to scrutiny in laboratory settings; findings from laboratory settings have been replicated and enhanced in field research. The result is sound practice informed by research in organizations such as J.P. Morgan.

Systematic job analysis ensures that people are evaluated on the knowledge, skills, and behaviors critical to performing effectively in their respective organizations. Involving job incumbents and their supervisors in an analysis that identifies the behaviors necessary to implement the organization's strategy and approved by senior management ensures that the appraisal instrument will be seen by all as relevant. Training programs that increase observer objectivity when using the appraisal instrument now exist. The value of getting appraisal input from multiple stakeholders has been shown.

With regard to the appraisal/coaching process, practice stemming directly from theory shows the necessity of setting specific difficult goals for improving performance. Theory, specifically social cognitive theory, provides a framework for understanding why the performance management process either takes place or fails to take place. When the outcome expectancies of conducting appraisals are neutral or negative, when there is no perceived relationship between the performance appraisal one receives and subsequent positive as well as negative outcomes, the entire process is seen as meaningless. A major reason why the outcomes are viewed as neutral or negative is organizational politics. A survey instrument now exists for assessing the political climate in an organization that may impede or enhance the coaching and developing of employees, and suggesting ways to improve them.

Few things can harm the relationship between a coach and members of a team than perceptions of unfairness. Again theory, organizational justice, explains why these perceptions occur and how they can be eliminated.

As HR managers have become increasingly educated in the behavioral sciences during the latter half of the twentieth century, the dawn of the twenty-first century should usher in an era for reciprocal effects of informed practice and research. The time has come for HR managers and I/O psychologists to examine potential additive and multiplicative benefits stemming from: (1) treatment packages; (2) ways to facilitate on-going coaching of self and others; (3) the reciprocal effects of appraisal systems on other organizational systems; (4) the inter-relationships among organizational savviness, tacit knowledge, and organizational citizenship behavior; and (5) how knowledge from one or more aspects of the above can be applied effectively to virtual teams where individuals never meet face to face, do not know one another, are separated geographically, yet work interdependently for a limited period of time.

ACKNOWLEDGMENTS

Preparation of this chapter was funded in part by a grant from the Social Sciences and Humanities Research Council to the first author. We gratefully acknowledge critical feedback on a preliminary draft from Edward Lawler and Roger Martin.

REFERENCES

Bandura, A. 1986: *Social foundations of thought and action*, Englewood Cliffs, NJ: Prentice-Hall.

Banks, C. G., and Murphy, K. R. 1985: Toward or narrowing the research–practice gap in performance appraisal. *Personnel Psychology*, 38, 335–45.

Bernardin, H. J., and Buckley, M. R. 1981: Strategies in rater training. *Academy of Management Review*, 6, 205–12.

Bernardin, H. J., and Pence, E. G. 1980: The effects of rater training: Creating new response sets and decreasing accuracy. *Journal of Applied Psychology*, 65, 60–6.

Campbell, J. P., Dunnette, M. D., Lawler, E. E., and Weick, K. E. 1970: *Managerial behavior, performance, and effectiveness*, New York: McGraw-Hill.

Dossett, D. L., Latham, G. P., and Mitchell, T. R. 1979: The effects of assigned versus participatively set goals, KR, and individual differences when goal difficulty is held constant. *Journal of Applied Psychology*, 64, 291–8.

Drucker, P. 1973: *Management: Tasks, responsibilities, and practices*, New York: Harper & Row.

Dunnnette, M. D. 1976: Mish-mash, mush, and milestones in organizational psychology. In H. Meltzer and F. R. Wicket (eds.), *Humanizing organizational behavior*, Springfield, IL: Charles C. Thomas.

Fay, C. H., and Latham, G. P. 1982: Effects of training and rating scales on rating errors. *Personnel Psychology*, 35, 105–16.

Flanagan, J. T. 1954: The critical incident technique. *Psychological Bulletin*, 51, 327–58.

Folger, R., Konovsky, M., and Cropanzano, R. 1992: A due process metaphor for performance appraisal. In B. M. Staw and L. L. Cummings (eds.), *Research in organizational behavior*, 14, 129–77.

Greenberg, J. 1986: Determinants of perceived fairness of performance evaluation. *Journal of Applied Psychology*, 71, 340–2.

Ilgen, D. R., Barnes-Farrell, J. L., and McKellin, D. B. 1993: Performance appraisal process research in the 1980s: What has contributed to appraisals in use? *Organizational Behavior and Human Decision Processes*, 54, 321–69.

Landy, F. J., and Farr, J. L. 1980: Performance rating. *Psychological Bulletin*, 87, 72–107.

Latham, G. P. 1986: Job performance and appraisal. In C. Cooper and I. Robertson (eds.), *Review of industrial and organizational psychology*, Chichester, England: Wiley.

Latham, G. P. 1998: *Correlates of executive education program revenue, repeat business, and the satisfaction of client organizations and individual participants*, Millington, NJ: UNICON.

Latham, G., Mitchell, T. R., and Dossett, D. L. 1978: The importance of participative goal setting and anticipated rewards on goal difficulty and job performance. *Journal of Applied Psychology*, 63, 173–81.

Latham, G. P., and Seijts, G. H. 1997: The effect of appraisal instrument on managerial perceptions of fairness and satisfaction with appraisals from their peers. *Canadian Journal of Behavioural Science*, 29, 275–82.

Latham, G. P., Skarlicki, D., Irvine, D., and Siegel, J. 1993: The increasing importance of performance appraisals to employee effectiveness in organizational settings in North America.

In C. Cooper and I. Robertson (eds.), *International review of industrial and organizational psychology*, Chichester, UK: Wiley.

Latham, G. P., and Wexley, K. N. 1977: Behavioral observation scales for performance appraisal purposes. *Personnel Psychology*, 30, 255–68.

Latham, G. P., and Wexley, K. N. 1994: *Increasing productivity through performance appraisal*, Reading, MA: Addison-Wesley.

Latham, G. P., Wexley, K. N., and Pursell, E. D. 1975: Training managers to minimize rating errors in the observation of behavior. *Journal of Applied Psychology*, 60, 550–5.

Latham, G. P., Wexley, K. N., and Rand, T. M. 1975: The relevance of behavioral criteria developed from the critical incident technique. *Canadian Journal of Behavioural Science*, 7, 349–58.

Lazer, R. I., and Wikstrom, W. S. 1977: *Appraising managerial performance: Current practices and future directions*, New York: Conference Board.

Levine, J., and Butler, J. 1952: Lecture versus group decision in changing behavior. *Journal of Applied Psychology*, 36, 29–33.

Locke, E. A., and Latham, G. P. 1990: *A theory of goal setting and task performance*, Englewood Cliffs, NJ: Prentice-Hall.

Longnecker, C. O., Sims, H. R., Jr., and Gioia, D. A. 1987: Behind the mask: The politics of employee appraisal. *Academy of Management Executive*, 1, 183–93.

Maier, N. R. F. 1958: *The appraisal interview: Objectives, methods and skills*, New York: Wiley.

Meyer, H. H., Kay, E., and French, J. R. 1965: Split roles in performance appraisal. *Harvard Business Review*, 43, 123–9.

Napier, N., and Latham, G. P. 1986: Outcome expectancies of people who conduct performance appraisals. *Personnel Psychology*, 39, 827–38.

Pursell, E. D., Dossett, D. L., and Latham, G. P. 1980: Obtaining valid predictors by minimizing rating errors in the criterion. *Personnel Psychology*, 33, 91–6.

Ronan, W. W., and Latham, G. P. 1974: The reliability and validity of the critical incident technique: A closer look. *Studies in Personnel Psychology*, 6, 53–64.

Smith, P., and Kendall, L. M. 1963: Retranslation of expectations: An approach to the construction of unambiguous anchors for rating scales. *Journal of Applied Psychology*, 47, 149–55.

Strouse, J. 1998: The brilliant bailout. *The New Yorker*, 74 (36), 62–72.

Sulsky, L. M., and Day, D. V. 1992: Frame-of-reference training and cognitive categorization: An empirical investigation of rater memory issues. *Journal of Applied Psychology*, 77, 501–10.

Thorndike, R. L. 1949: *Personnel selection: Test and measurement*, New York: Wiley.

Tziner, A., and Kopelman, R. 1988: Effects of rating format on goal-setting dimensions: A field experiment. *Journal of Applied Psychology*, 73, 323–6.

Tziner, A., Kopelman, R., and Joanis, C. 1997: Investigation of raters' and ratees' reactions to three methods of performance appraisal: BOS, BARS, and GRS. *Revue Canadienne des Sciences de l'Administration*, 14, 396–404.

Tziner, A., and Kopelman, R., and Livneh, N. 1993: Effects of performance appraisal format on perceived goal characteristics, appraisal process satisfaction, and changes in rated job performance: A field experiment. *Journal of Applied Psychology*, 73, 323–6.

Tziner, A., and Latham, G. P. 1989: The effects of appraisal instrument, feedback and goal setting on worker satisfaction and commitment. *Journal of Organizational Behavior*, 10, 145–53.

Tziner, A., Latham, G. P., Price, B. S., and Haccoun, R. 1996: Development and validation of a questionnaire for measuring perceived political considerations in performance appraisal. *Journal of Organizational Behavior*, 17, 179–90.

Wexley, K. N., Sanders, R. E., and Yukl, G. A. 1973: Training interviews to eliminate contrast effects in employment interviews. *Journal of Applied Psychology*, 57, 233–6.

Wherry, R. J., and Bartlett, C. J. 1982: The control of bias in ratings: A theory of rating. *Personnel Psychology*, 35, 521–51.

Wiersma, U., and Latham, G. P. 1986: The practicality of behavioral observation scales, behavioral expectation scales, and trait scales. *Personnel Psychology*, 39, 619–28.

Wiersma, U. J., van den Berg, P. T., and Latham, G. P. 1995: Dutch reactions to behavioral observation, behavioral expectation, and trait scales. *Group and Organization Management*, 20, 297–309.

chapter 9
GOAL SETTING:
THEORY AND PRACTICE

TERENCE R. MITCHELL, KENNETH R. THOMPSON, AND JANE GEORGE-FALVY

This chapter is about the use of goal-setting strategies and interventions in organizations. Our intention is to provide a summary of the theory that has been developed to explain how and why goal setting works, as well as a review of the practical issues involved in actually using goal setting successfully. Because this chapter straddles the theory and practice dichotomy it will not be an elaborate or detailed analysis of either. However, the chapter does provide a fairly comprehensive review and summary of what we know to date and provides current references for more detailed analyses of the topics covered.

■ GOAL SETTING IN CONTEXT

To understand more precisely what we will cover, we need to see organizational goal setting in relation to behaviour, to motivation, and to other theories and ideas involving goals. People are complex processors of information, both cognitive and emotional. They are constantly thinking, evaluating, and acting and switching back and forth as they go. Sometimes we are cold and reflective, other times hot and emotive and sometimes we simply carry on with what appears to be well-rehearsed or practiced behavior without much thought at all.

Observe your own actions for a while. You will probably find that you will work or be engaged by one activity for a while and then switch to another one, and then another and so on. Sometimes these shifts occur quickly, sometimes there are longer time periods between shifts (Atkinson and Birch 1970). These activity sequences are described by Ford (1992) as a "behavioral episode" that reflects "coherent sequences of unitary person-in-context functioning" (p. 23) or more simply, "a slice of life."

The question for researchers and organization theorists is, of course, to understand why we select some actions and not others and why we switch activities. To the extent to which the behaviors are voluntarily chosen, we usually invoke some sort of motivational explanation: "They want to behave that way." The definition of motivation at one level means "an inner desire to make an effort" (Dowling and

Sayles, 1978, p. 16). However, trying to reach agreement about what constitutes or represents an "inner desire" has led to more complex perspectives.

Perhaps the most frequently utilized definition revolves around four processes. My own definition 15 years ago (Mitchell, 1982) included those psychological processes involved in arousal, direction, intensity, and persistence of voluntary actions that are goal directed. Similar definitions are abundant in the literature (Atkinson, 1964; Bandura, 1986; Beck, 1978; Campbell and Pritchard, 1976; Ford, 1992; Franken, 1988; and Steers and Porter, 1991).

Our first key point is that at the center of almost all the major theories used to explain motivational processes and behavioral sequences is the concept of goals. Goals are internal psychological representations of desired states which can be defined as outcomes, events, or processes. They encompass terms like intentions, aim, purpose, and objective. It is the result we try to reach. It is part of the human condition, almost all voluntary human activity is at least partially caused by goals.

But "partially" and "caused" need a little more explanation. As outsiders, looking at someone else, all we can easily observe is behavioral action and self-reports. We have to assume that these actions and reports are multiply caused. Abilities, needs, values, desires, and goals all contribute to action, and the composite of causes (relative weights or contributions) varies across behaviors. Thus, attempts to find sole causes for all behaviours or for a particular behavior are probably futile.

Other theories of motivation address how needs, values, personality, rewards, and the work itself might influence goal selection or influence behaviour directly, independent of goals. Mitchell (1997) covers these other theories in a recent integrative review paper and concludes that "Goal setting is clearly the star performer. It is the single most researched topic in the field of motivation" (p. 72). Thus, while goals may be only part of the picture for understanding purposeful action, they are a very big part.

The causality issue also deserves comment. Note that goals are future-oriented. They represent desired futures and therefore it is the seeking, aspiring, and planning that influences present action. One has an idea of where they want to go (end state) and a desire to do so. These ideas and desires result in intentions which are the direct antecedents to action (Tubbs and Ekeberg, 1991).

We will close this section by simply pointing out the universality of goal constructs in psychological theory. Austin and Vancouver's (1996) review of goal constructs provides a listing of psychological theories that incorporate goals. Included are over 30 theories of attitudes, aspirations, control, achievement, images, reasoned action, and intentions. They start their review with a quote from William James in 1890 suggesting that the "pursuance of future ends" is central to understanding behavior and close their paper by stating that "the goal construct is central for the psychologist's nomological net" (p. 363).

Given that goals play such a central role in current psychological theorizing, it is not surprising that goal constructs have also been used to understand behavior in organizations. Why do people work as long or as hard as they do? Why do they choose one set of activities or actions rather than another? Goals are a major explanation for these questions and we turn now to a review of the theory and research on organizational goal setting.

▪ GOAL SETTING THEORY AND RESEARCH

Without a doubt, the major goal-setting resource, is the book written by Ed Locke and Gary Latham entitled *A Theory of Goal Setting and Task Performance* (1990). These two organizational scientists have devoted a large part of their distinguished careers to developing and testing a theory of goal setting. The book is a marvellous summary of their work plus the work of others. But, in addition, the book is a wonderful example of how theory is developed, tested, changed, and refined.

Major findings

The theory and research on goal setting is truly vast. The Austin and Vancouver (1996) and Locke and Latham book (1990) have around 1,000 different references. Since our objective in this paper is to review both academic and practitioner literatures we will impose some limitations on what we cite. With respect to the theory and research coverage we will usually refer to the Locke and Latham book (1990) as a starting point and then add important literature published since 1990 on each topic.

There are two main well documented propositions that indicate the importance of goals with respect to work behavior. These are:

1. Increases in the difficulty of assigned goals leads to increases in performance (assuming goal acceptance).
2. Specific, difficult assigned goals result in higher performance than do best or no assigned goals.

The first proposition predicts a linear relationship between goal difficulty level and job performance, given that the goals are accepted by the individual. Locke and Latham (1990) review the results from four major meta-analyses (Chidester and Grigsby, 1984; Mento et al., 1987; Tubbs, 1986; and Wood et al., 1987) that cover almost 200 studies using many thousands of subjects. Over 90 percent of the studies support this proposition with the effect size on performance being about a 10–15 percent increase as a result of goal level. Recent research (for example, by Tubbs et al., 1993) demonstrated a significant effect of assigned goal level on performance similar to what is reported above. In addition Gellatly and Meyer (1992) found that self-efficacy perceptions and higher arousal mediated the assigned goal level–performance relationship.

While we will discuss the theoretical explanations for these findings in more detail later, the assumption is that harder goals lead to greater arousal, effort, and persistence than easy goals. The critical question, of course, from a practitioner perspective is "how difficult is difficult?" and we will address this issue in our section covering practice. However, it is important to point out that goal difficulty can be defined in terms of some absolute level based on absolute task standards (such as 90 percent defect free). Difficulty levels can also be based on relative comparisons or improvement standards (for example, produce 20 percent more). A paper by Wright et al. (1995) suggests that these two types of goal difficulty operationalizations have different effects on performance over time. Increases in absolute goal difficulty levels tend to lead to performance increases initially which then flatten out while increases in relative improvements lead to initial increases in performance and then perform-ance drops off. This is also a practical issue we will discuss later.

The second proposition, that goal specificity is important, has also received sub-stantial empirical support. Referring to the same four meta-analyses plus one by Hunter and Schmidt (1983), Locke and Latham (1990) report again that about 90 percent of 200 studies show support for this proposition. Again, thousands of subjects were involved and the effect sizes range from 8–16 percent on performance.

The problem with these latter results is that they include both specificity and difficulty (level) effects (Wright and Kacmar, 1994). Presumably, specificity helps to clarify what is acceptable performance and *direct* activity towards the appropriate target. Having no goal or a do best goal is vague and may lead to considerable variance in self-set goals both in terms of content and level. People might set quality goals rather than quantity goals or easy goals rather than difficult ones. In many studies we simply cannot tease out the level versus the specificity effects. However, Locke et al. (1989) did demonstrate independent level and specificity effects, with the latter effects resulting in lower variance in performance.

There are a few recent research papers that address the goals versus no goals and specificity issues. The recent reviews by Rodgers and Hunter (1991, 1994) on MBO programs and the work by Pritchard (1995) with his PROMES system (that includes specific goals) show that introducing specific goals definitely has a positive impact on performance. However, these papers are reviewing large intervention systems that include issues of appraisal, feedback and other possible factors that can influence performance.

The Wright and Kacmar (1994) study demonstrated that goal specificity led to higher commitment to the goal and lower performance variability on one task and higher self-set goals on a second task. Thus, specificity may have an impact on per-formance through directing effort, clarifying what needs to be done and increasing commitment to the goal.

The results cited above mainly apply to studies where assigned goals are used for individuals and performance is an individual criterion. However, Locke and Latham (1990) review 41 studies that include group goals and they report that again, over 90 percent yield positive results for their main propositions. The issue of whether to use group or individual goals is obviously dependent upon the extent to which people work closely and cooperatively together. Weldon and Weingart (1988) sug-gest that group cooperation and information exchange are important for group goals to work and Mitchell and Silver (1990) showed that interdependence was also a key factor. Group goals worked best when people were interdependent and in fact, individual goals could reduce performance in these conditions. Doerr et al. (1996) strengthened this conclusion by showing that individual assigned goals worked best on a less independent push processing line while assigned group goals worked best on the more interdependent pull line.

The post-1990 work in group goal setting is supportive of these propositions. O'Leary-Kelly et al. (1994) did a meta-analysis and narrative review showing strong effects of assigned group goals on group performance. Individual studies by Weingart

(1992), Klein and Mulvey (1995), Weldon et al. (1991), and Crown and Rosse (1995) report positive effects of group goals and goal level on performance with goal commitment, effort, and planning serving as possible explanations. A study by Silver and Bufanio (1996) showed that group efficacy also mediated the group goal level–performance relationship.

Finally, we need to mention the 10 percent of the studies where effects were not found (and presumably all those file drawer studies that never got published, some of which may not have shown goal-setting effects). Locke and Latham (1990) review each of these published studies and conclude that there are a series of recurring themes that emerge from their analysis. The most frequent explanations for the lack of results were that the assigned goal level was not really difficult, commitment to the goal was low or questionable, the tasks were new and complex and the subjects had no task strategies to help them succeed, the feedback about their performance level was inadequate or the goal really did not match the performance criterion. Some of these issues bear directly on the mechanisms by which goal setting works and we will address that issue next. Suffice it to say that the results are overwhelming that having a difficult, specific assigned goal leads to better performance than having a vague or easy goal and this is true for both individuals and groups, laboratory and field studies and many different types of tasks.

Goal mechanisms

Given that goal setting works in terms of increasing performance, the obvious question that follows is "Why does it work?." We mentioned earlier that motivation is reflected by psychological processes reflecting arousal, direction, intensity, and persistence of voluntary actions. Not surprisingly, goal-setting theory utilizes similar constructs as explanatory mechanisms. That is, given that a goal is defined and accepted, its effects on behavior are mediated by motivational processes.

Arousal is generally seen as reflected in a person's effort or energy exerted and goal difficulty seems to have its major effect on performance through effort as a mediator. Locke and Latham (1990) and Latham and Locke (1991) review numerous studies that demonstrate goal effects on effort. Tasks requiring strength and energy like the arm ergometer, hand dynamometer, bike ergometer, and weight lifting have been used as well as more general effort criteria like physical exertion, rate of work, and effort ratings by one's self and outside observers.

There have also been studies that looked at arousal more directly. Sales (1970) found that a physiological indicator (heart rate) was associated with goal difficulty and a more recent study by Gellatly and Meyers (1992) found that heart rate was a mediator of the goal difficulty–performance relationship. Obviously, tasks vary on the extent to which sheer effort contributes to performance. In some cases ability, task strategies, or interdependencies with machines or people may also be major factors. However, the more that effort contributes to performance, the more powerful goal effects should be.

Sustaining one's effort over time, or persistence is also a key behavioral indicator of motivation. Such persistence often allows one to overcome distractions or continue in the face of the occasional setback. Goal setting is assumed to influence persistence through the duration or time spent trying to reach a goal. Note that time spent can be somewhat independent of the arousal or intensity construct that is reflected by effort exerted. While there is some tradeoff between intensity and duration, low or high levels of effort can be exerted over short or long time periods.

The research results presented by Locke and Latham (1990) and Latham and Locke (1991) confirm these predictions. More time is spent on tasks with difficult goals and people quit a task earlier with easy goals. Learning tasks, such as reading material, anagram tasks, bargaining tasks, study time and so on, have all been used to show goal-persistence effects.

Obviously, we want people to work hard and stick with it, but we also want them to work in the right direction, on the right thing. Goals provide such a direction. Not only do they suggest what constitutes an acceptable outcome to oneself or others, they also suggest by omission what is not to be pursued and what is not acceptable. Goals orient one's attention in a particular direction.

This attention directing property of goals is mostly associated with goal specificity. If a goal is ambiguous it has fewer directive properties. Locke and Latham (1990) and Latham and Locke (1991) review the research supporting this proposition. Learning tasks, driving a car, study activities, and managerial behaviour have all been researched, and goals have demonstrated directional effects.

A fourth and not so easily handled psychological result of goal setting that is important for task performance is the development of task strategies. In many cases, attention to the task at hand, sheer effort, and persistence are not enough to perform well. In addition to required skills or abilities, people must search their memory, learn, and try complex task strategies in order to perform well. More complex tasks are likely to call for such strategies.

We know that appropriate strategies moderate the goal difficulty–performance relationship (Chesney and Locke, 1991) and that challenging goals increase the likelihood that known strategies will be used (Earley et al., 1989). What appears to be important is that the person (given that they have the ability and knowledge) has the time to develop and test strategies. Given such time, difficult goals can lead to better strategy development and use, and subsequently, high performance (Earley et al., 1992).

Task strategy development seems to involve both the directing properties of specific goals and the arousing property of difficult goals. Given the time and goal acceptance, strategies can be developed and used. In this sense, strategy development appears to be a less direct and more contingent effect of goal setting on psychological mechanisms.

The results reviewed by Locke and Latham (1990) clearly show that specific, difficult assigned goals can lead to the development of effective task strategies, especially in the areas of planning one's task activities. In addition, specific, difficult quantity goals often lead to a strategy of reducing quality as a means of attaining quantity. We will return to this issue when we discuss the content of goals in our application section.

In summary, the goal level and specificity relationships with performance appear to be mediated by the arousal, persistence, and direction mechanisms and when time permits, the development of task strategies. As Locke and Latham (1990) point out, no one has actually tested whether these four mechanisms are *complete* mediators but they certainly explain most of the relationship. We turn now to a review of those variables that appear to moderate the goal–performance relationship.

Necessary contingency factors: commitment and feedback

The level and specificity variables discussed in the previous section are usually classified as *content* variables. They provide information about dimensions on which goals can vary. A second important goal attribute is *intensity*. Locke and Latham (1990) refer to intensity as goal commitment, the degree to which the person sees the goal as important, is attached to it and determined to reach it, even in the face of setbacks, distractions or obstacles. Austin and Vancouver (1996) use similar terms and include Ford's (1992) term relevance.

One initial confusion in the goal-setting literature focused on the meaning and interpretation of the commitment construct related to the idea of goal acceptance. Locke and Latham (1990) have clarified this issue. Acceptance refers to the commitment to assigned goals only (presumably one would accept self-set or jointly set goals). Commitment therefore is a broader construct and varies in intensity while acceptance appears to refer only to assigned goals.

The relationships among goal level, commitment and performance are complex, including both direct and moderator effects (Locke and Latham, 1990; Latham and Locke, 1991). It appears that when goal level is held constant there are direct effects of commitment on performance. For difficult goals the relationship is positive and this has been demonstrated repeatedly. For easy goals it may be negative since those with low commitment to easy goals may revise their self-set goals upwards while working on a task, while those with high commitment to an easy goal would stop when the goal was attained.

The moderating effect, across goal levels, shows that commitment is especially important when goals are difficult. That is, the relationship between goal level and performance is stronger with high commitment than with low commitment. The study by Wright (1989) shows both the direct and indirect effects of commitment on performance. Thus, goal commitment is a key factor in producing positive performance and we want that commitment to be high, especially where goals are moderately or extremely difficult.

Two additional issues about goal commitment need to be mentioned. First, there is an ongoing debate about how to conceptualize and therefore measure this construct. Tubbs (1994) and Tubbs and Dahl (1991) have argued that a discrepancy measure reflecting the difference between one's assigned goal and a self-set goal (the closer the two the higher the commitment) is best, while Wright et al. (1994) have developed and tested a more direct self-report measure using Likert-type scales. The latter probably reflects a more general motivational commitment while the former is more narrow and perhaps more precise in reflecting only a self-set versus assigned goal discrepancy. DeShon and Landes (1997) report that the Hollenbeck et al. (1989) scale measure includes both an expectation and a commitment dimension on complex tasks and that these different dimensions have different relationships with important goal-setting constructs. Thus, further measurement work on commitment is needed.

The second issue relates to all the research on what causes goal commitment (Locke and Latham, 1990; Latham and Locke, 1991). One set of factors has to do with how goals are introduced by managers or supervisors. The encouragement and support given by managers helps one think they can reach a goal, and one's trust in these people is important as well. Supervisors and managers also have the legitimate authority and power to set goals and employees want to meet these expectations. Peer group members and social influence are also important as is the public nature of the commitment and the instrumentability of the goal for reaching valued outcomes.

In addition, financial incentives can increase commitment to a goal but have other direct effects on performance and effects on other goal constructs as well. When moderately difficult goals are used, having a bonus for goal attainment seems to increase commitment. However, using such a bonus when goals are very difficult may backfire (most people would not get the bonus and therefore be upset). Locke and Latham (1990) suggest that having different bonus amounts for different performance levels might be a better overall system. We will return to this issue in our practice section. Recent research has confirmed many of these conclusions. Wofford et al. (1992), in reviewing 78 studies, found that high commitment to a goal was best predicted by task difficulty (moderate challenge), the intent to which the person felt they had the capability to reach the goal (for example, self-efficacy) and their actual expectation of goal attainment. Gollwitzer (1990) and Gollwitzer et al. (1989) suggest that the importance of a goal, reflected by the intensity and comprehensiveness of thinking about it, determine subsequent commitment and action towards reaching it.

The second major moderator of the goal–performance relationship is feedback. Feedback is information that tells someone how well they are doing and its effect on performance depends upon how it is interpreted and used. If feedback is related to the setting of difficult performance goals or to increased commitment to those goals then performance should increase. In this sense, goal-setting constructs mediate the feedback–performance relationship and feedback without goal setting has little impact on performance.

The finding of equal or perhaps greater importance is that goal setting appears not to work very well unless feedback is present (Erez, 1977). Locke and Latham (1990) review over 30 studies confirming that feedback moderates the goal setting–performance relationship. One needs to know how well they are actually performing to gauge what is left to achieve. Note that when one is achieving or surpassing a goal that feedback increases one's confidence and self-efficacy but it may also cause one to have little incentive to improve. Thus, feedback seems to have its most positive effect when one's performance is still short of goal attainment coupled with one's dissatisfaction with that state of affairs (Locke and Latham, 1990).

There are some more detailed issues surrounding feedback that are in the current literature. First, much of control theory (see Austin and Vancouver, 1996) postulates a negative control loop such that greater discrepancies between a target and current performance are the major force for directed action to reduce the discrepancy. Locke (1991, 1994) has criticized this perspective for a number of reasons, one of which is the idea that action stops when goals are met. He argues that humans create discrepancies by setting higher goals and he reasons that seeking and striving are part of this human condition. Phillips et al. (1996) provided positive empirical support for the idea that people create positive discrepancies.

The source and type of feedback are also important. Greller and Parsons (1992) found that task feedback seems to be used to evaluate one's own performance while more general organizational feedback helps individuals to frame their behavior in a larger perspective. Feedback messages also come in different forms or types. One's pay is seen as a feedback message as is one's performance evaluation (Bannister and Balkin, 1990). Earley et al. (1990) demonstrated that process feedback (how to do the task) influenced task strategies while outcome feedback influenced effort and self-efficacy.

Finally, while feedback is traditionally seen as downward flowing information, it can flow upward as well (Smither et al., 1995), and, of course, one's interpretation (attributions) of the feedback mediates its impact on performance (Tindale et al., 1991).

In summary, both commitment and feedback are necessary for goal setting to work. We turn now to some other moderators that clarify and provide boundaries for goal-setting effects.

Other contingency factors: ability, learning stage, and task complexity

There are three other moderators of the goal setting–performance association that need to be discussed. Ability seems to play a relatively complex role in goal-setting relationships. Most obvious is that ability has a direct and main effect on performance and ability is more important for performance on tasks that have a high ability component needed for good performance. These are straightforward. The two moderator effects are not entirely in agreement but not opposed to each other either. First, Locke and Latham (1990) report results that show that *when goals are difficult*, the goal–performance relationship is stronger for high ability subjects than low ability subjects. Second, Kanfer (1996) summarizes a few of her studies from the resource allocation paradigm that show that *for a relatively complex task* that had been learned, goal setting increased performance for low ability subjects more than for high ability subjects.

Both findings make sense. When goals are difficult and there is an ability component to the task, the correlation of goal level with performance should be higher for high ability people than for low ability people, because the association will be stronger at the high goal, high performance levels. In complex tasks that have been practiced, a relatively easy or moderately difficult goal will result in greater performance increases for the low ability subjects than for the high ability subjects, because of lack of variance at the low end of the relationship for the high ability subjects. More research is clearly needed on this topic.

The learning stage moderator effects initially came also from the resource allocation perspective suggested by Kanfer and Ackerman (1989). They found that setting goals for a relatively complex task was detrimental to learning and performance in the early stages of learning a task. The goals were seen as distracting and disruptive for concentrating on the learning of crucial stimulus–response relationships. Mitchell et al. (1994) replicated these results, showing that goal setting was more strongly related to performance after a task was well learned than in its early learning stages.

The third moderator is task complexity and the original meta-analysis of 72 studies by Wood et al. (1987) showed convincingly that goal setting seemed to have a less strong effect on performance for complex tasks than for simple ones. This result was true for both goal difficulty and goal specificity relationships with performance. The explanation for that effect has been attributed both to the fact that criterion reliabilities are lower on complex tasks (and when you correct for criterion unreliability, the differences are reduced) and to the fact that complex tasks are more likely to require complex task strategies. You will recall from our earlier discussion that goal effects on task strategies were somewhat indirect and less strong than effects on effort, persistence, and direction.

The key issue from recent research reveals that if the person has the time to learn and use appropriate task strategies, goal setting can still have a powerful effect on performance on complex tasks. The strategies are clearly important (Chesney and Locke, 1991) and when time is available for strategies to be learned, goals will help performance (Smith et al., 1990). In addition, DeShon and Alexander (1996) showed that goals will help on complex tasks where underlying models or strategies of successful task completion are available. On complex tasks where no such strategies are available, goals have little impact on performance. Findings from the resource allocation research are similar. For example, Kanfer et al. (1994) showed that goal setting has little impact on performance when massed practice (little time between trials) is used but does have an effect on performance with spaced practice where people have more time to learn relationships and strategies. Latham and Seijts (in press) also show that on a complex task, if goals are broken down to a very specific, proximal goal (different specific goals for each trial) that people perform better than where they are given a do best or distal goal (an overall performance goal across all trials). Thus, goals can help performance in complex tasks where time is given to learn strategies, where strategies are available and when the goals are broken down to fit with the stage of learning.

So, goal setting works but has some boundaries as well. There must be feedback and commitment for goals to work, and they work better on simple tasks and after a task is well learned. The moderating effects of ability are more confusing and still need clarification. We turn now to an examination of the underlying theoretical issues involved in understanding how and why goals are chosen and why some people select and become committed to harder goals than other people.

Goals and the larger theoretical context

We need to review a couple of issues before we attempt to place goals in a larger theoretical context. First, goals represent an outcome that one wants or is striving for. Second, remember that it is one's personal goal (the one they have chosen to try for) that is the direct antecedent of behavioral intention and action. Finally, remember that goals represent future states. As such, time unfolds between the moment of goal choice and goal attainment. It is important to know what causes goal choice *and* it is important to know how this chosen goal can be changed and can influence action taking place as one actually pursues the goal.

There are a variety of representations of striving for a future outcome in the motivational literature. Locke and Bryan (1968), for example, had people estimate four constructs – the outcome one would "try for," "hope for," "expect," and their "minimum." While these were all highly correlated (see also Wood and Locke, 1987) there were some differences. The hope and try for goals tend to be higher than the expect or minimum goal and these latter two are closer to the actual performance than the hope and try for goals.

Daniels and Mitchell (1995) used three constructs that represented the outcome people *wanted* to attain, *expected* to attain and thought that they *could* attain. These three constructs map nicely on to three main motivational theories with *want* seeming to fit the goal-setting idea best, *expect* is an integral part of expectancy theory and *can* or capacity is the variable that is represented by self-efficacy approaches. Daniels and Mitchell (1995) also found that these constructs were highly correlated and while "expect" had the lowest mean it was the most accurate predictor. Bandura's (1997) recent book also makes these distinctions among these constructs.

Thus, expectancy ideas and self-efficacy ideas appear to be similar to goal-setting ideas in the notion that beliefs about future performance can influence present action. The question is, how are they all related?

A number of theorists have attempted theoretical integrations, including Eden (1988), Garland (1985) and Locke and Latham (1990). Earley and Lituchy (1991) competitively tested these three approaches and while all three were supported, the Locke and Latham approach received the most support. A summary of their model is represented in figure 9.1. Note that there are two main constructs that are seen as direct antecedents of intention, action, and performance, and these are self-efficacy and one's personal goal (see Tubbs and Ekeberg, 1991). Locke and Latham (1990) have summarized these relationships by saying that "performance is affected not only by what one is trying to do but by how confident one is of being able to do it" (p. 72). In their model, the self-efficacy construct is seen as broader than the expectancy construct and since they are often measured in a similar manner, they focus on efficacy (Latham and Locke, 1991).

Two other things are worthy of note. Self-efficacy has a direct effect on performance as well as an effect on one's personal goal. We mentioned earlier that while goals indeed had a major impact on performance they were not the only variable that was important. One's assessment of their personal capability on a specific task, their self-efficacy, also has an independent effect on performance.

The second point to note is that there are other variables that are more "distal" that can influence self-efficacy and personal goal as well as performance directly. The assigned goal can obviously influence the personal goal. In addition, people who are assigned difficult goals "are more like to have high self-efficacy since assigning high goals is in itself an expression of confidence" (Latham and Locke, 1991, p. 221).

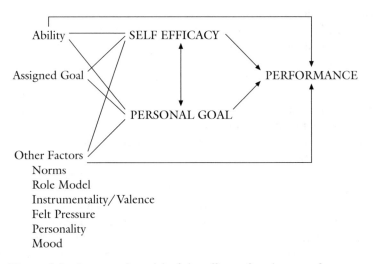

Figure 9.1 Integrated model of the effects of goals on performance

Ability (which is often reflected by assessment of previous performance) is a major contributor to self-efficacy and personal goals and can have an independent effect on performance. Finally, there is an "other factors" category that includes a set of variables that can influence efficacy, personal goal, and performance.

Locke and Latham (1990) review the research on these other factors and while they group them and discuss them in a somewhat different arrangement, for our purposes this list will suffice. Norms reflect the notion that in many cases there is an agreed upon expectation about performance levels that is communicated by co-workers. These norms usually reflect a level below that assigned by management and can influence one's personal goal (and may or may not influence efficacy). Modeling can influence how well one thinks they can do (efficacy) and their personal choice of a goal. Seeing someone else successfully accomplish a task boosts self-confidence as well as one's personal target. Instrumentality and valence are terms from expectancy theory and the former reflects the relationship between obtaining the goal and other outcomes (for example, if I increase sales by 20 percent I will receive a $5,000 bonus) and the latter reflects the value or importance of obtaining these outcomes. When these two are combined they reflect an overall evaluation of a particular goal and therefore influence the goal that is selected (presumably one selects a goal that is attractive in terms of the outcomes that accrue upon attainment). See Tubbs et al. (1993) for a recent example. The felt pressure variable is meant to capture both external and internal forces that influence goals and efficacy. Externally, one's supervisor or manager can provide support as well as put pressure on someone to accept an assigned goal. Internally, one can wish to prove themselves and reach a particular performance level.

There are also personality variables related to goal level and efficacy and performance and this literature is vast and growing. The major personality factors that are associated with these variables are the need for achievement (for example, see Phillips and Gully, 1997), conscientiousness (see, for example, Gellatly, 1996; and Barrick et al., 1993), and goal orientation (Dweck, 1986). People who have a "learning goal orientation" see ability and learning as malleable and changeable and are more likely to set higher goals and perform well than people who have a less malleable "performance goal orientation" (for example, see Button et al., 1996; Phillips and Gully, 1997). Other variables that have been studied include self-esteem, action-orientation and locus of control (for a review see Austin and Vancouver, 1996).

Locke and Latham (1990) also suggest that one's mood at the moment can influence goal choice and Bandura (1997) argues that mood influences self-efficacy. People with a more positive mood will report higher confidence levels and personal goal levels.

There are four relatively recent studies that test or summarize the multiple relationships presented in figure 9.1. Woofford et al. (1992) found that efficacy beliefs and expectations based on ability influenced goal level and that goal valence and outcomes like rewards and incentives increased goal commitment. Thomas and Mathieu (1994) confirmed the influence of ability and efficacy on personal goals. Moussa (1996) showed that difficult goals are selected if one thinks they are capable of reaching them and they are highly valued. Phillips and Gully (1997) showed that ability and learning goal-orientation, need for achievement, and locus of control influence efficacy and personal goals which are related to performance. While all the details and relative contributions of these relationships still need some clarification, we now have a pretty good idea about the nomological net surrounding goal-setting constructs and their effects on performance.

The second set of issues with respect to theory is focused on what happens after one has selected a goal. There has been substantial activity in this area over the last ten years and while different labels are often used we will refer to this body of work as self-regulation. Significant contributions can be found in the work of Gollwitzer (1990, 1993), Bargh (1994), Bargh and Gollwitzer (1994), Frese and Zapf (1994), Kanfer (1996), Kanfer and Ackerman (1989), and Kanfer and Kanfer (1991).

A number of issues are involved here. Once a goal is accepted one puts together plans and in some cases calls up fairly automatic scripts about how to proceed. These are described as implementation intentions by Bargh and Gollwitzer (1994) and are more or less conscious (Bargh, 1994). After this planning stage, one proceeds to acting and evaluating (Gollwitzer, 1993). Throughout the evaluating phase, one is constantly monitoring and evaluating their progress towards the goal (Frese and Zapf, 1994). When large differences are detected, goals or behavior may be revised (Frese and Zapf, 1994) and a fairly deliberate and conscious process will be involved. Differences in internal attributes (conscientiousness, attention) and external focus (actions, behaviors) can influence how well one adjusts and persists (Kuhl, 1992). People can also seek feedback in this process to clarify the need for future actions (Ashford and Tsui, 1991). They can also table or put aside the activity and temporarily disengage from pursuing the goal (Ford 1992). Kanfer (1996) has also found that people can be trained to avoid distractions and to use various internal attributional and self-talk mechanisms to stay on task and to continue in pursuit of a goal.

In summary, one's personal goal is caused by a variety of factors, chief among them being their self-efficacy, ability, and the assigned goal. Other social and personal factors can influence one's goal as well. Once the goal is selected it has an impact on action over time. Various personal orientations, task attributes and training can facilitate the motivational effects of goals and keep people striving for the goal. A key part of that process involves the monitoring of one's progress towards the goal (feedback) and their responses to this information. Thus goals are multiply caused, have a direct effect on intentions and actions, and have persistent motivational properties over time.

This concludes the theory and research summary. By necessity some issues were omitted and some received less thorough treatment than is available in the literature. In addition, some important topics like the use of participative versus assigned goals or quality versus quantity goals will be discussed in our practice sections when we discuss how one actually sets a goal and the type of content of the goal that should be used. We turn now to a review of these issues.

■ PRACTICAL ISSUES IN GOAL SETTING

The second half of the paper tackles the problems and issues associated with actually attempting to use goal setting in organizational situations. Each section will have a brief review of the empirical and theoretical perspectives but most of the focus will be on practical experience and actual examples.

Two preliminary topics that frame this practical section need to be discussed. First, doing work in actual organizations is different in some substantive ways from doing research. Most (about 70 percent) of the goal-setting studies were conducted as laboratory studies or simulations using students as subjects. Goals typically worked on simple tasks for short time periods. They mostly were studied when people worked independently.

Mitchell and Wood (1994) reviewed how most organizational settings are distinctly different from the typical study described above. Most people have multiple tasks that require switching and prioritizing. They have multiple goals for these tasks as well as short-term and long-term goals. The performance on their tasks may have multiple causes and may require different levels of personal and technological support. Tasks in the real world are dynamic and evolving. These changes often occur without warning or are caused by agents outside one's control. We firmly believe (and there are certainly enough studies to confirm it) that goal setting has a powerful impact on performance in these settings. However, these settings present a whole series of practical issues of implementation with which a manager must deal.

The second issue was addressed by Mitchell (1997) in a discussion of how certain settings are more or less appropriate for different motivational interventions. Notice what we have said about successful goal setting. It requires being able to set relatively specific and difficult goals. Both of these factors require a relatively precise and stable criterion. You also need feedback for goal setting to work. Feedback demands that you can monitor your own (or someone else's) performance *and* provide timely and accurate assessments of the progress towards the goal. Goals have to be integrated hierarchically and vertically with co-workers. All of this activity requires management, effort, cost, and time. Thus, we will start this section by simply saying that goal setting is an active and intensive intervention that may not always be the best motivational approach in terms of contextual fit or in terms of benefits compared to costs.

What goal should be set?

Goals have content. In a practical situation, you have to decide what standard or criterion you will actually use (Bobko and Colella, 1994). Locke (1997) suggests that one should start by looking at the factors (such as revenues and costs) and behaviors (such as attention to customers) that are most highly related to financial returns. In addition, top level management must agree upon a long-range plan and business strategy that reflects the importance of various factors like product quality, customer satisfaction, and employee happiness. The two specific dimensions that have received the most research attention on this topic have been quality versus quantity goals and process versus outcome goals.

Quantity/quality examples

Locke and Latham (1990) review the quantity/quality issue. In general, the research suggests that people often make tradeoffs between quantity and quality goals and that most frequently, with difficult quantity goals, quality can suffer. Research by Gilliland and Landes (1992), Locke et al. (1994) and Audia et al. (1996) has addressed these issues. These studies suggest that the quality reduction tradeoff strategy is less apparent in simple tasks than complex ones and that quality goals can help with strategy development.

The emphasis on both quality and quantity goals was quite evident at a Latter-Day Saints (LDS) hospital when it adopted a stronger customer-focused strategy using qualitative goals (Petzinger, 1998). The traditional goal-setting process focused on quantitative goals, such as number of beds filled (occupancy rate), number of procedures, and the number of staff per patient. Under a plan developed by Diane Kelly, a neonatal intensive-care nurse, and Joan Lelis, chief of surgical services (a nurse herself), the outpatient surgery processes were refocused around qualitative goals with less emphasis on the quantitative goals. As the staff developed a plan to re-engineer outpatient surgery, they realized that clinical competency, the ability to do the procedure well, was only part of the equation that leads to patient satisfaction. Health care is about personal encounters with the patient and the patient's family and loved ones. The re-engineering focused on small and large elements of that personal encounter. The qualitative aspects of various performance processes related to patient satisfaction were analyzed and improved. For example, doctors were often late in starting the first surgery in the morning. The late start increased the probability that subsequent surgeries would be delayed. This not only hurt staff and facility planning but it also created customer ill will. Objectives were set that improved the ratio of procedures started on time. In addition, other processes were modified. For example, a goal was set that encouraged blood to be drawn at the same time as inserting a needle for intravenous fluids. This reduced the time needed by having two procedures and reduced the need for a laboratory technician to draw a second sample of blood. Some procedures were eliminated altogether. For example, some patients were not pleased to be told they could not wear underwear under surgical gowns even if they were only having shoulder surgery. The reason for the practice was to curb infections. However, after eliminating the practice, the hospital found no increase in infection rates.

The hospital reports that focusing on qualitative goals in addition to quantitative operational goals led to shorter recovery times for patients, increased unit productivity as revised procedures led to shorter duration time for a surgical procedure, and patient satisfaction improved dramatically. What the hospital learned was that quality and quantity goals are essential to boosting patient satisfaction and that there is a positive relationship between quality goals and hospital profitability (Petzinger, 1998).

Roth et al. (1995) also provide a nice example of dealing with quantity and quality issues. They were working with a company that made several types of electronic components and, in particular, dealing with a team that was inspecting electronic components (such as loose wires, too much dirt, unclear labels) and correcting problems (for example, soldering loose pieces, applying protective coatings) and putting the components through a final inspection. One quality goal focused on the percentage of components that would pass final inspection, whereas a quantity goal was the percentage of the components completed that they received to inspect. The interesting point about this example was that the employees then assigned weights to the goal indicators, which clarifies the importance of the quality/quantity distinction.

Process/outcome

A process goal often focuses on the way one accomplishes a task, the learning of new relationships or task strategies, while an outcome goal focuses on output and things actually produced (Frese and Zapf, 1994). A learning or process goal appears to increase feedback seeking (VandeWalle and Cummings, 1997) and strategy development (Winters and Latham, 1996) and this activity is especially helpful on more complex tasks. Harackiewicz et al. (in press) note this distinction in an educational environment and that mastery or process goals resulted in greater interest and involvement with the material but outcome goals produced better performance. VandeWalle (1999) presents an overall review of how learning orientations and mastery goals affect a variety of meta-cognitive structures, self-regulation, knowledge, and performance.

Przygodda et al. (1995) provide an example of how a company can focus on daily internal processes as well as on outcomes. Working with a plant that produced circuit breakers, groups got together and decided on a variety of objectives emphasizing quality and process. They used indicators, such as the total amount of time to identify and repair machine breakdowns and the daily number of defective pieces identified that needed rework. They also had an overall productivity goal and the various goals were weighted by the team.

Levels/stages

Mitchell and Wood (1994) have also suggested that overall we can think about goals at multiple levels (organizational, group, individual) and for various stages of the performance cycle (input, process, output, and outcome). When AT&T

developed its Universal Card, it developed a hierarchy of goals for various dimensions of its service. One goal was customer satisfaction. They then translated customer satisfaction in terms of multiple operational objectives. For example, one operational goal, which related to customer satisfaction, was accessibility. Operational process goals that relate to accessibility include: number of abandoned calls (calls not answered); number of rings before the call was answered; and number of times the customer was transferred before their question was answered. As Alfred W. Kuebler, former chief information officer reports, the AT&T Universal Card carefully defined operational metrics or objectives for every aspect of customer satisfaction and then used these objectives as a means to assess system performance (Kuebler, 1998). This division won the Malcolm Baldrige National Quality Award, in part because of the comprehensive view of goals that they used to ensure superior customer satisfaction.

Thus, the content of goals can vary. Quantity, quality, and timeliness are key factors that can often be measured at different levels or different points in the performance cycle. Two main points emerge from practical examples. First, individuals and groups should use some sort of weighting to reflect the tradeoffs involved. The importance of quality and quantity or process and outcome should be explicit. Second, goals should be set for activities over which employees have substantial control. Pritchard's book (1995) contains numerous examples where employees balk when asked to meet objectives that they cannot control (for example, products are given to them to inspect that are built with defective parts). Indicators for which control is low should be discounted in terms of their importance weights.

Finally, different types of tasks may require different types of goals. For example, Matthews et al. (1994) demonstrated that outcome and output goals worked better than process goals when people worked independently but the reverse was true where people were interdependent. When people need to work together, it is often the process that causes performance losses, and setting process goals can help to remedy that problem.

How is the goal set?

For years there was an extensive debate on whether goals should be assigned, participatively set or self-set with the major comparisons between the first two (Locke and Latham, 1990). Latham et al. (1988) published a long monograph summarizing competitive tests and came to the conclusion that assigned goals can be just as effective as participatively set goals especially when one "sells" the assigned goals rather than simply "tells" them.

Three current studies add some qualifications to these conclusions. Latham et al. (1994) show that participative goals help in the development of self-efficacy and performance strategies on complex tasks and these strategies help performance. George-Falvy (1996) found that participation was helpful in the early stages of learning (consistent with the development of the task strategies idea) and also on complex tasks. Ludwig and Geller (1997) found that assigned goals increased performance on targeted behaviors but that non-targeted, but related, behaviors were increased by participation (pizza drivers learning safe driving techniques). Thus participation may have some cognitive and learning benefits, especially on complex tasks.

The need to get participation in the goal-setting process became very evident to Motorola in 1978. Motorola thought it was doing a very good job in the market. At an annual sales meeting each division was reporting their results and the executive group was working on planning for the future. One of the executives from one of the key divisions of the company got up during the meeting and told the group that they ought to get out of that business. The room was shocked. This was one of the most profitable divisions and was a major contributor to Motorola's total revenue. The executive went on to say that the quality of the product that Motorola was producing was terrible and it was only a matter of time before its competitors would provide a superior product that would outperform and deliver more customer satisfaction than Motorola's products. That meeting resulted in the "great quality awakening in 1981" at Motorola that exists today (Motorola, 1991).

Bob Galvin, then CEO, along with others decided that the company would only survive if it focused on meeting customer needs for a reliable and useful product. However, Bob Galvin realized very quickly that a cultural change of this magnitude would not come from assigning goals of quality improvement. First, even the executive committee was not sure how to change the culture of a company the size of Motorola. Second, they wanted a process that would tap the creative talent of the entire company. This would come only with the establishment of goals that would allow a degree of creative latitude on finding the best means to reach the goals and would encourage involvement in the goal-setting process.

The focus was on increasing participation in the goal-setting process and increasing involvement in the process of improving the culture of quality in the total organization. One of the major approaches used to do this was started in 1982, called the *quality system review* (QSR). The QSR is designed to increase participation in the quality process, improve the quality of goal setting in the organization, and to help other divisions learn about the quality efforts of the division that is under review. The QSR is designed to assess the quality efforts of each department.

For example, one category examines the quality of management systems. One sub-category under that title is concerned with the extent that management solicits, accepts, and rewards feedback from the work force. The scoring for this element ranges from poor (no system exists for solicitation of ideas from employees) to outstanding (individual and/or team recognition is part of the process). Virtually all employees are empowered to improve process, service, and administrative quality and are actively involved in quality improvement teams. Management provides active leadership of the employee's participation process for continuous improvement. To obtain a ranking above poor, the unit must be able to demonstrate that there is a functional approach that is deployed through the unit with results that are demonstrated.

The value of this process as it relates to goal setting is that it almost forces each individual from each unit to become involved in the goal-setting process. The QSR did not prescribe how the unit ought to develop the processes and procedures needed to reach an outstanding ranking. That forced the employees in the unit to determine what was best for the needs and environment of that unit. Also, by looking at process dimensions, it forced the unit to include process objectives along with outcome objectives. Motorola was deliberate in its choice of having people from different units of Motorola to be the team of examiners. This would help disseminate good ideas to other parts of the organization and aid the creative and empowering process. Having public rankings of points for units also encouraged specific actions and demonstrated results in order to improve the quality perspective of the organization.

So how should goals be set? Motorola determined that they needed to develop the talents of all its employees to help in deciding how to make better products, how to improve processes so that they are more reliable and reduce wasted time and effort (improve what is called the "cycle time of the process"). Bob Galvin and the executive committee wanted to get all employees involved in setting the direction of the organization. The QSR process was one of the ways that helped Motorola meet the needs of its customers and become the 1987 winner of the Malcolm Baldrige award for quality, the highest quality award given in the United States. In addition, by encouraging units and teams within those units to define quality in their own way, it assisted in developing participative goal setting that aided the creative and innovative growth that Motorola has experienced over the past decade (Motorola, 1991). It appears that while assigned goals can work very well, where teams are used participation is important, quality is important, and commitment is crucial.

How many goals?

Austin and Vancouver (1996) pay considerable attention to this issue: "When multiple goals are considered, their interrelations are critical. The dominant conceptualization of the structure of goals, across psychological domains is hierarchical" (p. 341). They cite numerous authors who incorporate this hierarchical idea (Beach and Mitchell, 1990; Freze and Zapf, 1994; Lord and Levy, 1994; Scheier and Carver, 1988). Broad and long-term (distal) goals are divided and compartmentalized into more specific short-term goals – specific plans to reach immediate targets that facilitate the attainment of long-term objectives and values. To do this effectively requires integration across goal levels.

One also has multiple tasks and the question is, does one set goals at the level of specific tasks and at a more global level? How do we prioritize these goals across horizontal and vertical levels (departments, groups, and tasks for individuals). Locke and Latham (1990) review this research and highlight a study by Edmister and Locke (1987) where subjects assigned weights (reflecting goal importance) to their different goals and the weights were associated with subsequent performance levels.

The theoretical issues often revolve around the switching from task to task and the resources involved in doing that. The Kanfer and Ackerman (1989) presentation of their resource allocation model suggests that such switching (and the resources involved in focusing on multiple goals for multiple tasks) does utilize important resources, while DeShon et al. (1996) suggest that it might not be as critical as we thought. However, when multiple goals cause conflict, performance can suffer (Locke et al., 1994).

The multiple goal issue becomes particularly troublesome as employee jobs are enlarged to include not only their regular task, but some additional tasks that may relate to the goals of the larger organization or in order to increase empowerment. Briefly, a conflict occurs between the performance goals of the normal task and those of the various work groups of which the individual is a part. Some of these are quite inevitable even as part of the work task. For example, many production jobs will have a quantity goal and a level of quality goal. The performance goal (quantity) is meaningless unless there is a quality goal to support it. However, as we have documented, conflicts can occur between quantity and quality.

Multiple goal conflict was such a problem at the Chicago Public Schools that the school system, under Paul Vallas, felt that there was a lack of focus of many of the school districts. It was unclear which goals were more important than others. Under the remarkable reorganization that was made when Paul Vallas became chief executive officer, that focus was changed to one major goal: standardized test scores. While they also encouraged the various schools to develop metrics to assess operational performance related to improving student test performance, it was clear that the overriding goal was the students' test scores for each school. The result of the refocus was a marked improvement in test scores for a majority of the 409,499 students that are in the system, according to Philip J. Hansen, Chief Accountability Officer for the school district (Hansen, 1998). In 1998, over 60,000 students attended summer school to try to meet the necessary test scores so that they could be promoted. The old practice, before Vallas, of social promotions without mastery of the material is over.

Having one overarching goal is one strategy that reduces goal proliferation and conflict. Another strategy, as we have mentioned, is to have goals weighted by importance. In addition, most examples we have seen or read about that have been successful keep the total number of goals relatively low and show how goals at different levels and stages are integrated and complementary. The tension seems to be between too few goals (and important activities are neglected) and too many goals (which results in a lack of focus and direction). Goal setting is a system that requires active and persistent management if it is to succeed.

How difficult is a difficult goal?

We have already discussed the linear relationship between assigned goal difficulty and performance, given that goals are accepted (Locke and Latham, 1990; Wood et al., 1987). The question, for a practitioner, is just how difficult is difficult and how do we represent that to an employee so that the goal will be accepted? If it is "very difficult" the goal may not be attractive (have a low valence) and employees will need time and resources (Mitchell and Wood, 1994) to reach it.

The early research on goal difficulty was not much help in this regard. "Goal theory is vague as to how hard a hard goal should be" (Locke and Latham, 1990, p. 39). There was an informal sort of rule of thumb that a difficult goal was one that you could reach 10–20 percent of the time or be reached by 10–20 percent of the people. This level of difficulty apparently is acceptable to most subjects.

The issue of how the goal difficulty is represented has been researched heavily by Wright (Wright, 1990, 1992; Wright et al., 1995). He has shown that there are two basic ways to operationalize difficulty. First, you can use what he calls an assigned goal level that reflects some sort of objective standard or normative standard. The second technique is to use what he calls performance improvement goals, which are based on an individual's past performance. This latter technique often feels like ratcheting to the employee; that is, they improve a lot and then are asked to improve a lot again. Wright et al. (1995) suggest that in the long run this latter technique may cause problems.

Motorola's experience with goal level issues is instructive. One of its first quality efforts led to the establishment of a 10 percent increase in quality per year for five years. The goal in almost all units was met but the executive committee was not pleased at how the goals were met. In the next set of goals, the executive established the goal of a 20 percent improvement in quality per year over the next five years. Unit leaders were incensed. Many complained that it was impossible to reach the objectives doing what they have been doing in the past, and they were right. They reached the objectives in the past by simply working harder and longer hours. This is not what Bob Galvin and the executive committee wanted (Thompson, 1992). They wanted their employees to rethink how things were done, find a new way to reach the quality goals. Hence, goals were dramatically raised in order to force the employees to find creative solutions to improve quality. The more difficult goals lead to the desired behaviors. Units were now focusing on new procedures and rethinking everything that they did. Not all experiments increased quality, but the revised goal did lead to the change in the focus of the employees' efforts. So one question to be asked in determining how difficult goals should be, ought to relate to the kinds of behaviors that the goal setters want to see exhibited in the organization.

"Stretch goals" is an idea that has been introduced over the past decade. Stretch goals are objectives that are very difficult to reach; some would call them impossible to reach. Conventional research would support the notion that stretch goals would not be accepted as they would be too difficult to achieve. Yet there are some excellent cases of dramatic progress made through the use of stretch goals. For example, the CSX Corporation railroad was concerned about the lack of profits occurring in the hauling of coal from West Virginia and Maryland. It simply was not worth it to improve track and equipment for hauling a product that was not receiving the return on investment that other commodities were experiencing. In one final effort to change the conditions, the CSX management sent a team down to Cumberland, Maryland, charged with reaching a stretch goal to earn the cost of capital on the equipment that was being used in the area. This idea was totally alien to the rail industry. Conventional wisdom supported the notion that direct costs such as labor and fuel were the important factors to consider in rail operations. Hence, long trains are used to reduce the cost of crews, and horsepower per ton of cargo is kept low to save on fuel. The end result is long and slow trains that lead to poor car utilization. Conventional wisdom leads to cars spending a lot of time doing nothing. Longer trains mean that it will take longer to load a train at the mine. Once underway, the train will take longer and be prone to more problems just because of the length and the desire to use locomotive power in the most economical fashion. Once at the unloading terminal, the long trains swamp the ability of the loading equipment to handle the coal, leading to delays in getting the train unloaded. The end result was that cars spent much of the time not moving and hence, not earning much money for its owner.

The stretch team immediately focused on improving car utilization. They proposed running shorter trains thereby getting a car loaded, moved, and unloaded in a much shorter time. Operating people, whose bonuses were based on keeping labor and fuel costs down objected. Upper management rearranged the incentive system for operations. The end result was much better car utilization leading the railroad to haul virtually the same amount of coal per year with 5,000 fewer coal cars. As engines were used more efficiently, and as they could get over the road quicker with shorter trains, there was a need for fewer engines. The rate of return on the remaining cars met the stretch goals imposed by management. The increase in profitability of the division led to a decision to increase the investment in improving tracks and other services in the region thereby making coal more competitive worldwide. As the costs associated with moving the coal were reduced and the railroad made a commitment to stay in the area and improve its infrastructure, the mining companies were encouraged to make further investment to improve their extraction processes (Thompson et al., 1997).

Stretch goals must be accepted by work groups, as well as by top level management. A prerequisite for acceptance seems to be that stretch goal teams must have support by management to make the changes in the system without the normal bureaucratic and political processes miring the group in debates and appeals for approvals rather than progress. Thompson and others call this idea "bureaucratic immunity." In addition, there must be adequate information flows that are accommodated to the needs of the stretch team (Thompson et al., 1997). In retrospect, stretch goals will lead to improved performance if the goals are accepted by the stretch team. The team will accept the goals if it is clear there is management support, they are free of some of the normal approval processes, and they are immune from the bureaucratic processes necessary with much of the change process in many organizations. Hence, the prospect of making substantial change that would be visible to management encourages acceptance of these "impossible" stretch goals.

One final point on goal difficulty. As one moves up the organizational hierarchy, people usually have more responsibility and more flexibility and discretion. Major changes in direction, process and procedures can be made at higher levels. It appears that the use of stretch goals may be more appropriate at that level than at lower levels where there is less flexibility and therefore less opportunity to make dramatic process or procedural changes resulting in dramatic performance increases. Difficult but obviously attainable goals are more appropriate at these lower levels.

Do you use incentives and rewards for goal attainment?

One way to increase the attractiveness of a goal (its valence) is to use incentives for goal attainment. In practice, this means a bonus is given when the goal is reached. How exactly should this be done?

Locke and Latham (1990) review the research on this issue and come to a rather "contingent" conclusion. Anticipated rewards definitely can increase the attractiveness of a goal. However, if the goal is too difficult, many people may not reach it and will be frustrated or angry as a result. They argue that in this situation an incentive "changes the subject's mental set" (p. 43). In addition, since incentives may have effects on other goal attributes (such as, self-set goal level) or direct effects on action through other mechanisms, it is hard to explain completely the effects of incentives on performance.

However, their review in 1990 and the Latham and Locke (1991) paper suggest the following. Use a bonus for goal attainment when the goals are moderately difficult. When difficulty is increased reward partial goal attainment or progress towards the goal. In addition, one can have increasing incentives matched to higher performance level goals. More current research seems to confirm these ideas. Seta et al. (1992) show that having too much invested in goal attainment can increase anxiety and hurt performance. Lee et al. (1997) show that an all-or-nothing bonus works better with moderate goals than difficult goals and Moussa (1996) found that the best performance is achieved by people with high task-specific self-esteem, who are encouraged to set difficult goals, using a piece-rate reward system.

The question is not whether there should be some connection between the goal and an incentive. It is clear that there should be. The difficulty relates to how to connect the incentive. If there is a binary relationship that the reward comes only with meeting the goal, then there may be discouragement when a difficult goal is not met. However, is there a loss of focus on reaching the goal if the reward is based on performance improvement? Is some sort of combination desirable in some situations, similar to a Taylor piece-rate plan where there was a strong incentive for reaching the goal, but reinforcement for progress in meeting the goal as well (Taylor, 1911).

The Chicago School District found the need to reinforce both reaching the goal, and progress toward the goal. The District as a whole has over 409,000 students, 82 percent of which come from low income families and 14 percent of which are limited in the use of the English language. As the reformed school board appointed in 1995 found, it would be difficult and demoralizing to develop a goal requiring, for example, 50 percent of the students to be above the national norms on standardized tests. While that goal might be attainable in some schools, other schools would simply give up as the goal was viewed as too difficult to reach. Philip J. Hansen, Chicago Public Schools Chief Accountability Officer, reported that the school board realized that while the focus is on bringing all schools to higher standardized test scores, it was imperative to match performance and rewards in a way that led to continuing high levels of effort in all schools. Hence, while it was still clear where the ultimate goal created the focus, there were still progress incentives to keep encouraging high levels of effort (Hansen, 1998).

This sensitivity toward sustaining effort was also evident at the AT&T Universal Card division (Kuebler, 1998). One of the main reasons for using goal setting is to provide clarity about what is the desired endpoint. The incentives ought to be a major driver in sustaining efforts toward that final endpoint. However, if the incentives are such that they only reward final endpoint attainment, this can lead to a degradation of effort with very difficult goals, and thus, the benefit of the incentive is lost. There is a desire, as well, to avoid the gamesmanship that often recurs in many MBO programs, where "if the rewards are based on goal attainment, let me make my goals easy to reach" (Mitchell and Wood, 1994). Hence, with the AT&T Universal Card, incentives were provided that encouraged goal attainment, but allowed for recognition of progress toward the goal as well. How to decide when to reward performance improvement over goal attainment becomes one of the skills of the art of management.

When should you use individual or group goals?

With the increased use of teams in the American workforce, there has been renewed attention on group dynamics and group performance. Most of the research on goal setting reviewed by Locke and Latham (1990) is with individuals, although they do suggest that the same motivational mechanisms should occur in groups, and cite studies that support these propositions. In addition, they suggest that in groups, other mechanisms and processes occur that can interact with goal level and commitment that are important for understanding the goal–performance relationship.

The recent research has been supportive of these ideas. The O'Leary-Kelly et al. (1994) review paper shows that group goals have strong effects on group performance and Weingart (1992) and Weldon et al. (1991) show that effort and planning function as mediators. Mitchell and Silver (1990) and Doerr et al. (1996) demonstrated that interdependence is a key moderator variable in terms of what type of goal should be set. The former study showed that individual goals can hurt performance where people are highly interdependent and the latter study suggested that a group goal works better on a more interdependent pull production line than a less interdependent push line. Crown and Rosse (1995) show that group-centered individual goals can complement group goals to increase group performance. Finally, Podsakoff et al. (1997) and Klein and Mulvey (1995) have shown that group cohesiveness increases group goal level and performance, while Silver and Bufanio (1996) show that group efficacy increases group goal level and performance.

The use of group goals seems to depend on the amount of interdependence required by the task. For example, many real estate brokers treat each of their agents as individual profit centers. The agents are charged overhead and administrative expenses, but then can keep all the proceeds from any sales that they make. The end result is that each agent is much more focused on doing those behaviors that will enhance selling their own properties. There are few agent behaviors focused toward doing what may lead to a more cohesive and cooperative agency. In contrast some real estate brokers set up goals that are based on group performance. All or some of the proceeds of any sale that an agent makes, goes into one fund that is then distributed to each agent at the end of the period. The aim of this communal goal setting is to focus the agents' efforts on working as a team and promoting the agency, less on the efforts of the individual. Individual self-reports support this process; however, a problem with the system relates to a behavioral concept called "social loafing." Social loafing occurs when a member of a team allows the others in the team to do the work while gaining the benefits of others doing the work. Social loafing is a problem in many organizations and can tend to create divisiveness in work teams, depending on how the reinforcement system is structured.

This was particularly true at the production unit at Levi Strauss & Co. (King, 1998). Since 1992, many of the factories switched from an individual incentive system to a work team incentive system. Work teams would consist of 10–35 workers who would share doing specific tasks associated with the production of trousers, and incentives would be paid as a function of the production of the total team. But note that while the incentives were for a group, people still did individual tasks. The change was designed to empower workers to find better ways of improving the quality and quantity of performance while reducing some of the injury rates that were occurring as employees, in the old system, did the same task over and over again.

Unfortunately, the team incentive approach led to increased conflict between slow and fast performers. High performers saw their pay decrease in 1993, a year after the change, as plant productivity dropped to 73 percent of pre-team levels. As a contrast, low performers got more money, creating feelings of injustice and anger. While plant productivity has increased since then, it has only increased to 93 percent of pre-team levels. The lack of improvement led to the company closing 11 factories in the United States affecting 6,000 employees. Conflict between some group members was so bad that there were threats against slow workers to "get out or face potential harm." In one case, a worker threatened to kill a low performing team member.

Group goals can also be troublesome in situations where the individual's effort cannot in some rather direct way be tied to the reward for reaching the goal. That is, the group goal is substantially removed from the impact of a specific individual's or unit's effort or performance. For example, much of the motivational rewards associated with working as a store manager for Wal-Mart was associated with profitability of the store and to a larger degree, the bonus that would result from the appreciation of the stock price for Wal-Mart common stock. Thus, the success of both store and company was the group goal. For many years, the success of Wal-Mart as an organization, helped to increase the stock price and store profits such that many store managers became quite wealthy. The growth in the number of stores aided in providing promotions for employees and success would excite employees to do even more to reach the goals of the organization. Reaching profit level goals that Sam Walton, founder of Wal-Mart, challenged his employees to reach, at one time, resulted in Sam Walton doing the hula on Wall Street.

In an upturn, everyone wins with such a distant group goal. However, if the group goal is tied to incentives and reaching the goal is outside the control of the individual, not reaching the goal can lead to a significant drop in morale and effort. At Wal-Mart, once the stock price began to stagnate in the early 1990s and store profits were eroded from stiffer competition, the incentives that propelled high levels of effort in the past were gone. An employee that expended high levels of effort found that the stock price was not appreciating and promotions were not as forthcoming as before. Some employees would take the view, "why should I work like crazy if my efforts don't affect the goal and my rewards that occur for reaching the goal?" A group goal is helpful in many cases as the research would support, but there is a pragmatic danger in having a group goal that is so removed that team members cannot see the relationship of their effort and reaching the goal.

Group performance goals are now being used in elementary education. Many schools now educate their students using the group method. The logic for forming students into "pods" or learning groups of four or so is that the teacher can then focus on perhaps seven groups in class instead of 28 individuals. Groups can be an effective means to teach members concepts that would be difficult if they did not have the feedback and knowledge of their peers as they work on problems. The use of these pods seems to support an enhancement of the learning that is possible because of the group members teaching other group members. In addition, if there are rewards for group goal achievement, other group members may take action for those members who may be acting at odds with the purposes of the assignment.

So, the effective application of group versus individual goals in organization settings seems to be closely related to the types of tasks and the structure of incentives and reinforcements. Group goals work where there is substantial interdependence. If they are used where people are independent, individual performance may suffer if people see a loss of positive personal outcomes from a group reward over an individual reward. A social loafer can also do much to demoralize and reduce the motivation in a group where group goals are used. Giving the group the power to reward and punish their members can sometimes correct this problem. If an individual does not see the connection between individual and team effort and reaching a group goal, then the goal will have little motivational properties as well. Both proximal and distal group goals can be used to solve this problem. In addition, group goals can lead to greater individual member support and the developing of a more nurturing environment. Social support may be important to encourage greater effort and commitment toward the goal. This important support seems to be a factor in the use of stretch goals as demonstrated in the CSX railroad example above. The appropriate use of group goals can be a powerful motivational strategy but if used incorrectly, a number of problems may occur.

How do you manage the goal-setting process?

Mitchell and Wood (1994) discussed a number of practical issues involved with managing a goal-setting intervention, as did Mitchell (1997). Goal setting requires lots of work to implement successfully. There has to be coordination across people and organizational units as well as up and down the organizational hierarchy. Monitoring has to take place to assess goal progress and when attainment or progress is achieved, feedback, rewards and bonuses need to be delivered. These are the nuts and bolts of using the system.

In addition, Locke and Latham (1990) and Mitchell (1997) point out that in practice, there is always a need for revision and change. Priorities change, competitors do unexpected things, new government regulations are revealed and so on. All of these types of complexities point out that goal setting occurs in a dynamic world.

It is also true that goal setting occurs in a political environment (Mitchell and Wood, 1994). It is often social, negotiated, and public. As such, goals can become political symbols, rallying points or objects of ridicule and criticism. As Rodgers and Hunter (1991) have pointed out in their meta-analyses of MBO programs, the support of top level management is a key predictor of whether such programs will succeed or fail. Goal-setting systems need political support and resources to be effective.

The Baldrige award criterion provides a good background for understanding aspects of managing the goal-setting environment pertaining to product quality and customer satisfaction. The first Baldrige award was presented in 1987. The award is designed to recognize those organizations that are successful in creating a total quality environment that is customer-focused. Some of the major core values that are the foundation of the Baldrige award are a focus on fact, results, and on defining and measuring key business requirements. Hence, it is essential, by the Baldrige criteria, that an organization must be driven by a strong goal-centered culture.

There are seven categories associated with the Baldrige criteria for performance excellence. These include: (1) leadership; (2) strategic planning; (3) customer and market focus; (4) information and analysis; (5) human resource focus; (6) process management; and (7) business results. The first three of these dimensions can be considered as the driver of the organization. Defining the customer and market focus are the major foundations of the strategic plans that give focus to the efforts of the organization. The personal involvement of all leaders in the organization, but particularly top leadership, is important in sustaining the values and culture while supporting the directions provided by the strategic plans. Item 4, information and analysis, can also be considered the platform that the organization operates. Providing the internal operational and external market information is central to knowing where the organization is and where it is going. Categories 5 and 6, human resources and process management, are considered the work core. It is people doing processes that gets things done in the organization that leads to category 7, business results (National Institute of Standards and Technology, 1998).

There are three major criterion dimensions for the Baldrige award: approach, deployment, and results. Approach relates to how the organization has established the mechanisms to address what is asked in the criteria. Deployment relates to the extent to which those means have been dispersed in the organization to include all members of the organization. Results relate to the quantified measures that have been made to assess the progress of the organization in addressing the various quality issues stated in the criteria. Categories 1–6 address approach and deployment issues. Category 7 addresses quantified results.

Several key issues that the examiner addresses relate to the concepts of alignment, prevention, and measurement. Alignment relates to the need to align elements across the categories. For example, there should be an alignment of what has been articulated as key business, customer, and operational performance requirements. These evolve from the key business requirement section of the application. The key business requirements are those requirements essential to the survival and success of the organization. From a review of these requirements and customer requirements the strategic plan is formed. Hence, there should be alignment between key business requirements, category 3, customer and market focus, and the strategic plan, category 2. There should be alignment between what is articulated in the strategic plan and the deployment of that plan with the other elements of the organization (categories 4–6). Finally, there should be alignment between what has been said as being important and what has been measured in the organization (category 7).

The Baldrige criterion and its scoring provide an example of managing the goal-setting environment. Objectives ought to be established in each of the major areas important to meet the needs of the customer. In addition, the various plans to meet the needs of the organization should be linked or aligned with the various other objectives in the organization so there is a consistent and concerted effort expended to meet organizational goals. This implies that there is a hierarchical relationship between goals (outcome versus process and outcome versus concurrent and preliminary control aspects) and that close monitoring of these antecedent objectives is critical in meeting the final outcome objective.

Lastly, in the scoring of the Baldrige criteria, a moderate degree of weight is placed on prevention and having cycles of improvement. Prevention relates to going beyond reacting to problems as they occur. It encourages a system that anticipates and tests to ensure that problems will not occur within the products and processes of the organization. In addition, it is important that the organization demonstrates that there has been a cycle of improvement. This means that the process under study has been in place, there are measures (objectives) to assess its performance, and that there has been at least one systematic review of performance. From this review there can be changes, if needed, to improve the reliability, cycle time (the time it takes to do the process once), or reduce the cost of the process.

Management of a quality process is similar to the management of the goal-setting process. A particular goal cannot be viewed in isolation of the other process, objectives, and capacities of the people in the organization. A systemic view must be taken that supports the inter-relationship involved and supports the development of the culture that will support the goal-setting processes and its corresponding benefits.

■ CONCLUSION

Both Locke and Latham (1990) and Latham and Locke (1991) summarize the theory and research in goal setting by describing what they call the "high performance cycle." One must start with a context that is conducive to goal setting (for example, can give feedback, have managerial support) and then choose goals that reflect behaviors and activities that are important for effective individual and organizational performance. These should be specific and difficult. Care should be taken to insure commitment and high self-efficacy and to provide feedback along the way. Time to develop appropriate task strategies must be available. Both partial success and goal attainment can be rewarded. When goal attainment leads to valued rewards, high satisfaction is the result and such satisfaction can increase organizational commitment and reduce turnover, leaving a workforce that is excited about pursuing new and stimulating challenges.

As we have seen in this chapter, however, the devil is in the details. When trying to actually use goal setting there is a long list of practical considerations. Can I measure goal attainment? Do I have the resources to implement and support this system? What sorts of tasks are people working on and how do I match goals to tasks? Are people working in teams or alone? What are the political implications of setting particular goals?

There is now a fairly substantial body of literature and practical wisdom around to help us with these issues. Papers by Locke (1997), Mitchell (1997) and the current paper cover a broad range of topics pertaining to when you can use goal setting and how you can implement it effectively. References have been provided to particular examples that deal with particular issues.

Like any body of knowledge there is always a two-way flow between theory and practice. Goal setting is clearly an approach that has informed our understanding of human behavior and increased effectiveness in the work place. There are still numerous issues that can be enlightened through further research and practical experience. But goal setting is clearly a success story for industrial and organizational psychology and one we can point to with pride.

REFERENCES

Ashford, S. J., and Tsui, A. S. 1991: Self-regulation for managerial effectiveness: the role of active feedback seeking. *Academy of Management Journal*, 34, 251–80.

Atkinson, J. W. 1964: *An introduction to motivation*, Princeton, NJ: Van Nostrand.

Atkinson, J. W., and Birch, D. 1970: *The dynamics of action*, New York: Wiley.

Audia, G., Kristof-Brown, A., Brown, K. G., and Locke, E. A. 1996: Relationship of goals and microlevel work processes to performance on a multiple manual task. *Journal of Applied Psychology*, 81, 483–97.

Austin, J. T., and Vancouver, J. B. 1996: Goal constructs in psychology: Structure, process, and content. *Psychology Bulletin*, 120, 3, 338–75.

Bandura, A. 1986: *Social foundations of thought and action: A social cognitive theory*, Englewood Cliffs, NJ: Prentice-Hall.

Bandura, A. 1997: *Self-efficacy: The exercise of control*, Freeman Publishing Co.

Bannister, R. D., and Balkin, D. B. 1990: Performance evaluation and compensation feedback messages: An integrated model. *Journal of Occupational Psychology*, 63, 97–111.

Bargh, J. A. 1994: The four horsemen of automaticity: Awareness, intention, efficiency, and control in social cognition. In R. S. Wyer and T. Srull (eds.), *Handbook of social cognition*, 2nd edn., Vol. 1, Hillsdale, NJ: Erlbaum, 1–40.

Bargh, J. A., and Gollwitzer, P. M. 1994: Environmental control of goal directed action: Automatic and strategic contingencies between situations and behaviors. In W. Spaulding (ed.), *Integrative views of motivation, cognition, and emotion*, Nebraska Symposium on Motivation, Vol. 41, Lincoln: University of Nebraska Press, 71–124.

Barrick, M. R., Mount, M. K., and Strauss, J. P. 1993: Conscientiousness and performance of sales representatives: Test of the mediating effects of goal setting. *Journal of Applied Psychology*, 78, 111–18.

Beach, L. R., and Mitchell, T. R. 1990: Image theory: A behavioral theory of decisions in organizations. In B. M. Staw and L. L. Cummings (eds.), *Research in organizational behavior*, Vol. 12, Greenwich, CT: JAI Press, 1–41.

Beck, R. C. 1978: *Motivation: Theories and principles*, Englewood Cliffs. NJ: Prentice-Hall.

Bobko, P., and Colella, A. 1994: Employee reactions to performance standards: A review and research propositions. *Personnel Psychology*, 47, 1–29.

Button, S. B., Mathieu, J. E., and Zajak, D. M. 1996: Goal orientation in organizational research: A conceptual and empirical foundation. *Organizational Behavior and Human Decision Processes*, 67, 26–48.

Campbell, J. P., and Pritchard, R. D. 1976: Motivation theory in industrial and organizational psychology. In M. Dunnette (ed.), *Handbook of industrial and organizational psychology*, Chicago: Rand McNally, 63–130.

Chesney, A. A., and Locke, E. A. 1991: Relationships among goal difficulty, business strategies, and performance on a complex simulation task. *Academy of Management Journal*, 34, 400–24.

Chidester, T. R., and Grigsby, W. C. 1984: A meta-analysis of the goal setting performance literature. *Academy of Management Proceedings*, 202–6.

Crown, D. F., and Rosse, J. G. 1995: Yours, mine and ours: Facilitating group productivity through the integration of individual and group goals. *Organizational Behavior and Human Decision Processes*, 64, 138–50.

Daniels, D., and Mitchell, T. R. 1995: Differential effects of self-efficacy, goals and expectations on task performance. Paper presented at the 55th Annual Meeting at the Academy of Management, Vancouver, BC, August.

DeShon, R. P., and Alexander, R. A. 1996: Goal setting effects on implicit and explicit learning of complex tasks. *Organizational Behavior and Human Decision Processes*, 65, 18–36.

DeShon, R. P., Brown, K. G., and Greenis, J. L. 1996: Does self-regulation require cognitive resources? Evaluation of resource allocation models of goal setting. *Journal of Applied Psychology*, 81, 595–608.

DeShon, R. P., and Landis, R. S. 1997: The dimensionality of the Hollenbeck, Williams and Klein 1989: Measure of goal commitment on complex tasks. Organizational *Behavior and Human Decision Processes*, 70, 105–16.

Doerr, K., Mitchell, T. R., Klastorin, T. D., and Brown, K. 1996: The impact of production policies and behavioral interventions on productivity, quality and job satisfaction. *Journal of Applied Psychology*, 81, 142–52.

Dowling, W. F., and Sayles, L. R. 1978: *How managers motivate: The imperatives of supervision*, New York: McGraw Hill.

Dweck, C. S. 1986: Motivational processes affecting learning. *American Psychologist*, 41, 1040–8.

Earley, P. C., Connoly, T., and Ekegren, G. 1989: Goals, strategy development and task performance: Some limits on the efficacy of goal setting. *Journal of Applied Psychology*, 74, 24–33.

Earley, P. C., and Erez, M. 1991: Time-dependency effects of goals and norms: The role of cognitive processes on motivational models. *Journal of Applied Psychology*, 76, 717–24.

Earley, P. C., Lee, C., and Lituchy, T. R. 1989: Task strategy and judgments in goal setting: The effects of a learning emphasis and training sequence on performance. Unpublished manuscript, Department of Management and Policy, University of Arizona.

Earley, P. C., and Lituchy, T. R. 1991: Delineating goal and efficacy effects: A test of three models. *Journal of Applied Psychology*, 76, 81–8.

Earley, P. C., Northcraft, G. B., Lee, C., and Lituchy, T. R. 1990: Impact of process and outcome feedback on the relation of goal setting to task performance. *Academy of Management Journal*, 33, 87–105.

Earley, P. C., Shalley, C. E., and Northcraft, G. B. 1992: I think I can, I think I can . . . processing time and strategy effects of goal acceptance/rejection decisions. *Organizational Behavior and Human Decision Processes*, 53, 1–13.

Eden, D. 1988: Pygmalion, goal setting and expectancy: Compatible ways to boost productivity. *Academy of Management Review*, 13, 639–52.

Erez, M. 1977: Feedback: A necessary condition for the goal setting–performance relationship. *Journal of Applied Psychology*, 62, 624–7.

Ford, M. E. 1992: *Motivating humans: Goals, emotions and personal agency beliefs*, Newbury Park, CA: Sage.

Franken, R. E. 1988: *Human motivation*, 2nd edn., Pacific Grove, CA: Brooks/Cole.

Frese, M., and Zapf, D. 1994: Action as the core of work psychology. In M. D. Dunnette, L. M. Hough, and H. Triandis (eds.), *Handbook of industrial and organizational psychology*, Vol. 4, Palo Alto, CA: Consulting Psychologist Press.

Garland, H. 1985: A cognitive mediation theory of task goals and human performance. *Motivation and Emotion*, 9, 345–67.

Gellatly, I. R. 1996: Conscientiousness and task performance: Test of a cognitive process model. *Journal of Applied Psychology*, 81, 474–82.

Gellatly, I. R., and Meyer, J. P. 1992: The effects of goal difficulty on physiological arousal, cognition and task performance. *Journal of Applied Psychology*, 77, 694–704.

George-Falvy, J. 1996: Effects of task complexity and learning stage on the relationship between participation in goal setting and task performance. Paper presented at the 56th Annual Meeting of the Academy of Management, Cincinnati, Ohio, August.

Gilliland, S. W., and Landes, R. S. 1992: Quality and quantity goals in a complex decision task: Strategies and outcomes. *Journal of Applied Psychology*, 77, 672–81.

Gollwitzer, P. M. 1990: Action phases and mind-sets. In E. T. Higgins and R. M. Sorrentino (eds.), *Handbook of motivation and cognition*, Vol. 2, New York: Guilford Press, 53–92.

Gollwitzer, P. M. 1993: Goal achievement: The role of intentions. In M. Hewstone and W. Stroebe (eds.), *European review of social psychology*, Vol. 4, Chichester, England: Wiley, 141–85.

Gollwitzer, P. M., Heckhausen, H., and Ratajczak, H. 1989: From weighing to willing: Approaching a change decision through pre- or post-decision mentation. *Organizational Behavior and Human Decision Processes*, 45, 41–65.

Greller, M. M., and Parson, C. K. 1992: Feedback and feedback inconsistency as sources of strain and self-evaluation. *Human Relations*, 45, 601–20.

Hansen, P. J. 1998: Personal interview conducted on June 11, 1998.

Harackewicz, J. M., Barron, K. E., Carter, S. M., Lehto, A. T., and Elliot, A. J. (in press): Predictors and consequences of achievement goals in the college classroom: Maintaining interest and making the grade. *Journal of Personality and Social Psychology*.

Hollenbeck, J. R., Williams, C. R., and Klein, H. J. 1989: An empirical examination of the antecedent of commitment to difficult goals. *Journal of Applied Psychology*, 74, 18–23.

Hunter, J. E., and Schmidt, F. L. 1983: Quantifying the effects of psychological interventions on employee job performance and work force productivity. *American Psychologist*, 38, 473–8.

Kanfer, R. 1996: Motivation from an integrated resource allocation perspective. Paper presented at the 11th Annual Conference of the Society for Industrial and Organizational Psychology, San Diego, April.

Kanfer, R., and Ackerman, P. L. 1989: Motivation and Cognitive abilities: An integrative/aptitude–treatment interaction approach to skill acquisition (monograph). *Journal of Applied Psychology*, 74, 657–90.

Kanfer, R., Ackerman, P. L., Murtha, T. C., Dugdale, B., and Nelson, L. 1994: Goal setting, conditions of practice, and task performance: A resources allocation perspective. *Journal of Applied Psychology*, 79, 826–35.

Kanfer, R., and Kanfer, F. H. 1991: Goals and self regulation: Applications of theory to work settings. In M. L. Maehr and P. R. Pintrich (eds.), *Advances in motivation and achievement*, Vol. 7, Greenwich, CT: JAI Press, 287–326.

King, R. 1998: Levi workers are assigned to teams, and morale takes a hit. *Wall Street Journal*, May 20, 1998, A1 and A6.

Klein, H. J., and Mulvey, P. W. 1995: Two investigations of the relationship among group goals, goal commitment, cohesion and performance. *Organizational Behavior and Human Resources Processes*, 61, 44–53.

Kuebler, A. 1998: Personal interview conducted on June 9, 1998.

Kuhl, J. 1992: A theory of self-regulation: Action versus state orientation, self-discrimination, and some applications. *Applied Psychology: An International Review*, 41, 97–129.

Latham, G. P., Erez, M., and Locke, E. A. 1988: Resolving scientific disputes by the joint design of crucial experiments by the antagonists: Application to the Erez–Latham dispute regarding participation in goal setting. *Journal of Applied Psychology (monograph)*, 73, 753–72.

Latham, G. P., and Locke, E. A. 1991: Self-regulation through goal setting. *Organizational Behaviour and Human Decision Processes*, 50, 212–47.

Latham, G. P., and Seijts, G. H. (in press): The effects of proximal and distal goals on performance on a moderately complex task. *Journal of Organization Behavior*.

Latham, G. P., Winters, D. C., and Locke, E. A. 1994: Cognitive and motivational effects of participation: A mediator study. *Journal of Organizational Behavior*, 15, 49–63.

Lee, T. W., Locke, E. A., and Phan, S. H. 1997: Explaining the assigned goal–incentive interaction: The role of self-efficacy and personal goals. *Journal of Management*, 23, 541–59.

Locke, E. A. 1991: Goal theory versus control theory: Contrasting approaches to understanding work motivation. *Motivation and Emotion*, 15, 9–28.

Locke, E. A. 1994: The emperor is naked. *Applied Psychology: An International Review*, 43, 367–70.

Locke, E. A. 1997: Motivation through conscious goal setting. *Applied and Preventive Psychology*, 5, 117–24.

Locke, E. A., and Bryan, J. F. 1968: Grade goals as determinants of academic achievement. *Journal of General Psychology*, 79, 217–28.

Locke, E. A., Chah, D. O., Harrison, D. S., and Lustgarten, N. 1989: Separating the effects of goal specificity from goal level. *Organizational Behavior and Human Decision Processes*, 43, 270–87.

Locke, E. A., and Latham, G. P. 1990: *A theory of goal setting and task performance*, Englewood Cliffs, NJ: Prentice-Hall.

Locke, E. A., Smith, K. G., Erez, M., Chah, D. O., and Schaffer, A. 1994: The effects of intra-individual goal conflict on performance. *Journal of Management*, 20, 67–91.

Lord, R. G., and Levy, P. E. 1994: Moving from cognition to action: A control theory perspective. *Applied Psychology: An International Review*, 43, 335–98.

Ludwig, T. D., and Geller, E. S. 1997: Assigned versus participative goal setting and response generalization: Managing injury control among professional pizza drivers. *Journal of Applied Psychology*, 82, 252–61.

Matthews, L. M., Mitchell, T. R., George-Falvy, J., and Wood, R. F. 1994: Goal selection in a simulated managerial environment. *Group and Organization Management*, 19, 460–80.

Mento, A. J., Steel, R. P., and Karren, R. J. 1987: A meta-analytic study of the effects of goal setting on task performance: 1966–84. *Organizational Behavior and Human Decision Processes*, 39, 52–83.

Mitchell, T. R. 1982: Motivation: New directions for theory, research and practice. *Academy of Management Review*, 7, 80–8.

Mitchell, T. R. 1997: Matching motivational strategies with organizational contexts. *Research in Organizational Behavior*, 19, 57–149.

Mitchell, T. R., Hopper, H., Daniels, D., George-Falvy, J., and James, L. 1994: Predicting self-efficacy and performance during skill acquisition. *Journal of Applied Psychology*, 76, 845–55.

Mitchell, T. R., and Silver, W. S. 1990: Individual and group goals when workers are interdependent: Effects on task strategies and performance. *Journal of Applied Psychology*, 75, 185–93.

Mitchell, T. R., and Wood, R. E. 1994: Managerial goal setting. *Journal of Leadership Studies*, 1, 3–26.

Motorola, 1991: *Motorola corporate quality system review guidelines*, Phoenix, Arizona: Motorola Literature Distribution Center.

Moussa, F. M. 1996: Determinants and process of the choice of goal difficulty. *Group and Organization Management*, 21, 414–38.

National Institute of Standards and Technology. 1998: *1998 Criteria for performance excellence: Malcolm Baldrige national quality award*, Gaithersburg, MD: United States Department of Commerce.

O'Leary-Kelly, A. M., Martocchio, J. J., and Frink, D. D. 1994: A review of the influence of group goals on group performance. *Academy of Management Journal*, 37, 1285–1301.

Petzinger, Jr., T., 1998. The front lines: Nurses discover the healing power of customer service. *Wall Street Journal*, February 27, 1998, 1B.

Phillips, J. M., and Gully, S. M. 1997: Role of goal orientation, ability, need for achievement, and locus of control in the self-efficacy and goal setting process. *Journal of Applied Psychology*, 82, 792–802.

Phillips, J. M., Hollenbeck, J. R., and Ilgen, D. R. 1996: Prevalence and prediction of positive discrepancy creation: Examining a discrepancy between two self-regulation theories. *Journal of Applied Psychology*, 81, 498–511.

Podsakoff, P. M., Mackenzie, S. B., and Ahearne, M. 1997: Moderating effects of goal acceptance on the relationship between group cohesiveness and productivity. *Journal of Applied Psychology*, 82, 974–83.

Pritchard, R. D. 1995: *Productivity measurement and improvement: Organizational case studies*. New York: Praeger.

Przygodda, M., Kleinbeck, U., Schmidt, K.-H., and Beckman, J. 1995: Productivity measurement and enhancement in advanced manufacturing systems. In R. D. Pritchard (ed.), *Productivity measurement and improvement*, New York: Praeger.

Rodgers, R., and Hunter, J. E. 1991: Impact of management by objectives on organizational productivity (monograph). *Journal of Applied Psychology*, 76, 322–36.

Rodgers, R., and Hunter, J. E. 1994: The discard of study evidence by literature reviewers. *Journal of Applied Behavioral Science*, 30, 329–45.

Roth, P. L., Watson, M. D., Roth, P. G., and Pritchard, R. D. 1995: ProMES in an electronic assembly plant. In R. D. Pritchard (ed.), *Productivity measurement and improvement*, New York: Praeger.

Sales, S. M. 1970: Some effects on role overload and role underload. *Organizational Behavior and Human Performance*, 5, 592–608.

Scheier, M. F., and Carver, C. S. 1988: A model of behavioral self-regulation: Translating intention into action. In L. Berkowitz (ed.), *Advances in experimental social psychology*, Vol. 21, New York: Academic Press, 303–46.

Seta, J. J., Seta, C. E., and Donaldson, S. 1992: The implications of a resource-investment analysis of goal value for performance in audience and solitary setting. *Basic and Applied Social Psychology*, 13, 145–64.

Silver, W. S., and Bufanio, K. M. 1996: The impact of group efficacy and group goals on group task performance. *Small Group Research*, 27, 347–59.

Smith, K. G., Locke, E. A., and Barry, D. 1990: Goal setting, planning and organizational performance: An experimental simulation. *Organizational Behavior and Human Decision Processes*, 46, 118–34.

Smither, J. W., London, M., Vasilopoulos, N. L., Reilly, R. R., Millsap, R. E., and Salvemini, N. 1995: An examination of the effects of an upward feedback program over time. *Personnel Psychology*, 48, 1–33.

Steers, R. M., and Porter, L. W. 1991: *Motivation and work behavior*, New York: McGraw-Hill.

Taylor, F. W. 1911: *Principles of scientific management*, New York: Harper & Brothers.

Thomas, K. M., and Mathieu, J. E. 1994: Role of causal attributions in dynamic self-regulation and goal processes. *Journal of Applied Psychology*, 79, 812–18.

Thompson, K. R. 1992: Conversations with Bob Galvin. *Organizational Dynamics*, 26(3), 56–69.

Thompson, K. R., Hochwarter, W., and Mathys, N. 1997: Stretch targets: What makes them effective? *Academy of Management Executive*, 11(3), 48–60.

Tindale, R. S., Kulik, C. T., and Scott, L. A. 1991: Individual and group feedback and performance: An attributional perspective. *Basic and Applied Social Psychology*, 12, 41–62.

Tubbs, M. E. 1986: Goal-setting: A meta-analytic examination of the empirical evidence. *Journal of Applied Psychology*, 71, 474–83.

Tubbs, M. E. 1994: Commitment and the role of ability in motivation: Comment on Wright, O'Leary-Kelly, Cortina, Klein and Hollenbeck. *Journal of Applied Psychology*, 79, 804–11.

Tubbs, M. E., Boehne, D. M., and Dahl, J. G. 1993: Expectancy, valence and motivational force functions in goal setting research: An empirical test. *Journal of Applied Psychology*, 78, 361–73.

Tubbs, M. E., and Dahl, J. G. 1991: An empirical comparison of self report and discrepancy measures of goal commitment. *Journal of Applied Psychology*, 76, 708–18.

Tubbs, M. M., and Ekeberg, S. E. 1991: The role of intentions in work motivation: Implications for goal setting theory and research. *Academy of Management Review*, 16, 180–99.

VandeWalle, D. 1999: Goal orientation comes of age for adults: A literature review. Paper presented at the National Meeting of the Academy of Management, Chicago, Illinois, August.

VandeWalle, D., and Cummings, L. L. 1997: A test of the influence of goal orientation on the feedback-seeking process. *Journal of Applied Psychology*, 82, 390–400.

Weingart, L. R. 1992: Impact of group goals, task component complexity, effort and planning on group performance. *Journal of Applied Psychology*, 77, 682–93.

Weldon, E., Jehn, K. A., and Pradham, P. 1991: Processes that mediate the relationship between a group goal and improved group performance. *Journal of Personality and Social Psychology*, 61, 555–69.

Weldon, E., and Weingart, L. R. 1988: A theory of group goals and group performance. Presented at Academy of Management meeting.

Winters, D., and Latham, G. P. 1996: The effect of learning versus outcome goals on a simple versus a complex task? *Group and Organization Management*, 21, 236–50.

Wood, R. E., and Locke, E. A. 1987: The relation of self-efficacy and grade goals to academic performance. *Educational and Psychological Measurement*, 47, 1013–24.

Wood, R. E., Mento, A. J., and Locke, E. A. 1987: Task complexity as a moderator of goal effects: A meta-analysis. *Journal of Applied Psychology*, 72, 416–25.

Wofford, J. C., Goodwin, V. L., and Premack, S. 1992: Meta-analysis of the antecedents of personal goal level and of the antecedents and consequences of goal commitment. *Journal of Management*, 18, 595–615.

Wright, P. M. 1989: Test of the mediating role of goals in the incentive–performance relationship, *Journal of Applied of Psychology*, 74, 699–705.

Wright, P. 1990: Operationalization of goal difficulty as a moderator of the goal difficulty–performance relationship. *Journal of Applied Psychology*, 75, 227–35.

Wright, P. M. 1992: A theoretical examination of the constraint validity of operationalizations of goal difficulty. *Human Resource Management Review*, 2, 275–98.

Wright, P. M., Hollenbeck, J. R., Wolf, S., and McMahan, G. C. 1995: The effects of varying goal difficulty operationalizations on goal setting outcomes and processes. *Organizational Behavior and Human Decision Processes*, 61, 28–43.

Wright, P. M., and Kacmar, K. M. 1994: Goal specificity as a determinant of goal relationship, *Journal of Applied Psychology*, 74, 699–705.

Wright, P. M., O'Leary-Kelly, A. M., Cortina, J. M., Klein, H. J., and Hollenbeck, J. R. 1994: On the meaning and measurement of goal commitment. *Journal of Applied Psychology*, 79, 795–803.

chapter **10**

RESEARCH ON THE EMPLOYMENT INTERVIEW: USEFULNESS FOR PRACTICE AND RECOMMENDATIONS FOR FUTURE RESEARCH

SARA L. RYNES, ALISON E. BARBER, AND GALE H. VARMA

The interview is a costly, inefficient and usually non-valid procedure, often used to the exclusion of far more thoroughly researched and validated procedures. The interview should be retired from its role as an assessment tool and be retained only as a public relations, recruiting, and information disseminating device. (Dunnette and Bass, 1963)

One important conclusion from the present analyses is that structured interviews may have some advantages over more traditional cognitive tests . . . Based on the expert judgments collected in the present research, the structured interview seemed to provide a more comprehensive assessment of relevant skills and abilities than the cognitive ability test which was more limited with respect to the constructs assessed. (Pulakos and Schmitt, 1995, p. 305)

The employment interview has long enjoyed great popularity among both employers and job applicants. Despite repeated warnings that interviews were both unreliable and invalid, employers persisted in using them more than any other method for selecting employees (Church, 1996; Hakel, 1982). Similarly, applicants continued to prefer them over less personalized or more objective forms of assessment.

While the popularity of the interview among practitioners is hardly a new phenomenon, the opening quotes illustrate the rather dramatic extent to which the employment interview has increased in scientific respectability in recent years. In part, the enhanced scientific respectability of the interview is the result of advances in meta-analytic techniques that have allowed for the aggregation of hundreds of small-sample studies and correction for statistical artifacts. Meta-analyses have shown not only that surprisingly high validities can be obtained from structured interviews, but also that even the much maligned unstructured interview has greater validity than was previously suspected (for example, McDaniel et al., 1994; Wiesner and Cronshaw, 1988).

Thus, meta-analytic findings have raised the intriguing possibility that practitioner use of the interview persisted in the face of scientific criticism, not solely because of irrationality on the part of practitioners or the desire for social forms of selection, but also in part because practitioners were more accurate in their beliefs about the interview than scientists gave them credit for. At the same time, scientific criticisms of the interview led employers to make improvements to the interview – particularly in terms of increased structure and job-relatedness – that have enhanced average interview validities over time.

In this paper, we review some of the major research developments that have led to a greater optimism about the interview, as well as a somewhat improved understanding of the specific factors associated with validity enhancement. Although empirical interview research has been concerned primarily with four broad categories of outcomes – reliability, validity, legal defensibility, and applicant reactions (see, for example, Campion et al., 1997; Williamson et al., 1997) – we focus only on the latter three in this review. Clearly, research on the factors associated with reliability is also important, in that evidence regarding correlates of reliability may provide clues about how interview decisions are made and how interview processes might be improved.[1] However, from a practical standpoint, reliability *per se* is of secondary importance to the outcomes of validity, legal defensibility, and applicant acceptability.

It should also be noted that there are likely to be important relationships *among* these three outcomes. For example, an interview's validity is likely to influence its legal defensibility, just as applicants' reactions to interviews are likely to influence their inclinations to file lawsuits. However, because research to date has examined these outcomes primarily in isolation from one another, we follow the same practice in this review. We begin with an overview of major research findings regarding interview validity, focusing most heavily on findings from the past decade.

■ FACTORS ASSOCIATED WITH INTERVIEW VALIDITY

Interview structure

Researchers have long speculated about the probable advantages for validity of using structured rather than unstructured interviews (for example, Janz, 1982; Latham et al., 1980). One of the most significant empirical developments in interview research over the past decade has been the meta-analytic confirmation of this speculation. For example, Wiesner and Cronshaw (1988) reported an average corrected validity coefficient (with respect to job performance ratings) of 0.62 for structured, versus 0.31 for unstructured interviews. Comparable figures from an even larger meta-analysis by McDaniel et al. (1994) were 0.44 for structured interviews and 0.33 for unstructured.

One offshoot of these empirical findings has been an increase in attempts to understand the precise practices or processes that contribute most heavily to the greater average validity of structured interviews, as well as to the higher validities of some structured interviews than others (such as Campion et al., 1997; Dipboye and Gaugler, 1993). From a practical standpoint, determining the specific characteristics that contribute most to validity is essential for determining the relative cost effectiveness of alternative interview design features or interventions (Dipboye and Gaugler, 1993).

In the process of speculating about the underlying determinants of variations in interview validities, it has become increasingly clear that interview structure is a multidimensional and non-dichotomous construct. Campion et al. (1997) define structure as "any enhancement of the interview that is intended to increase psychometric properties by increasing standardization or otherwise assisting the interviewer in determining what questions to ask or how to evaluate responses" (p. 656). Their review elaborates 15 potential components of structure, organized into two major categories: structuring of interview content (for example, using the same questions, limiting prompting, controlling ancillary information); and structuring of the evaluation process (for example, use of multiple scales, behavioral anchors, and mechanical scoring). Similarly, Dipboye and Gaugler (1993) discuss 12 "surface features" that differentiate highly structured from less structured interviews, and then use these as a basis for inferring possible underlying cognitive and behavioral processes that account for differences in average validities between structured and unstructured interviews.

At present, there is no definitive evidence as to which components of interview structure are most important to validity. However, based on a combination of previous research, psychometric arguments, and opportunity for gain over typical practices, Campion et al. (1997) suggest that the following *content* factors are probably most important for increasing validity: using job analysis; asking the same questions of all applicants; and asking better questions (that is, situational, behavioral, background, and job knowledge questions versus opinions, attitudes, goals, aspirations, self-evaluations, and self-descriptions). Similarly, they suggest that the most useful *evaluative* features are likely to be rating each answer or having multiple scales, using anchored scales, and training interviewers.

It is difficult to estimate the extent to which interviews, in practice, demonstrate the various recommended structural components. One problem concerns the fact that practitioners have been asked holistic questions about structure or standardization (for example, Ryan and Sackett, 1987; Rynes et al., 1997) that do not reflect the multidimensional nature of structure as we have come to understand it. The second difficulty is that interview practices have been self-reported by practitioners, rather than empirically observed by outsiders or reported by applicants. This is problematic because there may be a considerable element of social desirability in the reporting of structured versus unstructured interviews, as well as considerable slippage between official "policy" on interviews and their conduct in practice (Dipboye and Gaugler, 1993).

Keeping these caveats in mind, Ryan and Sackett (1987) reported that 15.2 percent of individual assessors (who typically screen for relatively high-level positions) use tightly standardized interviews, 72.8 percent use loosely standardized formats, and 11.9 percent use completely unstandardized interview formats. More recently,

Rynes et al. (1997) reported that among members of the National Association of Colleges and Employers, structured interviews were the second most extensively used selection devices (after reference checks) for screening both new college graduates (3.99 on a 5-point scale) and experienced workers (3.84). In contrast, reported usage of unstructured interviews was 2.92 for new college graduates and 2.98 for experienced workers. Finally, in a recent issue of *The Industrial Psychologist*, Philip Roth asserted that "roughly 70% of interviews are still unstructured" (Church, 1996, p. 110). Clearly, problems mentioned in the preceding paragraph as well as the lack of consistency in available estimates imply that more (and better) research is needed on this question.

Question content

One topic that has received a considerable amount of attention in recent years is whether higher validities are obtained using situational ("What would you do?") questions, past behavior description ("Tell me about a time in the past when you . . .") questions, or psychologically-oriented questions designed to assess personal traits. At this point in time, the evidence with respect to situational versus behavior description interviews remains equivocal, although both appear to be superior to psychologically oriented interviews (McDaniel et al., 1994).

For example, individual studies have reported conflicting results with respect to the validity of situational versus behavior description questions, with some studies finding stronger support for situational interviews (for example, Latham and Saari, 1984; Latham and Skarlicki, 1995; Maurer and Fay, 1988), and others finding stronger support for behavioral descriptions interviews (for example, Campion et al., 1994; Pulakos and Schmitt, 1995). Interpretation of these findings is complicated by a variety of potential confounding differences across studies (such as breadth versus specificity of questions, question-by-question versus dimensional or holistic scoring, low- versus high-level jobs, see Latham and Sue-Chan, 1999). Nor have meta-analyses shed much light on this question to date, due to insufficient numbers of behavioral description interview studies (McDaniel et al., 1994). Thus, additional research on this question would be desirable, including the eventual aggregation of future studies via meta-analysis. In the meantime, designers of future individual studies might look to Pulakos and Schmitt (1995) as an excellent example of a field experiment conducted under carefully controlled conditions.

Interviewer training

Similar to research on supervisory training to avoid errors in performance appraisal (for example, Latham and Wexley, 1981), interview research suggests that interviewer training is unlikely to improve validity unless it is rather extensive and involves active practice and feedback. For example, Maurer and Fay (1988) obtained no improvement in inter-rater reliability after eight hours of interviewer training (although low power represents a possible explanation, given only 22 interviewers in each condition).

Similarly, Vance et al. (1978) found no improvement in interviewer reliability following brief interviewer rating-error training. However, Dougherty et al. (1986) did obtain improvements in validity following extensive training including practice interviews with feedback.

More recently, Stevens (1998) provided interesting data suggesting differences between trained and untrained recruiters in the conduct of the interview process. Using content analysis of 39 campus interview transcripts, she found that trained interviewers were more likely to ask secondary, open, and performance-differentiating questions than were non-trained interviewers. Trained recruiters were also less likely to discuss non-job-related topics, and less likely to modify their evaluations of candidates on the basis of whether the interview was focused primarily on recruitment (attraction) or selection (screening) objectives. Although this study did not assess the actual validity of trained versus untrained interviewer judgments, all of the significant process differences observed suggest that trained interviewers were more likely than untrained ones to have produced job-related candidate evaluations.

Interview focus

Another difference that has been speculated to affect interview validity is the extent to which the interviewer is focused on recruitment and attraction versus screening or selection objectives. Specifically, Rynes (1989) hypothesized a number of ways in which validity might suffer as interviewers became more recruitment-oriented (for example, by talking more about the vacancy and inquiring less about the applicant, by asking fewer questions that are likely to disqualify applicants).

Recently, Stevens (1998) provided direct evidence for some of these propositions based on content analysis of 39 actual interview transcripts. Recruiters who were primarily recruitment-oriented (as opposed to screening or recruitment-plus-screening-oriented) were found to spend 50 percent more time talking, to volunteer twice as much information, and to ask half as many questions of applicants. Although this study stopped short of examining actual interviewer validities, all observed process differences are consistent with the hypothesis that interviews with a dominant recruitment orientation are likely to exhibit lower validity.

Multiple interviewers

Previous authors have offered a number of reasons as to why board or panel interviews are likely to produce superior validities relative to interviews conducted by single interviewers (Campion et al., 1988, 1997). For example, multiple interviewers may reduce the impact of idiosyncratic biases, improve reliability, elicit more information and better recall, and encourage more active information processing by exposing individual differences in recall and interpretation. In general, prior researchers have tended to adopt the perspective that although panel interviews are probably likely to be more valid than individual ones, the important practical question is whether they are *sufficiently* valid to justify their additional expense.

Recent evidence, however, suggests that even the relative validity of panel versus individual interviews is open to question. For example, an early meta-analysis by Wiesner and Cronshaw (1988) suggested that panel interviews were indeed more valid, at least for unstructured interviews (0.37 versus 0.20). However, McDaniel et al.'s later (1994) and larger meta-analysis found rather different results. Specifically, based on sample sizes of more than 11,000 in each category, individual interviews were found to have significantly higher corrected validities (0.43) than panel interviews (0.32) for a combination of structured and unstructured interviews. Moreover, in contrast to Wiesner and Cronshaw's (1988) results, this pattern was found to hold more strongly for structured (0.46 versus 0.38) than unstructured interviews (0.34 versus 0.33). Finally, Marchese and Muchinsky (1993) found no relationship between number of interviewers and interview validity.

Interpretation of the preceding results is hampered to some extent by the failure to control potential confounding variables associated with panel versus individual interviews (for example, degree of interview structure, method of arriving at panel decisions; see also Campion et al., 1997). Clearly, it would be useful for future researchers, at a minimum, to report these surrounding conditions for purposes of future meta-analyses. More optimally, future researchers should be encouraged to jointly manipulate alternative combinations of interview characteristics under tightly controlled conditions.

In designing future research of this type, we recommend that researchers review the excellent interview field research conducted by Pulakos and colleagues (for example, Pulakos and Schmitt, 1995; Pulakos et al., 1996). Pulakos et al. (1996) explicitly tested whether consensus discussions among panel members added incremental validity over mechanical averages of their individual ratings. Results suggested that although the validity coefficient for consensus ratings ($r = 0.35$) was statistically different from that associated with the average of individual ratings ($r = 0.32$), the difference was small enough to be of little practical significance. However, future researchers might wish to examine whether *averaging* the ratings of panel members, rather than conducting consensus discussions, might further enhance panel validities by preventing possible dominance by one or two assertive individuals.

In addition, Pulakos et al. (1996) tested whether individual interviewer differences in leniency, stringency, and central tendency had a detrimental effect on interview validities when aggregated with ratings from other raters (they did not; average validities were 0.32 for both actual ratings and ratings standardized within rater). Finally, the authors showed that what appeared to be substantial individual differences in validity (range = −0.10 to 0.65) could be completely accounted for by sampling error associated with differences in the number of candidates assessed per interviewer.

Ancillary information

Considerable evidence exists that interviewers' post-interview evaluations are highly correlated with their pre-interview impressions (Dipboye, 1989). However, as Dipboye (1989) correctly indicates, the existence of pre-interview impressions does not necessarily produce invalid interview results. Rather, to the extent that pre-interview impressions determine post-interview evaluations, the validity of the interview would be expected to depend on the validity of the specific information (for example, test scores, application blanks, letters of recommendation) that contributes to the pre-interview impression. Thus, if pre-interview impressions are formed on the basis of cognitive ability or job knowledge test scores, the interview might be expected to produce more valid results than if impressions are formed on the basis of letters of recommendation or personal appearance.

However, the fact that pre- and post-interview impressions are typically quite highly correlated does raise the question of the interview's *incremental* validity in relation to information already available from other sources. Dipboye (1989, p. 57) has argued that "the primary threat of pre-interview impressions is not to the basic validity of interviewer assessments considered alone, but to the incremental validity of these assessments."

Pre-interview impressions can influence incremental validity in a number of ways. For example, interviewers may place applicants in various "categories" (such as ideal candidate, poorly qualified candidate) prior to the interview. Like other forms of stereotyping, this categorization can then influence the way in which recruiters conduct the interview, as well as their processing and recall of information exchanged. In addition, differences in recruiter conduct can have self-fulfilling prophecy effects on applicants, who may discern the recruiters' initial impression and respond in ways that confirm the impression (Dipboye, 1989).

Limited empirical evidence supports the idea that incremental interview validities may be compromised by the provision of prior information, particularly information regarding applicant ability (such as cognitive test scores, rank in class). For example, Dipboye (1989, p. 47) uncovered two studies suggesting that when interviewers have access to prior test score information, the interview provides little if any incremental validity. In one of the studies (Kelly and Fiske, 1951) the mean validity for the interview was lower than the mean validity of the alternative predictors, while in the other study (Gorman et al., 1978) subjects typically made more valid judgments on the basis of paper credentials alone than they did on the basis of paper credentials plus interviews.

Further evidence suggests that not only incremental, but also *independent* interview validities, may be negatively affected by the prior availability of evidence regarding applicants' cognitive ability. Specifically, the McDaniel et al. (1994) meta-analysis identified 19 studies ($N = 2,196$) where cognitive test scores were available to recruiters, and 47 studies ($N = 6,843$) where they were not. Analyses suggested that knowledge of test scores had a detrimental effect on interview validities, in that corrected validities averaged 0.26 when scores were known versus 0.45 when they were not known. Furthermore, this pattern of results obtained for both structured and unstructured interviews.

In combination, the preceding results suggest that for whatever reason, interviewers appear to be less effective in assessing applicants when provided with prior information about applicants' cognitive ability. However, on the other side of the coin, there is evidence that the interview *can* contribute significant incremental validity to test scores when those scores are unknown to the interviewer. For example,

Campion et al. (1994) found that an interview comprised of 15 situational and 15 behavioral description questions added significant incremental validity (incremental $R = 0.28$; $p < 0.05$) to a battery of nine cognitive ability tests that were administered after, rather than before, the interview. Furthermore, both past behavior and future situational questions contributed significant incremental variance over test scores alone (incremental $Rs = 0.28$ and 0.2 for behavioral and situational questions, respectively). Similarly, Pulakos and Schmitt (1995) found that a behavioral description interview contributed significant incremental variance (incremental $R = 0.37$; $p < 0.05$) over a cognitive ability test battery. In contrast, the test battery improved incremental validity over the interview by a much smaller amount (incremental $R = 0.14$).

Finally, based on previous meta-analytic findings, Schmidt and Hunter (1998) reported that standardized interviews are likely to provide higher incremental validities (24 percent increase) in combination with cognitive ability tests than any other selection device except integrity tests. This result flows from the relatively high validities of structured interviews, combined with the relatively low correlations between cognitive ability and interview scores.

In combination, then, results suggest that interviews are capable of providing significant incremental validity over cognitive ability tests, but that this capability can be seriously eroded by "contaminating" the interview with prior knowledge of ability. Thus, from the narrow standpoint of enhancing validity, current research suggests that interviews should not be contaminated by prior knowledge concerning applicant ability.

Construct validity

Schuler (1989) has argued that "the employment interview does not exist," but rather is a "kind of cover that can be filled with different constructs, methods, and modes" (p. 344). At the present time, perhaps no interview research topic generates greater enthusiasm among the scientific community than that of examining the content and processes of actual interviews, and the implications of content and process differences for differential interview outcomes (for example, Campion et al., 1997; Dipboye and Gaugler, 1993; Harris, 1989; Smith, 1994).

This emphasis has been urged for both practical and scientific reasons. In a practical sense, knowledge about the relationships between what interviews actually measure and their empirical validity can be used to design more cost-effective interviews, as well as combinations of interviews and other selection devices. In a scientific sense, identification of construct–outcome relationships can be used to further develop theories of work performance and predictor–criterion dimensionality. In the words of Dipboye and Gaugler (1993): "From this broader perspective, all validation is essentially construct validation and should be guided by an a priori explication of why interviews may succeed or fail in selecting applicants" (p. 138).

A variety of preliminary approaches have been taken toward examination of interview content, constructs, and outcomes. For example, Smith (1994) has taken a theoretical approach to the problem, arguing that selection devices (including interviews) should be assessed according to the extent to which they tap the following three predictor categories: universals (characteristics required by all work, such as general mental ability, vitality, conscientiousness or will to achieve); occupationals (characteristics required by certain jobs, such as specialized knowledge and specific abilities), and relationals (person–environment fit, such as values fit and congruence of job interpretations). By categorizing interviews in this way and relating them to obtained empirical validities, Smith argues that a better understanding of why some interviews work better than others is likely to emerge.

Others have taken a more empirical approach to uncovering the constructs assessed by interviews. For example, Landy (1976) factor analyzed ratings on specific interview dimensions to extract more general factors. Others have investigated the correlations between interview scores and scores on other predictors (for example, cognitive test batteries or objectively scored work experience records) as a way of inferring the extent to which interviews tap these alternative, better-understood constructs (Campion et al., 1988; Kinicki and Lockwood, 1985).

In one of the most intriguing empirical studies to date, Huffcutt et al. (1996) meta-analyzed 49 studies ($N = 12{,}037$) for the purpose of: (1) determining the average correlation between interview scores and scores on cognitive ability tests; (2) examining various potential moderators of the strength of the ability–interview score relationship (degree of structure, content of questions, interviewer access to test score data, job complexity); and (3) assessing whether interviews with higher empirical validities are also more highly saturated with cognitive ability.

With respect to average interview–ability correlations, results revealed that the mean sample-weighted correlation between interview ratings and ability test scores was 0.25 (0.40 following corrections for statistical artifacts). Moderator analyses also revealed a number of intriguing variations in the strength of this relationship. For example, contrary to expectations, more highly structured interviews tended to exhibit lower (rather than higher) correlations with cognitive ability. Also contrary to expectations, interviews for low-complexity jobs tended to correlate more highly with ability test scores than did interviews for higher-complexity jobs. Consistent with predictions, future-oriented situational interview scores were more highly correlated with cognitive ability than were past-oriented behavior description interview scores. Making cognitive test scores available to interviewers also increased the correlation between test and interview scores. Finally, as expected, interviews that displayed high validities (0.30 or above) tended to show higher correlations with cognitive ability than did interviews with low or medium validities.

Finally, Pulakos and Schmitt (1995) adopted a combination content/construct validity approach to constructing a structured interview that was explicitly designed to tap a broader set of dimensions than those assessed by cognitive ability tests. Following thorough job analysis procedures, structured interviews were constructed to tap seven KSA (knowledge, skills, and abilities) categories (such as, planning, organizing, and prioritizing; relating effectively with others; adapting to changing situations; demonstrating integrity). Assessments of incremental validity showed that the interviews provided substantially greater incremental validity to the test scores than did test scores to the interviews.

In summary, the research summarized to this point paints a considerably more positive picture of the validity and potential usefulness of the employment interview than at any point since it was first subjected to empirical investigation. We turn now to an examination of the interview's legal history and current legal status.

■ LEGAL DEFENSIBILITY AND FAIRNESS

Early reviews of the interview's legal defensibility were based on narrative analyses of court cases involving the interview (Arvey and Faley, 1988). Reasons for successful (or unsuccessful) employer defenses were recounted and translated into prescriptive advice for employers. Based on one such review, Campion and Arvey (1989) recommended the following interventions for increasing the interview's legal defensibility: developing job descriptions; selecting and training multi-racial interviewers of both sexes; asking the same job-related questions of all applicants; implementing reviews of recruiter behaviors and decisions; keeping better records of interviews; and monitoring interview outcomes for adverse impact.

More recently, Williamson et al. (1997) employed empirical analyses of 99 court cases to determine the structural characteristics of interviews most closely associated with favorable versus unfavorable outcomes for the employer. Both disparate treatment ($n = 84$) and disparate impact ($n = 46$) cases were examined.

Given the multidimensionality of interview structure (for example, Campion et al., 1997), Williamson and colleagues began by creating three general categories of structural dimensions: job-relatedness or objectivity (such as basing questions on job analysis, training interviewers); standardized processes (asking the same questions of everyone, using specific rating scales and anchors); and use of multiple interviewers. For both disparate treatment and disparate impact cases, the largest correlate of a favorable decision for the defendant was job-relatedness or objectivity of the questions (simple correlation = 0.38; $p < 0.05$). This was followed by standardized procedures ($r = 0.27$; $p < 0.05$), and multiple interviewers ($r = 0.17$; $p < 0.10$).

These results held up in multivariate analysis (logistic regression) as well, with standardized coefficients for the three types of structure being 0.41 ($p < 0.05$), 0.12 (not significant) and 0.08 (not significant), respectively. In addition, the odds ratio (chances of a verdict for the defendant divided by chances of a verdict for the plaintiff) for job-related/objective questions was 2.93 in disparate treatment cases, and 10.96 for disparate impact cases. The addition of multiple control variables did not change the general pattern regarding the role of structure, although one control variable – political affiliation of the judge – had a large independent effect on verdict outcomes.

In addition to questions of legality, a few studies have looked at questions of likely interviewer bias, adverse impact (typically operationalized as differences in mean interview scores), and/or interview fairness (typically operationalized as differences in predictor–criterion slopes across various groups). Pulakos and Schmitt (1995) found small, if any, differences in interview performance across whites, blacks, Hispanics, males, and females. In addition, regressions of performance ratings on interview evaluations produced no statistically significant slope or intercept differences, suggesting little if any adverse impact or unfairness from using experience-based interviews. Two other studies also found little evidence of differential regression lines by sex (Arvey et al., 1987), or race and sex (Campion et al., 1988).

More generally, Campion and Arvey (1989) suggest that research evidence regarding interviewer bias seems considerably less negative now than in earlier reviews, where bias was widely assumed. They suggest that a variety of contextual factors may be responsible for these findings, such as increases in the amount of job-related information provided to interviewers (see, for example, Tosi and Einbender, 1985) and methodological richness of the research stimulus (Mullins, 1982). We turn now to examination of how interviews are regarded, not by courts of law, but by applicants themselves.

■ APPLICANT REACTIONS

Applicant reactions to interviews are important because interviews attempt to combine applicant screening and selection objectives with applicant attraction (Rynes, 1989). If applicants react negatively to interviews, they may drop out of the selection process early, reject job offers, or possibly file lawsuits based on perceived unfairness or lack of job-relatedness (Rynes et al., 1991; Schuler, 1989). In such cases, considerable overall utility may be lost from the interview process, even with impressive selection validities (Murphy, 1986).

Research on applicant reactions to the interview is positioned within a broader body of research examining applicant reactions to selection devices of various types (such as assessment centers, work samples, or ability tests; Cascio and Phillips, 1979; Rynes and Connerley, 1993; Schmidt et al., 1977; Smither et al., 1993). One framework for studying applicant reactions has been based on privacy concerns, suggesting that applicants resist procedures that do not allow them to control sensitive personal information about themselves (for example, Stone and Stone, 1990). A second framework has been based on justice theory, arguing that selection procedures will be viewed more favorably to the extent that both their processes and outcomes are perceived as fair or just (for example, Gilliland, 1993). Yet another perspective focuses on applicant motivation, suggesting that negative attitudes toward selection devices may reduce applicant motivation to perform well on them and, as a result, potentially affect the validity of such devices (for example, Arvey et al., 1990; Chan et al., 1998).

Applicant reactions research that has focused specifically on the interview has tended to examine either reactions to interviewers, or to interview content or processes. We turn first to research on applicant reactions to interviewers.

Applicant reactions to interviewers

Most research on applicant reactions to interviewers or recruiters has been conducted in the context of college placement offices. Two main streams of research exist, one focusing on interviewer personality traits and behaviors, and the other on interviewers' demographic characteristics.

Traits and behaviors

A significant number of studies have examined applicant reactions to interviewer traits (personality characteristics) and behaviors. While the earliest work on applicant reactions to interviewer traits and behaviors was primarily descriptive, more recent studies have offered (and in some cases tested) a theoretical rationale for these effects. Because job applicants often have limited information about jobs and organizations, they may use recruiter traits and behaviors as signals of important aspects of the employment opportunity. More specifically, as articulated by Rynes (1991), recruiters may serve as the basis for two types of applicant inferences: inferences regarding the applicant's probability of receiving a job offer; and inferences regarding job or organizational characteristics.

The traits or behaviors most commonly studied are warmth (or supportive behavior) and informativeness (that is, whether the interviewer provided adequate information about the job). The general conclusion drawn from these studies is that these traits and/or related behaviors are related to important outcomes including attraction to the job, willingness to pursue the job, likelihood of accepting an offer, and evaluations of both the interview and the interviewer. The findings are fairly robust, in the sense that they have been documented through survey research in field settings (for example, Alderfer and McCord, 1970; Harris and Fink, 1987; Liden and Parsons, 1986; Maurer et al., 1992; Powell, 1984; Schmitt and Coyle, 1976; Taylor and Bergmann, 1987; Turban and Doherty, 1992), as well as through experimental designs (for example, Goltz and Giannantonio, 1995; Kohn and Dipboye, 1998; Rynes and Miller, 1983) and qualitative research (Rynes et al., 1991). In addition, a number of studies provide evidence to support the signaling mechanism as an explanation for observed effects (for example, Goltz and Giannantonio, 1995; Rynes et al., 1991; Rynes and Miller, 1983).

Nevertheless, some limitations must be noted. First, the findings are not perfectly consistent. Many studies examine multiple outcomes and find effects for some outcomes but not for others. As one example, Schmitt and Coyle (1976) found that interviewer warmth was associated with all nine outcomes they assessed, but informativeness was associated with only seven of the nine outcomes. In addition, Rynes et al. (1991) found that some individuals reacted more strongly to interviewers than did others.

A second potentially important criticism of this line of research has to do with the duration or persistence of the observed effects. Reactions to interviewers appear to carry more weight immediately after the interview than they do later in the recruitment/selection process (Taylor and Bergmann, 1987). In other words, the impact of interviewer traits and behaviors on actual job choice decisions may be small or even trivial. Nevertheless, if negative reactions to interviewers cause applicants to drop out of the process early on (Rynes et al., 1991), the impact of these reactions could be quite significant.

Demographic characteristics

Interviewers' demographic characteristics (for example, gender, race, age, level in organizational hierarchy) may influence applicants for one of three reasons. First, the nature of the person conducting the interview can send signals about the organization or about the importance of the job for which the applicant is being interviewed. For example, applicants might make inferences about organizational diversity or the organization's commitment to equal opportunity based on the characteristics (gender and race in particular) of the interviewer. Alternatively, Rynes (1991) suggested that applicants may respond to interviewer demographic characteristics simply because they share the same general biases held by much of society. Finally, Maurer et al. (1992) have offered the "similarity" hypothesis: drawing from the marketing literature, they argued that applicants respond more favorably to influence sources, such as interviewers, who are similar to themselves.

Several studies have addressed the impact of recruiter demographic characteristics on applicant reactions, with results that can be described as mixed at best. Gender effects have been studied frequently, with weak and inconsistent results. For example, Liden and Parsons (1986) found that female interviewers were seen as more personable and informative than male interviewers, but also found that applicants interviewed by women had less favorable impressions of the job than applicants interviewed by men. Interviewer gender was unrelated to likelihood of accepting a job offer in their study.

Taylor and Bergmann (1987), Turban and Dougherty (1992), and Maurer et al. (1992) all found evidence that reactions to interviewer gender varied as a function of applicant gender. However, the nature of this relationship differed across studies. Turban and Dougherty (1992) found evidence of a similarity effect: male applicants were more attracted to the organization when they were interviewed by male interviewers. However, female applicants were unaffected by interviewer gender. In contrast, Taylor and Bergmann (1987) and Maurer et al. (1992) found that gender *dis*similarity was associated with attraction – in these studies, female applicants were more attracted to the organization when their interviewers were male, and male applicants were unaffected by interviewer gender. However, what is common to all three of the above studies is that, if anything, applicants have tended to favor male recruiters (or the jobs they are recruiting for).

Findings regarding demographic characteristics other than gender are even weaker. For example, Taylor and Bergmann (1987) found age effects, while Turban and Dougherty (1992) and Maurer et al. (1992) did not. Taylor and Bergmann (1987) and Turban and Dougherty (1992) both found evidence that applicants reacted to the interviewers' education level, although in Turban and Dougherty the effect was only marginally significant. Taylor and Bergmann (1987) found some evidence of reactions to recruiters' job type, but Turban and Dougherty (1992) did not.

Most research involving interviewers' demographic characteristics has taken place in the field. While this approach can enhance the external validity of findings, it may also limit our opportunities to find significant effects. First, actual interviewers may not vary widely in terms of race, level, or job type. Second, characteristics such as gender, race, or level are likely to be confounded with other personal characteristics in field settings, again inhibiting our opportunity to find anticipated effects. Therefore, one strategy for re-energizing this line of research might be to conduct experimental studies that avoid these limitations associated with field research. Such studies could examine main effects (that is, *whether* applicants respond to demographic characteristics) as well as process issues (that is, *why* applicants respond to these characteristics). If carefully designed and controlled experimental studies fail to find substantial relationships between interviewer demographics and applicant responses, we could more safely conclude that interviewer demographics are not particularly important to applicants.

Reactions to the interview process

Interviews can be differentiated on a number of dimensions besides the characteristics of the interviewers involved. Indeed, current research regarding interview validity focuses on elements of the interview process (such as degree of structure) rather than on the interviewer. However, as yet there is fairly little research on applicant reactions to the manner in which interviews are conducted. Three areas that merit additional research are interview focus, interview structure, and interview content.

Interview focus

One interesting aspect of the interview process is the degree to which the interviewer emphasizes recruitment or selection. Rynes (1989) clearly differentiated these two objectives, but noted that employment interviews generally contain some emphasis on each. In some cases (most likely, where labor shortages are severe), interviewers might devote the majority of their time to convincing applicants to work for their organization. In other cases (perhaps where the number of applicants far exceeds the number of jobs available), interviewers may devote more energy to screening out less desirable applicants. Logic would suggest that applicants should respond more favorably to recruitment-oriented interviews, since applicant attraction is their primary objective. However, the small amount of research available on this topic does not support this logical speculation.

For example, Taylor and Bergmann (1987) assessed how much time recruiters typically spent evaluating the applicant and how much time was typically spent "selling" the organization, and concluded that neither variable influenced applicant's perceptions of company attractiveness or the likelihood that they would accept a job offer. Similarly, Stevens (1998), in a study analyzing audio recordings of actual interviews, concluded that there was no relationship between interview focus and applicant attraction, despite the fact that interviewers exhibited different behaviors when their focus was on recruitment rather than selection.

Even more surprisingly, Turban and Dougherty (1992) found that when recruiters spent more time "selling" jobs, applicants perceived the jobs as less attractive. Similarly, Barber et al. (1994) found that applicants whose interviews focused solely on recruitment were less likely to persist in pursuing a job than were applicants whose interviews combined recruitment with selection.

Several reasons for these counterintuitive findings have been offered. Turban and Dougherty (1992) suggested that applicants may become suspicious of jobs that are "oversold," whereas Barber et al. (1994) suggested that applicants whose interviews involved some screening might have felt more committed to the employment process because they had passed an initial hurdle. However, neither study provided evidence to support these propositions. At this point, whether applicants respond at all to interview focus remains an open question, but it is interesting to note that there is no evidence that they respond positively to recruitment-oriented interviews.

Interview structure

A second aspect of the interview process relevant to applicant attraction is interview structure. Campion et al. (1997) discussed possible applicant reactions to a variety of aspects of interview structure. However, most of their discussion was speculative and there is little empirical evidence on this issue. The few studies that do assess reactions to structure are reviewed below.

To date, only one study has suggested that interview structure increases applicant attraction. Specifically, Taylor and Bergmann (1987) found that applicants whose interviewers reported using high levels of structure were more inclined to accept job offers than applicants whose interviewers were less structured. In contrast, Turban and Dougherty (1992) found no relationship between interview structure and applicant perceptions of organizational attractiveness, although it should be remembered that the absence of effects in any single study may be due to sampling error and low power.

At least three studies have suggested that applicants may react negatively to high degrees of interview structure. Latham and Finnegan (1993) found that college students showed clear preferences for unstructured interviews over behavior description and situational interviews. Subsidiary analyses suggested that they saw unstructured interviews as "allowing them to say everything they wanted to say, enabling them to feel relaxed, allowing the outcome to be based on their abilities rather than on the skill of the interviewer, and enabling them to show the interviewer that they are highly motivated" (p. 52). Overall, Latham and Finnegan conclude that this pattern suggests "a desire on the part of student applicants to control the interview."

More recently, Kohn and Dipboye (1998) conducted two laboratory experiments that focused in detail on reactions to interview structure. In these studies, students playing the role of job applicants were presented with either transcripts or descriptions of interviews. These documents manipulated various aspects of interview structure (for example, use of the same questions for all applicants, use of job-related questions). Like Latham and Finnegan, Kohn and Dipboye found that applicants responded negatively to highly structured interviews, and concluded that users of structured interviews should be quite wary of their impact on attraction outcomes.

However, it should be noted that both Latham and Finnegan (1993) and Kohn and Dipboye (1998) used transcripts or descriptions of interviews as stimuli, and therefore did not assess reactions to actual interviews. Overall it is difficult to draw a clear conclusion from this small body of research, particularly since methods and results have both varied across studies. However, there are both logical reasons and (some) empirical evidence to suggest that overly rigid structure can have a negative effect on applicants.

Interview content

A final aspect of the interview process likely to influence applicant attraction is interview content. As noted earlier, applicants generally respond favorably to recruiters who are perceived as more informative, suggesting that the amount of information provided is important. However, it is not clear whether the *type* of information provided is also important. Nor is it clear whether applicants also react to the type of information *collected*.

Surprisingly few studies have explicitly examined the question of interview content. Taylor and Sniezek (1984) provided one of the few studies to directly address this question. They surveyed 148 users of a campus placement office, assessing what was covered during their interviews as well as how they reacted to the interview (specifically, whether they felt they had a fair opportunity to present their qualifications, and whether the interview had influenced their evaluation of the organization's attractiveness). Factor analysis of 25 information content items revealed three factors, reflecting general qualifications, specific knowledge (such as, courses taken), and geographic mobility. Taylor and Sniezek (1984) concluded that applicants reacted positively to interviews that emphasized general qualifications, but that they were unaffected by the emphasis placed on specific knowledge or geographic mobility.

A limitation of Taylor and Sniezek's study is that they did not differentiate between information provided by the recruiter versus information sought by the recruiter. Their factor analyses resulted in three dimensions of information that appear to be oriented more toward selection (that is, gathering of information) than recruitment (dissemination of information). Thus, we can say little about what kind of information the recruiter should provide. None the less, their results do suggest that topics covered in the interview can influence applicant reactions.

While Taylor and Sniezek (1984) focused on general content areas and their impact on applicants, an extensive stream of research has implications for a different dimension of interview content: its accuracy or realism. Realistic job previews (RJPs), in which organizations provide both positive and negative information about positions they are attempting to fill, are associated with post-hire outcomes such as lower levels of turnover and higher performance among those who accept jobs (Phillips, 1998). RJPs are also related to applicant behavior: applicants who receive RJPs are less likely to drop out of the selection process than those who receive traditional (positive) recruitment messages. However, the average effects of realism tend to be very small (for example, -0.05 correlation with turnover and -0.03 with applicant attrition; Phillips, 1998; see also McEvoy and Cascio, 1985).

We know fairly little about the role of realistic information in the context of employment interviews, as most RJP research focuses on other means of delivering realistic information (for example, in writing or via videotape; Phillips, 1998). Barber et al. (1994) manipulated interview realism in a field experiment and examined its relationship to applicant attraction. They found no relationship between the RJP manipulation and applicant persistence in pursuing a job. Stevens (1998) found a positive correlation between interview realism and applicant attraction. Her data also suggest an explanation for this positive relationship: interviewers who were perceived as realistic were also perceived as more informative on other dimensions (for example, offered more positive information and more information about employees), as well as more personable. Given the well-documented relationships between informativeness, personableness, and applicant attraction (Rynes, 1991), it would be interesting to know whether Stevens' observed relationship between realism and attraction remained significant after other interviewer qualities were controlled.

Summary

We currently know a fair amount about how applicants respond to interviewers: that they prefer warm and informative interviewers; and that they do not appear to be consistently affected by recruiters' demographic characteristics. This knowledge has some practical value, in that organizations can certainly choose warm individuals for interviewer positions and then train them to be informative. It is not clear, however, whether much can be gained from additional research along these lines.

We know far less about applicant reactions to characteristics of the interview itself. This is unfortunate because the potential applied value of such knowledge is great: organizations certainly can modify interview processes to achieve desired recruitment outcomes. Our lack of knowledge in this area is also unfortunate because it falls far behind what we know about the validity of interview processes. For example, there is a wealth of evidence suggesting that structured interviews are "better" because they are more valid. However, there are also hints that overly structured interviews may interfere with employee attraction. In an environment in which there is increasing pressure not only to identify, but also to attract the most promising applicants, paying relatively more attention to the effects of interview content on applicant attraction would seem to be an important objective for future research.

■ NEEDED RESEARCH

As we have seen, existing research has already provided practicing managers and professionals with many ideas for increasing the likely validity, legality, and attractiveness to applicants of the employment interview. In this section, we suggest additional research directions that may contribute to even further improvements in interviewing practice. A summary of both previous findings and needed research can be found in table 10.1.

Construct and incremental validity

As earlier sections have revealed, recent progress has been made toward understanding the most appropriate ways in which to combine information from interviews

Table 10.1 Interview best practices and needed research with respect to validity enhancement, legal defensibility, and applicant reactions

Validity enhancement	Legal defensibility	Applicant reactions
Best practices: Use structured interviews based on job analysis – particularly situational and behavioral description interviews Train interviewers to ask job-related and performance-differentiating questions Emphasize selection over recruitment in the interview Do not reveal applicant's cognitive ability prior to interview Increase the extent to which the interview taps cognitive ability	*Best practices:* Use job-related, objective questions based on job analysis and delivered by trained interviewers Use standardized processes – ask the same questions of all candidates; use the same rating scales and anchors Use multiple interviewers	*Best practices:* Use warm, supportive, informed, and informative recruiters Have interviewers adopt a mixed selection-plus-recruitment orientation; do not neglect selection in favor of "selling" Avoid overly structured interviews
Needed research: Basic construct validity research Incremental validity when used in combination with other selection devices Consideration of interview structure, purpose, and timing as potential moderating variables Simultaneous examination of multiple criteria and tradeoffs Interviewer reactions to, and actual use of, alternative interview formats Search for interview content that simultaneously improves validity and applicant reactions Possibilities of similarity bias (for example, age and cognitive ability) Determinants of interviewer differences in mental models of ideal candidates and "fit"		*Needed research:* Research on applicant reactions to different types of interview content, including potential individual differences (for example, ability) in reactions to content Continued development of theoretical models of applicant reactions

with information from other selection devices, particularly tests of cognitive ability (for example, Campion et al., 1994; Dipboye, 1989; McDaniel et al., 1994; Pulakos and Schmitt, 1995). Generally speaking, recent research suggests that prior interviewer knowledge of a candidate's cognitive ability tends to reduce not only the interview's incremental validity, but even its stand-alone validity. This poses some interesting challenges for obtaining maximum validity from employment interviews, given the various ways in which an applicant's cognitive ability can be signaled to an interviewer prior to the interview, even where actual test scores are not provided (such as, colleges attended, grade point averages, dean's lists, academic scholarships).

As numerous other authors have indicated, questions concerning interview validity – and particularly incremental interview validity – cannot be satisfactorily answered in the absence of information about the underlying constructs tapped by each particular interview. Researchers have made a number of initial attempts toward grappling with this problem, ranging from factor analysis of interview content (Landy, 1976), to correlating interview scores with scores from instruments with clearer construct identification (for example, Huffcutt et al., 1996; Kinicki and Lockwood, 1985), to using a combination of construct and content validation procedures to design interviews that tap constructs other than cognitive ability (Pulakos and Schmitt, 1995).

These are all reasonable approaches that merit future application and extension. At present, the ability to obtain further insights about the interview through meta-analysis is limited not only by the relatively small number of studies that examine interviews in concert with other devices, but also by the even smaller number of studies that make serious attempts to identify the constructs tapped by the interview in question. It is possible that assessment center data may be of use in answering these questions, in that extensive interviews are often given in conjunction with simulation exercises and personality and ability tests, with target constructs identified for each assessment center component.[2] In any event, we recommend that future research on the combined validities of interviews plus other selection devices be required to address the question of underlying interview constructs as a prerequisite for publication.

Relatedly, there is a need to examine the construct and incremental validities of interviews conducted for different purposes, or at different phases of the selection process. For example, one goal for an increasing number of values-centered organizations is to use initial interviews, not so much to recruit and screen for particular jobs, but rather to decide whether the candidate is a good fit for the company in general (Cohen and Greenfield, 1998; Pfeffer, 1998). Similarly, many organizations with rapidly changing job requirements have shifted from basing initial interviews on specific KSAs to broader competencies. In addition, there are variations in the order in which different companies seek different kinds of information (for example, whether they primarily seek values, or competencies, in the first stage of the interviewing process).

More generally, it is possible that the very nature of employment interviews is changing, with more different types of interviews being employed to accomplish a broader range of purposes than in the past. More precise identification of the type of interview being investigated (for example, initial screening versus final hiring), along with the constructs underlying each, is important not only for applied purposes, but also to insure that we do not combine apples and oranges in narrative reviews and meta-analyses of research findings.

Expanding the criterion space: examining multiple criteria simultaneously

There is also a general need to increase the amount of research devoted to outcomes of the interview process other than empirical validity, legal defensibility, and applicant reactions. Additional outcomes that might be investigated include: cost and speed of the hiring process; performance and retention of eventual hires; and reputational damage or enhancement among those interviewed (as well as their friends and acquaintances). Because there is the potential for tradeoffs among competing objectives, simultaneous analysis of multiple outcomes would be particularly useful (see, for example, Boudreau and Rynes, 1985).

Although the preceding comments apply to all selection devices and procedures, there are a number of issues of specific interest with respect to the interview. For example, an increasing number of companies now use telephone or video interviews to reduce costs at initial hiring stages. Making a shift from in-person to telephone interviews can affect a variety of outcomes, all of which merit investigation (such as, empirical validity of hiring decisions, yield ratios at subsequent stages of the process, applicant reactions, speed of hiring, and overall costs).

In the only study of telephone interviews identified to date, Schmidt and Rader (in press) reported average validities (across 33 studies representing 2,539 observations) of 0.40 for supervisory ratings of performance, which is highly similar to the 0.44 reported by McDaniel et al. (1994) for face-to-face interviews. Moreover, this similarity in outcomes occurred despite the fact that the particular telephone interviews in question differed from typical structured interviews in a number of other respects as well (such as, empirically-based construction, separation of interviewer and scorer roles). Schmidt and Rader speculate that the similarity in outcomes, despite dissimilarity in development and implementation processes, occurs because different types of structured interviews all measure (to varying degrees) constructs with known generalizable validity, such as conscientiousness and general mental ability. Although Schmidt and Rader suggest a number of pros and cons of telephone interviews relative to more conventional structured interviews, they did not conduct a cost–benefit analysis or explicitly examine the tradeoffs involved (for example, less training for interviewers, but more for interview scorers).

At the same time that many employers are attempting to reduce screening costs at the front end of the interview process, they are simultaneously increasing the amount of screening that occurs in later phases (for example, multi-day site visits, mini-assessment centers). While such tactics can decrease the probability of making erroneous hiring decisions, they may also delay the extension of job offers and result in lost applicants, particularly among the most sought-after candidates (Rynes et al., 1991). Thus, multiple outcomes (speed of hiring, number and characteristics of dropouts from the applicant pool) should be assessed at multiple phases of the recruitment and selection process and, to the greatest extent possible, subjected to a comprehensive utility analysis (Boudreau and Rynes, 1985; Murphy, 1986).

Interviewer characteristics

Although a number of interviewer characteristics have been very well studied (for example, personableness, informativeness), there are a number of important things about interviewers that have not yet been well researched. One important piece of missing information concerns how interviewers feel about various types of interviews, such as structured versus unstructured, or behavioral description versus situational interviews. This is an important omission because the potential advantages of a particular interview format (such as behavior description interviewing) can only be obtained if interviewers actually adhere to the prescribed procedures while interviewing real applicants. Given the importance of this issue, it is somewhat surprising that so little research has focused on the interviewer's perspective of the interview (Barber, 1998).

Some evidence regarding this question was provided by Latham and Finnegan (1993), who assessed the perceived "practicality" of unstructured, behavior description, and situational interviews from a managerial perspective. Contrary to most previous speculation (see next paragraph), they found that managers regarded situational interviews as the most practical, followed by behavior description and unstructured interviews, respectively. In interpreting these results, it is important to note that of the 16 items used to assess practicality, five measured the ability of the interview to identify truly qualified applicants, five measured the extent to which the interview format could be successfully defended against a lawsuit, and six tapped the extent to which the interview was "easy and comfortable for the interviewer to use" (p. 45). Thus, the first segment of the scale seemed to assess perceived validity; the second, perceived legality; and the third, perceived desirability of use. Also important is the fact that this study did not assess actual *use* of these formats by the managers. Distinguishing between survey responses and actual usage is important because items concerning desirability of usage would seem to have a heavy component of social desirability, given the previous findings regarding validity and legal defensibility.

Therefore, despite Latham and Finnegan's findings, we suspect that gaining interviewer compliance with recommended procedures may be a more challenging task than is typically acknowledged. This is because many interviewers tend to regard successful interviewing as more of an "art" than a science (see, for example, Hakel, 1982), to have great confidence in their personal intuitions about candidates (Bretz et al., 1993; Hakel, 1982), and to resist attempts to limit their discretion in interviewing (Campion et al., 1997; Church, 1996). Given these realities, it would seem to be important to understand the sources of interviewer resistance (where it arises) and to develop ways of overcoming it.

For example, analyzing the sources of interviewer resistance might lead to further improvements in interview design by suggesting types of questions that are not only valid, but that also have higher interviewer and applicant acceptability (see also, Rynes, 1993). At the same time, it would be useful to assess the effectiveness of different types of training and feedback methods for persuading interviewers to apply a preordained interview format. Because of the importance of interviewer motivation to effective interviewing, we believe that developing a better understanding of the interviewer's perspective is one of the highest research priorities for improving interview practice.

A second (and related) priority with respect to interviewer research concerns how interviewers establish such concepts as "ideal" or "best-fitting" candidates. This is important because despite the increased use of structured interviews, interviewer training (Connerley and Rynes, 1997), and explicit organizational consideration of person–job fit (Cohen and Greenfield, 1998), research continues to show considerable individual differences with respect to how interviewers assess "fit" (Bretz et al., 1993), even for the same position within the same company (Kristof-Brown, 1997).

Thus, although the growth in the use of structured interviews is likely to have increased average interview validities, research continues to suggest that there is further room for improvement.

Qualitative research might prove helpful in this regard, with interviewers first providing their descriptions of "ideal" or "best-fitting" candidates, followed by explanations of the reasons for singling out those characteristics. Based on these descriptions, an attempt might then be made to determine the underlying origins of observed differences. For example, the fact that there is considerable idiosyncratic variance in fit descriptions, even for the same job within the same firm, suggests that identifiable individualistic phenomena may underlie these constructs (such as similar-to-me effects, or varying mental models of "good performance").

In addition, at least two specific variables would appear to merit investigation for the possibility of similarity biases in the current work environment: interviewer age and interviewer ability. Questions concerning the effects of interviewer age (in relation to applicant age) have become particularly interesting of late, given widespread assertions of a growing generational gap in attitudes and approaches to work (for example, Labich, 1995; Munk, 1998, 1999; Ratan, 1993), as well as the fact that applicants are increasingly being interviewed by individuals younger than themselves (Munk, 1999). To the extent that these trends continue, earlier (and limited) research on interviewer age (Rogers and Sincoff, 1978) is likely to be of little relevance in the current work environment.

Finally, given the increased organizational emphasis on hiring the "best and the brightest" (see, for example, Fishman, 1998; Reingold, 1998; Stross, 1997), it may be a good time to examine whether interviewers exhibit similar-to-me biases with respect to indicators of applicant ability, such as grade point averages, dean's lists, and academic honors. This is a potentially important question, in that there is some reason to believe that individuals with modest ability or achievement levels may exhibit biases against candidates with higher abilities or achievements (Stross, 1997; Whyte, 1956). Although evidence already suggests that sending high-achieving recruiters can be a considerable advantage in terms of applicant attraction (Rebello, 1992; Reingold, 1998; Rynes et al., 1991; Stross, 1997), there is little evidence concerning whether interviewer ability or achievement simultaneously affects interviewers' selection decisions. As such, we recommend this question for future research.

Applicant reactions

One of the bright spots in current human resource practice is that, due at least in part to empirical research findings (Janz et al., 1986; Schmidt and Hunter, 1998), employers are increasingly aware of the crucial importance to long-term organizational success of hiring the very best candidates possible (Snow and Snell, 1993). To date, however, the vast majority of research on improving hiring outcomes has focused on applicant selection, rather than attraction. Given the "war for talent" identified by McKinsey & Co. (Fishman, 1998) and others (for example, Stewart, 1997), additional research is needed to ascertain the effects of selection practices – particularly the interview – on applicant impressions and decisions.

To date, most of the research on applicant reactions to selection devices has focused on tests rather than interviews (Smither et al., 1993). For example, despite the ongoing debate about whether situational interviews are more or less valid than behavioral description ones, there has been only one study of whether one format is preferred by applicants over the other (Latham and Finnegan, 1993), and that did not involve actual interview participation by subjects. In addition, there has been no research on applicant reactions to "brainteaser" interviews (sample question: What is the sum of all integers from 1 to 100?) despite their rapidly growing use by software, consulting, and investment banking firms (for example, Kane, 1995; Stross, 1997; Sorkin, 1998). Nor has there been research on whether there are important individual differences in the types of interviews preferred by different kinds of applicants (for example, those with varying levels of general mental ability, different personalities, or different career interests), or whether certain types of interviews (such as, brainteasers) will be more acceptable when used by some firms (for example, Microsoft or McKinsey) than others.

In line with the increasing importance of attracting as well as selecting employees, we may also benefit from rethinking our theoretical base for applicant reactions research. Currently, the dominant framework for applicant reactions research is justice theory (see, for example, Gilliland, 1993; Greenberg, 1987), which focuses on whether or not selection procedures are regarded as "fair." In an environment of intense competition for the best and the brightest, it seems possible that merely aiming for fairness may fall far short of what is required to attract the best applicants. Rather, employers may need to be concerned not only with whether interviews are seen as fair (which will continue to be important), but also whether they are regarded as impressive, challenging, ethical, comfortable, or perhaps even "fun" (Munk, 1998).

■ CONCLUSIONS

We believe that the employment interview provides a wonderful example not only of the potential advantages of research for practice, but also of the value of practice for stimulating useful research questions. Specifically, despite very negative research findings over a long period of time, practitioners persisted in using the interview, insisting that they could learn important information from it that could not be acquired in other ways.

Now, after more than three-quarters of a century of disagreement between researchers and practitioners on this point (for example, Hakel, 1982), researchers have moved much closer to adopting the practitioner's perspective of the interview. This result would never have occurred had practitioners "listened" to early research and abandoned the interview. Rather, in response to practitioners' stubborn persistence, researchers continued to try to refine practices with respect to what they regarded as a poor selection device. In the process, many changes have been made to interviewing procedures that have succeeded in raising their validity considerably beyond original levels (which were in fact higher than originally believed). We hope this chapter will continue to advance the mutual benefits of interview research for practice, and of practice for interview research.

ACKNOWLEDGMENTS

We would like to thank Frank Schmidt and the editors of this volume for helpful comments on an earlier version of this chapter.

NOTES

1. For example, evidence presented by McDaniel et al. (1994, p. 604 and footnote, p. 605) suggests that greater unreliability is probably introduced into interviews by differences in *applicant* behaviors across interview occasions, than by differences in interviewer ratings of the same applicant on the same interview occasion. Specifically, average reliabilities among interviewers simultaneously viewing the same applicant performance were 0.81, as compared with reliability estimates of 0.52 when different raters interviewed the same applicant, but on different occasions. As such, McDaniel et al. conclude that on average, more variance (29 percent) in interviewer ratings is due to test–retest instability in applicant responses, than to inter-rater unreliability (19 percent of the variance) in judging the same applicant behavior.
2. We thank Frank Schmidt for this suggestion.

REFERENCES

Alderfer, C. P., and McCord, C. G. 1970: Personal and situational factors in the recruitment interview. *Journal of Applied Psychology*, 34, 377–85.

Arvey, R. D., and Faley, R. H. 1988: *Fairness in selecting employees*, Reading, MA: Addison-Wesley.

Arvey, R. D., Miller, H. E., Gould, R., and Burch, P. 1987: Interview validity for selecting sales clerks. *Personnel Psychology*, 40, 1–12.

Arvey, R. D., Strickland, W., Drauden, G., and Martin, C. 1990: Motivational components of test-taking. *Personnel Psychology*, 43, 695–716.

Barber, A. E. 1998: *Recruiting employees: Individual and organizational perspectives*, Thousand Oaks, CA: Sage Publications.

Barber, A. E., Hollenbeck, J. R., Tower, S. L., and Phillips, J. M. 1994: The effects of interview focus on recruitment effectiveness: A field experiment. *Journal of Applied Psychology*, 79, 886–96.

Boudreau, J. W., and Rynes, S. L. 1985: Role of recruitment in staffing utility analysis. *Journal of Applied Psychology*, 70, 354–66.

Bretz, R. D., Rynes, S. L., and Gerhart, B. 1993: Recruiter perceptions of applicant fit: Implications for individual career preparation and job search behavior. *Journal of Vocational Behavior*, 43, 310–27.

Campion, J. E., and Arvey, R. D. 1989: Unfair discrimination in the employment interview. In R. W. Eder and G. R. Ferris (eds.), *The employment interview: Theory, research and practice*, Newbury Park, CA: Sage, 61–73.

Campion, M. A., Campion, J. E., and Hudson, J. P., Jr. 1994: Structured interviewing: A note on incremental validity and alternative question types. *Journal of Applied Psychology*, 79, 998–1002.

Campion, M. A., Palmer, D. K., and Campion, J. E. 1997: A review of structure in the selection interview. *Personnel Psychology*, 50, 655–702.

Campion, M. A., Purcell, E. D., and Brown, B. K. 1988: Structured interviewing: Raising the psychometric properties of the employment interview. *Personnel Psychology*, 41, 25–42.

Cascio, W. R., and Phillips, N. F. 1979: Performance testing: A rose among thorns? *Personnel Psychology*, 32, 751–66.

Chan, D., Schmitt, N., Sacco, J. M., and DeShon, R. P. 1998: Understanding pretest and posttest reactions to cognitive ability and personality tests. *Journal of Applied Psychology*, 83, 471–85.

Church, A. H. 1996: From both sides now: The employee interview – the great pretender. *The Industrial Psychologist*, 34(1), 108–17.

Cohen, B., and Greenfield, J. 1998: *Ben and Jerry's double-dip*, New York: Fireside.

Connerley, M. L., and Rynes, S. L. 1997: The influence of recruiter characteristics and organizational recruitment support on perceived recruiter effectiveness: Views from applicants and recruiters. *Human Relations*, 50, 1563–86.

Dipboye, R. L. 1989: Threats to the incremental validity of interviewer judgments. In R. W. Eder and G. R. Ferris (eds.), *The employment interview: theory, research and practice*, Newbury Park: Sage, 45–60.

Dipboye, R. L., and Gaugler, B. B. 1993: Cognitive and behavioral processes in the selection interview. In N. Schmitt and W. Borman (eds.), *Personnel selection in organizations*, San Francisco: Jossey-Bass, 135–70.

Dougherty, T. W., Ebert, R. J., and Callender, J. C. 1986: Policy capturing in the employment interview. *Journal of Applied Psychology*, 71, 9–15.

Dunnette, M. D., and Bass, B. M. 1963: Behavioral scientists and personnel management. *Industrial Relations*, 2, 115–30.

Fishman, C. 1998: The war for talent. *Fast Company*, 16, August, 104–10.

Gilliland, S. W. 1993: The perceived fairness of selection systems: An organizational justice perspective. *Academy of Management Review*, 18, 694–734.

Goltz, S. M., and Giannantonio, C. M. 1995: Recruiter friendliness and attraction to the job: The mediating effect of inferences about the organization. *Journal of Vocational Behavior*, 46, 109–18.

Gorman, C. D., Clover, W. H., and Doherty, M. E. 1978: Can we learn anything about interviewing real people from "interviews" of paper people? Two studies of the external validity of a paradigm. *Organizational Behavior and Human Performance*, 22, 165–92.

Greenberg, J. 1987: A taxonomy of organizational justice theories. *Academy of Management Review*, 12, 9–22.

Hakel, M. D. 1982: Employment interviewing. In K. M. Rowland and G. R. Ferris (eds.), *Personnel Management*, Boston: Allyn and Bacon, 129–55.

Harris, M. M. 1989: Reconsidering the employment interview: A review of recent literature and suggestions for future research. *Personnel Psychology*, 42, 691–726.

Harris, M. M., and Fink, L. S. 1987: A field study of applicant reactions to employment opportunities: Does the recruiter make a difference? *Personnel Psychology*, 40, 765–83.

Huffcutt, A. I., Roth, P. L., and McDaniel, M. A. 1996: A meta-analytic investigation of cognitive ability in employment interview evaluations: Moderating characteristics and implications for incremental validity. *Journal of Applied Psychology*, 81, 459–73.

Janz, T. 1982: Initial comparisons of patterned behavior description interviews versus unstructured interviews. *Journal of Applied Psychology*, 67, 577–80.

Janz, T., Hellervik, L., and Gilmore, D. C. 1986: *Behavior description interviewing: New, accurate, cost effective*, Boston: Allyn and Bacon.

Kane, K. 1995: The riddle of job interviews. *Fast Company*, 1, November, 50–4.

Kelly, E. L., and Fiske, D. W. 1951: *The prediction of performance in clinical psychology*, Ann Arbor: University of Michigan Press.

Kinicki, A. J., and Lockwood, C. A. 1985: The interview process: An examination of factors recruiters use in evaluating job applicants. *Journal of Vocational Behavior*, 26, 117–25.

Kohn, L. S., and Dipboye, R. L. 1998: The effects of interview structure on recruiting outcomes. *Journal of Applied Social Psychology*, 28, 821–43.

Kristof-Brown, A. 1997: *The Goldilocks pursuit in organizational selection: How recruiters form and use judgments of person-organization fit*, College Park, MD: University of Maryland.

Labich, K. 1995: Kissing off corporate America. *Fortune*, 131(3), February 20, 44–52.

Landy, F. J. 1976: The validity of the interview in police officer selection. *Journal of Applied Psychology*, 61, 193–8.

Latham, G. P., and Finnegan, B. J. 1993: Perceived practicality of unstructured, patterned, and situational interviews. In H. Schuler, J. L. Farr and M. Smith (eds.), *Personnel selection and assessment: Individual and organizational perspectives*, Hillsdale, NJ: Lawrence Erlbaum Associates.

Latham, G. P., and Saari, L. M. 1984: Do people do what they say? Further studies on the situational interview. *Journal of Applied Psychology*, 69, 569–73.

Latham, G. P., Saari, L. M., Pursell, E. D., and Campion, M. A. 1980: The situational interview. *Journal of Applied Psychology*, 65, 422–7.

Latham, G. P., and Skarlicki, D. P. 1995: Criterion-related validity of the situational and patterned behavior description interviews with organizational citizenship behavior. *Human Performance*, 8, 67–80.

Latham, G. P., and Sue-Chan, C. 1999: A meta-analysis of the situational interview: An enumerative review of reasons for its validity. *Canadian Psychology*, 40, 56–67.

Latham, G. P., and Wexley, K. N. 1981: *Increasing productivity through performance appraisal*, Reading MA: Addison-Wesley.

Leavitt, H. J. 1995: Hot groups. *Harvard Business Review*, 73(4), 109–16.

Liden, R. C., and Parsons, C. K. 1986: A field study of job applicant interview perceptions, alternative opportunities, and demographic characteristics. *Personnel Psychology*, 39, 109–23.

Marchese, M. C., and Muchinsky, P. M. 1993: The validity of the employment interview: A meta-analysis. *International Journal of Selection and Assessment*, 1, 18–26.

Maurer, S. D., Howe, V., and Lee, T. W. 1992: Organizational recruiting as marketing management: An interdisciplinary study of engineering graduates. *Personnel Psychology*, 45, 807–33.

Maurer, S. D., and Fay, C. 1988: Effect of situational interviews, conventional structured interviews, and training on interview rating agreement: An experimental analysis. *Personnel Psychology*, 41, 329–44.

McDaniel, M. A., Whetzel, D. L., Schmidt, F. L., and Maurer, S. D. 1994: The validity of the employment interviews: A comprehensive review and meta-analysis. *Journal of Applied Psychology*, 79, 599–616.

McEvoy, G. M., and Cascio, W. F. 1985: Strategies for reducing employee turnover: A meta-analysis. *Journal of Applied Psychology*, 70, 342–53.

Mullins, T. W. 1982: Interviewer decisions as a function of applicant race, applicant quality, and interviewer prejudice. *Personnel Psychology*, 35, 161–74.

Munk, N. 1998: The new organization man. *Fortune*, 137(5), March 16, 63–74.

Munk, N. 1999: Finished at forty. *Fortune*, 139(2), February 1, 52–66.

Murphy, K. R. 1986: When your top choice turns you down: Effect of rejected offers on the utility of selection tests. *Psychological Bulletin*, 99, 13–8.

Pfeffer, J. 1998: *The human equation: Building profits by putting people first*, Boston: Harvard Business School Press.

Phillips, J. M. 1998: Effects of realistic job previews on multiple organizational outcomes: A meta-analysis. *Academy of Management Journal*, 41, 673–90.

Powell, G. N. 1984: Effects of job attributes and recruiting practices on applicant decisions: A comparison. *Personnel Psychology*, 37, 721–32.

Pulakos, E. D., and Schmitt, N. 1995: Experience-based and situational interview questions: Studies of validity. *Personnel Psychology*, 48, 289–308.

Pulakos, E. D., Schmitt, N., Whitney, D., and Smith, M. 1996: Individual differences in interviewer ratings: The impact of standardization, consensus discussion, and sampling error on the validity of a structured interview. *Personnel Psychology*, 49, 85–102.

Ratan, S. 1993: Why busters hate boomers. *Fortune*, 128(8), October 4, 56–70.

Rebello, K. 1992: How Microsoft makes offers candidates can't refuse. *Business Week*, 3253, February 24, 65.

Reingold, J. 1998: And now, extreme recruiting. *Business Week*, October 19, 97–100.

Rogers, D. P., and Sincoff, M. Z. 1978: Favorable impression characteristics of the recruitment interviewer. *Personnel Psychology*, 31, 495–504.

Ryan, A. M., and Sackett, P. R. 1987: A survey of individual assessment practices by I/O psychologists. *Personnel Psychology*, 40, 455–88.

Rynes, S. L. 1989: The employment interview as a recruitment device. In R. W. Eder and G. R. Ferris (eds.), *The employment interview: Theory, research, and practice*. Newbury Park, CA: Sage, 127–42.

Rynes, S. L. 1991: Recruitment, job choice, and post-hire consequences. In M. D. Dunnette and L. M. Hough (eds.), *Handbook of industrial and organizational psychology*, 2nd edn., Palo Alto, CA: Consulting Psychologists Press.

Rynes, S. L. 1993: Who's selecting whom? Effects of selection practices on applicant attitudes and behavior. In N. Schmitt and W. Borman (eds.), *Personnel selection in organizations*, San Francisco: Jossey-Bass, 240–74.

Rynes, S. L., Bretz, R. D. Jr., and Gerhart, B. 1991: The importance of recruitment in job choice: A new way of looking. *Personnel Psychology*, 44, 487–521.

Rynes, S. L., and Connerley, M. L. 1993: Applicant reactions to alternative selection procedures. *Journal of Business and Psychology*, 7, 261–77.

Rynes, S. L., and Miller, H. E. 1983: Recruiter and job influences on candidates for employment. *Journal of Applied Psychology*, 68, 146–54.

Rynes, S. L., Orlitzky, M. O., and Bretz, R. D. 1997: Experienced hiring versus college recruiting: Practices and emerging trends. *Personnel Psychology*, 50, 309–40.

Schmidt, F. L., Greenthal, A. L., Hunter, J. E., Berner, J. G., and Seaton, F. W. 1977: Job sample versus paper-and-pencil trades and technical tests: Adverse impact and examinee attitudes. *Personnel Psychology*, 30, 187–97.

Schmidt, F. L., and Hunter, J. E. 1998: The validity and utility of selection methods in personnel psychology: Practical and theoretical implications of 85 years of research findings. *Psychological Bulletin*, 124, 262–74.

Schmidt, F. L., and Rader, M. (in press): Exploring the boundary conditions for interview validity: Meta-analytic validity findings for a new interview type. *Personnel Psychology*.

Schmitt, N., and Coyle, B. W. 1976: Applicant decisions in the employment interview. *Journal of Applied Psychology*, 61, 184–92.

Schuler, H. 1989: Construct validity of a multimodal employment interview. In B. J. Fallon, H. P. Pfister and J. Brebner (eds.), *Advances in industrial organizational psychology*, Amsterdam: North-Holland.

Smith, M. 1994: A theory of the validity of predictors in selection. *Journal of Occupational and Organizational Psychology*, 67, 13–51.

Smither, J. W., Reilly, R. R., Millsap, R. E., Pearlman, K. E., and Stoffey, R. W. 1993: Applicant reactions to selection procedures. *Personnel Psychology*, 46, 49–76.

Snow, C. C., and Snell, S. A. 1993: Staffing as strategy. In N. Schmitt and W. Borman (eds.), *Personnel selection in organizations*, San Francisco: Jossey-Bass, 448–78.

Sorkin, A. R. 1998: The Wall Street recruiting bowl. *The New York Times*, November 29, Bu-1 and 10.

Stevens, C. K. 1998: Antecedents of interview interactions, interviewers' ratings, and applicants' reactions. *Personnel Psychology*, 51, 55–85.

Stewart, T. A. 1997: *Intellectual capital: The new wealth of organizations*, New York: Currency-Doubleday.

Stone, E. F., and Stone, D. L. 1990: Privacy in organizations: Theoretical issues, research findings, and protection mechanisms. In K. R. Rowland and G. R. Ferris (eds.), *Research in personnel and human resource management*, Vol. 8, Greenwich, CT: JAI Press, 349–411.

Stross, R. E. 1997: *The Microsoft way*, Reading, MA: Addison-Wesley.

Taylor, A. 1998: Consultants have a big people problem. *Fortune*, 137(7), April 13, 163–6.

Taylor, M. S., and Bergmann, T. J. 1987: Organizational recruitment activities and applicants' reactions at different stages of the recruitment process. *Personnel Psychology*, 40, 261–85.

Taylor, M. S., and Sniezek, J. A. 1984: The college recruitment interview: Topical content and applicant reactions. *Journal of Occupational Psychology*, 57, 157–68.

Tosi, H. L., and Einbender, S. W. 1985: The effects of the type and amount of information in sex discrimination research: A meta-analysis. *Academy of Management Review*, 28, 712–23.

Turban, D. B., and Dougherty, T. W. 1992: Influences of campus recruiting on applicant attraction to firms. *Academy of Management Journal*, 35, 739–65.

Vance, R. J., Kuhnert, K. W., and Farr, J. L. 1978: Interview judgments: Using external criteria to compare behavioral and graphic scale ratings. *Organizational Behavior and Human Performance*, 22, 279–94.

Whyte, W. H. 1956: The fight against genius. In W. H. Whyte, *The organization man*, New York: Touchstone Books, 205–17.

Wiesner, W. H., and Cronshaw, S. F. 1988: A meta-analytic investigation of the impact of interview format and degree of structure on the validity of the employment interview. *Journal of Occupational Psychology*, 61, 275–90.

Williamson, L. G., Campion, J. E., Malos, S. B., Roehling, M. A., and Campion, M. A. 1997: Employment interview on trial: Linking interview structure with litigation outcomes. *Journal of Applied Psychology*, 82, 900–12.

chapter 11

INTELLIGENCE, MOTIVATION, AND JOB PERFORMANCE

*John E. Hunter, Frank L. Schmidt,
John M. Rauschenberger, and
Michele E. A. Jayne*

■ INTRODUCTION

The purpose of this chapter is to evaluate competing models of the effect of personality on job performance using data gathered for Army Project A. In particular, we re-analyzed the correlations presented in McHenry et al. (1990) using data pooled over nine US army jobs with a total sample size of $N = 4,500$.

Personality experts have generated many speculative hypotheses linking job performance to personality. The most extreme use of such hypotheses was made by Raymond Cattell in the construction of his 16PF personality inventory. He used many job preference items as indicators for various traits. However, most of those items have very poor reliability and more recent inventories have dropped all such items. Some of the speculative hypotheses may be true, but the size of the relationships appears to be tiny.

The most widely accepted theory linking performance to personality is the lay theory of performance. This theory assumes that ability plays little role in the determination of individual differences in performance. The dominant determinant of individual differences for this theory is effort. In this theory, there is a causal path from personality to motivation to effort to performance. This is one of the competing theories to be tested here.

The main alternative theory is based on conscientiousness rather than motivation (Hunter and Schmidt, 1996). This theory assumes that there are two very different dimensions to work: job performance and citizenship behavior. It assumes that personality has little influence on performance but has a huge impact on citizenship behavior (Borman and Motowidlo, 1997). This theory is starkly different from the lay theory in that effort is assumed to make little difference in performance outcome. Rather the influence of conscientiousness is on citizenship behavior. For example, the person with low conscientiousness irritates supervisors and others by being late, by making personal calls in working time, by being slipshod about rules, and so on.

Motivation and effort

Many laypeople believe there is only a limited relationship between intelligence and job performance. The theory is that people are all approximately equal in ability; everyone can do the job. But people differ enormously in how hard they work and hence how much they get done. Thus, the prediction is that while the correlation between ability and performance will be small, the correlation between motivation and performance will be large.

This theory is extremely important because it is the dominant theory among supervisors, managers, and others who make decisions about those who work under them. Since they do not recognize differences in ability, they attribute any failings in performance to inadequate motivation. This means that all evaluations become moral evaluations as well as performance evaluations. This can be especially damaging to beginning workers who may come to have low general self-esteem to go along with their work-related self-esteem which is already under attack because of poor performance.

It is important to note that the lay theory is strongly influenced by experience at school and in activities like sports and music. All of these activities have an extremely large voluntary component; a person can freely decide how much time to spend on the activity. For people with equal or nearly equal ability, learning is determined primarily by time on the task (Bloom, 1964). So people who put in a lot more time studying or practicing will learn more and thus perform at a higher level. If motivation and effort are the dominant determinants of time spent on an activity, then they will be large causal determinants of performance at that activity. According to this hypothesis, effort is important because it creates differences in preparation for performance rather than directly creating differences in the actual performance itself.

This situation is, in general, very different on most jobs. Most modern jobs have no voluntary aspect to performance. Work is assigned and monitored. Everyone puts in approximately 40 hours a week. There is no opportunity for individual differences in time on task; there is no homework, there are no recommended weight lifting or running exercises. Thus it is possible that the lay theory is correct for school and other early activities while having little applicability to performance on most jobs.

The critics – emphasis on learning

There are those who think that the influence of motivation is overstated. They argue that job analysis shows military jobs – like most jobs – to be much more complex than they seem to outside superficial observers. They argue that the main determinant of job performance is how much the person has learned about how to do the job well. Since intelligence is highly correlated with learning, these critics predict that intelligence will be highly correlated with performance.

The predicted high correlation between intelligence and performance has been extensively validated using meta-analysis (Hunter and Hunter, 1984; Hunter and Schmidt, 1996). Hunter (1986) found a construct level correlation between intelligence and objectively measured performance of 0.80 for civilian work and 0.73 for military work. By contrast, the correlation for supervisor ratings of performance is considerably smaller and it varies with job complexity. For medium complexity work (the middle 68 percent in 1983), the correlation is only 0.57.

The critics hypothesize that personality enters the evaluation of job performance only because supervisors cannot distinguish between performance and citizenship behavior. Even with direct and well-designed instructions, supervisor ratings of performance correlate with personality variables. On the other hand, objectively measured performance has little correlation with personality.

Personality measures

The major personality variable that is highly correlated with performance ratings is conscientiousness (Barrick and Mount, 1991; Mount and Barrick, 1995; Ones et al., 1993; Schmidt and Hunter, 1998). However, this finding is less clear than it might be because there are considerable variations in the definition of conscientiousness. Could what is currently called "conscientiousness" be the "motivation" variable from the lay theory?

As part of Project A, Hough et al. (1990) conducted an extensive meta-analysis on the relationship between personality and performance. They used their meta-analysis findings to put together an extensive battery of the personality tests that had proved effective and included them in the Project A research design. They thought in terms of two main dimensions – dependability and achievement:

- dependability measures: conscientiousness, and non-delinquency (that is, delinquency reverse scored);
- achievement measures: self-esteem, work orientation, and energy level.

Dependability corresponds to the narrow definition of conscientiousness – rule following. The achievement dimension is more closely related to the concept of motivation. The two dimensions are logically distinct, but highly correlated. Even without any correction for attenuation, the correlation between the Project A composites is 0.58 (McHenry et al., 1990).

From the viewpoint of performance theories, the key question is this: should the construct underlying these dimensions be called "motivation" or should it be called "conscientiousness?" Our path analysis tests this issue. It can be viewed as a use of the Cronbach and Meehl (1955) "nomothetic net" method for construct validation.

▪ PROJECT A CORRELATIONS

The correlations to be used in testing our path models were presented in one of the early reports on the US Army Project A (McHenry et al., 1990). We used confirmatory factor analysis to compute the correlation matrix for six constructs. We used the correlations for 12 variables from McHenry et al. to do this. The 12 variables are identified in table 11.1 along with the corresponding correlations. Confirmatory factor analysis implicitly corrects the construct correlations for attenuation due to error of measurement.

Table 11.1   The key variables from McHenry et al. (1990); data pooled over nine US army jobs; $N = 4,500$

Variable list by factor:
501 = Ability (1–4)
   1. VERB   = ASVAB Verbal composite
   2. MATH = ASVAB Quantitative composite
   3. TECH = ASVAB Technical composite
   4. SPAT   = Spatial ability composite
502 = Motivation (5–6)
   5. ACHEV = Achievement composite
   6. DEPND = Dependability composite
504 = Performance (7–8)
   7. TPROF = Core technical proficiency
   8. SPROF = General soldiering proficiency
506 = Rating (9–10)
   9. EFF&L = Effort and leadership
  10. DISC   = Personal discipline
505 = Bearing (11)
  11. FIT&B = Military fitness and bearing
503 = Physical condition (12)
  12. COND = Physical condition

Correlations between variables (decimals omitted):

		1 V	2 M	3 T	4 S	5 A	6 D	7 TP	8 SP	9 E	10 D	11 F	12 C
VERB	1	100	52	56	41	5	−2	32	36	7	5	−11	−6
MATH	2	52	100	45	56	11	5	33	38	12	10	−1	−2
TECH	3	56	45	100	50	8	−3	34	40	18	8	−9	−3
SPAT	4	41	56	50	100	7	1	38	47	14	7	−4	−4
ACHEV	5	5	11	8	7	100	58	11	11	30	18	28	37
DEPNB	6	−2	5	−3	1	58	100	11	9	22	30	22	14
TPROF	7	32	33	34	38	11	11	100	58	28	19	3	−3
SPROF	8	38	38	40	47	11	9	58	100	28	17	5	0
EFF&L	9	7	12	18	14	30	22	28	28	100	59	46	11
DISC	10	5	10	8	7	18	30	19	17	59	100	33	0
FIT&B	11	−11	−1	−9	−4	28	22	3	5	46	33	100	30
COND	12	−6	−2	−3	−4	37	14	−3	0	11	0	30	100

Intelligence

The US Military devotes considerable time to the initial appraisal of recruits reporting for duty; including an extensive cognitive ability test battery. Thus the military data furnishes an excellent measure of intelligence.

The intelligence measures are:

1. ASVAB Verbal composite
2. ASVAB Quantitative composite
3. ASVAB Technical composite
4. Spatial aptitude composite

Personality: conscientiousness or motivation?

The research team for Project A (McHenry et al., 1990) selected their personality measures based on the meta-analysis conducted by Hough et al. (1990). They put together an extensive battery of the personality tests that had proven effective and included them in the Project A research design. From our point of view, their battery created one of the best measures of motivation ever put together – it taps the successful elements from a wide variety of prior research studies.

The key theoretical question is: is the personality construct in table 11.1 to be regarded as "motivation" or as "conscientiousness?" The construct used in our analysis is defined by the two composite scores since data for the individual scales was not reported. These composites are:

- Achievement composite: self-esteem, work orientation, and energy level.
- Dependability composite: conscientiousness, and non-delinquency (that is, delinquency reverse scored).

Job performance: objective measures

The US Military is one of the few organizations willing to spend the money required to create and use objective measures of job performance, such as work sample tests and extensive job analysis-based job knowledge tests. Two such measures were reported by Project A. Both are composite scores across job knowledge tests and work sample tests.

- Core technical proficiency;
- General soldiering proficiency.

Our performance construct was defined by these two composite measures. The military refers to this construct as "proficiency."

Fitness and bearing

The military has always sharply distinguished between job performance and overall military evaluation. In part, this stems from worries about the difference between job performance during peace and maintaining competence in the face of combat. A key element of military evaluation is physical fitness and general appearance or demeanor.

Project A presented data for ratings of fitness and bearing. However, they presented only a single composite score. Since there is only one measurement of fitness and bearing, the reliability cannot be computed from their report. The confirmatory factor program implicitly assumes perfect reliability for such a measure. Hence, the correlations for fitness and bearing are systematically underestimated since it was not possible to correct for attenuation due to error of measurement.

Physical conditioning

The Project A designers were well aware of the military emphasis on physical fitness so they tried to create a predictor for it. However, the reader is warned that the predictor is indirect. What they actually measured was how much heavy exercise the applicant reports. Thus the phrase "physical conditioning" actually means "self-reported physical exercise."

Project A presented data only for a single composite score measuring "conditioning." Since there is only one measurement of physical conditioning, the reliability cannot be computed from their report. The confirmatory factor program implicitly assumes perfect reliability for such a measure. Hence, the correlations for physical conditioning are actually correlations for self-reported exercise. These correlations are systematically underestimated since it was not possible to correct for attenuation due to error of measurement.

Overall evaluation

In most research, supervisor performance ratings are so highly correlated that only one dimension is defined. In the Project A data, this was not true. The ratings for fitness and bearing were not only nominally different from ratings for general evaluation, but this distinction held up statistically as well. Thus, overall evaluation was based only in part on fitness and bearing and was based also on proficiency. That is, the military consider both fitness and job performance in their overall evaluation. The overall evaluation (performance ratings) measures were: effort and leadership, and personal discipline.

Confirmatory factor analysis

Six constructs were identified as underlying the 12 measurements selected from Project A. The correlations for the 12 manifest variables are presented in table 11.1. Confirmatory factor analysis was used to compute the construct correlations. These correlations are reported in the bottom part of table 11.2.

■ TESTING THE MOTIVATION MODEL

Our confirmatory factor model has one construct for personality. According to the lay theory, this construct should be motivation. So, in testing the lay model, we will call the construct "motivation." The reader is warned that the lay theory shows poor fit for this data. Thus the label "motivation" does not really fit the data.

Table 11.2 Confirmatory factor analysis on the data from McHenry et al. (1990); that is, the correlations in table 11.1

Factor list and reliabilities:

	Factor	Alpha
501 =	Ability (1–4)	0.80
502 =	Motivation (5–6)	0.73
503 =	Physical condition (12)	1.00[a]
504 =	Performance (7–8)	0.73
505 =	Bearing (11)	1.00[a]
506 =	Overall rating (9–10)	0.74

Factor correlations:

		501 A	502 M	503 C	504 P	505 B	506 R
501	Ability (1–4)	100	7	−5	68	−9	18
502	Motivation (5–6)	7	100	33	18	32	42
503	Physical condition (12)	−5	33	100	−2	30	7
504	Performance (7–8)	68	18	−2	100	5	38
505	Bearing (11)	−9	32	30	5	100	51
506	Overall rating (9–10)	18	42	7	38	51	100

[a] Reliability estimated at 1.00 because there was only one measure available to estimate the factor.

Objectively measured performance

According to the lay theory, individual differences in performance are almost entirely due to differences in effort. Therefore there should be a high predictive validity for motivation and a low predictive validity for intelligence. The simple correlations are 0.18 for motivation and 0.68 for intelligence. The standardized multiple regression is

Performance = 0.67 Intelligence + 0.13 Motivation + else

with a multiple correlation of 0.69.

This result is disappointing for the lay theory. Motivation adds little to the prediction of performance; the correlation for intelligence alone is 0.68 while the multiple correlation is 0.69. Thus, while motivation has a positive weight, that weight is much smaller than would be predicted by the lay theory.

Performance ratings

Consider overall performance evaluation using supervisor ratings. According to the lay theory, evaluation is only indirectly related to the predictors. Motivation determines effort which in turn determines performance and performance ratings.

Consider first the predictor correlations. Motivation correlates 0.42 with overall evaluation while intelligence correlates 0.18. The standardized multiple regression equation is:

Evaluation = 0.15 Intelligence + 0.41 Motivation + else

with a multiple correlation of 0.45.

These findings are much more comfortable to the lay theory. Motivation is the big predictor and ability is the small predictor.

On the other hand, the findings for overall evaluation must be considered in relation to the findings for performance. If supervisor ratings are based on performance, then the findings for ratings should match the findings for performance in relative terms. This is far from reality.

Ratio: Weight for ability over weight for motivation
    Performance: Ratio = 0.67/0.13 = 5.15
    Ratings: Ratio = 0.15/0.41 = 0.36

The ratios are completely opposite in direction. This contradicts the lay theory.

■ THE CONSCIENTIOUSNESS MODEL

The more recent models of the influence of personality on job performance assume that performance ratings are heavily based on citizenship behavior as well as on actual performance. Conscientiousness is highly correlated with performance ratings because it is highly predictive of citizenship behavior. We now consider the same findings as before but with the personality construct labeled "conscientiousness" instead of "motivation."

Objectively measured performance

According to the recent theory, performance is largely based on job knowledge and job mastery. In a work setting, there is little opportunity for differences due to voluntary participation; little opportunity for extra practice or preparation. Thus intelligence should have high predictive validity while the validity for conscientiousness should be small.

The simple correlations are 0.18 for conscientiousness and 0.68 for intelligence. As we saw earlier, the standardized multiple regression is:

Performance = 0.67 Intelligence + 0.13 Conscientiousness + else

with a multiple correlation of 0.69.

This result fits the expectations of learning theory. Conscientiousness adds little to the prediction of performance; the correlation for intelligence alone is 0.68 while the multiple correlation is 0.69. Thus, while conscientiousness has a positive weight, that weight is much smaller than would be predicted by the lay theory.

The question for the learning theorist is this: why is there a positive weight for conscientiousness? If all trainees are put through identical training, the work week is the same for everyone, and all work is monitored; then why does conscientiousness correlate with performance? One answer stems from Bloom's (1964) work on time-on-task. Consider two people who are attending a training lecture. Both are nominally present, but the conscientious person will make sure that they listen carefully. The slipshod person may daydream rather than listen. Schmidt and Hunter (1998) report an average correlation of 0.30 between conscientiousness and amount learned in training.

Performance ratings

Consider overall performance evaluation using supervisor ratings. According to learning theory, evaluation is only indirectly related to the predictors. Intelligence determines performance, which in part determines overall evaluation. Differences in conscientiousness determines differences in citizenship behavior, which in turn is a determinant of performance ratings.

In the military, one dimension of citizenship behavior is particularly stressed and is separately evaluated: physical fitness and bearing. One main effect of conscientiousness should operate indirectly through differences in fitness.

Consider first the predictor correlations. Conscientiousness correlates 0.42 with overall evaluation while intelligence correlates 0.18. The standardized multiple regression equation is:

Evaluation = 0.15 Intelligence + 0.41 Conscientiousness + else

with a multiple correlation of 0.45. Since intelligence is the main determinant of performance, this reversal of relative weight suggests that the military places more importance on citizenship behavior than on performance.

This proposition can be tested directly by considering the multiple regression of overall evaluation onto performance and onto fitness and bearing. Note first that fitness and performance are almost entirely uncorrelated: $r = 0.05$. The correlation between performance and overall evaluation is 0.38 while the correlation between fitness and evaluation is 0.51. The standardized multiple regression equation is:

Evaluation = 0.36 Performance + 0.49 Bearing + else

with a multiple correlation of 0.62.

According to the theory, the effect of intelligence on evaluation is indirect: intelligence determines performance which determines evaluation. The predicted weight for intelligence on evaluation is thus predicted to be the product $(0.67)(0.36) = 0.24$ which is not far from the observed weight of 0.15.

According to the theory, the effect of conscientiousness is indirect. The main impact is indirect through citizenship behavior. However, since conscientiousness also has an impact on performance there will be a secondary indirect impact on evaluation through performance. If we partial out both performance and bearing, the correlation between conscientiousness and evaluation drops from 0.42 to 0.27. This is a large drop but it is far from a drop to zero.

Consider a multiple regression where we add conscientiousness as an additional predictor to performance and bearing. The standardized equation is:

Evaluation = 0.32 Performance + 0.42 Bearing + 0.23 Conscientiousness + else

with a multiple correlation of 0.66. This shows that conscientiousness makes a contribution to evaluation above and beyond that made through its impact on performance and bearing.

One simple interpretation of these results is that bearing is an imperfect measure of citizenship behavior; some other important aspect is missing. The apparent direct link from conscientiousness to evaluation is an artifact due to the fact that this other aspect of citizenship behavior is missing.

Conditioning, fitness, and evaluation

Fitness was anticipated to be an important component of the overall evaluation process. So conditioning was assessed as a predictor. The conditioning variable was measured by asking the recruits how much exercise they get. Fitness is in part the level of physical conditioning while in the service. Because of the specific nature of athletics (some like it and some don't), conditioning before joining should specifically predict conditioning after joining. Because the military puts heavy emphasis on fitness and bearing, highly conscientious people should stress conditioning after joining because it is asked for. Thus we would expect fitness to be predicted by both conditioning and by conscientiousness.

The simple correlations of conscientiousness with fitness are 0.30 for conditioning and 0.32. However, this is complicated by the fact that there is a correlation of 0.33 between conscientiousness and conditioning. That is, even before military recruitment, those who are conscientious are likely to exercise more than those who are not. This may reflect a general societal emphasis on exercise or it may reflect anticipation of joining the military.

The standardized multiple regression of fitness onto conditioning and conscientiousness is:

Fitness = 0.22 Conditioning + 0.25 Conscientiousness + else

with a multiple correlation of 0.38. Thus, fitness in the military is in part due to a prior commitment to fitness along with an acquired commitment due to the military view of fitness as part of the soldier profile.

The path model

Consider now a path model derived from the learning theory of performance. First, there is the traditional part of the theory having to do with performance as mastery and learning. There is an arrow from intelligence to performance and an arrow from performance to evaluation.

Key regression results:
PERFORM = 0.67 ABILITY   + 0.13 CONSC   + u1
CONDITN =   0.33 CONSC   + u2
BEARING =   0.25 CONSC + 0.22 CONDITN + u3
OV RATG = 0.32 PERFORM + 0.23 CONSC + 0.42 BEARING + u4

Multiple correlations:
  Job performance $R = 0.69$
  Physical conditioning $R = 0.33$
  Fitness and bearing rating $R = 0.38$
  Overall evaluation $R = 0.66$

The path diagram:

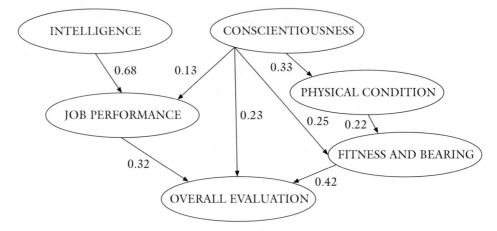

Figure 11.1 A path analysis of the McHenry et al. (1990) Project A data using the factor correlations from table 11.2

Second, we have the impact of conscientiousness. There is an arrow from conscientiousness to conditioning; conscientious people are more likely to exercise even before they join the military. There are then arrows from conditioning to fitness and from conscientiousness to fitness. The arrow from conditioning represents the carry-over of good or bad exercise habits from pre-military life. The arrow from conscientiousness reflects the fact that conscientious people will be more likely to adopt the military's recommendations for full-time exercise.

Third, we have the arrows representing the evaluation process. There is an arrow from performance and an arrow from fitness. These fit the theory perfectly. However, there is also an unanticipated arrow directly from conscientiousness to evaluation representing an impact above and beyond the impact through performance and fitness. Presumably there is some other aspect of citizenship behavior which is the missing intervening variable for conscientiousness.

The path model is presented in figure 11.1 and the results of the path analysis are presented in table 11.3.

Table 11.3 The test of the path model shown in figure 11.1 using the data from table 11.2

	1 A	2 M	3 C	4 P	5 B	6 R
Original correlations:						
1　Ability (1–4)	100	7	–5	68	–9	18
2　Conscientiousness (5–6)	7	100	33	18	32	42
3　Physical condition (12)	–5	33	100	–2	30	7
4　Performance (7–8)	68	18	–2	100	5	38
5　Bearing (11)	–9	32	30	5	100	51
6　Overall rating (9–10)	18	42	7	38	51	100
Reproduced correlations:						
1　Ability (1–4)	100	7	2	68	2	24
2　Conscientiousness (5–6)	7	100	33	18	32	42
3　Physical condition (12)	2	33	100	6	30	22
4　Performance (7–8)	68	18	6	100	6	38
5　Bearing (11)	2	32	30	6	100	51
6　Overall rating (9–10)	24	42	22	38	51	100
Errors: (actual – reproduced)						
1　Ability (1–4)	0	0	–7	0	–11	–6
2　Conscientiousness (5–6)	0	0	0	0	0	0
3　Physical condition (12)	–7	0	0	–8	0	–15
4　Performance (7–8)	0	0	–8	0	–1	0
5　Bearing (11)	–11	0	0	–1	0	0
6　Overall rating (9–10)	6	0	–15	0	0	0

■ THE THREE PREDICTOR VARIABLES

The six variables in our model can be split into the three predictor variables (intelligence, conscientiousness, and conditioning). The predictors are *not* uncorrelated with each other. Rather we have:

		I	C_s	C_n
Intelligence	I	1.00	0.07	–0.05
Conscientiousness	C_s	0.07	1.00	0.33
Conditioning	C_n	–0.05	0.33	1.00

The correlations between the predictors require explanation. The explanations are consistent with the original process model but add further complexity.

The correlations between the predictors also have methodological implications. They introduce a large number of small departures in the computations above; especially the masking effects. Some masking effects that were small now become zero effects. But the main outlines of the results are the same.

Intelligence and conscientiousness

The correlation between intelligence and conscientiousness is 0.07, small but definite (given the sample size of 4,500). Why might intelligence and conscientiousness be correlated?

Consider the role of success in the development of conscientiousness. Children try all sorts of things. Consider any kind of competence. The child tries a simple version of the task. Given success, the child tries a more difficult version. The child also becomes more motivated toward mastery in general because of the positive effect associated with success. Given too many failures, the child quits trying. The child is also likely to become a little less motivated to try things in general.

In particular, consider the impact of suggestions by adults. If those suggestions typically lead to success, the child will become more conscientious. If suggestions typically lead to failure, the child will become less conscientious. Since high intelligence generates success for more suggestions, the child with higher intelligence will be somewhat more conscientious.

Is a correlation of 0.07 trivial? Consider the extremes: the top and bottom 1 in 1,000 (the military employs millions). This is a 6 standard deviation difference in intelligence. The difference in conscientiousness would be 0.42 standard deviations; about the size of our very large laboratory effects.

Conscientiousness and conditioning

The correlation between conscientiousness and conditioning is not zero but a moderately large 0.33. Why might there be a correlation between conscientiousness and conditioning?

Consider people who apply to join the military. It is likely that they think of the military at least partly in terms of combat. If they are motivated to look good as soldiers, then they would be motivated to make sure that they are physically fit even before they join. That is the suggested explanation of the correlation of 0.33 between conscientiousness and physical conditioning.

An effect of 0.33 is very large when you consider extremes. For the top versus the bottom 1 in 1,000 soldiers, this would mean a difference of 1.98 or nearly 2 standard deviations (using the whole military population as the reference). Nearly all those with high conditioning would be above average in conscientiousness.

Intelligence and conditioning

The correlation between intelligence and conditioning is not zero but −0.05. Furthermore, that relationship is masked by differences in conscientiousness. The partial correlation is more negative:

$$r_{IC_n} = -0.05$$

$$r_{IC_n \cdot C_s} = -0.08$$

Consider the multiple regression of conditioning onto conscientiousness and intelligence:

$C_n = 0.34\ C_s - 0.07\ I$

$R_{C_n \cdot C_s I} = -0.34$

The multiple regression also shows a small but definite negative impact of intelligence on conditioning.

Why? Consider leisure time. A person with high intelligence might be more likely to have intellectual interests such as politics, history, or technical hobbies. As a result, a person with high intelligence might spend more leisure time in sedentary activities such as reading newspapers, magazines, and books. The person with high intelligence might thus on average have less leisure time in which to pursue sports or other active hobbies. This is the suggested explanation.

Note that the effect of intelligence is -0.07 within groups matched for level of conscientiousness. This effect becomes a difference of -0.42 standard deviations for the top versus bottom 1 in 1,000 such soldiers.

◼ PREDICTING THE DEPENDENT VARIABLES

There are six constructs identified in the Project A data; three predictors and three dependent variables. In this section, we consider the prediction of each dependent variable from the three predictor variables.

Performance as a dependent variable

Intelligence and conscientiousness were expected to have an impact on job performance. Conditioning was introduced as a predictor for predicting fitness, not because it was expected to influence job performance.

The three predictor correlations are 0.68 for intelligence, 0.18 for conscientiousness, and -0.02 for conditioning. The three variable multiple regression is:

$Performance = 0.67\ I + 0.14\ C_s - 0.03\ C_n + else$

with a multiple correlation of 0.69. For a sample size of $N = 4{,}500$, the tiny beta weight of -0.03 is too large to be due to sampling error.

If there is an effect, it probably has to do with time. Suppose that the people who are extremely active in sports spend some of their work time thinking about sports. Suppose that some of the extremely sedentary people spend some of their extra leisure time thinking about their work. A tiny effect needs a tiny explanation!

Fitness and bearing as a dependent variable

The process model claims that conscientiousness and pre-army conditioning will have an impact on fitness and bearing in the army. On the other hand, intelligence was expected to have little or no impact on fitness. The simple correlations are 0.30 for conditioning, 0.32 for conscientiousness, and −0.09 for intelligence. The standardized multiple regression equation is:

$$\text{Bearing} = 0.26\ C_s + 0.21\ C_n - 0.10\ I + \text{else}$$

with a multiple correlation of 0.39. The beta weight for intelligence is −0.10 which is not trivial. So intelligence does have a negative effect on fitness.

Why? Consider the finding for intelligence and conscientiousness on pre-army physical conditioning:

$$\text{Conditioning }(C_n) = 0.34\ C_s - 0.07\ I + \text{else}$$

The suggested explanation was that people with high intelligence are more likely to spend large portions of their leisure time in sedentary pursuits such as reading newspapers, magazines, and books. This explanation would seem equally likely to apply to life after joining the army.

Overall evaluation ratings as a dependent variable

All three predictors are expected to have a positive impact on overall evaluation ratings. The three correlations are 0.18 for intelligence, 0.42 for conscientiousness, and 0.07 for conditioning. The standardized multiple regression is:

$$\text{Evaluation} = 0.15\ \text{Intelligence} + 0.42\ \text{Conscientiousness} - 0.06\ \text{Conditioning} + \text{else}$$

with a multiple correlation of 0.45.

Why is the regression weight for conditioning negative? This seems strange. The regression weight for fitness was a positive 0.49 and conditioning has a moderately large positive impact on fitness. So the implied beta weight is positive. We can offer no immediate explanation. It may be that this fact is some kind of clue as to the missing intervening variable; the missing aspect of citizenship behavior. At the moment, we do not know how to use that clue.

◼ CONCLUSION

Project A generated unparalleled data for testing our model. All of the results fit a model in which the major personality variable is conscientiousness rather than motivation. This fits the assumption that differences in effort play little role in modern work contexts. This was predicted from the fact that there is no large voluntary participation component to most current jobs.

The model which fits the data suggests a wide gulf between performance and citizenship behavior as determinants of final work evaluation. Performance is mostly determined by intelligence with only a small impact from conscientiousness. On the other hand, consider our one measure of citizenship behavior; that is, fitness and bearing. Fitness was heavily influenced by conscientiousness with little impact from intelligence. Indeed the impact of intelligence was a small negative influence. Matched for conditioning and conscientiousness, soldiers with high intelligence tended to be rated as somewhat less fit than those with low intelligence. This may be a real finding stemming from differences in leisure time activities. On the other hand, it may be that highly intelligent soldiers are held to higher expectations than soldiers of low intelligence.

When supervisors in civilian settings are asked to rate workers on separate dimensions for performance and citizenship behavior, there is some slight factor separation but most items of the two classes are highly correlated with each other. There is more separation in military data than in comparable civilian data. Supervisors are heavily influenced by a general impression and citizenship behavior has at least as large an effect on that general impression as does actual job performance. The continued use of supervisor ratings of job performance will thus continue to create problems for theoretical understanding. Despite the fact that supervisors have difficulty distinguishing between performance and citizenship, that difference is very large and extremely important to the full understanding of behavior in work settings.

■ PRACTITIONER PERSPECTIVES ON THE ROLE OF INTELLIGENCE AND MOTIVATION IN JOB PERFORMANCE

Managers and supervisors in today's increasingly global economy show indications of understanding more deeply the nature of the relationship that worker intelligence and motivation play in the ongoing success of the organization. What major organization today fails to extol "our people" as a, if not *the*, source of "competitive advantage?" Managers and supervisors have always known that every worker, at every organizational level, has always brought both "head" and "heart" to a job – as "intelligence" and "motivation/conscientiousness" are often expressed in managerial vernacular. The lay theory, which postulates equal ability, may no longer be an adequate representation of managerial and supervisory perceptions for most jobs. Learning theory, which articulates a more complex relationship between intelligence and motivation may be a more accurate general representation of managerial and supervisory beliefs. The degree to which managers and supervisors perceive a causal role for intelligence and motivation (conscientiousness) in explaining job performance and their ratings of that performance can be examined further by exploring both a historical context for this issue and then by reviewing how this role is reflected in the operation of human resource systems in many, especially larger, organizations today.

Historical context

In the depths of the industrial revolution as epitomized, perhaps, in the creation of the assembly line, *both* "head" and "heart" had become an increasingly unnecessary component of work. To increase productivity, work itself had been successfully reduced to a routinized process with specified rules, simple requirements, and controlled outcomes – taxing little of either worker intelligence or motivation. "Ability" was substantively diminished to the possession of physical characteristics such as hand strength and capacity for physical fatigue. "Motivation" was limited to managing boredom. A "strong back" and "weak mind" had become the primary requirements of successful job performance.

The lessons of the assembly line were also successfully transferred to the "white collar" work experience. Organizations reified bureaucracy and prescribed policies and practices that formalized white-collar work in excruciating detail so as to adequately explicate every operational contingency of consequence. An accountant, for example, was rewarded more for merely applying the organization's prescribed accounting practices to problems than by bringing to bear accounting knowledge and/or experience gained from extra-organizational associations. That accountants were recruited by organizations out of accounting schools was to some extent almost more a matter of convenience than necessity. Virtually anyone who could read and follow prescribed practice could perform the task with at least an elementary level of success. While expertise had its place, the wont was to eliminate it as much as practicable. Those who knew and embodied the organization's practices best were the most valued workers. W. Edwards Deming (1982) wrote extensively on the impact of organizational practices in suppressing individual differences in job performance in both white- and blue-collar work settings.

The consequence of assembly line social contracting was eventually made manifest in worker motivation. While still possessing little opportunity to materially alter the contract in ways related to knowledge or ability, workers impacted the motivational element with behavior designed to attack the ennui of the environment. Legendary are stories of Coca-Cola bottles rattling inside the door panels of automobiles moving down American assembly lines. Events such as this, however, began to teach managers and supervisors that despite the seeming impenetrability of the rational "assembly line" process, worker motivation/conscientiousness was capable of impacting both outcome and output.

Little wonder, then, that the lay theory became increasingly popular among managers and supervisors. While ability was still largely operationalized as a non-factor in the equation, worker motivation had found a way to impact desired results, and thus became an aspect of the work situation managers and supervisors needed to "manage."

As organizations continue to evolve and change, so too do workplace and worker requirements. It was not until the late 1970s that organizations began serious experimentation with human resource initiatives, such as quality circles, participative management and employee involvement as mechanisms for gaining worker input to increase organizational productivity, and with it, competitiveness. As some organizations sadly discovered, advances in technology alone, such as computers or robotics, could not overcome inept organization/worker relationships or workplace environments that stifled opportunities for collaborative worker contribution.

A new social contract, therefore, continues to evolve and with it new implications for understanding managerial and supervisory perceptions of intelligence and motivation as causal agents of objective measures of job performance and ratings of that performance.

Changing work environment

Many organizations today are downsizing and de-layering, dramatically increasing the worker-to-manager/supervisor ratio. Workers in many more organizational environments, even the assembly line, have "bosses" spending less and less time "looking over their shoulders." In some large global organizations, the direct supervisor for some workers may not even be in the same country. Matrix reporting schemes are also changing the nature of "boss–subordinate" relationships, as part of a worker's responsibilities are managed by one boss, while a different boss is involved with other duties. In the auto industry today, for example, an engineer may have a direct reporting relationship to a functional engineering manager responsible for ensuring that company engineering practices are followed across all engineering projects, while also having a matrix relationship with a vehicle program manager who will oversee the engineer's day-to-day duties associated with engineering projects on a particular car design. Anyone failing to perceive a potential conflict in what will constitute "good" job performance for each of these bosses has spent little time, indeed, in such working relationships. To evaluate the engineer's "total job performance" one would need input from a minimum of two different supervisors and understand two different sets of criteria of "good" job performance.

Consequently, workers have more time and freedom to "think on their feet." Managers and supervisors are simply "not around" or, at a minimum, more removed from day-to-day situations to answer questions and solve problems for workers. In many assembly line jobs, for example, workers often serve as their own quality control inspector by collecting quality data, analyzing it, making adjustments on the line, and graphing the results on quality control charts as data for other shifts. The value of having "intelligent" workers (that is, who can be creative and problem solve themselves out of trouble) in these jobs is becoming more apparent to managers and supervisors.

The changing nature of the workplace is causing managers and supervisors to reflect more on the "people" requirements associated with jobs. The lay theory appears to be becoming less popular as an overall explanation of their perceptions. A review of the elements of human resource systems in operation today in many large organizations also offers insights into their changing perceptions. Competency models are becoming popular mechanisms for outlining managerial and supervisory perceptions of worker requirements.

Competency modeling

Many organizations today are linking the elements of their human resource systems (recruiting, selection, compensation, performance appraisal, training and development) together by developing competency models that articulate the expectations which managers and supervisors have for worker performance (see, for example, National Academy of Public Administration, 1997 for a list of different competency models used by American companies and US government offices). Across organizations, these models generally express in different words very similar worker requirements.

The choice of words or terms used says more about an organization's culture than about inherent differences in worker requirements across organizations.

With regard to managerial and supervisory perceptions of intelligence required for jobs, these models typically include descriptions of worker traits or behaviors such as visioning, systemic or strategic thinking, creativity, innovation, problem solving, technical capability, and the like. Most of the definitions for these concepts are basically restatements of many of the factors already measured in most available tests of intelligence. Managers and supervisors often mention that "intelligence" (as expressed in these organizationally appropriate ways) is required more in complex jobs than in entry-level ones. However, greater numbers of managers and supervisors today are noticing that, even for entry level jobs in both the hourly and salaried arena, some non-zero level of these "intellectual" abilities will, at a minimum, enhance worker performance, even if it would be too bold to state that such capabilities are "required." As one reaction to the workload and stress levels that accompany work in downsized and de-layered structures, managers and supervisors are admonishing workers to "work smarter, not harder." Such admonishments suggest that managers and supervisors perceive that "intellectual" capability at some level is a necessary requirement for performing successfully in today's organization – at any level. More research on the applicability of competency model components to non-complex jobs would be helpful.

Equally obvious in these models, however, are those characteristics related to managerial and supervisory concern with motivation (conscientiousness), especially citizenship behavior. Here, descriptions of worker traits or behaviors include such items as customer/service orientation, teamwork, interpersonal skills, negotiation skills, flexibility, openness, empowerment, and so on. Managers and supervisors often summarize these competencies as measures of organizational "fit." The fact that these citizenship behavior elements often appear more frequently in many of these models is probably not conclusive evidence that managers and supervisors weight them more heavily as predictors of performance or their ratings of perform-ance. Rather, managers and supervisors seem to be indicating that citizenship behavior, and its relationship to performance, is far more complex than they realized. The reason for the proliferation of these citizenship competencies relates more to some managers and supervisors placing more emphasis on one or more of them in their own organizational contexts. So as not to "leave out" any important elements, these models often merely incorporate them into the structure of the model, even if the intercorrelation of these elements is obvious on a rational, let alone statistical, basis. The US government's Office of Personnel Management, for example, has a com-petency model that includes 27 competencies. What is obvious in all of these models, however, is that both "intelligence" and "motivation" constructs are increasingly being viewed as essential by managers and supervisors in today's organizations. Goleman (1998), for example, analyzed competency models from 188 companies and identified three categories of competency: technical, cognitive, and a third he called "emotional intelligence", which contains such citizenship behaviors as self-awareness, self-regulation, motivation, empathy, and social skill. He found emotional intelligence to be a critical factor at all job levels, but increasingly important in higher level positions.

Recruiting

An examination of changing recruiting practices in many organizations offers further insights into managerial/supervisory perceptions of intelligence and motivation as predictors of objective and rated performance. While most large organizations have always tended to do their salaried recruiting from the "best schools," a number of them now are using their most senior management personnel as recruiters. The logic espoused is that most people naturally tend to "recruit those like themselves" with regard to both "intelligence" and "motivation." By using those senior managers with a proven successful track record in the organization, the next generation of leadership is ensured through such recruiting practices. This practice is intended to not only guarantee a selection of the most "intelligent" or "best and brightest," but also reinforces the importance managers and supervisors today place on organizational "fit" (citizenship behavior).

As further evidence of the growing respect for the complexity and expertise required in many of today's jobs, some organizations are engaging in "boutique" recruiting. These are efforts to identify very specialized schools with specialized programs and establish early relationships between the organization and students and faculty to lure graduates to the firm. Again, the appreciation here is that the skill and ability profiles of future workers produced by these schools will be very difficult, if not impossible, for the organization to cultivate "in-house."

Further, some recruiter training sessions now include an economic analysis of the long-term investment costs associated with each recruit. Salary, benefit, and other investment costs are projected over the organization's tenure statistics to demonstrate how each hire decision can often represent millions of dollars in investment. These figures are provided as evidence that if "unintelligent" or "unmotivated" candidates are hired, the organization's long-term productivity is jeopardized. In many organizations, gone are the days when "who you know," rather than "what you know," determined the candidate pool. In downsized and de-layered organizations, managers and supervisors know that there are fewer and fewer places to "hide" or "shelf-sit" non-performing employees. Knowing that work environments now require greater degrees of employee decision-making freedom, candidates are being reviewed by managers and supervisors with far greater scrutiny. These concerns are also reflected in organizational selection practices.

Selection

Managers and supervisors increasingly appreciate that the evaluation of most of the "intelligence" and "motivation" elements of the competency models they use require selection techniques far more sophisticated than the unstructured interview. Consequently, many large organizations are adopting multi-faceted assessment approaches, like assessment centers, to provide more comprehensive and objective data. There is an increasing realization that an adequate evaluation of the "whole person" requires such rigor. This is especially true for salaried jobs. Again, as with recruiting, organizations are involving some of their more senior members to serve as assessors and interviewers in the selection process, for the same reasons as mentioned above for recruiting. More popular today is the use of techniques such as situations inventories or exercises, in which candidates react to "real life" organizational scenarios created by managers and supervisors themselves. The idea is to give candidates an opportunity to "live a day in the life" in the new job so that managers and supervisors can gather data on, or witness first hand, the candidate's citizenship behavior. Many of these situational assessments specifically void themselves of job specific "content" issues so that an "unbiased" measure of citizenship behavior can be made. The "intelligence" competencies are evaluated in other components of the process.

This evolution in selection practice is consonant with another increasingly popular option for evaluating candidate performance: the internship. Many organizations are using internships and other similar types of working relationships as opportunities to gain competency data on candidates. One-time internship performance appraisals at the conclusion of internships are being augmented or replaced with more sophisticated internship evaluations based on organizational competencies. In some organizations, candidates for internships must first be evaluated through the organization's assessment process before being chosen for an internship.

Assessor/interviewer training programs for these selection processes offer their own insights into how managers and supervisors perceive the link between intelligence and motivation and performance. Managers and supervisors often state their desire to separate issues of "head" versus "heart" in the assessment. They relate tales of previous hires who were "brilliant" in their field, but who proved to have no "heart" or "passion" or "fire in the belly" for doing the work, or could not "get along" with their colleagues. Rarely, however, does one ever hear the reverse. This suggests that many organizations have always been relatively successful with traditional selection processes in securing worker "intelligence" at sufficient levels, but have missed the increasingly important aspect of citizenship behavior.

As a result of the increasing use of multi-rater assessment processes, candidate evaluations increasingly involve consensus decision-making processes. As with assessor/interviewer training, these forums provide opportunities to observe managers reconciling candidate intelligence and motivation in deciding job offers. As with performance appraisal processes to be noted below, some selection processes provide weighting schemes for the competencies. Assessors and interviewers often debate the extent to which a given behavior reflects "head" or "heart."

Selection practices for hourly workers are also beginning to include elements related to both the "intelligence" and "motivation" competencies. As blue-collar jobs grow in complexity and as changes in workplace environment provide more opportunity for independent decision making, selection practices for these jobs will likely also change. Some Japanese auto plants in the United States, for example, have begun "pre-employment training" programs in attempts to ensure that workers can "absorb" required training and demonstrate the necessary citizenship behaviors required to "fit" in the Japanese-style production culture. Research on this growing trend would also prove helpful.

Compensation

Pay-for-performance compensation incentive systems have been popular in organizations for many years. These are plans that compensate more generously those workers who differentiate themselves from other workers by obtaining more organizationally relevant outcomes. As the workplace environment changes, however, there is growing discussion about the future relevance of pay-for-knowledge incentives. These discussions are prompted by a realization among managers and supervisors that many jobs increasingly require performance elements that depend not only on the particular type of knowledge a worker possesses, but also the ability of the worker to manage information and know where to find information. Thus, "intelligence" is to some degree finding its way into managerial and supervisory consideration as a compensatable factor of performance. Also, as will be noted below, performance appraisal systems that operationalize pay-for-performance incentives are including competency evaluations of citizenship behavior as elements of performance. Little has been said about "pay-for-behavior" incentives systems, but such an option would seem to be in keeping with changing managerial and supervisory thinking about worker performance on the job.

Performance appraisal

An evolution to "results-based" versus "objective-based" evaluations of performance is taking place in many organizational settings. Much as in the educational world's debate on the effectiveness of "outcome-based" education theory, managers and supervisors are beginning to explore appraisal schemes that evaluate workers more on the basis of their ability to "produce results" rather than achieve pre-agreed upon objectives. (Again, see Deming, 1982 regarding the role that management-by-objectives (MBO) schemes have played in limiting worker performance.) To be successful in these workplaces, it is not enough to merely "do what you are told," which is what is at the heart of the MBO process. Workers are increasingly being expected to demonstrate the ability to "judge" what needs to be done on the job, and then demonstrate the initiative do it – often without the opportunity to "check" with a manager or supervisor first. This is also a natural consequence of the increasing freedom and flexibility associated with the changing work environment.

Finally, just as the military has always sharply distinguished between job performance and overall military evaluation, the instructions for evaluating overall performance are changing for some performance appraisal systems. Overall performance ratings are being increasingly tempered by motivation (conscientiousness) concerns prompted by the link of these variables to the competency models included in the appraisal processes. For example, a measure such as "amount sold per quarter" may be used as one objective measure of salesperson performance, but a competency measuring citizenship behavior (for example, customer-orientation) would also evaluate the degree to which the salesperson obtained those results through behaviors consonant with the organization's values and principles (such as not deceiving customers). Overall ratings of performance in many of these competency-based appraisal systems specifically assign a unique weight for job performance and citizenship behavior. Most of these weighting schemes provide greater weight for performance than citizenship behavior (60/40, 70/30) – opposite of the weights found for the learning theory model. There still exists a debate among some managers and supervisors as to the wisdom of "adding" the citizenship behaviors to objective measures of worker performance. For many organizations, however, ratings of job performance are changing to include these "soft-side" evaluations.

Because of the changing work environment described earlier, 360-degree performance appraisals are also becoming more popular. These systems attempt to include input on worker performance from multiple sources. In addition to peers and subordinates, information is often requested of customers. This is further evidence that managers and supervisors believe that citizenship behaviors play a key role in understanding worker performance in today's organizational settings.

Performance appraisal training sessions also offer insights into managerial and supervisory perceptions of the role that intelligence and motivation play as causal agents of performance and ratings of performance. In seeking assistance in dealing with the coaching and counseling responsibilities often associated with performance appraisals, supervisors and managers are increasingly asking for advice and tools for providing feedback to workers. They want to know what to say or do when they believe a worker isn't "bright enough" to perform the job adequately or how to help someone "get the guts" to make decisions on the job without needing to check first with a supervisor or manager. Many companies are formalizing empowerment training to assist managers and supervisors in communicating to workers the conditions that allow for greater worker involvement in the decision-making process.

Training and development

In addition to the training and development implications already outlined for recruiting, selection, and performance appraisal as evidence of the link managers and supervisors see between intelligence and motivation and job performance and performance ratings, other training efforts in organizations today also help substantiate the link. Most of the competencies contained in an organization's competency model find their way as subject matter into training and development programs.

As discussed previously regarding pay-for-knowledge compensation incentives, today's jobs increasingly require greater degrees of information management. Workers are no longer necessarily expected to "know it all" when it comes to the information, especially technical knowledge, required to perform the job. The half-life of engineering knowledge for many fields, for example, is now counted in months. There is, however, evidence that managers and supervisors do expect workers to know where and how to obtain any information needed. The proliferation of the worldwide web, and internal organizational web systems, is making access to information sources easier. Again, competencies such as "information management" in many competency models require workers to exercise independent judgment as to where to go to obtain job relevant information. Increasingly popular are organizational training offerings related to "learning how to learn." These training efforts reflect managerial and supervisory concern that job performance suffers when workers are ill equipped to "manage" information.

Equally popular, however, are training and development efforts related to citizenship behavior. Courses on empowerment, teambuilding, interpersonal skills, and a host of other similar citizenship behavior competencies abound. Again, all reflect managerial and supervisory belief that workers who fail to demonstrate organizational "fit" will not be successful in today's workplace.

These training and development efforts apply equally to both white- and blue-collar work. In many organizations today, work sites have worker "learning centers" to help bring necessary "just in time" training to workers. Job and work requirements often change so often and quickly, that without learning centers, workers would be unable to access the information they need to keep up with work schedules. The value of a worker who can "learn quickly" is becoming very apparent to managers and supervisors. They know that "intelligence" is the essential element that allows workers to "absorb the training."

Finally, there also exist growing concerns in some organizations that schools and universities are not fully preparing students for the "world of work." While some of these arguments center on the need for further grounding in the fundamentals (reading, writing, and math skills), more and more organizations bemoan the lack of preparation in citizenship behaviors. Many organizations are taking active roles in communities to help students and faculty understand more fully the changing nature of the workplace, and the human capabilities, both "intellectual" and "motivational," that are needed.

Implications for learning theory

Observation of the changing workplace environment and the operation of modern human resource systems seems to provide ample evidence that the lay theory is becoming less descriptive of the perceptions which managers and supervisors in today's organizations have of the roles that intelligence and motivation play as causal agents of job performance and their ratings of that performance. Less clear, however, is support for the degree to which the weights contained in the present path model adequately reflect those in managerial perceptions. It seems apparent that a growing number of managers and supervisors today concede that actual job performance is greatly impacted by worker "intelligence." Whether it is, in their perception, five times as great as the role motivation (conscientiousness) plays is unclear.

The learning theory model's approximate equal weighting of job performance and citizenship behavior in predicting overall evaluations seems more in line with the observational evidence from managers and supervisors, although if performance appraisal process indications are any yardstick, the weight for performance should be larger than that for either conscientiousness or citizenship behavior. For managers and supervisors in this human resource system, performance data seems to far outweigh motivation data as a basis for making performance appraisal ratings. The unanticipated path between conscientiousness and overall evaluation, with its significantly large weight, is also inexplicable from these observations. If there is a particular aspect of conscientiousness underlying this relationship, it is likely that it might vary by organizational context. Beyond a generalized citizenship behavior factor, many organizations often specify a unique aspect of conscientiousness, such as "customer-oriented" in retailing firms, that managers and supervisors are asked to assess in their overall evaluations.

Changes in the workplace, behavioral observations of managers and supervisors, and the changes in human resource systems being made to link worker competency to organizational productivity and competitiveness make clear that the role that intelligence and motivation play in understanding job performance, and ratings of performance, will continue to be an evolving one for quite some time. At present, generalizations based on these information sources are tenuous at best. It is not difficult, for example, to find a supervisor who will explain that "citizenship behavior" is the primary determiner of successful job performance of a customer service representative, who largely does nothing more than read information from computer screens to customers who call in with a question. "As long as they can read, they've got all the brains I need," would be a typical insight from such a supervisor. It is also easy to find a manager of scientists in a research laboratory who will avow that the only thing of concern is the scientist's ability to problem solve, with little regard for whom the scientist "gets along" with, even other scientists. These are, perhaps, extreme examples, but they tend to demonstrate that sweeping generalizations about the perceptions of managers and supervisors are difficult.

REFERENCES

Barrick, M. R., and Mount, M. K. 1991: The big five personality dimension and job performance: A meta-analysis. *Personnel Psychology*, 44, 1–26.

Bloom, B. S. 1964: *Stability and change in human characteristics*, New York: Wiley.

Borman, W. C., and Motowidlo, S. J. 1997: Task performance and contextual performance: The meaning for personnel selection. *Human Performance*, 10, 99–109.

Cronbach, L. J., and Meehl, P. E. 1955: Construct validity in psychological tests. *Psychological Bulletin*, 52, 281–302.

Deming, W. E. 1982: *Out of the crisis*, Cambridge, MA: MIT Press.

Goleman, D. 1998: What makes a leader? *Harvard Business Review*, 76, (6), 93–102.

Hough, L. M., Eaton, N. K., Dunnette, M. D., Kamp, J. D., and McCloy, R. A. 1990: Criterion-related validities of personality constructs and the effect of response distortion on those validities. *Personnel Psychology*, 75, 581–95.

Hunter, J. E. 1986: Cognitive ability, cognitive aptitudes, job knowledge, and job performance. *Journal of Vocational Behavior*, 29, 340–62.

Hunter, J. E., and Hunter, R. F. 1984: Validity and utility of alternate predictors of job performance. *Psychological Bulletin*, 96, 72–98.

Hunter, J. E., and Schmidt, F. L. 1996: Intelligence and job performance: Economic and social implications. *Psychology, Public Policy, and Law*, 2, 447–72.

McHenry, J. J., Hough, L. M., Toquam, J. L., Hanson, M. L., Ashworth, S. 1990: Project A validity results: The relationship between predictor and criterion domains. *Personnel Psychology*, 43, 335–54.

Mount, M. K., and Barrick, M. R. 1995: The big five personality dimensions: Implications for research and practice in human resources management. In G. Ferris (ed.), *Research in personnel and human resource management*, Vol. 13, Greenwich, CT: JAI Press, 153–200.

National Academy of Public Administration 1997: *Managing succession and developing leadership: Growing the next generation of public service leaders. Phase III. Practical tools*, Washington, DC: National Academy of Public Administration.

Ones, D. S., Viswesvaran, C., and Schmidt, F. L. 1993: Comprehensive meta-analysis of integrity test validities: Findings and implications for personnel selection and theories of job performance. *Journal of Applied Psychology*, 78, 679–703.

Schmidt, F. L., and Hunter, J. E. 1998: The validity and utility of selection methods in personnel psychology: Practical and theoretical implications of 85 years of research findings. *Psychological Bulletin*, 124, 262–74.

chapter **12**

ORGANIZATIONAL RECRUITMENT: ENHANCING THE INTERSECTION OF RESEARCH AND PRACTICE

M. Susan Taylor and Christopher J. Collins

"In the old days, hiring was a leisurely affair. The résumés would dribble in by mail and the first candidates wouldn't be called for weeks. It might take two months for the whole process to run its course. The new era is about speed. Résumés are sent by fax. Managers rush through the applications. Employees are hired within a week." (White, 1998)

"Cambridge, Mass. – Totally Apocryphal Technologies (TAT), a fast-rising player in the rapidly expanding field of genetic engineering, recently announced that it would proceed with a controversial program to take tissue samples from top-performing members of its engineering, sales, and management staff. Rather than using the samples to screen for illegal drug use or pre-existing medical conditions, TAT hopes to use its recently developed human-cloning technology to address a critical lack of available talent. In a recent statement, TAT CEO Hugh R. Keating described the project as 'a logical application of our core technology in what continues to be an extremely tight labor market'." (Caggiano, 1998)

The expanding economy of the 1990s is experiencing its ninth straight year of growth in the United States (Smart and Berselli, 1998). Unemployment levels have fallen to their lowest levels in the last 25 years, and the ratio of probable workers to probable retirees is predicted to fall from its current rate of 4:1 to 3:1 by 2020 (Caggiano, 1998). In the midst of these significant environmental changes, recruitment has emerged as arguably the most critical human resource function for organizational survival and success. Firms in a variety of sectors, including banking, and food service, in addition to the well-recognized high technology industries, are finding themselves engaged in fierce, and continuing battles with their competitors for the recruitment of the best and brightest new hires. By definition, these individuals must possess state-of-the-art knowledge and skills that will allow their firms to compete effectively in an increasingly global and sophisticated marketplace. In addition, they also must possess the potential to shape a future where human resource demands are largely unknown at this point. For many companies, recruiting has become an essential tool in ensuring that they have the human resources necessary to achieve their current strategic direction and to continue innovating and growing in the future.

Perhaps not surprisingly given these developments, the bar has been raised significantly for organizational recruitment programs. Employer after employer has found that established recruitment sources are no longer adequate to compete for talented employees in a highly competitive and sophisticated marketplace (White, 1998). Thus, growing numbers of organizations are experimenting with new methods and sources of recruitment, although to the best of our knowledge, none has attempted the employee cloning strategy noted in the second lead quotation (a spoof vignette published by *INC. Magazine*).

How have recruitment practices changed in response to the tight labor market pressures? A few brief examples will suffice for the present. Cisco Systems, a rapidly growing California-based networking firm, has replaced virtually all of its prior recruitment advertising (for example, newspaper, radio, etc.) with the Internet-based recruiting programs that are specially targeted to the desired applicant population. Based on their own market research that most job-related web entries are received from employed candidates searching the Internet during work hours, Cisco provides job browsers easy to access fake computer screens in case a boss or co-worker enters the room unexpectedly. However, web-based recruiting is not Cisco's only foray into non-traditional recruitment sources. The firm routinely acquires five to six new companies per year in order to fuel its rapid growth with the proven and talented employees of other firms. Recognizing that acquisitions in and of themselves do nothing to prevent valued talent from walking out the door when another employer takes over, Cisco has identified a method of orientation, accommodation, and enculturation that allows them to retain virtually the entire technical staffs of its acquisitions (Nakache, 1997). Another example of innovative recruitment can be found in the practices of the well-known McKinsey Consulting Group. In response to the chronically tight consulting market, McKinsey now places "open" advertisements in international business publications, such as *The Economist* (1997). The ads state that in order to obtain the "right candidate" (whose characteristics are described in detail in the ad), McKinsey will now accommodate the candidate's own availability, rather than its own timetable for recruitment.

The previous examples encourage one to ask whether organizations struggling to revamp their recruitment programs can receive much assistance from the existing conceptual and empirical recruitment literature. Specifically, how closely do newly evolving recruitment practices follow the body of existing? What is known about the strategic impact that recruiting has on organizations as entities? Looking toward the future, what can be done to bring the domains of recruitment research and practice closer together? These are some of the questions addressed in this chapter.

■ DEFINITION, CHAPTER SCOPE, AND ROADMAP

In examining the intersection of recruitment research and practice, we have followed a common practice of limiting our discussion to the topic of external recruitment, the attraction of those not yet employed by the organization to apply for membership (Barber, 1998; Rynes, 1991; Taylor and Giannantonio, 1993). We also exclude the topic of employee selection, which is covered in another chapter within this text (see chapter 10). We incorporated these boundaries in order to provide a more in-depth discussion of external recruitment (hereafter referred to as, simply, recruitment), rather than a relatively weaker coverage of a larger body of content.

Concurring with Barber (1998) that it is more appropriate to define recruitment by its intent, rather than by its effects, we propose the following definition:

> Recruitment includes the set of activities undertaken by the organization for the primary purpose of identifying a desirable group of applicants, attracting them into its employee ranks, and retaining them at least for the short term.

This definition borrows heavily from Barber's (1998) own while also incorporating our belief that at least short-term, if not long-term, employee retention is a recruitment objective.

A roadmap of the chapter shows it beginning with a summary of academic recruitment literature in order to establish what is known about the effects of recruitment practices and what remains unknown. However, in light of the recent publication of a major and comprehensive research book on recruitment (Barber, 1998), we have chosen not to develop this review in the depth and detail that already appears elsewhere. In the following section, we provide several examples of recruitment practices developed in the last three years by organizations operating in highly competitive marketplaces and in the midst of an expanding economy. The latter part of this section examines the relationship between newly emerging recruitment practices and the body of existing research findings, drawing conclusions about how closely related the two are and the desirability of strengthening their inter-relationship. The third section of the chapter proposes a change in perspective for recruitment research, recommending that it become more macro and strategic in nature. Using the resource-based view of the firm as a theoretical foundation, we address the question of why the practice of recruitment might be expected to add value to organizations by providing them with a sustained competitive advantage. This section also reviews existing empirical evidence relevant to this analysis. Finally, the chapter concludes with a series of recommendations for both recruitment research and practice that are intended to bring the two domains closer together in the future. We turn now to a summary of the research literature.

■ RECRUITMENT RESEARCH IN THE LAST DECADE

Much like the practice of recruitment, the volume and nature of recruitment research has changed dramatically in the last two decades. As Rynes noted in a 1991 handbook chapter, the volume of empirical literature on recruitment at that time required a 50-page review paper that far exceeded the single page of coverage given to the topic in the 1976 handbook (Rynes, 1991). She also concluded that in the 15-year interim between the two publications researchers had made great strides in explaining how recruitment may impact applicant and employee behavior.

Table 12.1 Evaluation of current knowledge base

Major topics	Activity
Actor	
Applicants	Substantial information available; generally the focal point of research
Organizations	Little understanding of their actions; better understanding of how they are affected
Organizational agents	Often treated as passive; rarely considered as unique actors
Outsiders	Minimal knowledge of potential effects
Activity	
Defining a target population	Almost no information
Choice of source/medium	Some knowledge of consequences of choice
Message delivery	Substantial information on some topics
Closing the deal	Some knowledge of why and how applicants choose job, little understanding of recruitment activities dealing with job offers/choice
Administrative processes	Limited knowledge on some issues
Outcomes	
Attraction	Good understanding of effects of some aspects of recruitment, e.g. reactions to recruiters; little understanding of effects, other aspects, e.g. image
Post-hire outcomes	Good understanding of effects of some aspects of recruitment, e.g. RJPs and sources; little understanding of effects, other aspects, e.g. recruitment activities subsequent to initial job interviews
Organizational performance	Little knowledge
Other outcomes	Relatively little knowledge of long-term impact on agents or other employees
Context issues	
Internal	Almost no knowledge
External	Almost no knowledge
Phases	
Generating applicants	Significant knowledge of some issues, e.g. recruitment source effects; little or no knowledge of others, e.g. image
Maintaining applicant status	Focus of most recruitment research, but little attention to anything beyond the initial interview
Influencing job choice	Significant knowledge of some issues, e.g. choice process; little or no knowledge of others, e.g. impact of post-offer recruitment activities

Source: Used with permission, Barber (1998).

More recently, Barber (1998), found sufficient conceptual and empirical literature to devote an entire book to the topic of recruitment. Organizing her review around five dimensions of recruitment (actors, activities, outcomes, context, and phases), she concluded the text with a summary of what is known and what knowledge is needed in each of the five areas (see table 12.1 for a summary). As table 12.1 indicates, recruitment researchers have amassed a great deal of knowledge about the way applicants respond to particular recruitment activities (especially about recruiter effects in the early stages of the process), about recruitment source effects, and about the impact of realism in recruitment message (primarily the realism they contain). There is also a limited amount of information on how and why applicants choose a job. However, there is little or no research at the macro or organizational level of analysis, as opposed to the individual applicant level, and virtually no attention has

Table 12.2 Principles obtained from recruitment research

Finding	Confidence level
Attracting applicants	
1. Informal recruitment sources yield more positive outcomes than do formal sources with respect to performance, job satisfaction, absenteeism, and turnover	Low
2. Recruitment sources have an effect on the characteristics of applicants' attracted	Medium
3. Recruitment materials have a more positive impact on applicants' reactions when they contain more, rather than less, specific information about job and organizational characteristics, such as salary, location, and diversity/fairness	Medium
4. Organizational image influences applicants' initial reactions to potential employers	Medium
Maintaining applicants' interest and involvement	
5. The effects of initial recruitment activities are likely to be strongest for applicants who have a greater number of job market opportunities	Medium
6. Recruiter demographics have a relatively small effect on applicants' attraction to the organization	Medium
7. Selection predictors used during recruitment influence applicants' reaction to the organization, with more invasive (e.g., personality, drug tests), and seemingly less accurate predictors yielding more negative effects	Medium
8. Realistic job previews (RJPs) have a negative effect on subsequent turnover	High
9. RJP Effects on turnover are stronger for more intelligent, more committed and more experienced applicants	Medium
10. Applicants' early recruitment experiences with activities and recruiters provide signals about hidden or missing job and organizational information	High
Influencing job choice	
11. RJPs negatively affect job acceptance decisions although whether this is due to the intended self-selection effect is unknown	Medium
12. Recruiter warmth has a large and positive effect on applicants' decisions to accept a job	High
Conceptual	
13. Both the individual differences and realistic information hypotheses seem to explain part of the recruitment source effects	Medium
14. RJP effects are explained at least in part by the fact that employees become more committed to employers who are honest enough to provide them with realistic information and enable them to make their job decision based on a complete set of information	Medium
15. Applicants' beliefs about the existence of a "good fit" between their subjective factors such as needs, values, and interests and personality" influence their job choice decisions	High
16. Both compensatory and non compensatory decision models explain applicants' job acceptance decisions, indicating that situational factors may be moderating when a particular model is used	Medium

been given to the impact that contextual issues (for example, the level of unemployment) may have on recruitment practice effectiveness. Using Barber's conclusions as a starting point, in table 12.2 we summarize the knowledge principles underlying these findings, as well as the degree of confidence that appears warranted at this stage of the research. For a further explanation of these findings, we refer the reader to Barber (1998).

Despite clear advances in recruitment research findings, however, it is important to realize that both Rynes (1991) and Barber (1998) independently noted that recruitment research had generally fallen short in terms of its contribution to practice.

Concluding that recruitment research has ignored central issues of critical importance to employers, Rynes (1991) identified the following unanswered questions:

1. How to invest a limited amount of money to spend on recruitment so as to reap the greatest return?
2. What content to include in recruiter training in order to recoup the investment in training expense through enhanced acceptance rates or higher applicant quality?
3. How to attract high quality applicants despite a firm's inability to pay market wages and salaries?
4. How to enhance the organization's distinctiveness in the recruitment market for applicants?
5. What is the utility of recruiting for applicants at first, rather than second tier universities?
6. When to begin campus recruiting in order to attract the greatest number of quality applicants?
7. What are the components of organizational image, and how does a firm go about changing a poor one?

Similarly, Barber's summary of the known and unknown recruitment areas (see table 12.1) reveals a paucity of research about how organizations:

1. Make recruitment decisions or are affected by them;
2. Define applicant populations and motivate applicants to apply;
3. Persuade applicants to accept offers once the hiring decision is made;
4. Initiate recruitment activities in order to affect their own performance;
5. Respond to the external and internal context for recruitment such as the external labor market or their own business strategies.

In summary, two major reviews of the recruitment literature published in the last decade indicate that the majority of research to date has focused on applicants and their reactions, rather than on organizations, their external or internal context factors, or their performance. While agreeing with Barber (1998) that some level of focus on applicants' reactions is appropriate and important for recruitment research, we are alarmed by a continuing preoccupation with this level of analysis. Research focused around how applicants react to individual recruitment practices, rather than the effects of practices at the organizational level seems to us to hold strong negative implications for the practical usefulness of recruitment research findings. If so, we might expect to find evidence to this effect in a review of current recruitment practices and a comparison of these practices to the recruitment knowledge principles in table 12.2, taken from research findings. We turn now to a review of the applied recruitment literature during last three years.

■ CURRENT RECRUITMENT PRACTICE

Without question, one of the most important contextual issue facing US employers today is the tightness of the labor market. After more than nine straight years of economic expansion, the US unemployment rate has fallen to its lowest level in

25 years, hovering around 4.5 percent, with some areas characterized by rates below 3 percent (May, 1998). Because tremendous economic growth has occurred in high technology industrial sectors, these firms were some of the first to feel the pinch of a labor market that was under-supplied with critical skilled employees (such as computer scientists, engineers, software programmers). However, the high-tech sector is far from the only industry experiencing recruitment problems. In a recent article on recruiting in a tight labor market, May (1998), an industrial psychologist working in the private sector, identified several new strategies that employers have developed to better cope with these contextual factors, including: (1) casting a wider net to hire applicants; (2) capitalizing on technology; (3) using financial incentives; and (4) creating better places to work. In the following sections, we examine a variety of recruitment practices that companies have devised within each strategy.

Casting a wider net

This strategy typically includes targeting a broader range of potential applicants than has previously been considered, and the use of new, innovative practices to reach potential applicants whose existing qualifications meet position requirements.

Joe Martineq, the CEO of Productive Data Systems, an IT staffing and services company in Colorado, provides an example of the first type of "casting a wider net" strategy. Martineq formed a non-profit company called Technology Transfer Solutions that helps high school-equivalency students obtain entry-level IT jobs. Although Martineq's company does not directly benefit from the non-profit organization because it does not hire entry-level IT employees, he recognizes that a strong recruitment program requires a long-term effort (Caggiano, 1998).

Similarly, Tracor, a defense contractor, has undertaken a more instrumental approach to casting a wider net. Experiencing difficulties in hiring database programmers at its Maryland facilities because of the extremely tight labor market, Tracor now takes unskilled workers and teaches them database skills in a newly developed training program (Behr, 1997). Bosch, an auto parts manufacturer in Charleston developed a two-year apprenticeship program for high school students. Successful completion of the program provides them with an associate degree and the skills needed to manufacture sophisticated products (Siekman, 1998). Targeting a different non-traditional group, Protek Electronics, a $9 million electronics designer and manufacturer in Florida, found that, with some additional training, physically and mentally challenged individuals obtained through a local Easter Seals office became tremendous assets on the assembly line. Ultimately the demand for these employees grew so high over time that it exceeded the supply in the local Sarasota Florida area.

Still other companies have developed recruitment practices for attracting applicants across large geographical areas. Tired of struggling to recruit new production employees in an already tight Arizona labor market, Allied Signal targeted qualified workers currently living in cold weather cities and plied them with stories about the warmth of Arizona (Siekman, 1998). The firm placed advertisements in newspapers in several cold weather cities and then paid for the relocation of qualified production employees who were willing to make the move.

In perhaps the most sophisticated approaches to long-distance applicant attraction, Boston-based Fleet Inc. decided to broaden its geographic net by choosing new metropolitan statistical areas (MSAs) from which to recruit. The company used a four-factor model to select appropriate MSAs from which to recruit: high concentrations of desired knowledge and skills; existing favorable migration patterns from the targeted area to Fleet's home location in Boston; higher than average unemployment levels; and comparable housing costs. Fleet's results revealed that the best yielding areas were those having a large employment base with strong target SIC concentrations, high total northeastern mover ranks, above-average unemployment, and housing costs comparable to the northeast (McBride, 1997).

In a different version of this "cast a wider net" strategy, other firms have chosen to move their manufacturing plants to locations where an abundant and qualified workforce already exists. Siemens Automotive moved one of its manifold assembly plants from Windsor, Ontario to Lima, Ohio because this area had a large pool of skilled manufacturing employees who were looking for work after their employer lost its government defense contract (Siekman, 1998).

In yet another version of the "cast a wider net" strategy, employers are now initiating the intense networking activities that formerly were left up to an abundant applicant population in times of looser labor markets. Kathi Jones, a recruiting manager at Aventain Corp., arrives at the airport an hour early when traveling for business in order to search the business luggage tags of other travelers for competitors' names. She then attempts to involve the luggage owners in employment-related conversations. Barry Brodson, co-founder of Domino Equipment Co., constantly searches for talented construction specialists, one of his firm's core positions. He gathers as much information as possible about appropriate individuals and searches for opportunities to become acquainted and entice the person into changing companies (Munk, 1998).

Cisco Systems, the rapidly growing San José networking company mentioned earlier in this chapter, treats its recruitment program as a marketing campaign, where it pulls out all stops to market its jobs to talented outsiders. This approach has apparently worked well since Cisco has been able to grow at the rate of 1,000 new employees per quarter in the last two years. Targeting passive people who are happy and successful in their present companies, the firm has carefully studied this population to learn the nature of individuals' hobbies, when they would look for work, whose recommendations they would trust with respect to accepting a new position, and so on. Based on this research Cisco relies heavily on the Internet as a recruiting source, supplemented by newspaper ads that list the Internet address. The firm's recruiters frequently visit micro brewery festivals and antique shows (identified as hobbies of the target applicant pool) and hand out business cards with the company's web address. Although Cisco's innovative recruitment practices are now being copied by many of its competitors, the company's human resources staff report that they are not worried because, much like Cisco's regular customer products, it is common practice to make HR practices obsolete in six to twelve months (Nakache, 1997).

Another aspect of taking a marketing orientation to recruiting is to treat it as a continuing ongoing activity that never stops. Cathy Lanier, president and owner of Technology Solutions Inc., a $3.3 million technology-staffing firm in South Carolina, never discards a résumé once received. Rather, every résumé is entered into a database and updated every two years via a mailed query to the potential applicant in order to see what knowledge and skills individuals have added to their repertoire, along with current location, salary range, references, and a permanent contact address (Caggiano, 1998).

Other organizations are casting a wider net by varying either the content or source of their recruitment advertisements. Signal Corp., an information-technology services provider in Fairfax, Virginia, places humorous ads poking fun at its founder (for example, getting hit in the face with a pie to emphasize casual day, etc.) in the *Washington Post*. i-Cube, an IT consulting firm located in Boston, dropped its traditional recruitment ads in the *Boston Globe* in favor of renting billboard space right outside Logan Airport. Touting the company as a great place to work, the billboards have yielded many more applicants than did the far less visible, one time newspaper ads (Caggiano, 1998).

Finally, firms like Indus Corporation, a Vienna Virginia systems integration company, have chosen to cast a wider net through acquisitions in order to obtain desired high-tech talent. In 1996 alone, Cisco acquired 12 companies, retaining virtually all their employees, including 1,300 from one company alone. However, Indus CEO Shiv Krishnan warns that the cultural fit between the two firms has to be right, or newly acquired employees will leave, sticking the employer with nothing but huge acquisition costs (Caggiano, 1998; Nakache, 1997).

Capitalizing on technology

This strategy uses previously unknown recruitment sources, such as the company's web page, Internet-based job search services, specialized chat rooms (for example, those for Java programmers), etc., to recruit highly sought after professionals. Often these techniques can tap into applicants who were difficult or impossible to reach with traditional recruitment methods. Cisco Networking has been a leader in this respect, developing a "push-pull" technology to attract potential applicants. Through a combination of computer programs and hardware, the firm can determine where visitors to its web site have logged on from and direct those from rival companies to a special site announcing job openings at Cisco. Once further advanced, the technology could be applied to any one of a number of popular web sites (such as ESPN, Dilbert, and the like).

Note, however, that employers do not have to be from high-tech industries to benefit from computer-based recruitment technologies. Tiffany and Co. recently recruited applicants for two corporate sales positions by using a computer-based search of an online database in addition to running traditional newspaper advertisements. The database source yielded over 600 potential fits, which were later narrowed down to 25 ideal candidates. Overall, the computer-based search yielded a very workable pool of applicants in a much more efficient and timely manner than the more traditional newspaper advertisements (Weingarten, 1998).

Use of financial incentives

This strategy attempts to attract potential employees through the payment of financial incentives to new employees themselves, current employees who refer them to the company for hire, or to third parties who help make contact with desirable applicants. Many firms are using derivatives of this strategy. Schneider National, a Green Bay Wisconsin trucking firm, pays a $1,000 signing bonus to new recruits in areas with tight labor markets, such as Baltimore. Schneider also allows its best (safest and most productive) drivers to choose the company's dedicated accounts, thus giving them a more regular work schedule than its other drivers. Revenue Systems Inc., a Georgia software firm, has leased new BMW roadsters for its entire workforce of 40-odd employees as well as the 30 or so new employees it will hire this year. Why? The prestigious, highly visible, and fun-to-drive bonus will provide employees with a daily reminder that "life in general and their jobs at RSI are G-O-O-D" (Smart and Berselli, 1998). In the MBA labor market, signing bonuses are a well-institutionalized means of attracting sought after MBAs to a company's workforce. Recently a top graduate from Harvard received his choice of either a $40,000 sign-on bonus or full tuition remission from a recruiting company. High-tech organizations that cannot afford to pay high starting salaries are using a different type of incentive, stock options offering employees the potential to become millionaires if the company is successful and goes public. This particular recruitment strategy has been so effective that the large consulting firms have been losing top MBA candidates to high-tech startups (Taylor, 1998).

Other companies are simply using higher pay levels to attract potential employees (Siekman, 1998). Proctor and Gamble relies on its higher wage level, which pays about $4 above the local market average, to build a huge pool of potential employees and thus be more selective in hiring. Nucor Steel which pays well above the market average in its regional area, recently received 3,700 applications in five days for 90 openings. Carpenter Technology, a stainless steel producer in Pennsylvania, credits its wage level (paying $3 above market average) as the primary determinant of its ability to attract a large pool of potential applicants.

Better place to work

Increasingly firms are also focusing on enhancing their desirability as places to work as a recruitment strategy. This may be done in a variety of ways: by matching people to jobs more carefully to increase their likelihood of success; enhancing the intrinsic rewards present in the work itself; training managers to lead more effectively; helping people cope with workplace change; increasing employee involvement in organizational decisions; creating more career opportunities within the firm; and facilitating employees' ability to balance life and work such as telecommuting and casual dress. Bill Ziercher, CEO of Sterling Direct Inc., a direct-marketing and communications company in Missouri, successfully made his firm a fun place to work with the help of ongoing "contests" that promoted cooperation and teamwork. Brett Brewster of

Mitec Controls repeatedly lost high-tech recruits to larger firms. He responded by dividing the firm into five limited-liability corporations headed by a single account manager who worked with one to three test teams. Brewster paid teams based on the profitability of their contracts, a process that gave employees greater insights into how profits are produced in the business and thus, greater control over their own income levels (Caggiano, 1998). Progressive Car Insurance, based in Mayfield Village, Ohio, drastically increased its pool of interested applicants by changing to a casual dress environment allowing employees to work flexible hours, and offering telecommuting options (Munk, 1998). Finally, Corning has successfully lured workers away from higher paying jobs to work in its Charleston, South Carolina, fused silica production facility because of its work environment and potential long-term career opportunities (Siekman, 1998).

◼ HAS RECRUITMENT RESEARCH INFORMED RECENT PRACTICE?

The creativity and persistence displayed in many of the above recruitment practices are quite impressive. Yet, to what extent have these employers been able to draw on recruitment research findings in development? Our bottom-line assessment is "some but not nearly enough." In the following paragraphs, we explain the basis for this conclusion.

The stimuli for much of the development of new recruitment practices has been rapid and large-scale changes in the contextual or environmental factors that firms face while trying to compete in their marketplaces. A growth economy, record low unemployment rates, and increasingly sophisticated job requirements are all ex-amples of such contextual factors. Yet as Barber (1998) concluded, there has been virtually no research on the way various contextual factors affect the nature of recruitment activities or whether they moderate the impact of various practices on organizational-level performance. It should be noted that several of the recruitment strategies cited in the practice section of this chapter were proposed in prior concep-tual papers on recruitment. For example, a paper by Rynes and Barber (1990) proposed that organizations may rely on both special applicant groups (for example, physically or mentally challenged, high school equivalency applicants) and the broad use of financial incentives to enhance their ability to fill position vacancies. These strategies are clearly present in the "cast a wider net" and "use of financial incent-ives" practices mentioned earlier. Yet despite the fact that they were advanced almost a decade earlier, Rynes and Barber's (1990) proposals have stimulated virtually no research. Nor does existing research provide much insight into the relative utility of recruiting less qualified applicants and training them on the job versus recruiting fully qualified ones, or recruiting proven employees currently working in other areas of the firm and retraining them to meet position requirements in tight labor markets.

Similarly, while there is a moderate body of work on the effectiveness of different recruitment sources (for example, Blau, 1990; Breaugh and Mann, 1984; Williams et al., 1993), many findings about source effectiveness are weak and inconsistent across studies (Barber, 1998). Furthermore, the effects of new sources, such as web-based recruiting or the searching of résumé databases have not been examined, much less compared to those of more traditional sources (such as search firms, newspaper). In summary, we are aware of no empirical research that has examined the vast majority of recruitment practices described earlier. Further, existing research does not inform practitioners about the relative utility of using one particular strategy over any of the others or over a combination of different strategies.

Nevertheless, it is quite possible and very likely that the knowledge principles identified from recruitment research may explain why some of the newly emerging recruitment practices are reportedly so successful. For example, from past research findings we know that providing more, rather than less, information about job vacancies and about life inside the organization tends to result in more positive or favorable applicant reactions, both attitudinal and behavioral (see table 12.2, principle 3). Further, such effects are often strongest for highly sought after applicants who have greater job market opportunities, such as those in high technology industries (see table 12.2, principle 5). In addition, the networking activities undertaken by recruiters like Kathi Jones at Aventain Corp., seem likely to stimulate strong applicant perceptions of recruiter warmth, perceptions repeatedly found to yield positive applicant reactions in a number of studies (see table 12.2, principle 12). It is also true that recruitment activities have been shown to affect applicants' reactions and their subsequent job decisions, by providing signals about the status of other, as of yet, unseen job attributes (see table 12.2, principle 10).

The effects of many of the recruitment practices described above may also be explained by the fact that they build awareness of, and/or an initial attraction to, the organization among a population of applicants who were previously unaware of it. For example, Barber and Roehling (1993) found that postings containing extreme or unusual information about job attributes were more likely to attract individuals' attention, causing them to pay attention to the relevant attributes. This finding may account for the success of tactics like Signal Corp.'s humorous ads stressing the casual nature of its work place or i-Cube's use of recruitment billboards outside Logan Airport in Boston.

The new recruitment practices discussed above also may be successful because they provide potential applicants with complete or unique information about attributes that, in turn, increase their interest and desire to pursue the company. Research findings suggest that this may be particularly true for incentive-based recruitment strategies or better place to work ones. At least three studies (Cable and Judge, 1994; Rynes et al., 1983; Williams and Dreher, 1992) found that pay policies had a significant effect on the decision to apply. Honeycutt and Rosen (1997) reported that companies promoting a flexible career path were seen as more attractive by executive MBAs and MBA alumni. Thus, it appears that recruitment practices depicting unusually good working conditions may increase applicants' attraction to a given organization.

In summary, although findings from recruitment research have potential for explaining the effects of many of the newer recruitment practices reviewed in this section, there is virtually no direct empirical evidence. Thus, the research–practice gap continues to loom large in the area of recruitment, with very little actually known about the effects of these practices on applicants' reactions and/or on company performance, the types of companies that tend to implement them or about the environmental contexts that they face. A discrepancy of this size in a practical, rather than a basic, research area such as recruitment is simply unacceptable. Thus, we propose that a change of noticeable scope is long overdue for recruitment research, a change that is reflected in the level of analysis, conceptual background, and methodology of this area. The following section develops the logic behind our recommendation that researchers begin to view recruitment from a macro or organizational perspective, study the ways in which recruitment practices add value to the organization and help it sustain an advantage over competing firms, and examine a wider variety of practices from different organizations and environmental contexts in order to identify relative and combined effects. These proposals are explained more fully in the next section of the chapter.

■ STRATEGIC RECRUITMENT

Increasingly, managers and human resource professionals have become interested in the ways in which an organization's employees may contribute to its performance and in how human resource practices may be used to develop the employee attributes that subsequently yield strategic advantage for the firm (Pfeffer, 1998). During the last decade, this area of research, termed strategic human resource management, has flourished. It examines human resource systems from a macro or organizational perspective and asks whether the set or bundle of human resource systems that organizations design and implement subsequently impacts their financial performance, and if so, how.

A growing number of strategic human resource researchers (Barney and Wright, 1998; Becker and Huselid, 1998; Wright et al., 1994; Lado and Wilson, 1994) have argued that this area of study is best grounded theoretically in a resource-based view of the firm (Barney, 1991; Wernerfelt, 1984). This view focuses on how resources and competencies internal to the firm can be a source of sustained competitive advantage. Thus, it is arguably an appropriate conceptual framework for understanding recruitment effects at a macro or organizational level of analysis. According to the resource-based view, the resources of a firm can lead to competitive advantage when they create value for customers by lowering costs, providing something of unique value for them, or some combination of the two (Porter, 1985). Thus, if the programs, policies, and practices that firms use in managing their human resources are able to create value, they must do so by either decreasing the costs of its products/services, enhancing product/service differentiation in the eyes of customers or both (Barney, 1991).

Resources that lead to strategic advantage can be either tangible or intangible and include any number of assets, capabilities or processes that are both within the firm's control and capable of increasing either its efficiency or effectiveness in producing value for customers (Barney, 1991). Three distinct types of resources have been identified – physical and capital resources (for example, manufacturing plants, equipment, and finances), organizational capital resources (for example, systems of planning, controlling, and coordinating), and human capital. The organization's human capital, generally conceptualized as its employees, may add value through their skill levels, experience, judgment, intelligence, social relationships, insights, and so on. Wright and McMahan (1992) argued that systems or "bundles" of human resource practices can lead to sustained competitive advantage by helping firms to develop, integrate, and leverage their human resources in a manner that is consistent with the firm's business strategy. However, a resource can only be a source of sustained competitive advantage if the benefits it generates for a firm's customers cannot be duplicated or replaced by another resource held by a competitor (Barney, 1991). To more fully understand how a practice like recruitment can lead to sustained competitive advantage, we must consider the characteristics that are hypothesized to underlie this process.

Barney (1991) originally proposed that in order to provide an organization with sustainable competitive advantage, a resource must satisfy four criteria: value; imitability; rareness; and substitutability. Recently, in extending the resource-based view to human resource management practices, Barney and Wright (1998) added a fifth criterion, organization. While concurring with the importance of viewing human resource practices as congruent bundles, rather than just as independent practices (Becker and Gerhart, 1996; Becker and Huselid, 1998), we also believe that recruitment must be studied as one of, if not the, most important human resource systems. Note that by occurring early in the temporal chain of interactions that applicants have with a firm, recruitment becomes, in effect, a gatekeeper, influencing whether individuals have the opportunity or the desire to continue their relationship with the organization, and thus whether they ever experience any other human resource systems (such as selection, compensation, or training and development). Furthermore, several studies have now demonstrated that recruitment activities and the agents who conduct them provide both direct information (Bretz and Judge, 1994) and signals about the nature of the firm's other human resource systems (Rynes and Miller, 1983; Goltz and Giannantonio, 1995; Harris and Fink, 1987; Rynes et al., 1991). These signals undoubtedly shape new employees' initial reactions toward the firm's other HR systems, once encountered (Bretz and Judge, 1994). Thus, we argue that it is quite important to consider how recruitment activities, in and of themselves, may be a source of competitive advantage.

Can recruitment be a source of sustained competitive advantage?

In this section, we explore recruitment's contribution to organizations' sustained competitive advantage in greater detail by showing how it satisfies the five criteria proposed by Barney (1991) and Barney and Wright (1998).

Value

According to resource-based researchers, human resource practices can create value for an organization if they create greater efficiencies in labor costs or impact customers' perceptions of the product or service that they are receiving. Seemingly, recruitment has the potential to create value through both mechanisms. In the case of costs, published estimates of recruitment costs routinely place them in the thousands of dollars per hire (for example, Martin and Raju, 1992). Yet literature reviews and anecdotal evidence have frequently shown that a rigorous evaluation of recruitment, one going beyond the assessment of whether vacancies have been filled (Rynes and Barber, 1990), is apparently rarely conducted. Thus, survey research (Ostroff, 1995; Rynes and Boudreau, 1986) offers little evidence that recruitment source effectiveness is routinely assessed or that recruiters receive training on how to accomplish their tasks or feedback on their success in generating talented applicants. In short, it appears quite likely that organizations might enrich the quality of their applicant pools while simultaneously reducing their staffing costs through the more thoughtful design and follow-up assessment of their recruitment activities.

What might a thoughtfully designed recruitment system look like? Seemingly, it should focus on practices such as the efficient targeting of particular applicant populations, the identification of convenient, credible, and economical sources, the provision of abundant information about the firm that is desired by targeted applicants in order to make a job decision, and the rapid processing and evaluation of applicants so that job offers can be generated quickly, while the best candidates remain in the labor pool. Certainly, anecdotal evidence provided about the recruitment programs at highly touted firms such as Cisco Networking Systems, and Fleet Mortgage support this conjecture.

Similarly, it is likely that organizations also can reduce the typical costs of their recruitment programs by targeting applicant populations who are most likely to fit a given context and thus remain and succeed in that organization. Recently, a Center of Creative Leadership study reported that about 40 percent of all new management hires fail within the first 18 months on the job because of poor personal chemistry and cultural incompatibility (Fisher, 1998). Such job failures are clearly costly to both the organization and the individual managers. Anecdotal evidence from the study suggests strong recruitment influences. Many of the "failing" managers had multiple job offers from which to choose, and a strong vested interest in succeeding at the new position, rather than being back on the job market in 18 months. Yet they apparently failed to recognize that the new job was a poor fit in terms of personal chemistry and cultural compatibility. Given literally volumes of research on the effects of realistic job previews (that is, information such as how they work, what media make them work best, and so forth), it seems that a thoughtfully developed recruitment program also might reduce the costs associated with job failure.

Beyond the reduction of staffing costs, an organization's recruitment systems may create value indirectly, by attracting employees who are capable of enhancing the differentiation of the organization's products/services. This effect may be most likely in the case of service firms, where separating the service from its provider is recognized as a difficult discrimination for customers to make. The service provided by Southwest Airlines provides a good example. Additionally, such product/service differentiation is also likely to result from recruitment programs in firms that rely heavily on product innovation for their continuing growth and success. In summary, recruitment programs that market an organization's jobs to targeted applicant populations chosen specifically because they possess the attributes considered central to the implementation of its strategy seem likely to enhance the level of differentiation present in its products and services and, thereby, its performance. Investors apparently recognize this linkage between product differentiation capability and recruitment program effectiveness. A recent Ernst and Young study reported that institutional investors are now more likely to buy stock based on a company's ability to attract talented people (Grant, 1998).

Furthermore, over time, one might also expect synergies to occur between strong recruitment programs yielding desirable candidates, and the organization's ability to recruit effectively in the future. That is, developing a reputation as an employer of choice should make it easier for firms to recruit other new applicants with these specialties, due to both word-of-mouth and the social networks of current employees.

Rareness

According to a resource-based view of the firm, value creation, although important, is insufficient to yield sustained competitive advantage. Human resource practices also must enable a firm to acquire or develop a rare set of attributes in its workforce that are not possessed by the employees of the firm's major competitors, Otherwise, the application of such characteristics would simply enable the organization to maintain parity with major competitors, not to outperform them.

As described previously, a firm's recruitment practices may allow it to both attract, and retain, at least in the short term, a workforce possessing rare combinations of valuable attributes. As an example, consider the labor shortages among high technology positions in the Silicon Valley. Some sources report as many as 50,000 openings in Silicon Valley firms, despite the fact that these are some of the highest paid positions in the nation (Chandrasekaran, 1997). Firms that have effectively developed a strategic set of recruitment practices are able to attract this rare talent, fill positions with qualified employees, and retain these individuals over time, in order to meet growth objectives. Cisco Systems has a current vacancy rate in technology positions of only 3 percent, very low compared to the regional average of 10 percent. The ability to attract rare talent at a much greater rate than its competitors allows Cisco to continue developing new innovations and to grow at a phenomenal rate.

Imitability

Both value creation and rareness are considered insufficient to increase competitive advantage in the long term, unless rare and valuable human resource characteristics prove difficult for competitors to imitate. A number of factors determine the imitability of a firm's human resources. These include the availability of unique attributes in the labor market, the causal ambiguity surrounding which human resource practices contribute most strongly to the acquisition or development of rare employee characteristics, the difficulty of replicating human resource practices that are deeply embedded in social relationships, such as team-based appraisal or compensation, and the impact of the organization's unique history in shaping its culture.

As an example of the role played by a combination of these factors, Southwest Airlines uses a multitude of recruitment practices including advertisements in their own inflight magazine, job fairs, the Internet, and employee referrals in order to generate huge applicant pools (over 126,000 applications last year). While any of these individual practices are easily imitated by competitors, the combined set of activities, including the way they are implemented by Southwest and the nature of the company's culture, yields an overall recruitment strategy that is virtually impossible to imitate. Thus, Southwest's recruitment program is a source of sustained competitive advantage. Employment managers at Southwest carefully select a group of recruitment tools that are matched to the types of employees they are trying to target. In addition, the firm relies on its reputation as a "fun and challenging place to work" to attract individuals who will be well fitted to the customer-oriented culture that drives the company's success. Further, Southwest's reputation as a growing company that is very committed to its employees (no layoffs in its history) convinces potential employees that making an investment in this firm will be reciprocated on the part of the employer. Thus, while competitors may imitate some aspects of Southwest's recruitment activities, they are unable to integrate them with the other contextual elements, such as culture or reputation, that make Southwest's strategy so successful (Sunoo, 1995).

Substitutability

In order to be a source of sustained competitive advantage, there can be no strategically equivalent substitute for the relevant resource (Barney, 1991). This is the case because substitutes may be used by competitors to complete the same function or implement the same strategy. However, even when competitors are unable to duplicate the exact skills and abilities of a given firm, they can sometimes develop another resource and achieve the same advantage (for example, an employee decision-making ability may be replaced by an artificial intelligence system).

Recruitment appears to meet the criteria of non-substitutability in several ways. First, it seems unlikely that firms will be able to develop other resources to core skills and abilities that are particularly rare and valuable. For example, high-technology firms will be unable, at least in the foreseeable future, to develop replacements for software engineers or research scientists. Thus, the substitutability issue for these types of positions seems to depend on a firm's ability to develop a set of innovative practices that are equally as effective as their competitors. However, it may be proposed that the ability of a firm to develop an effective recruiting strategy for its context is, of itself, a unique competency requiring considerable effort and innovation. Thus, we expect that few firms are willing to make the investment necessary to develop innovative recruitment practices well-fitted to their context. Rather, most simply adopt fadish practices that appear to have worked effectively for other organizations. Therefore, by making a high initial investment in the development of appropriate recruitment practices, continuing to experiment with new practices chosen in light of the particular environmental context, and being willing to replace obsolete practices over time, firms should be able to avoid threats from competitors searching for substitutable practices.

Organization

Finally, if human resources are to be a source of sustained competitive advantage, firms must be organized to make full use of the value-creating, rare, and inimitable human resources that they employ. As Barney and Wright (1998) noted, it is common to find inconsistencies in the set of human resource activities implemented by organizations (for example, between the recruitment, selection, compensation, and appraisal systems used). Yet, a poor fit between practices often causes them to work at cross-purposes to one another. As an example, if recruitment practices target bright, motivated, team-oriented professional employees, while reward systems are individually-based, such a combination of structure and HR practices is likely to constrain an organizations' ability to fully utilize the valuable and rare human resources that it is able to recruit. As Barney and Wright (1998) concluded, the horizontal integration of human resource systems (such as compensation, selection, appraisal), rather than their isolated development and administration, is a critical requirement of the organization component of the resource-based view. At Cisco Systems, it appears that recruitment, an organizational culture stressing independence and achievement, and a supportive reward structure all contribute to the firm's ability to attract some of the most talented individuals in the networking industry, retain these individuals over time, and maintain high levels of performance. As company leaders describe it, "Our philosophy is very simple – if you get the best people in the industry to fit into your culture and you motivate them properly, then you're going to be an industry leader" (Nakache, 1997).

In summary, this section utilized the resource-based view of the firm as a conceptual framework for explaining how an organization's recruitment practices may contribute to its sustained competitive advantage. Although these proposals may be theoretically supported, it is also important to determine how well supported they are within the small but significant body of empirical research examining recruitment from the organization's perspective.

Empirical research on recruitment from an organizational perspective

A growing number of studies have empirically examined the impact of recruitment activities, often in conjunction with other HR practices, on measures of organizational performance. Because these studies have generally not investigated the ways in which recruitment or other HR practices affect performance, they cannot offer any evidence regarding the validity of our analysis of recruitment's contribution to organizations' sustained competitive advantage. However, they do provide a test of the overall impact of these practices at the organizational level.

Terpstra and Rozell (1993) conducted one of the first such studies. Assuming that key staffing practices yield better employees, who in turn contribute to higher levels of organizational performance, these researchers investigated the relationship of five staffing practices, including one in the area of recruitment (the use of follow-up studies of recruitment source effectiveness) to four indices of firm performance (annual profit, profit growth, sales growth, and an overall combined performance). Findings showed that firms conducting studies of recruitment source effectiveness also tended to display higher levels of performance in three separate industries, manufacturing (annual profit), service (sales growth, and overall performance), and wholesale/retail (annual profit and overall performance). Thus, the findings of Terpstra and Rozell (1993) provide some evidence that one recruitment practice (the evaluation of recruitment source effectiveness) is related to a firm's overall performance. It also suggests that recruitment effects may be stronger in some industries than others, perhaps due to contextual factors that limit how well recruitment practices are able to satisfy the criteria of sustained competitive advantage.

A study by Koch and McGrath (1996) proposed that organizations may gain competitive advantage from HR practices that lead to the development of a superior workforce with knowledge, skills, abilities, and personal traits that are more closely aligned with the firm's strategy. Using a cross-industry sample selected at the business level, the researchers examined the relationships between labor productivity and three HR practice sets: (1) investments in planning (operationalized as the use of procedures to identify the number of workers and skills needed to meet future business plans and as a firm's evaluation of its recruitment and selection systems); (2) investments in hiring (measured as the selection ratio and screening techniques to yield better individual–job fit); and (3) investments in employee development and productivity (measured as net sale/number of employees). Results revealed that of the three bundles of activities, planning had the greatest impact on productivity (measured as net sales/number of employees) although the effects of hiring were also significant. Overall, findings indicated that front-end HR activities such as planning, recruitment, and selection explained a significant percentage of variance in firms' productivity.

In a third study, Delaney and Huselid (1996) utilized data from the National Organizations Survey (NOS) to examine the relationship of five staffing practice clusters to the performance of more than 700 profit and non-profit organizations. The inclusion of profit and non-profit organizations in the same sample necessitated the use of perceptual measures of performance: (1) perceived organizational performance; and (2) perceived market performance. Applicant pool size significantly and positively related to the organization's market performance. Thus, their findings lend further support to our proposition that recruitment practices may influence organizational performance.

Huselid (1995) also conducted a cross-industry, national survey that tested for linkages between a cumulative index of HR practices and organizational performance. He examined a broad array of HR practices, including appraisal, compensation, employee involvement and voice, promotion system policies, staffing (selection ratio, use of formal job analysis, employment testing), and training and development. Clearly, the item closest to recruitment in this set is that concerning the firm's selection ratio, the number of hires to applicants per key position vacancy. Controlling for a number of firm and industry characteristics, Huselid found that the group of practices clustered into two HR system indices, skills/structure and motivation/human resources, each of which was related to different measures of firm performance. The skills/structure index was positively related to turnover and productivity, while the motivation/human resources index was related to productivity. Although examining only combined indices of practices, this study did provide further evidence that recruitment activities, in conjunction with other HR practices, may affect firm performance.

Huselid and Becker conducted a similar study in 1996, refining their measure of HR policies and practices to obtain a more comprehensive picture of the firm's HR system and its relationship to competitive strategy. This study included both the earlier recruitment item (selection ratio) and a second one on the percentage of the workforce covered by a formal written human resource or staffing plan including recruitment and succession (Becker and Huselid, 1998). Results continued to reveal strong and significant relationship between HR practices and performance, again suggesting that recruitment activities, in conjunction with other HR practices, are related to organizational performance.

A final study at the organizational level of analysis, Williams and Dreher (1992), also is relevant because it examined the relationships between pay and benefit levels (recruitment practices that fall under the financial incentives and better place to work strategies) and organizational level measures of recruitment effectiveness (number of applicants attracted to an opening, time taken to fill a position, and job offer acceptance rate). Using a sample of 352 banks with teller position openings, Williams and Dreher (1992) found that both the number of applications received and acceptance rates were positively related to pay level. Although the amount of time a position remained vacant was negatively related to pay level, the authors speculated that this result was caused by a time lag between bank's observation that positions were remaining unfilled and their decision to increase the pay level. The level of benefits offered by the banks was not significantly related to any of the three outcomes. Thus, the research provides strong evidence for the existence of a positive relationship between pay level and several different short-term indicators of recruitment effectiveness at the organizational level.

In summary, six studies (Delaney and Huselid, 1996; Huselid, 1995; Huselid and Becker, 1997; Koch and McGrath, 1996; Terpstra and Rozell, 1993; Williams and Drehrer, 1992) have examined the relationship between recruitment and firm-level measures of performance. Each study provided support for the hypothesized positive effects of recruitment activities, although in two cases recruitment effects were combined with those of other practices as an overall index, rather than assessed separately. Thus, there appears to be fairly strong and consistent evidence regarding the role of recruitment as a correlate of firm performance, including one set of recruitment effectiveness measures. Given this fact, it is somewhat surprising to find that so many of the empirical studies investigating linkages between HR systems and performance have failed to include measures of recruitment activities (for example, Delery and Doty, 1996; Huselid et al., 1997; Wellborne and Andrews, 1996; Youndt et al., 1996). The absence of recruitment measures from such studies is particularly suprising given Becker and Huselid's (1998) conclusion:

"On the one hand . . . the conceptual literature strongly suggest that an interrelated system of practices and policies forms an inimitable capability for strategy implementation. There is broad consensus that such HPWS (high performance work systems) would include rigorous recruitment and selection procedures, performance-contingent incentive compensation systems, management development and training activities linked to the needs of the business and significant commitment to employee involvement." (p. 63)

Unfortunately, despite existing support for the contribution of recruitment to firm's strategic advantage, few of the studies cited above actually examined the variables meditating the impact of HR systems such as recruitment on firm-level performance. Only Huselid (1995) has researched this issue and provided evidence that firm performance effects are at least partially mediated through employee turnover and productivity. These interim outcomes are certainly consistent with the notion that recruitment may add value to organizations by both decreasing their labor costs and providing a greater level of product or service differentiation. However, there is still a great need for further research that examines the relationship between recruitment and organizational performance, while also investigating the mediating variables that would provide further evidence on the validity of the "value-added" explanation. In the following section we offer recommendations for both research and practice in the hopes of strengthening the inter-relationship between these two domains.

■ RECOMMENDATIONS: RECRUITMENT RESEARCH AND PRACTICE

Prior sections of this chapter have illustrated that the body of recruitment research findings seems only tangentially related to current recruitment practices, suggesting that existing findings provide few insights for firms attempting to develop innovative practices that enhance employment yields as well as organizational effectiveness. Other sections in the chapter proposed changes in the level of analysis at which researchers study recruitment, and in the conceptual basis around which research is designed. A subsequent section showed that findings from a small number of studies conducted from this perspective consistently support the proposed effect of recruitment practices on organizational performance. Moving forward, the purpose of this section is to advance several specific recommendations for both research and practice that will serve to narrow the gap between the two domains in the future. We turn first to the area of recruitment research.

Research

Change the predominant level of analysis in recruitment research from individual to organizational

In order to make substantial progress in strengthening the linkage between recruitment practice and research, it is critical to switch to the organizational level of analysis in the majority of studies, rather than the small minority as is currently the case. Such a shift would allow researchers to examine recruitment practices across a population of organizations, permitting the assessment of context as a determinant of the kinds of practices implemented, and providing opportunities to determine practice effects on organizational level outcomes. Seemingly, the implementation of this one recommendation, in and of itself, would significantly increase the relevance of recruitment research for those involved in practice. Exactly what percentage of recruitment studies are we suggesting should be conducted at the organizational level of analysis? If pressed to provide a guideline, we propose a clear trend reversal, 70 percent versus 30 percent. Our intent is not to ignore or minimize the importance of applicant-level research and its accompanying outcomes, but simply to place more emphasis now in identifying knowledge about how organizations recruit and the relative and absolute results of their efforts at the firm level of analysis.

Conduct multi-industry focus groups of organizations emphasizing current and future recruitment issues, problems, and practices

It is telling that there appear to have been only four published surveys of organizational recruitment practices during the last 15 years (Ostroff, 1995; Rynes and Boudreau, 1986; Rynes et al., 1997; Terpstra and Rozelle, 1993). Seemingly, if recruitment researchers are unaware of the way organizations try to attract employees and of the problems they face in this area, it would be very difficult for them to conduct studies that prove relevant for employers. Furthermore, existing surveys have rarely tapped newly emerging but reportedly effective recruitment practices, such as the use of web-based recruiting, the application of a marketing approach, or the acquisition of other firms in order to acquire experienced and rare talent. Our conclusion is that researchers must be brought closer in proximity to recruitment as it is conducted by organizations who increasingly report that it is a key determinant of their survival in an extremely tight marketplace. The use of employer focus groups should not only permit researchers to make more informed choices about the variables they choose to study but also may provide many opportunities for data collection and other collaborations.

Prepare/read case studies of organizations recognized for recruitment excellence/sub-par performance

Firms like Cisco Networking and Southwest Airlines come quickly to mind as excellent candidates in this respect. Researchers can use such case studies as opportunities to gain more in-depth knowledge about the origin of a firm's level of emphasis (or lack thereof) on recruitment, the practices or activities that are believed to contribute to its effectiveness (ineffectiveness), the relationship between the organization's business strategy and its recruitment practices, and the level of consistency existing between different recruitment practices, as well as between other HR systems. Case studies seem a helpful but heretofore rarely used avenue for generating hypotheses about recruitment practices and inter-relationships.

Assess intermediate level outcomes of recruitment systems, as well as firm financial performance

The task of writing this chapter has led us to concur strongly with the recommendations of Rynes and Barber (1990) and Barber (1998) who emphasized the importance of examining intermediate level outcomes of recruitment effects at the organizational level of analysis (for example, the number of applicants yielded per position, the amount of time taken to fill the position, the acceptance rates of job offers, the knowledge skills and abilities of candidates in the applicant pool as well as those possessed by new hires, and the six-month and one-year turnover rates of new employees). The collection of both intermediate outcomes and financial performance at the organizational level should permit researchers and organizations to better track the impact of different recruitment practices, and hopefully, to understand how they may interact with one another in affecting firms' financial performance.

Compare the relative effectiveness of recruitment sources and practices

We also urge recruitment researchers to design studies that permit comparisons between the relative effectiveness of various practices, such as web-based versus newspaper or billboard advertising, traditional versus humorous recruitment messages, on intermediate level outcomes such as applicant pool size, time to fill vacancy, acceptance rate, and applicant characteristics. Thus, researchers may gain insight into the relative efficacy of various recruitment practices.

Use the resource-based view of a firm as a framework for designing multi-industry surveys examining firms' recruitment systems in combination with other HR systems

We also recommend that recruitment researchers utilize the resource-based view of the firm to conduct multi-industry studies of bundles of HR practices, including recruitment, and including measures of hypothesized mediating variables such as reduced labor costs or greater product/service differentiation (Rynes and Barber, 1990).

This more comprehensive approach would enable researchers to examine a more varied set of recruitment practices, examine environmental context as a moderator of both the use and effects of different practices, test the resource-based view of the firm as an explanation for recruitment and other HR practice effects. Following the research of Huselid and Becker (Becker and Huselid, 1998; Huselid, 1995; Huselid and Becker, 1996, 1997) we believe that researchers also must assess recruitment systems at the policy or philosophy level in order to better determine the external consistency between practices and firm's competitive strategy.

Strive to enhance the contribution of micro-level recruitment research to practice

While micro- or individual-level research has led to the development of a fairly extensive knowledge base about recruitment effects, these studies have often been too far removed from the practice of recruitment. We believe the usefulness of micro-level findings would be significantly enhanced by making three distinct changes within this body of work. First, we suggest that researchers examine focus group, case study, and survey data to identify recruitment practices that are of significant interest to practitioners. Second, micro-level studies should place greater emphasis on assessing individual attributes and behaviors (for example, the profile of know-ledge, skills, and abilities of new hires; the filing versus not filing of an initial application; the acceptance or non-acceptance of a site visit or a job offer remaining with versus leaving the hiring organization for 6–12 months) as outcomes of recruitment. Correspondingly, we recommend that researchers focus less attention on the prediction of attitudes such as attractiveness and recruiter liking that have previously received heavy emphasis in this literature. Finally, we urge recruitment researchers to increase their efforts to test various conceptual explanations for recruitment effects: the signaling phenomenon (Barber, 1998; Goltz and Giannantonio, 1995), the individual difference versus realistic job preview explanations (Schwab, 1982; Taylor and Schmidt, 1983), etc. Such tests will require the operationalization and measurement of appropriate process variables and the use of causal modeling techniques. Nevertheless these changes appear likely to enhance the usefulness of micro-level research findings for practitioners because of the immediate relevance and future generalizability of these findings.

Publish summaries of academic research in practitioner journals

Even large-scale changes in the nature and perspective of recruitment research are unlikely to affect practice unless they catch the attention of organizational leaders and human resource managers. Yet we suspect few practitioners relish the opportunity to curl up with an issue of the *Academy of Management Journal*, the *Journal of Applied Psychology*, or *Personnel Psychology* in their limited spare time. Researchers must take responsibility for making their work accessible to those who practice recruitment. Thus, they must periodically seek out a variety of forums where recruitment research is most likely to be read or heard by practitioners (for example, by publishing in practitioner journals or newsletters, making presentations at meetings or conferences). While such activities have rarely been directly encouraged by past academic reward systems, this practice is changing in some business schools. Equally as important is the realization that efforts to take research findings to those who can apply them in practice bring their own set of rewards, including: access to research sites; the identification of interesting hypotheses for future research; and the sense of knowing that one's research has made a difference in the lives and work of others.

The above recommendations notwithstanding, the review for this chapter made it even clearer to us that researchers are not the only group who must take more responsibility for bringing recruitment research and practice closer together. We turn now to several additional recommendations for those who practice recruitment.

Practice

Link recruitment to strategic goals of the organization

A primary theme of this chapter has been that recruitment systems can result in sustained competitive advantage for work organizations through stimulating the creation of a valuable, rare, inimitable set of human resources and through organizing to use them effectively. There is consistent evidence, however, that many organizations continue to view recruitment from an institutional perspective ("this is the way we have always done it") that greatly constrains its potential effectiveness and also incurs large and unnecessary costs (Ostroff, 1995; Pfeffer, 1998; Rynes et al., 1997). Our first recommendation urges organizations to consider the potential contribution that recruitment might make to the attainment of their business objectives by carefully considering what they wish to accomplish strategically, and how recruitment may add value to these efforts. Firms are also urged to examine the activities of organizations that are well-recognized as strategically excellent recruiters (such as Nordstroms or Southwest Airlines) as well as those of similar firms within their own industry.

Note, however, that this recommendation does not suggest that firms endorse and implement recruitment activities simply because they have worked well in other companies. Rather, we urge organizations to carefully avoid the faddish implementation of practices that offer no clear advantage. Unfortunately, we have observed several violations of this recommendation from a painfully close vantage point. One manufacturing firm with which we worked, decided to recruit on the Internet for its production workers, in lieu of its traditional newspaper advertisements, despite the fact that the majority of its past hires were from the local geographic area and rarely had either a home computer or access to the Internet. The Internet recruiting yielded only 20–25 applicants, most of whom lived too far away to make relocation justifiable, while past newspaper yields were generally more than 200 applicants, over 75 percent of whom were qualified for the position and lived close enough to take advantage of employment without relocating. The decision to pursue a recruitment practice because other firms are implementing it is unlikely to offer any strategic advantage but may incur high costs in terms of poor fitting new employees or unnecessarily high recruitment expenses.

In addition, we urge firms to recognize that recruitment practices must be thoughtfully linked to other key human resource activities (such as selection, compensation, training and development) in order to achieve desired strategic results. Thus, it is very important that they periodically assess the level of consistency between the body of HR practices, making certain that they are not working at cross-purposes with one another.

Involve current employees at all levels in recruitment activities

Our literature review revealed considerable qualitative support for this practice. For example, Pfeffer's (1998) research identified a set of seven best HR principles. He noted that successful companies often involve their top leaders in the recruitment process because it signals to applicants and current employees that the organization considers its recruitment program to be vitally important for its future success. In addition to top-leader involvement, we previously reported that more detailed information about job vacancies and life in the organization (in particular that information provided by current employees) has repeatedly been shown to favorably impact applicant reactions. Finally, results from the recruitment source studies have consistently shown that employee referrals are one of the more effective sources of new hires. Thus, although an organization's human resources staff must take direct responsibility for recruitment, there are a number of good reasons for involving many employees at all levels of the firm in this process.

Regularly track recruitment effectiveness and feedback results

Existing surveys of recruitment practices (Ostoff, 1995; Rynes and Boudreau, 1986) and anecdotal evidence (Rynes et al., 1991) suggest that organizations do very little evaluation of their recruitment systems, although there is some evidence that the number of organizations that do evaluate is increasing (Terpstra and Rozell, 1993). Given the high level of competitiveness in virtually all labor markets, this practice is simply unacceptable. In the prior set of recommendations for research, we identify a number of intermediate level outcomes that are relevant for assessing recruitment effectiveness. In addition to these, we recommend that organizations annually undertake qualitative assessments of the level of fit within its recruitment activities with respect to: (1) the consistency of practices within these systems (for example, the allocation of large referral bonuses to current employees while permitting long lag times before hire decisions are actually made); and (2) the internal fit between the recruitment and other HR systems (for example, aggressive recruitment systems involving top executives, applicant databases and financial incentives, coupled with pay levels that are below market or leadership skills that are recognizably abysmal). Assessments of recruitment effectiveness and the fit between and within recruitment, other HR systems, and the organization's strategic objectives must then be fed back to the appropriate levels of the organization so that rapid improvements can be made.

Experiment thoughtfully but regularly with new recruitment practices

Changing environmental conditions are likely to require accompanying changes in recruitment practices over time. Firms well recognized for their recruitment expertise are continually experimenting with new recruitment practices, because they recognize that competitors will identify and adopt some of their existing practices over time, thus making them less effective for sustained competitive advantage. Thus, organizations that thoughtfully experiment with new practices that seem consistent with their environmental context, strategic objectives, and other recruitment and HR practices, are likely to achieve a great deal of success in responding to changing environmental conditions.

Shape and sponsor relevant academic research

Increasingly organizational leaders are receiving invitations to learn more about and to shape academic research agendas. Not surprisingly, they also receive frequent opportunities to sponsor empirical studies that are relevant to their concerns and interests. These opportunities for input come in a variety of forms: through invitations to participate in surveys and interviews; joining alumni, executive boards or visitor boards that are associated with academic programs or centers; serving as classroom or student organization speakers; by funding academic research that is relevant to their business missions; purchasing membership in university-formed HR research networks, etc. Organizational participation is critical in order to bring research and practice closer together, even though avenues of participation must be chosen carefully. Organizational leaders are urged to investigate the reputations of researchers sponsoring the projects in which they are asked to participate and the purposes of the visitor boards they are asked to join. Nevertheless, by clearly articulating the needs and problems of their organizations and being willing to invest in research that is relevant to their organizational interests, either through the donation of participant time or money, leaders can play a major role in strengthening the relationship between research and practice.

■ CONCLUSIONS

During the course of this chapter we have examined the evolution of recruitment research over the last two decades and the knowledge principles that have developed out of that body of work. Through the use of the popular media, contacts with recruitment professionals and practitioner journals, we also compared recruitment findings to the set of practices and sources that have been developed by recruiting organizations during a decade-long period of economic expansion. Even though several of the newly emerging recruitment practices are quite consistent with existing knowledge principles gleaned from recruitment research, we suspect that this resulted more from chance factors, rather than from the exchange of information between the two groups. Overall, in assessing the extent to which recruitment practice has been informed by a growing body of recruitment research, we concluded, disappointingly, "not much." Yet, given a practical area such as recruitment, we are unable to believe that such a large disconnect is in any way appropriate or healthy.

Our recommendations for bringing recruitment research and practice closer together centered around conducting recruitment research at the organizational, rather than the individual, level of analysis, and being guided in the design of this research by a resource-based view of the firm that asks how recruitment practices can contribute to an organization's sustained competitive advantage. The foci of prior recruitment research suggests that this view is currently not widely held by recruitment researchers. Further, we suspect that only recently have practitioners, struggling with tight labor pools in a time of rapid economic expansion, become convinced of recruitment's critical role as a determinant of organizational performance. Yet, if both parties adopt a strategic perspective of recruitment, we believe that they will find themselves speaking an appealing and common language that may facilitate more frequent and direct communication. Hopefully these conversations will lead to discussions of future research topics, the implications of recruitment findings, and possibly, to research collaborations.

In looking toward the future, we urge researchers to recognize that there has probably never been a more critical period for recruitment research than the present, in terms of both needs and opportunities. After experiencing the pain of understaffing and the frustration of ineffective recruitment programs, many companies have developed an entirely new set of practices and implemented them side-by-side with more traditional recruitment activities. These naturally occurring experiments are just waiting for an interested researcher to study. Subsequently, study findings that also provide sufficient detail to facilitate adaptive organizational responses have enormous potential for impacting organizational performance during this period of high growth. Seemingly, organizations have never had a greater incentive to cooperate with and even sponsor such research.

However, even if recommended changes in recruitment research are implemented, they are unlikely to yield significant benefits unless recruiting organizations too undertake some change in their modus operandi. Traditionally, firms have consistently avoided both the evaluation of recruitment results and the feeding back of findings. The continuation of either practice constitutes a significant threat to the potential benefits that might otherwise result from the adoption of recruitment research findings. Thus, we urge organizational leaders to recognize the strategic importance of recruitment and accept responsibility for organizing in a way that enhances its effectiveness.

In researching this chapter, we became aware of an analogy used by public relations executive, Lou Hoffman, to describe the changes he made in his organization's recruitment practices in response to an increasingly tight job market coupled with rapidly escalating business opportunities. By introducing a number of new actors and many new practices, Hoffman essentially transformed his agency from a "hire as needed" organization to a business that is "as much a recruiting firm as a PR agency" (Caggiano, 1998). In speaking about the firm's recruitment process today, Hoffman likens it to the painting of the Golden Gate Bridge – when the painting crews finish the final bridge span, it is time to start the process all over again. We believe that this analogy is also appropriate for describing the appropriate interrelationship between recruitment research and practice. Recruitment practitioners must assist researchers at the beginning of the research process by identifying relevant practices and issues to study, and during the research process by both participating and sponsoring the activity. Once a given study has been completed, the data analyzed, results interpreted, the implications for recruitment programs returned to participating firms, and responsive changes made, it is time to start the cycle again.

If this process, or a similar one is followed, we believe the next chapter examining the linkages between recruitment research and practice will be far more positive in nature.

REFERENCES

Barber, A. E. 1998: *Recruiting employees: Individual and organizational perspectives*, Thousand Oaks, CA: Sage Publications.

Barber, A. E., and Roehling, M. V. 1993: Job postings and the decision to interview: A verbal protocol analysis. *Journal of Applied Psychology*, 78, 845–56.

Barney, J. 1991: Firm resources and sustained competitive advantage. *Journal of Management*, 17, 99–120.

Barney, J. B., and Wright, P. M. 1998: On becoming a strategic partner: The role of human resources in gaining competitive advantage. *Human Resource Management*, Spring, 1998, 31–46.

Becker, B. E., and Gerhart, B. 1996: The impact of human resource management on organizational performance: Progress and prospects. *Academy of Management Journal*, 39, 779–801.

Becker, B. E., and Huselid, M. A. 1998: High performance work systems and firm performance: A synthesis of research and managerial applications. In G. R. Ferris (ed.), *Research in personnel and human resource management*, 16, 53–102.

Behr, P. 1997: Cultivating a new crop of workers. *The Washington Post*, December 1, A01.

Blau, G. 1990: Exploring the mediating mechanisms affecting the relationship of recruitment source to employee performance. *Journal of Vocational Behavior*, 37, 303–20.

Breaugh, J. A., and Mann, R. B. 1984: Recruiting source effects: A test of two alternative explanations. *Journal of Occupational Psychology*, 57, 261–7.

Bretz, R. D., and Judge, T. A. 1994: The role of human resource systems in the job applicant decision processes. *Journal of Management*, 20, 531–51.

Butler, J. E., Ferris, G. R., and Napier, N. K. 1991: *Strategy and human resources management*, Cincinnati, OH: South-Western.

Cable, D. M., and Judge, T. A. 1994: Pay preferences and job search decisions: A person-organization fit perspective. *Personnel Psychology*, 47, 317–48.

Caggiano, C. 1998: Recruiting secrets. *INC. Magazine*, October, 30–42.

Chandrasekaran, R. 1997: The tech boom: Help wanted. *The Washington Post*, November 30, A21.

Delaney, J. T., and Huselid, M. A. 1996: The impact of human resource management practice on perceptions of organizational performance. *Academy of Management Journal*, 39, 949–69.

Delery, J. E., and Doty, D. H. 1996: Modes of theorizing in strategic human resource management: Tests of universalistic, contingency, and configurational performance predictions. *Academy of Management Journal*, 39, 802–35.

Fisher, A. 1998: Don't blow your new job. *Fortune Magazine*, June 22, 159–63.

Gatewood, R. D., Gowan, M. A., and Lautenschlager, G. J. 1993: Corporate image, recruitment image, and initial job choice. *Academy of Management Journal*, 36, 414–27.

Goltz, S. M., and Giannantonio, C. M. 1995: Recruiter friendliness and attraction to the job: The mediating role of inferences about the organization. *Journal of Vocational Behavior*, 46, 109–18.

Grant, L. 1998: Happy workers, high returns. *Fortune Magazine*, January 12, 81–95.

Guion, R. M. 1976: Recruiting, selection, and job placement. In M. D. Dunnette (ed.), *Handbook of industrial/organizational psychology*, Chicago: Rand-McNally, 777–828.

Harris, M. M, and Fink, L. S. 1987: A field study of applicant reactions to employment opportunities: Does the recruiter make a difference. *Personnel Psychology*, 40, 765–86.

Honeycutt, T. L., and Rosen, B. 1997: Family friendly human resources policies, salary levels, and salient identity as predictors of organizational attraction. *Journal of Vocational Behavior*, 50, 271–90.

Huselid, M. A. 1995: The impact of human resource management practices on turnover, productivity, and corporate financial performance. *Academy of Management Journal*, 38, 635–72.

Huselid, M. A., and Becker, B. E. 1996: Methodological issues in cross-sectional and panel estimates of the HR-firm performance link. *Industrial Relations*, 35, 400–22.

Huselid, M. A., and Becker, B. E. 1997: The impact of high performance work systems, implementation, effectiveness and alignment with strategy on shareholder wealth. Paper presented at the 1997 Academy of Management Annual Conference, Boston, MA.

Huselid, M. A., Jackson, S. E., and Schuler, R. S. 1997: Technical and strategic human resource management effectiveness as determinants of firm performance. *Academy of Management Journal*, 40, 171–88.

Koch, M. J., and McGrath, R. G. 1996: Improving labor productivity: Human resource management policies do matter. *Strategic Management Journal*, 17, 335–54.

Lado, A. A., and Wilson, M. C. 1994: Human resource systems and sustained competitive advantage: A competency-based perspective. *Academy of Management Review*, 699–727.

Martin, S. L., and Raju, N. S. 1992: Determining cutoff scores that optimize utility: A recognition of recruiting costs. *Journal of Applied Psychology*, 77, 15–23.

May, K. 1998: Work in the 21st century: Recruiting in a tight labor market. *The Industrial/ Organizational Psychologist* (TIP), 36, July, 39–41.

McBride, P. 1997: Luring them in. *Business Geographics*, 30–2.

Mueller, F. 1996: Human resources as strategic assets: An evolutionary resource-based theory. *Journal of Management Studies*, 33, 757–85.

Munk, N. 1998: The new organization Man. *Fortune*, 137(5), 63–74.

Nakache, P. 1997: Cisco's recruiting edge. *Fortune Magazine*. September 29, 275–6.

Ostroff, C. 1995: 1995 SHRM/CCH Survey: Bottom-line reasons support HR's place at the CEO's table. *Human Resource Management*, 356, 1–12.

Pfeffer, J. 1998: *The human equation: Building profits by putting people first*, Boston: Harvard Business School Press.

Porter, M. E. 1985: *Competitive advantage: Creating and sustaining superior performance*, New York: Free Press.

Rynes, S. L. 1991: Recruitment, job choice, and post-hire consequences. In M. D. Dunnette and L. M. Hough (eds.), *Handbook of industrial and organizational psychology*, 2nd edn., Vol. 2, Palo Alto, CA: Consulting Psychologists Press, 399–444.

Rynes, S. L., and Barber, A. E. 1990: Applicant attraction strategies: An organizational perspective. *Academy of Management Review*, 15, 286–310.

Rynes, S. L., and Boudreau, J. W. 1986: College recruiting in large organizations: Practice, evaluation and research implications. *Personnel Psychology*, 39, 729–57.

Rynes, S. L., Bretz, R. D., and Gerhart, B. 1991: The importance of recruitment in job choice: A different way of looking. *Personnel Psychology*, 44, 487–521.

Rynes, S. L., and Miller, H. E. 1983: Recruiter and job influences on candidates for employment. *Journal of Applied Psychology*, 68, 146–54.

Rynes, S. L., Orlitzky, M. O., and Bretz, R. D. 1997: Experienced hiring versus college recruiting: practices and emerging trends. *Personnel Psychology*, 50, 309–39.

Rynes, S. L., Schwab, D. P., and Heneman, H. G., III. 1983: The role of pay and market pay variability in job application decisions. *Organizational Behavior and Human Performance*, 31, 353–64.

Schwab, D. P. 1982: Recruiting and organizational participation. In K. Rowland and G. Ferris (eds.), *Personnel management*, Boston: Allyn and Bacon, 102–28.

Siekman, P. 1998: The hunt for good factory workers. *Fortune*, 137(12), 138B–J.

Smart, T., and Berselli, B. 1998: Workers move into the driver's seat. *The Washington Post*, July 16, A-1.

Sunoo, B. P. 1995: How fun flies at Southwest Airlines. *Personnel Journal*, 74(6), 62–73.

Taylor, A. 1998: Consultants have a big people problem. *Fortune*, April 13, 162–6.

Taylor, M. S., and Giannantonio, C. M. 1993: Forming, adapting, and terminating the employment relationship: A review of the literature from individual, organizational and interactionist perspectives. *Journal of Management*, 19, 461–515.

Taylor, M. S., and Schmidt, D. W. 1983: A process-oriented view of recruitment source effectiveness. *Personnel Psychology*, 36, 343–54.

Terpstra, D. E., and Rozell, E. J. 1993: The relationship of staffing practices to organizational level measures of performance. *Personnel Psychology*, 46, 27–48.

The Economist. 1997: A survey of management consultancy. March 22, 1–21.

Weingarten, T. 1998: The all-day, all-night, global, no-trouble job search. *Newsweek*, 131(14), 17.

Wellborne, T. M., and Andrews, A. O. 1996: Predicting the performance of initial public offerings: Should human resource management be in the equation? *Academy of Management Journal*, 39, 891–919.

Wernerfelt, B. 1984: A resource-based view of the firm. *Strategic Management Journal*, 171–80.

White, J. 1998: Labor market in N. Va. is kind to workers, cruel to employers. *The Washington Post*, June 28, A1.

Williams, M. L., and Dreher, G. F. 1992: Compensation system attributes and applicant pool characteristics. *Academy of Management Journal*, 35, 571–95.

Williams, C. R., Labig, C. E., and Stone, T. H. 1993: Recruitment sources and posthire outcomes for job applicants and new hires: A test of two hypotheses. *Journal of Applied Psychology*, 78, 163–72.

Wright, P. M., and McMahan, G. C. 1992: Theoretical perspectives for strategic human resource management. *Journal of Management*, 18, 295–320.

Wright, P. M., McMahan, G. C., and McWilliams, A. 1994: Human resources and sustained competitive advantage: A resource-based perspective. *International Journal of Human Resource Management*, 5, 301–26.

Youndt, M. A., Snell, S. A., Dean, J. W., and Lepak, D. P. 1996: Human resource management, manufacturing strategy, and firm performance. *Academy of Management Journal*, 39, 836–66.

chapter **13**

CONCLUSION: THE CHALLENGE OF LINKING THEORY TO PRACTICE

EDWIN A. LOCKE AND CARY L. COOPER

To be useful a theory must first be true – that is, it must correspond to the facts. (This does not mean a theorist must be omniscient – only that he has many relevant facts and that his conclusions are fully consistent with them and with all his other knowledge.) A theory that is true is potentially useful to practitioners. We say potentially because the theory may or may not deal with issues of interest to any given practitioner. Newton's Laws are true (of large objects) and they are of great importance to people who design rocket ships, but they are of little relevance to people who design retirement programs. Conversely, investment theories are of no relevance to the daily work of space engineers.

A related point is that all theories are limited – they explain only a limited range of phenomena. There is no such thing as a theory of everything in general but of nothing in particular. Thus, it is incumbent on the theorist to specify the domain to which his theory applies and for the practitioner to know to what phenomena a given theory applies. Furthermore, the theorist (or someone) has to communicate his findings in a form that practitioners can understand and use.

Even a theory that is true and relevant may not be applied or may only be applied with difficulty, for a variety of reasons to be addressed below. Thus, understanding the relation of theory to practice poses continual challenges to theorists and practitioners alike.

The chapters in this volume nicely illustrate the above issues. Let us consider several facets of the theory–practice relationship.

■ COMPLETENESS

A theory about a given topic does not necessarily encompass everything relevant to that topic. For example, Taylor and Collins note that recruitment research has mainly focused on the micro (individual) level of analysis, for example, the job choice process, RJPs, reactions to recruiters. However, it has not addressed all micro issues and has not addressed macro issues (how to recruit the right people in a tight labor market; how to tie recruitment to corporate strategy, such as how to use it for competitive advantage; how to use technology to recruit; how to determine the most cost-effective recruitment methods) at all. Existing recruitment theory is of very little use to practitioners because most of their concerns are of a macro nature. Thus Taylor and Collins suggest *a total re-orientation of recruitment research* to focus more on these macro issues.

■ DISSEMINATION

In the case of the employment interview, Rynes, Barber and Varma find a somewhat better fit between theory and practical need. Interview research has discovered a great deal of practically useful information about the benefits of different interview types (for example, structured versus unstructured), what type of interviewer training helps, and what the interview can add to other sources of information (such as ability test scores). Researchers have also discovered what interview procedures are most legally defensible and even what interview procedures and interviewer qualities make the most favorable impression on interviewees. Nevertheless, there are gaps in our knowledge, for example, how interview content affects applicants, how best to combine interview information with other applicant information.

An interesting observation of these authors, however, is that despite the existence of much useful information, most employers do not use it; for example, about 70 percent of interviews are unstructured, even though structured interviews are more valid than unstructured ones. (Greenberg and Lind argue that unstructured interviews are more likely to be seen as fair because interviewees are more able to express their opinions.) The irony here is that in the past it was the researchers who denigrated the validity of the interview and the practitioners who insisted that it was useful. Now that the researchers have proved that the practitioners were right, the latter do not use the type of interview that has been shown to be most valid. *This suggests that what is needed is better dissemination of what is known.* Here, unfortunately, the problem is that academics who do most of the research typically get no reward at all for publishing in practitioner journals! (Greenberg and Lind note the bias against applied research.)

■ RELEVANCE

A theory may be true but may have no effect on practice, because managers themselves do not believe that it is important. The chapter on job satisfaction by Judge and Church illustrates this point. There is ample evidence that high job satisfaction is beneficial to organizations but most practicing managers are not convinced, so they typically pay little attention to it. As one manager put it, "The concepts [of satisfaction and morale] are not used here." It is considered a "soft" measure having little to do with "hard" results such as productivity and profits. To be sufficiently convinced to take satisfaction seriously, managers want data showing the economic value of having a satisfied work force. The principle here is that *if one wants managers or executives to apply a theory, one has to show that it will help them achieve their goals.*

In the case of job satisfaction this suggests a specific strategy. The psychologist or consultant should work with an economist or accountant to estimate and document the financial benefits of a more versus a less satisfied work force. Its effect on turnover could presumably be documented; measuring other benefits quantitatively might be more difficult. Judge and Church do point out, based on an updated database of studies, that satisfaction and performance are somewhat correlated, but this does not show which is the cause of which. Ben Schneider at Maryland has shown a relationship between employee satisfaction and quality of customer service, so that might be another opening.

■ RISK

Some interventions are less risky than others, as the chapter by Ganster and Murphy reveals. Managers are quite willing to run programs on stress management and practitioners are quite willing to give them. However, neither is very anxious to try to reduce stress by changing organizational policies and procedures. Managers fear that such programs may undermine efficiency – perhaps with good reason. One of the most frequent causes of stress is work overload, but reducing the work load could lower productivity, thus making the manager look bad to his own boss. Furthermore, since there is less evidence that such organizational change programs work, practitioners are less willing to undertake a project that might make them look bad. *It is probable that the less risky the intervention, the more willing the company will be to allow it.* Thus practitioners need to limit risk. Of course, in the case of work overload, the psychologist could work with a process re-engineering expert. This might appeal to managers if the decreased workload could be tied to increased productivity.

■ POLITICS

Related to risk is the issue of organizational politics. A striking illustration of this was noted in the Aditya, House and Kerr article in which Kerr notes that the trait of intelligence is a taboo subject, "In today's United States there are some things that are dangerous even to think about, and career-ending to employ as independent or moderating variables." Of course, this is quite true despite the fact that intelligence is one of the powerful independent variables in the field of psychology (see the chapter by Hunter, Schmidt, Rauschenberger and Jayne). The immediate cause of this is that the government will come down hard if it finds that different groups perform differently on selection tests. The deeper cause of this problem is the philosophy of egalitarianism – the premise that it is somehow not quite moral if some people are more able than others. The principle here is: *a theory will not be applied, even if true, if it contradicts cherished values (especially if those values are defended by government agencies).*

■ SELF-CONCEPT OF MANAGERS

Closely related to the issue of values is the observation that managers may not agree to an intervention that implies they are not already good managers. Greenberg and Lind observed that many companies they contacted wanted nothing to do with "justice training," because that would imply that they were not already fair in their treatment of employees. Here the challenge to the theorist or consultant is to *frame the proposed intervention in such a way that it promises practical benefits without implying that the managers in question are morally deficient.*

■ MULTIPLE THEORIES

The complexity of application is exacerbated by cases in which there are many different theories pertinent to a given phenomenon. Take the case of money incentives. Bartol and Durham identify six different theories that deal with the issue of incentives (equity, expectancy, goal, agency, prospect, and institutional theory). These theories are, by and large, not contradictory but rather deal with different aspects of the phenomenon. In a case like this the practitioner is faced with a very difficult task: how to combine relevant aspects of the different theories to make practical decisions about incentive systems, for example, which type of incentive system to use in which context, including what level to apply them to (individual, group, organizational).

When there are multiple theories relevant to a given phenomenon, what the theorist needs to do is to help the practitioner with the integrations, that is, identify the key principles and show how they apply to specific cases. For example, expectancy theory can suggest that a key benefit of group incentive plans is that they will motivate cooperation but a key risk factor is that they may undermine the individual's belief that what he does will affect the outcome. This, in turn, will suggest steps that the practitioner might take, for example, show employees specifically how what they do affects group performance. This ties in with the discovery that cognitive factors, such as information exchange, can be critical to the effectiveness of incentive plans.

To take other examples, expectancy theory suggests that skill-based pay, though it facilitates flexibility, may not motivate high performance. Similarly, prospect theory suggests that people may resist variable pay, because they are adverse to losses in relation to their normal pay baseline.

The problem of the motivation of top executive continues to baffle theorists and practitioners alike, even though agency theory warns that agents will attempt to avoid risk unless principals convince them otherwise. Stock options seem like an ideal agency theory solution, because the CEO's main task is to increase shareholder value and owning stock would motivate them to do just this; unfortunately such motivation is often undermined when the stock drops and directors reset the option price at a lower level, thus, in effect, excusing failure. Such a policy, in effect, *rewards success most if it is preceded by failure* since the stock price can then run up from a lower base. Certainly one antidote that expectancy theory would suggest here is to require CEOs to personally own a substantial amount of stock (with no possibility of compensation if the price drops). In this case, the natural aversion to loss will still be respected: those who do not want to take the risk need not apply.

In the case of performance appraisal, the dynamic duo of Latham and Latham provide a fascinating example of the bringing to bear of multiple theories to a specific organizational context. Justice theory, goal theory, training theory, and findings from cognitive psychology were all brought to bear on the problem of how to design an effective performance appraisal system. J.P. Morgan's system looks to be exemplary: the standards are clearly specified in advance, the system is clearly tied to the organization's goals and strategy, multiple sources of information are used to insure objectivity, raters are trained, and communication between parties is extensive. Even here, however, the Lathams urge that more research is needed on issues such as appraisal in virtual relationships. What can we learn from the Lathams? Obviously, *theorist-practitioners should marry practitioners.*

■ CONTEXT

All theories must be applied in a specific context. A theory cannot specify all possible context factors because these are virtually unlimited. In reality, everything connects to everything else, so nothing literally stands alone in the universe. Here is where art or judgment meets science. *The practitioner has to figure out how to use viable theories in the context of the particular organization in question.*

Consider the goal-setting theory which Mitchell, Thompson and George-Falvy describe in such exquisite detail. But how to apply it? For example, how would you tie it in with incentives? – another example of multiple theories being applicable. But consider a more fundamental issue: what should you set goals *for*? Nothing in goal theory really answers this and, in a way, it could not, because that does depend on the particular organization or work unit involved. If goals are set for the wrong outcome, disaster will ensue. The practitioner has to figure out what is key, critical, important and also how the various goals will affect each other and other organizational systems (for example, cooperation and coordination).

Another context issue is organizational culture. Some perfectly good theories cannot be applied in a given setting, because the local cultural norms would reject it (for example, individual incentives in many unionized plants). A creative practitioner, however, may be able to modify the basic idea to fit the culture (for example, use group incentives). Another factor noted by Mitchell et al.: goal-setting systems usually need top management support; without it, the goals may simply be ignored. Of course, just about everything needs top management support so management has to make its priorities very clear. This issue becomes even more critical in multinational companies, because what works in one culture may not work so well, or work in a quite different way, in another culture.

There are many other context factors that bear on various theories, for example, recruitment methods may need to vary depending on the tightness of the labor market and the economy, legal factors may limit or control how performance appraisal is done, and technology may affect recruitment methods and feedback systems.

Hunter, Schmidt, Rauschenberger and Jayne show that selection systems and characteristics need to be integrated with training systems, incentive systems and performance appraisal systems as well as with technological changes. For example, if more and more people are to do higher level work under low supervision, an increasingly greater premium will have to be put on selecting people with high ability and self-motivation.

Aditya, House and Kerr bring up another context issue, that of consistency. The Vroom–Yetton model of decision making is taught at General Electric (GE) but the model implies much more variability in leadership style than managers can permit themselves if they want to avoid being seen as inconsistent. Thus, what GE takes away from the theory is the importance of decision acceptance, rather than the full contingency model. *It is as if practitioners deliberately choose to pick the ripe fruit (in their context) of the theory tree and leave the rest on the vine.* In a supreme irony, Kerr shows that organizations also can apply theories, in the case of achievement motivation theory, that are not supposed to apply to their (large) firms at all by creating systems, such as goal setting and feedback, that foster such motivation.

Probably the best example in this volume of the difficulties of applying theory in a given context is the chapter by Hackman, Wageman, Ruddy and Ray on team effectiveness. Hackman and Wageman lay out an elegant (and we believe fundamentally correct) theory or model of group effectiveness focused on four elements: clear direction; an enabling team structure; a supportive organizational context; and available, expert coaching. Then Xerox executives Ruddy and Ray, who agree with the substance of the theory, proceed to show how difficult it is to put all these principles into practice consistently. Some examples: it may be very hard to get managers with conflicting agendas to give groups a clear direction; finding enough people with the needed skills to staff all the requisite teams may be impossible; organizational support in the form of team rewards may motivate some teams and not motivate others; and managers may be willing and able to coach but may be unable to do it and also fulfill their other managerial responsibilities. This suggests that, *in addition to building a basic theoretical model, you may also need to build a theory of application if the theory is to be practically useful.*

▨ THEORY BUILDING

Some comments need to be made here about theory building.

The Academy of Management, in my opinion, has had a pernicious influence on the process of theory building, though their problems stem from other sources, especially bad philosophy of science. (I/O psychology is not quite so bad but still a victim of some bad philosophy.) The theory of theory building that is widely promulgated (and enforced by journal editors) is that you start by inventing a theory, then make deductions from it, and then test it (allegedly revising it later). This we submit is fundamentally wrong. You cannot build a sensible theory without facts. Theory building should be an inductive process. You should start by gathering facts pertinent to the issue you want to study from observation of reality. Such facts do not necessarily have to be based on quantitative measurement. They can be based also on qualitative data and can reflect information gained from all available sources, including field observations. The facts should be integrated and the theory should be the end result of the integration of those facts. This was, incidentally, the way goal-setting theory was developed, although quantitative data were dominant. However, there is no need for theory building to start in the laboratory.

Building theories inductively will make application easier and more natural, because you will have looked at the real world already to get your facts. So it will not become the case of ivory tower academics inventing a theory that has no tie to reality and then finding that somehow, material reality is too corrupt to accommodate itself to the theory that looked so pure and perfect in the ivory tower. (This, incidentally, is how the theory of socialism/communism was developed.)

It is no wonder that practitioners almost never read the academic literature. Aside from the jargon and mind-numbing statistics, the theories developed may have very little to do with the real world, or, if they do, they may deal with such minute segments of it, that it is not worth the manager's time to study them.

Consider a specific I/O example. How should we build a theory of organizational change? Should we deduce it from theories about other phenomena? What if those phenomena are only indirectly relevant? Should we study it in the laboratory? Not in this particular case, because we cannot easily abstract out the key elements and isolate them in the laboratory (as we can with some phenomena). Here there are just too many factors involved. The way we would start would be to look at successful and unsuccessful organizational change programs and find out what went on in each case and isolate the distinguishing features of each, namely those that were common to the successful programs and absent in the unsuccessful programs. This would not be the final story, but it would be a good start. The theory might then be tested prospectively and even quantitatively. Later it could be tested cross-culturally. There have been small-scale attempts to do this but nothing systematic so far as we know. Such a theory, once validated, could flow quite readily back into practice.

I/O psychology is in a unique position within the broad field of psychology, because it, at the same time, values practice but does not eschew theory. No subfield of psychology is better equipped than our own to develop valid theories that are practically useful and to base practice on theories that are valid. We just need to learn how to do it better. We hope this volume will provide some clues.

NAME INDEX

SUBJECT INDEX